A GRAMMAR WITH READINGS

KATHRYN F. BUTCHER/BARBARA M. GAFFNEY
UNIVERSITY OF NEW ORLEANS

Prentice Hall Regents
Englewood Cliffs, New Jersey 07632

Editorial Director: Arley Gray
Manager of Development Services: Louisa Hellegers
Development Editor: Kathy Ossip
Director of Production and Manufacturing: David Riccardi
Editorial Production/Design Manager: Dominick Mosco
Production Supervision: Janet Johnston
Interior Design, Page Composition, and Electronic Art: Ken Liao
Production Coordinator: Ray Keating
Cover Coordinator: Merle Krumper
Cover Design: Tom Nery
Cover Illustration and Interior Art: Linda Mellott
Permissions appear on page x, which constitutes a continuation of the copyright page.

Prentice-Hall, Inc.
A Simon & Schuster Company
Englewood Cliffs, New Jersey 07632

Printed in the United States of America

10 9 8 7 6 5 4 3 2 1

ISBN 0-205-15315-1

Prentice-Hall International (UK) Limited, London
Prentice-Hall of Australia Pty. Limited, Sydney
Prentice-Hall Canada Inc., Toronto
Prentice-Hall Hispanoamericana, S.A., Mexico
Prentice-Hall of India Private Limited, New Delhi
Prentice-Hall of Japan, Inc., Tokyo
Simon & Schuster Asia Pte. Ltd., Tokyo
Ediitora Prentice-Hall do Brasil, Ltda., Rio de Janeiro

Printed on Recycled Paper

To
Bruce and Kristen Butcher

To
The Dolly Sisters
(Barbara, Rita, and Toots)

and

Marty Curtin

CONTENTS

PREFACE

This text was conceived more than seven years ago as a result of our sharing an office and teaching the same groups of students at the University of New Orleans. The project grew out of our frustration with existing texts and our commitment to the central role of reading, particularly in academic preparation programs. Since that time, the quality of texts for ESL programs has improved greatly. Nevertheless, we trust that our book will find a place in ESL and EFL programs and perhaps developmental programs as well.

American Contexts is based on the principle, confirmed repeatedly by research, that second-language students master grammar and syntax rules best when they are presented in context. Moreover, whenever possible, those rules should be presented inductively and/or interactively, and they should be integrated with other skills.

Organization of the Text

Each unit contains three major parts: The Context, The Target Structure(s), and Integration:

1. The Context includes Pre-reading Questions, a Preview of Key Terms and Concepts, the Reading Passage used for contextualizing the target structure, Comprehension Questions, and Discussion Questions. This section introduces a "theme," such as Families and Neighborhoods in the U.S., which is carried throughout the unit. The theme of each unit relates to an aspect of U.S. culture or history that is of interest to ESL and EFL students.
2. The Target Structure covers the grammar itself and is divided into relatively brief "chunks" or "Focus on..." sections that can be covered in class a few at a time or assigned for homework. Following each major point is a checkpoint exercise intended to review the grammar and reinforce the students' understanding of it. Most checkpoints can be done by pairs or groups, as indicated by the ikons that accompany each exercise. Some are oral, some written. All the checkpoints relate in some way to the theme of the chapter introduced in the context section.
3. The Integration section, as its name implies, includes numerous activities that help students consolidate their understanding of grammar with other language skills, especially speaking and writing. Among the activities in this section are games, roleplays, debates, dialogues, and short written assignments, as well as comprehensive review exercises. More advanced students might go directly from the Context to the Integration section, which can be used as a review; these students could be directed to the Target Structure section for specific rules as needed.

Each unit concludes with suggested writing assignments, including journal entries and composition topics. These writings relate to the theme of the unit, such as Neighborhoods and Families, Humor and Imagination, or Native Americans.

The Nature of the Text

The Reading Base. We have chosen reading rather than conversation as the means of contextualization for a number of reasons.

First, authentic readings by skilled authors provide a rich source of information about the language: its grammar, syntax, style, and rhetoric. Students may discover and intuit these features while they are reading, whereas in speech they must concentrate on communicating effectively. Reading also provides students a chance to analyze, reflect, and generalize.

The second benefit of using readings in our text is the introduction of a central theme for each unit. Subsequent examples, exercises, and activities relate to the theme, which integrates all the material in the unit and makes it more meaningful.

Third, the readings we have chosen give students information about and insight into North American culture and various groups, such as Asian-Americans, African-Americans, and Hispanics, within that culture.

Finally, the high interest level of the content stimulates students to exchange ideas and expand their knowledge while they are gaining proficiency in the English language.

The Method: Induction, Interaction, Integration. The opening of each unit invites the students to discover rules of grammar and syntax inductively through examining the reading passage and also previewing the material to be presented in the chapter. For example, in Unit Four on tenses, students preview the target structure by examining the present tense verbs in the first paragraph of "My Name" by Sandra Cisneros and discussing the differences in their use.

Many Checkpoint exercises likewise involve induction; students are frequently asked to find certain structures in a paragraph and make generalizations about them. In the tense unit, for example, Checkpoint One asks students to analyze the simple present tense verbs and divide them into two groups according to whether their meaning is 1) permanent or general or 2) habitual or repeated.

The text is interactive in two ways. First, it employs reading as a vehicle to present structure so that students must interact with a text to learn rules. Second, the checkpoint exercises and Integration activities require students to interact with each other in pairs or small groups. In addition, teachers may ask students to work through the grammar explanations together in groups; for example, one group might work on sentence structure while others discuss article usage or passive verbs.

Group and pair work in all three parts of each unit, particularly the explicitly integrative activities like role plays, debates, and games in the final section, promote assimilation and consolidation of knowledge.

Suggestions for Teaching

The Context. The pre-reading questions and preview of the reading passage should be done in class either in groups or as a whole class. The Reading Passage can be assigned for homework once the preliminary in-class work has been done. Students will gain greater understanding of the passage if the teacher also reads it aloud either before or after the students have worked with the reading. The vocabulary exercise may be done by the whole class or in small groups or pairs. If time allows, lexical items could be reinforced by classroom activities. For example, small groups or pairs could write original sentences using the target words or phrases. Another activity might involve finding synonyms or antonyms.

Discussion questions may be covered as a whole-class activity or may be answered in small groups and reported to the class. Alternatively, groups can choose which question(s) they would like to discuss and report on; they can also change the order of the questions if they wish.

Teaching the Target Structure Section. The students' first exposure to the target structure usually involves their interacting with the text to discover and generalize rules. This task is performed in pairs or small groups with the teacher's assistance and guidance.

When this step is completed, teachers may want to explain the target structure in their own words, using their own examples or some from the students' work on the board. In this way, they *supplement* the material in the text rather than repeating it. As reinforcement, sections of the text with accompanying charts and examples may be assigned as homework before or after the teacher has explained key points and clarified the material.

If they prefer, teachers can take the students through the explanations in the text, paraphrasing the rules, adding examples where necessary, and prodding the students with questions to rouse interest and monitor their comprehension. Of course, the students should be required to raise their own questions as well.

Using the Checkpoint Exercises. The checkpoint exercises occur in the text after a "chunk" of grammar explanation. They serve two purposes: to give students a chance to practice the target rule and to give teachers a means of checking students' grasp of the new material. These checkpoints can be done in pairs or small groups or occasionally individually. Many of these exercises call for original answers; some are open-ended or role play. For especially difficult material or when more practice on a particular grammar point is necessary, the "Additional Practice" following the checkpoint may be assigned for classwork or for homework.

Teaching Integration. The final section of each unit provides a wealth of activities of different types; its purpose is to allow students to practice what they have learned and to employ all language skills in doing so: speaking, listening, reading, writing. The Integration section may be all that is needed for more advanced students to brush up on basic grammar, especially in the earlier units.

Teachers may want to pick out certain exercises and activities they feel will work especially well with certain groups, depending on the personality and composition of the class. Some activities are geared to classes of heterogeneous learners whose English language proficiency is at different levels. Some are for class-time, some for homework. Many exercises in this section are designed for ESL students who enjoy participating in activities that allow them to express their individual personalities and demonstrate a sense of humor and play.

ACKNOWLEDGMENTS

The authors appreciate the use of the following copyrighted material.

Unit 1: Passages from *Saint Maybe* by Anne Tyler (copyright © 1991 by Anne Tyler Modaressi) are reprinted by permission of Random House, Inc., and, in the British Commonwealth, by the author and Chatto & Windus.

Unit 2: "The Unicorn in the Garden" by James Thurber (©1957) originally appeared in *The New Yorker* (1939) as a "Fable for Our Times." It is reprinted by permission of Rosemary A. Thurber.

Unit 3: Katharine Brush's "Birthday Party" (©1946) was published in *The New Yorker* in 1946 and is reprinted by permission of the author. Judith Viorst's poem " . . . And Then the Prince Knelt Down and Tried to Put the Glass Slipper on Cinderella's Foot" (©1981 by Judith Viorst) is reprinted from *If I Were in Charge of the World and Other Worries,* published by Atheneum, an imprint of the Macmillan Publishing Company, and in Australia by A.M. Heath.

Unit 4: Sandra Cisneros' "My Name" and "Papa Who Wakes Up Tired in the Dark," are from *The House on Mango Street,* published in New York by Vintage Books, a division of Random House, in 1991, and in hardcover by Alfred A. Knopf in 1994. © 1984 by Sandra Cisneros and reprinted by permission.

Unit 5: Passages from *I Know Why the Caged Bird Sings* by Maya Angelou (©1969 by the author) are reprinted by permission of Random House, Inc.

Unit 6: Exerpts from "Tomorrow Is Coming, Children" from *Yokohama, California* by Toshio Mori are reprinted by permission of the Caxton Printers, Ltd., Caldwell, Idaho.

Unit 7: Joanne Sherman's "No Longer New York Cool" originally appeared in the *Southern Journal,* February 1991. It is reprinted by permission of the Southern Progress Corporation, Birmingham, Alabama.

Unit 8: "From Song to Sound: Bing and Elvis" by Russell Baker is copyright ©1977 by the New York Times Company and is reprinted by permission.

Unit 9: Sections of John G. Neihardt's *Black Elk Speaks (*copyright 1932, 1959, and 1972 by John G. Neihardt; copyright ©1961 by the John G. Neihardt Trust) are reprinted by permission of the University of Nebraska Press.

Unit 10: Susan Tifft's "Sticker Shock at the Ivy Tower" and the article "Is an Ivy Degree Worth Remortgaging the Farm?" appeared in the September 25, 1989, issue of *Time* Magazine and are copyright 1989 by Time Inc. and reprinted by permission.

We would like to thank the team at Prentice Hall Regents for their valuable editorial suggestions. In particular, we thank Arley Gray, Louisa Hellegers, Janet Johnston, Ken Liao, and Kathy Ossip. We are also indebted to Joe Opiela for his faith in and support of our project.

The advice and encouragement of Catherine Summers Lindenman and Mary Ruetten helped us to improve the manuscript and see the project through to its completion.

We thank Josette Beaulieu-McFaull and Lia Kushnir, our colleagues at UNO, for classroom-testing our materials through several reincarnations.

Finally, we thank our families and the friends, colleagues, and students who took an interest in our work.

AMERICAN CONTEXTS

A GRAMMAR WITH READINGS

Unit One

Basic Sentence Structure

READING: from *Saint Maybe* by Anne Tyler

THEME: Traditional Families and Neighborhoods in the United States

PART ONE. The Context

The reading that follows is the opening of *Saint Maybe* (1991) by Anne Tyler, a novel about the Bedloe family and their neighbors and friends on Waverly Street in Baltimore, Maryland. Tyler is a popular author who writes with humor and sensitivity about American culture, especially family life.

PRE-READING QUESTIONS

1. What are the characteristics of a traditional family in the United States? Are families in the United States different from those in other cultures? If so, what are some of the differences?
2. Describe the neighborhood you grew up in. Who were your neighbors? What was your relationship with them like?
3. What are the characteristics of good neighbors? bad neighbors?
4. In what ways are neighbors in the United States different from those in other cultures?

PREVIEW OF KEY TERMS AND CONCEPTS

The following key words and ideas appear in the reading. Guess the meaning of each term on the left by matching it to a definition on the right. Put the correct letter after each term. Discuss your answers with a partner or group, and ask your teacher about any terms you're not sure of.

1. Johns Hopkins ____
2. an apple-pie household ____
3. newlyweds ____
4. Orioles ____
5. clapboard houses ____
6. bobby socks ____

a. professional baseball team in Baltimore
b. thick white socks worn by teenage girls in the 1950s
c. famous university in Baltimore
d. typical middle-class American family
e. houses covered with horizontal rows of overlapping pieces of wood
f. just-married couple

Reading: From *Saint Maybe* by Anne Tyler

NOTE: The words followed by asterisks are defined at the bottom of the page.

(1) On Waverly Street, everybody knew everybody else. It was only one short block, after all—a narrow strip of patched* and repatched pavement,* bracketed* between a high stone cemetery wall at one end and the commercial clutter* of Govans Road at the other. The trees were elderly maples with lumpy, bulbous* trunks. The squat* clapboard houses seemed mostly front porch.

(2) And each house had its own particular role to play. Number Nine, for instance, was foreign. A constantly shifting assortment of Middle Eastern graduate students came and went, attending classes at Johns Hopkins, and the scent of exotic* spices drifted from their kitchen every evening at suppertime. Number Six was referred to as the newlyweds', although the Crains had been married two years now and were beginning to look a bit worn around the edges. And Number Eight was the Bedloe family. They were never just the Bedloes, but the Bedloe *family*, Waverly Street's version of the ideal, apple-pie household: two amiable* parents, three good-looking children, a dog, a cat, a scattering of goldfish.

(3) In fact, the oldest of those children had long ago married and left—moved out to Baltimore County and started a family of her own—and the second-born was nearing thirty. But somehow the Bedloes were stuck in people's minds at a stage from a dozen years back, when Claudia was a college girl in bobby socks and Danny was captain of his high-school football team and Ian, the baby (his parents' big surprise), was still tearing* down the sidewalk on his tricycle with a miniature license plate from a cereal box wired to the handlebar.

(4) Now Ian was seventeen and, like the rest of his family, large-boned and handsome and easygoing, quick to make friends, fond of a good time. He had the Bedloe golden-brown hair, golden skin, and sleepy-looking brown eyes, although his mouth was his mother's, a pale beige mouth quirking* upward at the corners. He liked to wear ragged jeans and plaid shirts—cotton broadcloth in summer, flannel in winter—unbuttoned all the way to expose a stretched-out T-shirt underneath. His shoes were high-top sneakers held together with electrical

---

* patched	repaired
pavement	material used for roads and streets
bracketed	enclosed on two opposite sides
clutter	a crowded area
bulbous	having bulb-like shapes or lumps
squat	short and wide
exotic	unusual
amiable	pleasant
tearing	racing
quirking	turning

tape. This was in 1965, when Poe High School still maintained at least a vestige* of a dress code, and his teachers were forever sending him home to put on something more presentable. (But his mother was likely to greet him in baggy,* lint*-covered slacks and one of his own shirts, her fading* blond curls pinned scrappily* back with a granddaughter's pink plastic hairbow. *She* would not have passed the dress code either.) Also, there were complaints about the quality of Ian's schoolwork. He was bright, his teachers said, but lazy. Content to slide through with low B's or even C's. It was the spring of his junior year and if he didn't soon mend his ways,* no self-respecting* college would have him.

(5) Ian listened to all this with a tolerant, bemused* expression. Things would turn out fine, he felt. Hadn't they always? (None of the Bedloes was a worrier.) Crowds of loyal friends had surrounded him since kindergarten. His sweetheart, Cicely Brown, was the prettiest girl in the junior class. His mother doted on* him and his father—Poe's combination algebra teacher and baseball coach—let him pitch in nearly every game, and not just because they were related, either. His father claimed Ian had talent. In fact sometimes Ian daydreamed about pitching for the Baltimore Orioles, but he knew he didn't have *that* much talent. He was a medium kind of guy, all in all.

(6) Even so, there were moments when he believed that someday, somehow, he was going to end up famous. Famous for what, he couldn't quite say; but he'd be walking up the back steps or something and all at once he would imagine a camera zooming in on him, filming his life story. He imagined the level, cultured* voice of his biographer saying, "Ian climbed the steps. He opened the door. He entered the kitchen."

(7) "Have a good day, hon?" his mother asked, passing through with a laundry basket.

(8) "Oh," he said, "the usual run of scholastic* triumphs* and athletic glories."* And he set his books on the table.

(9) His biographer said, "He set his books on the table."

---

* **vestige**	small amount
baggy	loose-fitting
lint	small fibers of fabric, fuzz
fading	becoming lighter (grayer)
scrappily	carelessly
mend his ways	reform himself, change bad habits
self-respecting	having high standards
bemused	preoccupied, distracted
doted on	spoiled, treated with excessive affection
cultured	educated, especially in fine arts
scholastic	related to school or studying
triumphs	victories
glories	honors

Comprehension Questions

1. What kind of family are the Bedloes? Discuss their characteristics.
2. What do the different houses on Waverly Street represent? What kind of people live in Number Nine? Number Six?
3. How would you describe the personality of Ian Bedloe? of Mrs. Bedloe?
4. What kind of neighborhood do the Bedloes live in? Discuss its characteristics.

Discussion Questions

1. The Bedloes seem to be a typical middle-class U.S. family of the 1960s. Describe a typical U.S. family of the 1990s.
2. One popular definition of a family is "a circle of friends who love you." What is your definition of a family? Do people have to be related to be considered a family?
3. The neighborhood on Waverly Street consists of single-family houses. Other types of residences also exist: two-family or multi-family houses, apartment buildings, condominiums, mobile homes, houseboats. Discuss the advantages and disadvantages of each. How does living in a certain kind of residence affect people?
4. What are some features of a "good" neighborhood? Describe your ideal neighborhood.
5. Discuss how families in the United States are portrayed in different movies and TV programs you've seen.

PART TWO. The Target Structure: Basic Sentence Structure

I Focus on Sentence Elements

Preview of Independent Clauses

With a partner or group, read the following groups of words. Then answer the questions.

He was bright but lazy.

Content to slide through with low B's and C's.

1. Which group of words is a complete sentence? Which is an incomplete sentence (sentence fragment)?
2. Is the sentence fragment longer or shorter than the complete one?
3. What elements are necessary to make a complete sentence?

Elements of a Sentence: Clause, Subject, Predicate

Every English sentence contains at least one independent clause: a structure with a *subject* and a *predicate* that can stand on its own, like the following.

Subject	**Predicate**
Time	flies.
The wind	blew.
Ian	set his books on the table.
An assortment of students	came and went.

A *subject* is what a sentence is about, and a *predicate* tells something about the subject. A predicate must contain a verb (for example, *flies*, *blew*, or *set*). It may contain two or more verbs (*came* and *went*) as well as other structures.

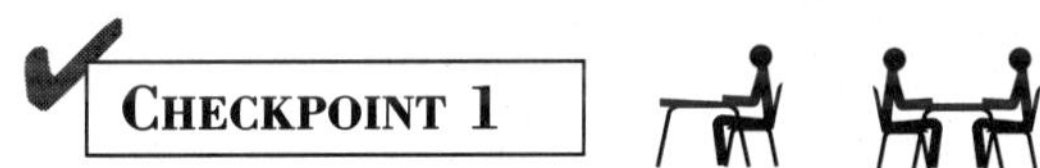

A. Draw a line between the subject and predicate in the following sentences, and then underline the verb in each predicate. Example:

Everybody / <u>knew</u> everybody else.

1. The trees were elderly maples with lumpy, bulbous trunks.
2. Each house had its own particular role to play.
3. Number Six was the newlyweds'.
4. Poe High School still maintained a vestige of a dress code.
5. Crowds of loyal friends had surrounded him since kindergarten.

B. Return to Paragraph 2 of the reading (page 6) and analyze the subjects and predicates as you did in Part A above. (Two sentences contain more than one clause, with a subject and predicate in each.)

Sentence Conventions

In addition to containing a subject and a predicate, a sentence must follow certain rules.

- **Capital Letter.** The first word of every sentence must begin with a capital letter; it cannot begin with a small letter or a number in digits.

- **End Punctuation.** Every sentence must end with appropriate punctuation, usually a period. Other final marks of punctuation are the question mark (?) and the exclamation point (!).
- **Word Order.** Normal word order in a statement is *Subject* + *Predicate* + the rest of the sentence. In questions, the subject comes *after* the first word in the verb, called an *auxiliary* or helping verb:

Statement: The Bedloes are living on Waverly Street.

Question: Are the Bedloes living on Waverly Street?

CHECKPOINT 2

A. With a partner or small group, discuss how the groups of words do not follow sentence conventions. Decide how they could be corrected.

1. 8 Waverly Street was the Bedloes' address.
2. Ian entered the kitchen
3. Had moved away the older children.
4. the newlyweds had been married for two years.
5. The foreigners were attending Johns Hopkins?

B. Write a paragraph giving your opinions about the neighborhood in *Saint Maybe.* Exchange your paragraph with another student; then check each other's work to make sure each sentence conforms to the sentence rules described above.

II Focus on Sentence Patterns: SVO and SVC

PREVIEW OF SENTENCE PATTERNS

With a partner, unscramble the following sentences.

1. books he set table on his the
2. sneakers his hightop shoes were
3. hug mother gave a Ian his
4. kitchen scent the drifted spices from of their

The sentences that you unscrambled illustrate common patterns in English sentences. These patterns differ in the kinds of predicates they contain.

SVO PATTERN

S + V + O = Subject / Verb / Object / rest of sentence
He / set / his books / on the table.

In this type of sentence, the subject *acts on* the object, and the object receives the action of the verb. The subject and object refer to different people or things.*

S + V + O Pattern		
Subject	**Verb**	**Object**
Ian	was riding	his bicycle.
Mrs. Bedloe	wore	old clothes.
The Bedloes	had	a clapboard house.
Ian	imagined	the voice of his biographer.

SVC Pattern

S + V + C = Subject / Verb / Complement
His shoes / were / high-top sneakers.

A complement is different from an object in that it is not acted upon by the subject; instead, a complement *completes* the meaning of the subject. The subject and object do not refer to different people or different things, as they do in an SVO sentence. They refer to the same person or thing. The verb in an SVC sentence is usually called a "linking" verb because it links the subject and complement. Some common linking verbs are *be*, *seem*, *look*, *feel*, *taste*, and *smell*. The part of the predicate after the verb either describes the subject or gives another name for it.

S + V + C Pattern		
Subject	**Verb**	**Complement**
Waverly Street	was	one short block.
The trees	were	maples.
The houses	seemed	mostly front porch.
His eyes	looked	sleepy.

---

* A small group of verbs called *reflexives* are exceptions to the rule that subjects and objects are different. The objects of reflexive verbs are always pronouns ending in *-self* (singular) or *-selves* (plural) that refer to the subject.

Ian always *enjoyed himself* when he played baseball.
(*himself* = Ian)

The Bedloes *considered themselves* good neighbors.
(*themselves* = The Bedloes)

CHECKPOINT 3 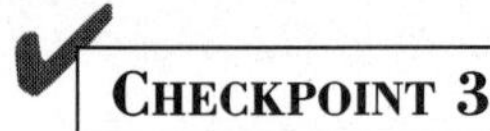 

A. Underline the verb in each of the following sentences, and label each sentence as SVO or as SVC. Remember that if what follows the verb is *different* from the subject, it is an object; if it is *not different*, it is a complement. Example:

Waverly Street *was* only one short block. <u>SVC</u>

1. Ian was large-boned and handsome and easy-going. ______
2. He liked ragged jeans and plaid shirts. ______
3. He had the Bedloe golden-brown hair, the golden skin, and sleepy-looking eyes. ______
4. She wouldn't have passed the dress code either. ______
5. Cicely Brown was the prettiest girl in the junior class. ______

B. Analyze the first six sentences of the reading (page 6). Which follow the SVO pattern, and which follow the SVC pattern?

III Focus on Patterns with Indirect Objects and the SV Pattern

SENTENCE PATTERNS WITH INDIRECT OBJECTS

Clauses that have *two* objects often follow this pattern.

S + V + IO + DO = Subject/Verb/Indirect Object/Direct Object
Ian / told / his mother / a story.

In this pattern, the indirect object appears *before* the direct object.

S + V + IO + DO Pattern

Subject	Verb	Indirect Object	Direct Object
The teacher	wrote	his parents	a note.
Cicely	bought	Ian	a gift.
Mrs. Bedloe	made	him	some lunch.

The sentences above can also follow a pattern that uses the prepositions *to* or *for* (S + V + DO + *to*/*for* + IO).

Indirect Objects with *To* or *For*				
Subject	**Verb**	**Direct Object**	***to/for***	**Indirect Object**
Ian	gave	a hug	to	his mother.
The teacher	wrote	a note	to	his parents.
Cicely	bought	a gift	for	Ian.
Mrs. Bedloe	made	some lunch	for	him.

Some verbs, such as *ask* and *cost*, always follow the first pattern.

Subject	Verb	Indirect Object	Direct Object
Claudia	asked	Ian	a question.
The sneakers	cost	him	thirty dollars.

Other verbs, such as *describe*, *explain*, and *say*, always follow the second pattern and always use *to* with the indirect object.

Subject	Verb	Direct Object	*to*	Indirect Object
Ian	described	his day	to	his mother.
She	explained	the recipe	to	him.
He	said	nothing	to	her.

Verbs that can follow either pattern (S+ V+ IO+ DO or S + V + DO + *to/for* + IO) include *bring, give, lend, pass, send, show, take, teach, tell,* and *write* (used with *to*); and *buy, cook, get,* and *make* (used with *for*).

Two Patterns Used with Indirect Objects	
Ian lent his friend a book.	He lent a book *to* his friend.
Ian wrote Cicely a note.	He wrote a note *to* Cicely.
Mr. Bedloe bought Ian a shirt.	He bought a shirt *for* Ian.
Mrs. Bedloe made Ian a cake.	She made a cake *for* Ian.

Two special rules must be followed in sentences with indirect objects.

1. When the indirect object comes before the direct object, do not use a preposition.

   INCORRECT: He bought for his girlfriend a blouse.
   CORRECT: He bought his girlfriend a blouse.

2. When the indirect object is a pronoun, use *to* or *for* before the pronoun.

   INCORRECT: He bought her it.
   CORRECT: He bought it *for* her.

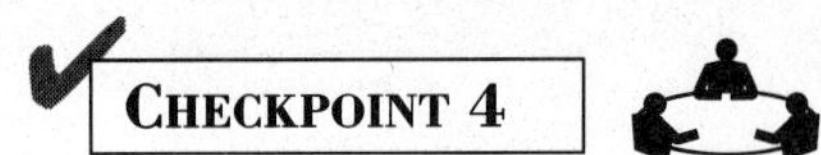

Checkpoint 4

Divide into teams of four to six members, and choose one student in your group to write the team's answers. Write requests that show the way direct and indirect objects follow each verb in the list below. A point will be given for each correct sentence, and the team with the most points wins. Time limit: 10 minutes.

Follow these patterns. (Remember that some verbs follow only one pattern and others follow two.)

bake Please bake me a cake.
Please bake a cake for me.

lend Please lend me $100.
Please lend $100 to me.

bake	get	pass	cook	make
send	give	show	write	buy
teach	explain	take	ask	lend
tell	say	describe	bring	

SV Pattern

Another sentence pattern occurs with verbs that do not take objects (intransitive verbs).

S + V Pattern = Subject / Verb / rest of sentence
The scent of spices / drifted / from their kitchen.

Although they don't take objects or complements, intransitive verbs are often followed by prepositional phrases that indicate time or location and begin with prepositions such as *to*, *for*, *in*, *at*, *before*, *after*, *with*, *about*, and *on*. Not all intransitive verbs are followed by prepositional phrases; the clause may end with the verb or another word or phrase, as the examples show.

S + V Pattern		
He	walked	*up* the back steps.
An auto accident	happened.	
An auto accident	happened	yesterday.
An auto accident	happened	*in* the evening.
It	occurred	*at* the end *of* Waverly Street.

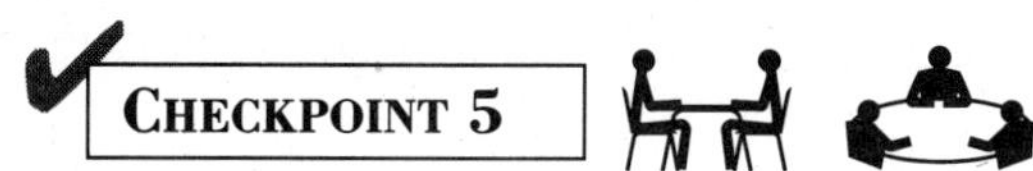

Read the following passage from *Saint Maybe* and circle all the main verbs. Then make a list of the verbs. Discuss whether each verb takes an object or not. If you're not sure whether a verb on your list is transitive or intransitive, check a dictionary.

The spring of 1988 was the wettest anyone could remember. It rained nearly every day in May, and all the storm drains overflowed and the gutters* ran like rivers and the Bedloes' roof developed a leak directly above the linen closet. One morning when Daphne went to get a fresh towel she found the whole stack soaked through. Ian called Davidson Roofers, but the man who came said there wasn't a thing he could do till the weather cleared.

MORE RULES ABOUT PREPOSITIONAL PHRASES

Prepositional phrases often follow intransitive verbs in the final position, but they can also occur in other positions in a sentence.

In the kitchen, Ian had lunch with his mother.

Ian had lunch *in the kitchen* with his mother.

Ian had lunch with his mother *in the kitchen*.

In the preceding sentences, the prepositional phrase *in the kitchen* acts as an adverb indicating a place. Prepositional phrases can also modify nouns; in that case, they act as adjectives and follow the noun.

The neighbor *on the corner* was an old man.

He was watching the boy *on the bicycle*.

When analyzing the structure of a clause or sentence, you may find it useful to eliminate the prepositional phrases. Removing them helps to reveal the major parts (subject and verb) of the clause.

(Subject) (Verb)
(After six o'clock) *Most people went* (into their houses).

(Subject) (Verb)
The foreign students (on Waverly Street) *were studying* (in the city).

A. Read the following passage from *Saint Maybe* and draw a line through all the prepositional phrases. Then label the subject and verb in each clause. Discuss your answers with the class.

---

* **gutters** low areas at the edges of streets or on roofs to carry off water

They passed the house that said MRS. GOODE, PALMIST—FORTUNES CHEERFULLY TOLD, but their mother didn't stop. Agatha was glad. Mrs. Goode was gray all over and her parlor smelled of mothballs. They came to . . . shoe repairs and laundromats. At Luckman's Pharmacy Thomas and Agatha slowed hopefully, but their mother said, "We'll go to Joyner's this time." She rotated her drugstores because she didn't want people thinking she bought too many pills. It was a pity, though. Luckman's had one of those gumball machines with plastic charms intermingled. Thomas and Agatha let their feet drag and sent a longing gaze backward.

B. Read the passage and draw a line through all the prepositional phrases. Then label the subject and verb in each clause. Discuss your answers with the class.

The Bedloes resemble the traditional white middle-class family in the United States during the 1960s, but such families are less common in the 1990s. In the traditional family, the husband was the sole bread-winner; the wife stayed at home, took care of the children, and did housework. Nowadays, relatively few families could afford this arrangement if they wanted it, and many do not want it. It is very common for mothers to work outside the house; in fact, many families could not make ends meet without two incomes. Moreover, with the increase in divorce, many families are headed by one parent, usually a woman.

IV Focus on Subject Fillers

It as a Subject Filler

In many sentences, the words *it* and *there* occur in the subject position but are not true subjects. Instead, their only purpose is to fill the subject position, which cannot be empty.*

It is often used as a subject filler in sentences about time, distance (in space or time), and weather. This *it* is not the same as the pronoun *it*, which is used to refer to a specific thing.

Ian had to change his shirt because *it* had holes in *it*.

(Here *it* refers to *shirt*.)

---

* The only exception to this rule is the imperative sentence in which the subject is omitted but understood to be "you": *Go home and change your clothes. Pass me the salt, please.*

It as a Subject Filler	
Time:	*It* is exactly three P.M. *It* was the spring of his junior year.
Distance:	*It's* about 40 miles from Baltimore to Washington, D.C. *It* only takes about an hour to drive from Baltimore to Washington.
Weather:	*It* is extremely cold today. *It* gets hot and humid in Baltimore in the summer.

Another type of sentence that occurs with the filler *it* contains this pattern.

It + linking verb + adjective + rest of sentence

It was *nice* hearing from you.

It feels too *hot* to go out today.

It was *fortunate* Ian was so popular.

Sometimes nouns are used instead of adjectives with this pattern.

It's been a *pleasure* meeting you.

It's a *shame* that you couldn't visit Baltimore with us.

CHECKPOINT 7  

Make a sentence using *it* as the subject filler with the expression provided. Identify the pattern used (time, distance, weather, adjective, or noun). Examples:

. . . three o'clock in the morning . . .

It's three o'clock in the morning. (time)

It was three o'clock in the morning when I woke up. (time)

1. . . . pleasant to . . .
2. . . . much too cold to . . .
3. . . . rarely hot in . . .
4. . . . incredible that you . . .
5. . . . earlier than . . .
6. . . . more than a thousand miles from . . .
7. . . . a fact that . . .

THERE AS A SUBJECT FILLER

Like *it, there* is not the true subject of a sentence. In *there*-sentences, the subject always occurs after the verb.

There + *be* + subject + rest of sentence

There were several different *neighbors* on Waverly St.

There was usually a spicy *aroma* drifting from the foreigners' house.

Note that the form of *be* agrees with the true subject.

The true subjects of these sentences can be moved to the subject position in sentences equivalent in meaning.

Several different neighbors were on Waverly Street.

A spicy aroma was usually drifting from the foreigners' house.

CHECKPOINT 8 

A. Write sentences beginning with *there is* or *there are* about your neighbors and compare them with those of a partner. You may want to refer to the list of people below. Examples:

There is a newlywed couple in my neighborhood.

There are several older couples in my neighborhood.

lots of nice people	noisy teenagers
pretty girls	several older couples
a newborn baby	a few large families
many children with bikes	a family from __________ (China, etc.)

B. Write several sentences using *There was/were* about a neighborhood you lived in before now or about how your present neighborhood has changed. Exchange your sentences with another student and check each other's sentences. Discuss differences between your neighborhoods. Examples:

There was a grocery store.

There were some children next door.

V Focus on Adding Information to Basic Sentence Patterns

Writers create variety and pack sentences with meaning by filling positions before, in the middle of, and after independent clauses. The types of structures that occupy different positions will be discussed in more detail in Unit 7; this section introduces them.

FRONT FILLERS

Front fillers are words, phrases, and clauses that begin sentences and precede independent clauses. They add meaning but do not affect the basic structure of the clause they precede. Except in some cases when they are short, front fillers are usually followed by a comma. The following are examples of *words and phrases* in the front position.

In the afternoon, Ian came home from school.

Then he set his books on the table.

Thinking of what his biographer would say, Ian greeted his mother.

Considered poorly dressed by his teachers, Ian was often sent home to change.

Unlike words and phrases, a *clause* in the front position contains a subject and a verb. Front clauses are different from independent clauses in that they cannot occur alone. Therefore, they are called "dependent" clauses. (Types of dependent clauses will be discussed in detail in Units 8–10.)

Because international students live there, one house is called "the foreigners'."

When Ian thought about his future, he sometimes felt he would be famous.

Read the passage from *Saint Maybe* and underline all the front fillers. Make three lists of front fillers: words, phrases, and clauses.

Walking home through the twilight, he kicked at clumps of old snow and muttered* to himself. Once or twice he groaned out loud. When he entered the front hall Bee said, "Hi, hon! How was our little Daffodil?" But Ian merely brushed past her and climbed the stairs to his room.

B. Read the following passage and underline all the front fillers. Divide them into words, phrases, and clauses.

According to some estimates, whites will no longer be a majority in the United States by the year 2050. Because minority populations and the number of non-white immigrants are increasing, typical families of the future will look very different from the Bedloes. Like other institutions in modern society, the family is changing. Clearly, it will keep changing to reflect social and economic developments.

MIDDLE FILLERS

Words, phrases, or clauses that begin sentences can usually occupy the position in the middle of the sentence (after the subject) also.

The foreigners *often* cook spicy food.

Everyone *on Waverly Street* knew everyone else.

Waverly Street, *although it was short,* contained a variety of neighbors.

---

* **muttered** spoke quietly, usually unhappily

Appositives, which are descriptive words or phrases, can sometimes be interchanged with the nouns they modify. Appositives are set off with commas when they occur in the middle position.

> Claudia, *the oldest child*, had moved to Baltimore County.
>
> (The oldest child, Claudia, had moved to Baltimore County.)

Other middle fillers, such as adjective clauses, refer to the subject but cannot be interchanged with it.

> Ian's brother, *who had been captain of his high school football team*, was nearing thirty.

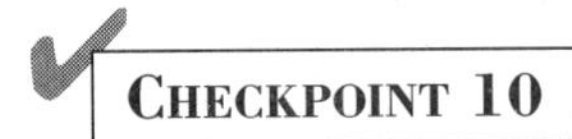

Checkpoint 10

A.

Read the following paragraph about Anne Tyler, author of *Saint Maybe*. Find and underline the middle fillers. Decide which are phrases and which are clauses. Which can also be used in the front position? Discuss your answers.

Anne Tyler, the author of *Saint Maybe*, was born in Minneapolis, Minnesota, but grew up in Raleigh, North Carolina. Tyler, after graduating at nineteen from Duke University, did graduate work in Russian Studies at Columbia University. *Saint Maybe* is Tyler's twelfth novel; her previous one, *Breathing Lessons*, was awarded the Pulitzer Prize in 1988. She is a member of the American Academy and Institute of Arts and Letters. She and her husband, whose name is Taghi Modarressi, live in Baltimore, Maryland.

B.

Write a paragraph describing the members of your immediate family and exchange it with a partner. Find all the middle fillers in your partner's paragraph and divide them into three groups: words, phrases, and clauses.

End Fillers

Many words, phrases, and clauses that may occur in the front or middle positions can also appear at the end of the sentence, after the predicate.

> The neighborhood was changing *very gradually.*
>
> They raised their children *during the 1950s and 1960s.*
>
> Number Six was referred to as the newlyweds', *although the Crains had been married for two years.*

Checkpoint 11

Read the following passage from *Saint Maybe.* Then underline the end fillers and put a circle around the front fillers. Discuss your answers with other students.

That summer, Ian got a job with Sid 'n' Ed's A-1 Movers—a very local sort of company consisting of a single van. Each morning he reported to a garage on Greenmount, and then he and two lean, black, jokey men drove to some shabby* house where they heaved* liquor cartons and furniture into the van for a couple of hours. Then they drove to some other house, often even shabbier, and heaved it all out again. Ian managed to enjoy the work because he thought of it as weight lifting. He had always been very conscious of muscles. As a small boy, admiring Danny and his friends at sports, he had focused upon their forearms—the braiding* beneath the skin as they swung a bat or punched a volleyball. There, he thought, was the telling difference, more than whiskers or deep voices. And he had examined his own reedy* arms and wondered if they would ever change. But when it happened he must have been asleep, for all at once two summers ago he had noticed as he was mowing the lawn—why, look at that! The ropy* muscles from wrist to elbow, the distinct blue cords of his veins. He had flexed a fist and gazed down, hypnotized, till his mother hallooed from the porch and asked how long he planned to stand there.

VI Focus on Coordination

Coordinating Conjunctions

Independent clauses can be joined with one of the following conjunctions: *and, but, or, yet, for, so,* and *nor.* A comma usually precedes a coordinating conjunction that connects two independent clauses, especially long clauses.

> Poe High School still maintained a dress code, *and* Ian's teachers were forever sending him home to put on something presentable.
>
> Ian was handsome, *but* his clothes were ragged.
>
> He felt that things would turn out fine, *so* he didn't worry about getting into a self-respecting college.
>
> He knew he would be famous, *or* at least he thought so.

---

* **shabby**	worn and dirty
heaved	lifted and moved with great effort
braiding	having the appearance of braids or interwoven strands of hair or fabric
reedy	thin, like a stick
ropy	like ropes or cords

The Semicolon

A semicolon may also join two independent clauses. It is used only when the two clauses are closely related in meaning.

> Bee Bedloe was a sloppy dresser; in fact, she looked as ragged as her son.
>
> Claudia was the oldest Bedloe child; she had married and moved to Baltimore county.

Independent clauses cannot be joined with a comma alone. This type of sentence error is called a "comma splice."

INCORRECT: Claudia was the oldest Bedloe child, she had married and moved to Baltimore.

Another type of sentence error is the "run-on." This occurs when independent clauses are joined without any punctuation or coordinating conjunction.

INCORRECT: Claudia was the oldest Bedloe child she had married and moved to Baltimore.

Checkpoint 12

A. 

Read the paragraph and circle the coordinating conjunctions. Underline the subjects once and the verbs twice. Then determine which conjunctions are used to join independent clauses. With your group, discuss the coordinating conjunctions. Could a different conjunction be substituted in any of the sentences?

The lights were still on, and the radio was playing a Beatles song. Ice cubes clinked in a glass. The cloppy footsteps came down the hall, and there was her mother outlined in the doorway. From the ankles up she was thin and fragile, but on her feet she wore two huge shoes from Danny's closet. She came over to Agatha's bed, shuffling slightly, so the shoes wouldn't fall off. "Are you awake?" she whispered.

B. 

Decide which of the following are complete sentences. Some may be fragments or incomplete sentences. Others may be comma splices or run-ons—incorrectly joined sentences. Rewrite items 1–5 as a paragraph consisting of correctly punctuated sentences.

1. Then along came June.
2. Dry as a bone.
3. Only one brief shower fell that entire scorching month.
4. The yard turned brown the cat lay stretched on the cool kitchen floor.
5. As flat as she could make herself.

C.

The following paragraph from *Saint Maybe* is punctuated incorrectly: it contains several incomplete sentences. With a partner, rewrite the passage so that it is punctuated properly.

Now Ian was seventeen. And, like the rest of his family, large-boned and handsome and easygoing, quick to make friends, fond of a good time. He had the Bedloe golden-brown hair, golden skin, and sleepy-looking brown eyes. Although his mouth was his mother's, a pale beige mouth quirking up at the corners.

Coordination of Sentence Parts

Besides independent clauses, coordinating conjunctions can join other structures in a sentence, such as subjects, verbs, objects, complements, or phrases. Usually a comma is not used before the conjunction joining these structures.

> The Bedloes *and* the Crains were neighbors.
> (subjects joined with a coordinator)
>
> Ian was bright *but* lazy.
> (complements joined with a coordinator)
>
> Ian could pitch *or* hit for the baseball team.
> (verbs joined with a coordinator)

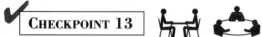

In this paragraph from *Saint Maybe*, identify the sentence parts that are joined with a coordinating conjunction.

For Doug's birthday, Bee made his favorite hors d'oeuvres*—smoked oyster log and spinach balls and Chesapeake crab spread. Claudia made a coconut cake that looked like a white shag bathmat. She and her family were the first to arrive. She had Ian come out to the kitchen with her to help put on the candles—fifty-nine of them, this year. Ian wasn't in a very good mood, but Claudia kept joshing* him so finally he had to smile. You couldn't stay glum* around Claudia for long; she was so funny and slapdash* and comfortable, in her boxy tan plaid shirt the same color as her skin and the maternity slacks she was wearing till she got her figure back. They ran out of birthday candles and started using other kinds—three tall white tapers* and several of those stubby votive lights their mother kept for power failures. By now they had the giggles. It was almost like

---

* **hors d'oeuvres**	appetizers, snacks served before dinner
joshing	teasing, joking with
glum	sad-looking
slapdash	casual and quick
tapers	thin candles

the old days, when Claudia wasn't married yet and still belonged completely to the family.

VII Focus on YES/NO Questions and Short Answers

Preview of YES/NO Questions

Read the following imaginary situation and dialogue to preview how questions are formed.

Situation: It is May, and some Johns Hopkins students from the Middle East are discussing how to spend their summer vacation in the United States.

Hassan: Are you taking a trip this summer?

Hamad: Maybe. Why? Do you want to go somewhere?

Hassan: Yes, I do. I want to see as much of the U.S. as I can. Are your exams over?

Hamad: Yes, they are. Is your last one this afternoon?

Hassan: That's right. Isn't it incredible that we're free for two months? Is the car running okay?

Hamad: Yes, it is. For the moment anyway. Does Abdulla have the summer off from his job? Don't you think he'd like to come along?

Hassan: Sure, I do. Let's start making plans. Does your map of the U.S. show all the national parks?

Abdulla: Hi! Are you going somewhere? Am I invited?

Checkpoint 14

Find all the questions in the dialogue that could be answered "yes" or "no" and circle the word that begins each question. These words are called *auxiliary verbs.* Divide them into two groups by completing the lists below. Then answer the questions that follow.

Group 1	Group 2
Are	*Do*

1. How is the word order in the questions you analyzed different from the word order in statements?
2. How did you divide the auxiliaries? Can you identify two patterns used in yes/no questions?
3. Do the auxiliaries in each list change according to the subjects that follow them?

Two Types of YES/NO Questions

Unlike statements, YES/NO questions use inverted word order: the subject follows the auxiliary verb instead of preceding it. For example, the statement *You are going somewhere* becomes *Are you going somewhere?*

Two auxiliary verbs that begin questions are *be* and *do*. If you put the words *am, is, isn't,* and *are* together, you formed one group of words that begin questions, the *be* verbs. In the other group, you should have put *do, does,* and *don't*; these words begin many present-tense questions that contain verbs other than *be*.*

YES/NO Questions with Forms of *Be*

Questions that begin with a form of *be* follow this pattern: *Be*-form + subject + main verb (if needed) + rest of sentence. Forms of *be* change according to the subject.

I *am*

We, they, you (singular or plural) *are*

He, she, it (or a singular noun) *is*

Be Verbs with YES/NO Questions

Be	Subject	Main Verb (if needed)	Rest of Sentence
Are	you	taking	a trip this summer?
Are	your exams		over?
Is	your last one		this afternoon?
Isn't	it		incredible that we're free for two months?
Is	the car	running?	
Am	I	invited?	

Checkpoint 15

Begin each question with the appropriate form of *be* (*am, is,* or *are*).

1. ____ all national parks open in the summer?
2. ____ I going to drive?
3. ____ the car in good condition?
4. ____ we leaving soon?
5. ____ the foreign students happy about their trip?

* Modal auxiliaries can also begin YES/NO questions. These verbs are explained in Unit 5.

YES/NO Questions with Forms of *Do*

Forms of the verb *do* are used to make questions when no other auxiliary verb occurs in the verb phrase. For example, the statement *You want to go somewhere* becomes *Do you want to go somewhere?* In questions beginning with *do*, this pattern is followed: form of *Do* + subject + main verb + rest of sentence.

The form of *do* changes according to the subject.

I, we, they, you (singular or plural) *do*

He, she, it (or singular noun) *does*

Forms of *Do* with YES/NO Questions

Do	Subject	Main Verb	Rest of Sentence
Does	Abdulla	have	the summer off from his job?
Don't	you	think	he'd like to come along?
Does	your map	show	all the national parks?

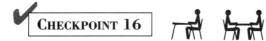

Checkpoint 16 

Begin each question with the appropriate form of *do*.

1. ____ we own a good map of the United States?
2. ____ your friends want to see some national parks?
3. ____ Abdulla have a job?
4. ____ the foreign students all come from the Middle East?
5. ____ she have friends in other states?

Short Answers

YES/NO questions are often answered with either *Yes* or *No* followed by the pronoun subject and the first verb form (auxiliary verb) of the question. Only negative answers may be contracted, or shortened.

Short Answers with *Be*

Yes, I am.	No, I'm not.	
Yes, he/she/it is.	No, he's/she's/it's not.	(No, he/she/it isn't.)
Yes, they are.	No, they're not.	(No, they aren't.)
Yes, we are.	No, we're not.	(No, we aren't.)
Yes, you are.	No, you're not.	(No, you aren't.)

To form short answers with *do*, the base form is used with all subjects except *he*, *she*, and *it*, which require *does*.

SHORT ANSWERS WITH *DO*

Yes, I (you, we, they) do.	No, I (you, we, they) don't.
Yes, he (she, it) does.	No, he (she, it) doesn't.

✔ CHECKPOINT 17 

A. Take turns asking and answering YES/NO questions about yourselves. Use short answers to respond. Example:

You/a good/student

Student A: Are you a good student?

Student B: Yes, I am. (or No, I'm not.) Are you a good . . .?

1. You/a good/dancer
   driver
   athlete, etc.
2. Most of your friends/students
   men/women
   intelligent/happy/friendly/fun, etc.
3. Your mother/tall
   father/short
   brother/like you
   sister/different from you
   at home

B. Form YES/NO questions using the cues. Add other information if you wish.

1. Foreigners/be free/three months

   Are the foreigners free for three months?

   No, they aren't. (No, they're not.) They're free for two months.
2. Hassan/want to travel
3. Hamad's last exam/be tomorrow
4. Abdulla/have the summer off
5. Their car/be running all right

VIII Focus on Information Questions

Preview of Information Questions

Read the following situation and dialogue.

Situation: The students have looked at their map and guidebook. They have made a plan for their summer trip that includes visiting five national parks, which are shown on the map.

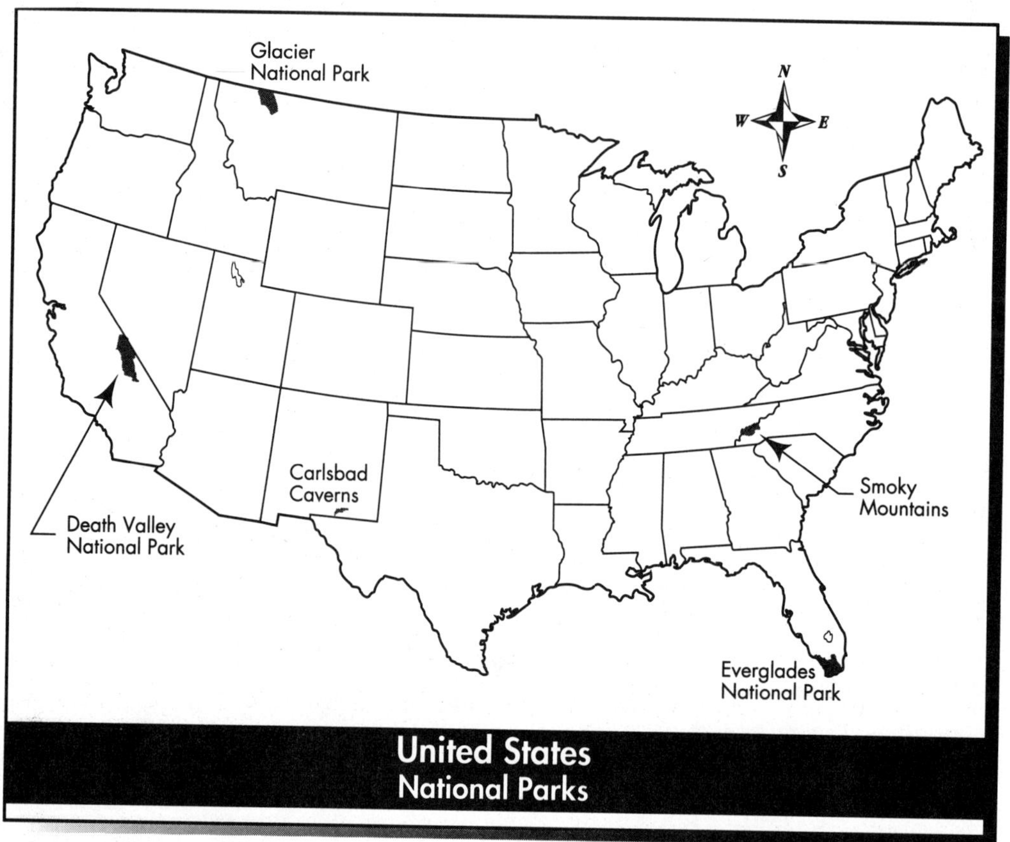

Abdulla: Where do you want to go, Hamad? There are lots of national parks. Which look best?

Hamad: These five look good to me.

Abdulla: But I don't know anything about these places. What do people wear when they go to a national park? How does a visitor make arrangements?

Hassan: Calm down. It's all in the guide book. How much insurance do you have, Abdulla?

Abdulla: Why are you asking me that? Who's driving this summer?

Types of Information Questions

Information questions ask for new information and begin with a question word, such as *Where, Why, When,* or *Who.* A list of question words with their meanings follows.

Where . . .?	What *place*?
When . . .?	What *time*?
Why . . .?	What *reason*?
How . . .?	In what *way*?
	To what *extent*?
Who(m) . . .?	What *person*?
Which . . .?	What *thing* or *activity*?
What . . .?	
How often . . .?	With what *frequency*?
How much, many . . .?	What *quantity*?
What . . . do?	What *occupation*?
What kind . . . ?	What *type* or *category*?
What (be) . . . like?	What *qualities* or *features*? (used in a description or characterization)

Checkpoint 18

Go back to the dialogue on page 28. Circle all the question words and identify the type of new information each question calls for. Example:

(Where) do you want to go? = What *place*

Object-Type Information Questions

Most information questions are formed like YES/NO questions, except that they begin with question words (*Who, What,* etc.). Information questions follow this pattern:

> Question word + auxiliary verb + subject + main verb + rest of sentence. The auxiliary agrees with the subject.

The questions in the box are called "object-type" because the question word and information that is provided in the answer are objects (of verbs or prepositions) or subject complements.

What do people wear in the Great Smoky Mountains?

They wear ____________ (object of verb).

To what national park do they plan to go?

They plan to go to ___________ (object of preposition).

What color are the mountains?

They are ___________ (subject complement).

Object-Type Information Questions

Question-word	Auxiliary	Subject	Verb	Rest of Sentence
Where	do	you	want	to go?
What	do	people	wear	when they go to a national park?
How	does	a visitor	arrange	guided tours?

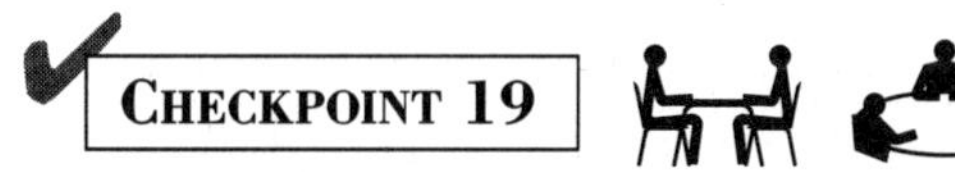

Read the description of the Great Smoky Mountains from the students' guidebook, and then do the exercise.

Great Smoky Mountains

800 square miles in Tennessee and North Carolina

Features: These rolling green mountains are called the "roof" of the eastern United States. The impressive forests contain more than 1200 varieties of trees and plants, more than 50 types of fur-bearing animals, and 200 kinds of birds.

Activities: Visitors enjoy white-water rafting down mountain streams and wilderness trails for cars and horses. The park contains 70 miles of the famous Maine-Georgia footpath, the Appalachian Trail.

What to Bring: Year-round rain and fog make rainproof clothing necessary. Hiking shoes and sturdy clothes are recommended.

Form questions using the cues. Then find the answer. Example:

Why/visitors/go/to the Smoky Mountains

Why do visitors go to the Smoky Mountains?
They go to see the forest, birds, and other animals.

1. How many/trees and plants/Great Smoky Mountains
2. How many/fur-bearing animals/Great Smoky Mountains
3. How many/birds
4. Where/tourists/walk
5. What/traveler/need to bring

Subject-Type Information Questions

In subject-type questions, the question word acts as a subject, and the new information that the question calls for is the subject in the answer. No verb precedes the subject in this type of question; the question word is followed by the auxiliary and main verb and then the rest of the sentence.

Subject-Type Information Questions

Question-word	Verb	Rest of Sentence
Which	looks	best?
Who	is driving	this summer?
What	makes	a national park enjoyable?

Return to the description of the Great Smoky Mountains on page 30. Make up a question for each answer. Example:

ANSWER: visitors

QUESTION: Who enjoys white-water rafting?

1. Fur-bearing animals
2. Wilderness trails for cars and horses
3. The park
4. Year-round rain and fog

IX Focus on Questions about the Past

Preview of Past-Tense Questions

Imagine that the students have just returned from the trip. Hassan and an American neighbor, Mr. Anderson, are discussing the students' experiences.

Mr. Anderson: Hi, boys. How were the parks?

Hassan: Great. We saw five.

Mr. Anderson: Which was your favorite?

Hassan: My favorite was Glacier, but it wasn't Abdulla's. He had a terrible time there.

Mr. Anderson: What happened?

Hassan: He hit a moose.

Mr. Anderson: Oh, no. Was he speeding?

Hassan: No, he wasn't. But the police came.

Mr. Anderson: Did they arrest him?

Hassan: Yes, they did.

Mr. Anderson: How long did they keep him?

Hassan: Overnight.

Mr. Anderson: Poor Abdulla.

✔ **Checkpoint 21**  

A. In the dialogue between Mr. Anderson and Hassan, locate the following: YES/NO questions, information questions, and short answers. Divide each category into *be* and *do*. Then divide information questions into subject-type and object-type.

B. Write your own past-tense questions about your partner's family or neighborhood. Make up as many questions as you can in 10 to 15 minutes. Then exchange papers and write short answers to each other's questions. Possible questions: Where did you live when you were a child? Did you like your neighborhood? How many brothers and sisters did you have? Were you the oldest?

Auxiliary Verbs in Past Questions

In the past tense, *be* verbs change according to their subject.

I, he, she, it *was*.

you, we, they *were*.

With many other past-tense verbs, however, the same auxiliary, *did*, is used for all questions.

Past Questions				
Question-word	Auxiliary	Subject	Main Verb	Rest of Sentence
	Was	he	speeding?	
How	were	the	parks?	
Which	were	your favorites?		
	Did	they	arrest	him?
How long	did	they	keep	him?

CHECKPOINT 22

Form past-tense questions using the cues and provide short answers. Refer to the dialogue to find answers if necessary. Example:

How many parks/students/see

How many parks did the students see?
Five.

1. What/be/Hassan's favorite
2. What/Abdulla/hit
3. Who/come
4. Abdulla/be speeding
5. The police/arrest/Abdulla
6. How long/police/keep/Abdulla
7. Abdulla/enjoy/Glacier Park

PART THREE. Review and Integration

Springtime in Baltimore: Sentence Identification

A. Some of the structures in the following passage from *Saint Maybe* are fragments. Combine the clauses and fragments to make complete sentences and rewrite the paragraph correctly.

It was near the end of March. That period when spring approaches jerkily. And then backs off a bit. The light was hanging on longer. Than it had a week ago. But a raw, damp wind was moving in. From the north. Ian zipped his jacket. And turned up the collar. He circled a group of Waverly Street children. Playing hopscotch.* Bulkily wrapped little girls. Planting their feet in a no-nonsense, authoritative way. Down a ladder of chalked squares. He performed a polite minuet.* With one of the foreigners. Dodging* right. Then dodging left. Till the foreigner said, "Please to excuse me." And laughed and stepped aside. Ian nodded. But he didn't stop to talk. Talking with the foreigners could tie up half the evening. What with the habit they had. Of meticulously* inquiring after every possible relative.

B. Read the following passage from *Saint Maybe* and label each S (complete sentence), F (fragment), RO (run-on), or CS (comma splice). Then rewrite items 1–8 as a correctly punctuated paragraph.

1. One of the Bedloe traditions was that important dinners, on holidays and such. ______
2. Were not the usual boring assortment of meats and vegetables. ______
3. Instead, Bee served their favorite course: hors d'oeuvres. ______
4. Oh, there'd be a turkey at Thanksgiving, cakes for birthdays, but those were just a nod to convention.* ______
5. What mattered were the stuffed mushrooms. ______
6. The runny cheeses, the spreads and dips and patés and shrimps on toothpicks. ______
7. The family was secretly proud of this practice, they enjoyed watching guests' reactions. ______
8. That Christmas they had oysters on the half shell the look of horror on Lucy's children's faces made everybody laugh. ______

---

* **hopscotch**	a children's game that involves hopping on squares drawn on the street or sidewalk
minuet	(from French) a type of formal dance
dodging	moving to the side to avoid bumping into someone
meticulously	conscientiously or carefully
nod to convention	something done only because it is traditional

Foreign Affairs: Using Indirect Objects

Expand the information below into complete sentences with indirect objects. Use two patterns if possible. Sample patterns:

They bought their friends some presents.

They bought some presents for their friends.

A. The Bedloes like to learn about the native countries of the foreign graduate students in the neighborhood. What are some things the students do to explain their culture?
   1. tell stories
   2. show pictures
   3. bring objects
   4. cook meals
   5. describe customs

B. Foreign students who come to the United States to study must adjust to the culture of this country. What do they have to learn in order to live on their own?
   1. buy groceries
   2. ask questions
   3. pay bills
   4. give gifts
   5. write letters

Neighborhoods: Subjects, Predicates, Fillers

Write at least five sentences describing your neighborhood. Give as many details as possible. Exchange papers with a partner and perform the following tasks.

1. Put a line between the subject and predicate.
2. Circle any front filler that precedes the subject of a sentence.
3. Underline any middle constructions that occur between the subject and predicate of a sentence.
4. Put a rectangle around any end filler.

Example:

(Because the houses are new,) my neighborhood / feels quite modern.

Residents of Waverly Street: Front, Middle, and End Fillers

A. Match elements from the four columns below to make complete sentences about Waverly Street. Add punctuation where necessary. Discuss your choices with the group. You may want to refer to the reading on pages 6 and 7.

Married for two years	foreign graduate students	live	with Ian and their pets
From the Middle East	elderly maples	have surrounded	Waverly Street
In Number Eight	the Crains	line	worn around the edges
Lumpy and bulbous	loyal friends	look	to attend Johns Hopkins
Since elementary school	the Bedloes	come	Ian

Example:

Married for two years, the Crains look worn around the edges.

B. The following excerpt from *Yankee* magazine (March 1991, p. 70) is about an artist who enjoys painting pictures of buildings in old Boston neighborhoods. Read the passage and underline the front fillers, circle the middle fillers, and draw a rectangle around the end fillers. Discuss your answers with other students.

Early in the morning, before the commuters* in Concord and Georgetown have even finished showering, an old van of drab* and vaguely military green slowly cruises the streets of Boston's Back Bay. The driver, a 63-year-old man named George Nick, carefully studies the brick and brownstone facades* along Commonwealth Avenue as though looking for an address. The lettering on the truck reads "Orpheus Landscapes," but Nick is not a gardener. When he locates a scene that interests him, he pulls his mobile studio over, switches on the old bus heater he had installed to take the chill off the Bay State* winter, sets up his easel* in the back of the van, and paints.

"I've been double-parked since 1969," he jokes.

---

* **commuters**	people driving to work
drab	dull, lacking color
facades	fronts, faces
Bay State	nickname for Massachusetts
easel	frame to support an artist's canvas

Game: Scrambled Sentences

Arrange the groups of words below to make sentences. Insert the commas where necessary and add correct capitals and punctuation. Put your group's sentences on the board and then discuss the structures in them, such as indirect objects, complements, and different types of fillers.

1. , , prepared a each Mrs. night her homemaker dinner Bedloe family's
2. , wasn't cook however she good a particularly
3. , grades were his but smart was ordinary Ian
4. his cultured biographer imagined the of Ian voice
5. exotic foreigners night themselves at the made meals the

National Parks: Questions

Read the descriptions of four national parks visited by the foreign students and do the exercises.

1 Everglades National Park

2,188 square miles in southern Florida

Features: Subtropical wildlife and vegetation live in this wet area; fish, alligators, and rare birds can be seen as well as unusual plants (mangrove, cypress, ferns, and orchids).

Activities: Visitors enjoy nature talks and walks through junglelike land. Boating trips for big-game fishing are available.

What to Bring: Light clothing and hats, insect repellent, and sunglasses.

2 Carlsbad Caverns

72 square miles in southeastern New Mexico

Features: The attraction includes the most remarkable limestone cavern in the world; it contains large rock formations in strange shapes. The "big room" is the largest underground space in the world.

Activities: Visitors can arrange four-hour trips into the cavern with a guide. Lunch is available on the tour. Special photographic trips are possible.

What to Bring: A jacket is necessary inside the cave; boots or sturdy shoes are important for climbing. Flash attachments improve cave pictures.

3 Death Valley Monument

2,981 square miles in Nevada and California

Features: Because this place has the lowest altitude in the Western Hemisphere, it is called "North America's basement." Sand dunes and desert scenery attract many visitors.

Activities: Illustrated talks, breath-taking views, horseback riding, and foot trails are the attractions here.

What to Bring: A jacket is needed for the cool evenings, and sunglasses and hats are essential during the day. Binoculars and cameras with light meters help visitors enjoy the scenery.

4 Glacier National Park

1,583 square miles in northwestern Montana

Features: This park is in a rough, glacier-cut mountain region filled with icy lakes and snow-covered mountains. Similar to central Alaska, it contains large mountain animals such as moose, deer, bear, big-horn sheep, and mountain goats.

Activities: Many horseback and hiking trails are laid out to view the wonderful scenery. In addition, overnight horseback trips into the wild animal territory can be arranged.

What to Bring: Cold, rainy weather makes warm, waterproof clothing essential. Binoculars and cameras are useful to view and record the spectacular scenery.

A. As a group, make up ten YES/NO questions based on the reading and have one person write them. Exchange papers with another group and answer the groups' questions with short answers. Example:

Are the Everglades in Florida?

Yes, they are.

B. Write a question that begins with each of the following words: *Where, Who, What, How, When, Why, How many, What kind.* Exchange papers with another group and let the other group answer your questions. Example:

Where is Glacier National park?

Game: Answer First

Brainstorm and write down a list of ten places or things from the reading about national parks. Give your list to another team. Each team has ten minutes to provide a question for each answer.

When the time is up, a member of each team reads the team's questions. A team receives one point for each correct question. The team with the most points wins. Examples:

ANSWER: Southeastern New Mexico.
QUESTION: Where is Carlsbad Caverns National Park?
ANSWER: Fish, alligators, and rare birds.
QUESTION: What kind of animals live in the Everglades National Park?

Game: Who Am I?

Divide into teams. The teams will compete in pairs. Each team thinks of famous people, places, and things and writes each on an index card. Pin one card to the back of each member of the opposite team. Each team member has two minutes to find out *who/what/where* he/she is by asking his/her teammates YES/NO questions. A successful participant receives a point, and the team with the most points at the end of the game wins. Examples: a diamond, Christopher Columbus, Shakespeare, the Pacific Ocean, China.

Suggestions for Writing

1. If you are keeping a journal, write an entry about one of the following: good neighbors, bad neighbors, neighborhoods or houses in your native country.
2. Write a description of the traditional American family. Divide your description into important characteristics, and give examples (from *Saint Maybe*, if you wish).
3. Compare the characteristics of a traditional American family with those of a traditional family from another culture that you know about.
4. Write a composition comparing two neighborhoods: (a) one in the United States vs. one in another country, or (b) the one where you live now vs. one where you used to live.
5. Discuss problems foreign students may have in becoming accustomed to life in another country, such as differences in food, clothing, driving, shopping, and the monetary system.
6. Write a description of one or more national parks or recreational areas you have visited. Make it as detailed as possible. Include descriptions of the scenery and an account of what you did there.

Unit Two

Nouns, Articles, and Pronouns

READING: "The Unicorn in the Garden" by James Thurber

THEME: Humor and Imagination

PART ONE. The Context

The following story by James Thurber (1894–1961) originally appeared in *The New Yorker* magazine as part of a series called "Fables for Our Times" (1939–40) and has been reprinted often. Well-known for his humorous fiction and cartoons, Thurber wrote a number of stories in the form of fables or fairy tales. Although "The Unicorn in the Garden" is about a married couple, it is not a serious depiction of American marriage, but instead is an amusing and ironic tale.

Pre-Reading Questions

1. Did you enjoy reading fairy tales when you were a child? What were some of their characteristics? For example, were they frightening, humorous, romantic? Did they teach lessons about good and bad behavior?
2. Western (European and American) literature includes many stories with imaginary animals like unicorns (horselike creatures with a single horn in the middle of their foreheads) and dragons that breathe fire. What other kinds of imaginary animals appear in fairy tales?
3. Many fairy tales in English begin with the phrase "Once upon a time" and end with "and they lived happily ever after," followed by a "moral," or lesson. How do fairy tales that you have read begin and end?

Preview of Key Terms and Concepts

The following words and ideas appear in the story. Guess the meaning of each term on the left by matching it to a definition on the right. Put the correct letter after each term. Discuss your answers with a partner or group, and ask your teacher about any terms you're not sure of.

1. breakfast nook ____
2. booby-hatch ____
3. psychiatrist ____
4. strait-jacket ____
5. "Don't count your chickens before they are hatched." ____
6. tulips, lilies, roses ____

a. types of flowers that require considerable care to grow

b. corner of a kitchen with a table and chairs or benches

c. garment with arms crossed in front and tied in back, used to control a person who might become violent

d. expression that warns against expecting good results before they happen

e. medical doctor whose specialty is treating emotional or mental disorders

f. slang term for a hospital for mental patients

Reading. "The Unicorn in the Garden" by James Thurber

(1) Once upon a sunny morning a man who sat in a breakfast nook looked up from his scrambled eggs to see a white unicorn with a gold horn quietly cropping* the roses in his garden. The man went up to the bedroom where his wife was still asleep and woke her. "There's a unicorn in the garden," he said. "Eating roses." She opened one unfriendly eye and looked at him. "The unicorn is a mythical* beast," she said, and turned her back on him.

(2) The man walked slowly downstairs and out into the garden. The unicorn was still there; he was now browsing* among the tulips. "Here, unicorn," said the man, and he pulled up a lily and gave it to him. The unicorn ate it gravely.* With a high heart, because there was a unicorn in his garden, the man went upstairs and roused* his wife again. "The unicorn," he said, "ate a lily." His wife sat up in bed and looked at him, coldly. "You are a booby," she said, "and I am going to have you put in the booby-hatch." The man, who had never liked the words "booby" and "booby-hatch," and who liked them even less on a shining morning when there was a unicorn in the garden, thought for a moment. "We'll see about that," he said. He walked over to the door. "He has a golden horn in the middle of his forehead," he told her. Then he went back to the garden to watch the unicorn; but the unicorn had gone away. The man sat down among the roses and went to sleep.

(3) As soon as the husband had gone out of the house, the wife got up and dressed as fast as she could. She was very excited and there was a gloat* in her eye. She telephoned the police and she telephoned a psychiatrist; she told them to hurry to her house and bring a strait-jacket. When the police and the psychiatrist arrived they sat down in chairs and looked at her with great interest. "My husband," she said, "saw a unicorn this morning." The police looked at the psychiatrist and the psychiatrist looked at the police. "He told me it ate a lily," she said. The psychiatrist looked at the police and the police looked at the psychiatrist. "He told me it had a golden horn in the middle of its forehead," she said. At a solemn* signal from the psychiatrist, the police leaped* from their chairs and seized* the wife. They had a hard time subduing* her, for she put up a terrific struggle, but they finally subdued her. Just as they got her into the strait-jacket, the husband came back into the house.

(4) "Did you tell your wife you saw a unicorn?" asked the police. "Of course not," said the husband. "The unicorn is a mythical beast." "That's all I wanted

---

* **cropping**	removing the upper parts from
mythical	imaginary, make-believe
browsing	wandering
gravely	very seriously
roused	awakened
gloat	a look of self-satisfaction
solemn	serious
leaped	jumped
seized	took by force
subdue	restrain, overpower

to know," said the psychiatrist. "Take her away. I'm sorry, sir, but your wife is as crazy as a jaybird." So they took her away, cursing and screaming, and shut her up in an institution.* The husband lived happily ever after.

(5) Moral: Don't count your boobies before they are hatched.

Comprehension Questions

1. What was the unicorn doing when the man saw it?
2. How did the wife react to her husband's news about the unicorn?
3. Why did the wife make a phone call when her husband went back outside? How did she feel?
4. Why did the police and the psychiatrist take away the woman instead of the man?
5. What does the proverb that concludes the story mean?

Discussion Questions

1. Fairy tales aren't usually funny, but they are predictable. The humor in this story arises from its **un**predictability. In what ways is the ending unexpected?
2. Readers who are familiar with proverbs in the U.S. expect to read "Don't count your chickens before they are hatched" as the moral of the story. What effect does the substitution of the word *booby* have?
3. Another source of humor in the story is the use of word play or puns. Puns are words or expressions that either have two meanings or that suggest another similar-sounding word or expression. What is the double meaning of *hatch* in Thurber's story?
4. Humor has been found to have a positive role in curing diseases and helping people recover from illnesses. Why do you think laughing and a sense of humor could contribute to good health?
5. People consult psychiatrists to overcome emotional problems, to improve relationships, and to gain more satisfaction from their lives. What are some other ways to achieve these goals? What do you think of psychiatry or psychotherapy as a means of helping people to improve their lives?

---

* institution   mental hospital

PART TWO: The Target Structures: Nouns, Articles, and Pronouns

I Focus on Types of Nouns

Preview of Nouns

How would you complete the following sentence?

The ________ saw a ________ in the ________.

If you had just read "The Unicorn in the Garden," you might have answered:

"The man saw a unicorn in the garden."

But there are other possibilities, such as

The woman saw a policeman in the driveway.

The psychiatrist saw a booby in the window.

The words that have been filled in are nouns. If you put words like these in the blank spaces, you showed that you recognize nouns and the way they are used. Two important clues indicated that the missing words were nouns.

1. Many nouns are preceded by articles (*a*, *an*, or *the*).
2. Most nouns act as *subjects*, *complements*, or *objects* of various kinds.

Checkpoint 1

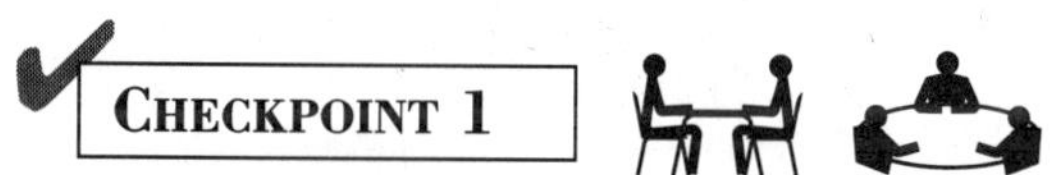

Circle the nouns in the first paragraph of "The Unicorn in the Garden" and discuss your choices with other students. Then answer the questions that follow the passage.

Once upon a sunny morning a man who sat in a breakfast nook looked up from his scrambled eggs to see a white unicorn with a gold horn quietly cropping the roses in his garden. The man went up to the bedroom where his wife was still asleep and woke her. "There's a unicorn in the garden," he said. "Eating roses." She opened one unfriendly eye and looked at him. "The unicorn is a mythical beast," she said, and turned her back on him.

1. The paragraph from the story contains thirteen nouns, including four (*man*, *unicorn*, *roses*, and *garden*) that are used more than once. Make two lists of nouns: those preceded by the indefinite article *a* and those preceded by the definite article *the*. Can you make any generalizations about the differences

between the two groups of nouns? Why are some "definite" and others "indefinite"?

2. Find five phrases that follow the pattern *article* plus *modifier* plus *noun*, and write them on a piece of paper. (The first is *a sunny morning.*) In which of the phrases is a noun used as a modifier to describe another noun?
3. Which nouns are used as subjects? Which are used as complements? (Remember that complements follow "linking" verbs.) Make two lists of these two groups.
4. Make a third list of the remaining nouns. All of these nouns are used as objects. Which are objects of verbs? (The rest of the nouns are objects in other structures that will be explained in later units.)

Types of Nouns

Nouns sometimes refer to people, like *man* and *wife*. Other nouns refer to things, such as *roses* and *unicorn*. The nouns *garden* and *nook* refer to places (or things). Another type of noun names an abstraction, concept, or idea.

Filled with *concern*, the police hurried to the house.

The woman's *behavior* caused the psychiatrist to put the strait-jacket on her.

Nouns like *concern* and *behavior*, which name ideas or qualities rather than concrete objects, often appear without articles.

The following chart shows examples of nouns used in "The Unicorn in the Garden."

Four Types of Nouns

People	Places	Things	Abstractions
a *booby*	the *booby-hatch*	a *unicorn*	great *interest*
police	the *garden*	a *lily*	*excitement*
the *man*	a *breakfast nook*	*glasses*	*behavior*
the *wife*	a *hospital*	*eggs*	*joy*

Because singular nouns that can be counted always appear with articles or other "determiners," those nouns are shown with articles in the box. Determiners include numbers (*one* unicorn, *three* lilies), possessives (*his* wife, *her* back), demonstrative adjectives (*this* woman, *those* police), and quantity words (*many* flowers, *some* husbands, *no* unicorns).

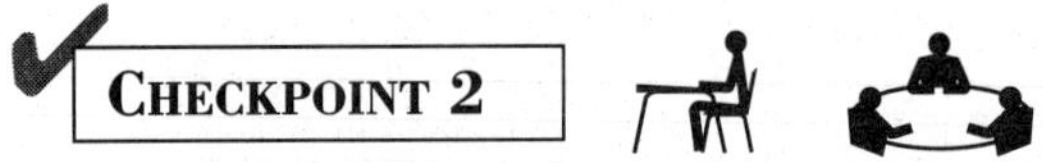

Circle the nouns in each of the following sentences. Then put the nouns in groups: persons, places, things, abstractions. Some nouns may belong in more than one group. Discuss your answers with classmates. Examples:

(person) (place or thing)
The (wife) was taken to the (booby-hatch).

1. The couple lived in that big empty house across town.
2. That man had been their psychiatrist for years.
3. Her husband had little respect for her.
4. Why would such a beast come into this unhappy environment?
5. The unicorn appeared in the garden.
6. Why did the police walk on the roses and lilies?
7. The horn on its forehead was made of gold.
8. Throughout history, gentleness and innocence have attracted these horselike creatures.

Singular and Plural Nouns

Most nouns have a plural form. Typically, *-s* is added to the singular noun to form the plural. *A* or *an* is never used with a plural noun, but *the* can be used with both singular and plural nouns.

Nouns with Regular Plurals

Singular	Plural
a terrific *struggle*	terrific *struggles*
a *psychiatrist*	three *psychiatrists*
a gold *horn*	gold *horns*
the *rose*	the *roses*

When a singular noun ends in *ss*, *x*, *z*, *sh*, *ch*, or *o*, the plural noun usually ends in *-es*.

Nouns with *-es* in the Plural

Singular	Plural
booby-hatch	booby-hatches
dish	dishes
fox	foxes
kiss	kisses
hero	heroes
mosquito	mosquitoes
potato	potatoes
tomato	tomatoes

EXCEPTIONS: *memo/memos*, *piano/pianos*, *radio/radios*, *solo/solos*, *zoo/zoos*

Some nouns have irregular plurals. Examples are *child/children*, *woman/women*, *man/men*, *tooth/teeth*, and *mouse/mice*. The rules for irregular noun plurals are explained in the Appendix on pages 383–385.

CHECKPOINT 3

The Greek writer Aesop, who lived in the sixth century B.C., wrote fables—short stories, often about animals, that taught a moral or lesson. Read Aesop's fable "The Dogs and the Fox," and circle all the nouns. Make two lists, one of singular nouns and one of plural nouns.

The Dogs and the Fox

Some dogs found the skin of a Lion and began to tear it wildly with their teeth. A Fox saw them and laughed at them.

"If that Lion had been alive," he said, "it would have been a very different story. He would have made you feel how much sharper his claws are than your teeth."

Moral: There's no honor in defeating a weaker opponent.

POSSESSIVE NOUNS

Nouns that express possession or ownership can be singular or plural. Singular possessive nouns are formed by the addition of *-'s* (apostrophe plus *s*).

the *woman's* eye	the *husband's* imagination
the *couple's* bedroom	the *wife's* surprise

The plural possessive is formed by the addition of only an apostrophe. Irregular plural forms (those that do not end in *s*) are made possessive by adding *-'s*.

two *psychiatrists'* patients	the *women's* movement
children's toys	two *boys'* secret

Notice that the number of the possessive noun and that of the noun it modifies do not have to be the same: one can be singular and the other plural.

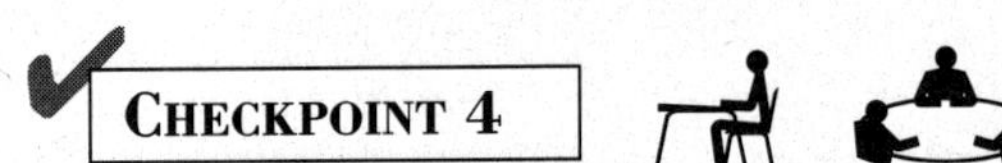

Answer the following questions with one **(1)** or more than one **(1+)**. You may have to refer to a dictionary or to the Appendix on pages 383–385 for information on irregular plurals.

1. women's husbands — How many women? ____ How many husbands? ____
2. this woman's husband — How many women? ____ How many husbands? ____

3. their husbands' surprise	How many husbands? ____ How many surprises? ____
4. the husband's surprises	How many husbands? ____ How many surprises? ____
5. the hospital's services	How many hospitals? ____ How many services? ____
6. the hospitals' service	How many hospitals? ____ How many services? ____
7. the people's choice	How many people? ____ How many choices? ____
8. the unicorn's horn	How many unicorns? ____ How many horns? ____

Proper and Common Nouns

Nouns can be classified as "proper" or "common." A proper noun is the actual name or title of a person, place, or thing; proper nouns are capitalized. Proper nouns include days of the week (*Monday*, *Tuesday*, etc.), months (*January*, *February*, etc.), holidays (*Thanksgiving*, *Christmas*, *Easter*), and languages and nationalities (*American*, *Arabic*, *Chinese*, *French*, etc). A common noun is a less specific person, place, or thing, and it is not capitalized.

Proper Nouns	**Common Nouns**
Winston State Hospital	a hospital
Mrs. Johnson	the woman
Dr. Watson	the psychiatrist
Office Sanchez and Officer Wilson	the police
March	last month
Thursday	one day last week

Capitalize the proper nouns in the following hospital promotional material.

winston state hospital has been serving emotionally troubled patients in the twin city area since january 1, 1955. Many doctors in morgan city and new london have confidence that their patients will receive the finest care at our hospital. The head of psychiatry, dr. ralph johnson, has been recognized as an expert in the treatment of paranoia and schizophrenia by the american psychological association. He was elected to several professional honor societies,

including the circle of hippocrates. Visitors are welcome at the hospital, and family members of patients can arrange to stay overnight on fridays and saturdays as well as the holidays of thanksgiving and christmas.

II Focus on Articles

There are many rules (and exceptions) about article use; only some of the most common and useful are covered here. (For rules about articles used with place names, see the Appendix on page 389.)

Indefinite Articles

A and *an* are indefinite articles. *A* is used before a noun that begins with a consonant sound; *an* is used before a noun that begins with a vowel sound: *a, e, i, o,* or *u* (except when it sounds like "you"). *An* is also used in a noun phrase when a modifier beginning with a vowel precedes the noun. When the consonant *h* is silent, it is preceded by *an* because the word really begins with a vowel sound (*an* honor, but *a* hotel).

A* versus *An

She looked at him with *an* unfriendly eye.

A fork is *a* utensil used for eating. (*u* sounds like "you")

A unicorn is *an* imaginary animal.

He made *an* honest mistake. (*h* is "silent)

She scrambled *an* egg.

Checkpoint 6

In this composition written by a nephew of the husband and wife in the story (Sam and Mary) on the topic "My Most Interesting Relative(s)," the indefinite articles have been left out. Fill in the blanks with *a* or *an*.

____ uncle of mine, Uncle Sam, always says that ____ university education is important for ____ child to think about, even at ____ early age. I think he's crazy. He must be because he told my mother he saw ____ unicorn in his garden and then convinced ____ psychiatrist to take my aunt, ____ very sane person, to ____ hospital for the insane. The next thing you know, he'll be telling us he found ____ big octopus in his bathtub!

My Aunt Mary told me about ____ electrical failure at the hospital yesterday. The patients became so wild that ____ police officer was called. He brought along ____ union representative to tell him what to do. They spent ____ hour trying to calm down the patients.

Auntie also said the food in the hospital is terrible. She wants me to bring her ____ appetizing snack the next time I visit. I wonder if she'd prefer ____ avocado salad or ____ stuffed eggplant. Maybe I'll just take her ____ oyster cocktail.

USING *A/AN*

Three common situations require the indefinite article *a* or *an*.

- *A* or *an* precedes most singular nouns when they are mentioned for the first time. In the following sentences, the article *a* is used to introduce a noun.

  They were *a* couple in their late thirties.

  He sat in *a* breakfast nook, eating breakfast.

- The indefinite article is used when a noun is not distinguished from others in its class; it refers to any one of its kind.

  The man saw *a* unicorn.

  Have you ever seen *a ghost*?

- *A/an* sometimes means *one*. When it has this meaning, it can be used with a noun that has already been identified. For example, Thurber wrote, "The unicorn," he said, "ate *a* lily," even though the noun *lily* had already been mentioned.

CHECKPOINT 7

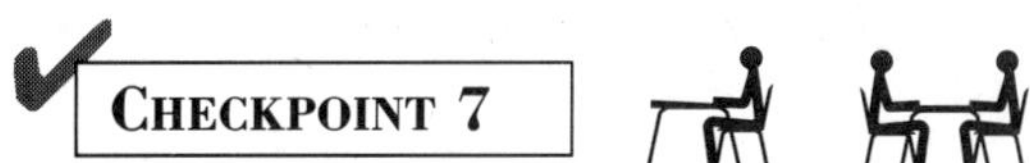

Circle the indefinite articles in this Aesop's fable, "The Monkey and the Cat." List the articles and nouns in three categories: first usage, indefinite, and *one*. Begin with *a cat*. Compare answers with a partner.

The Monkey and the Cat

Once upon a time, a cat and a monkey lived as pets in the same house. They were great friends and were constantly in all sorts of trouble together. What they seemed to think of more than anything else was getting something to eat, and it did not matter much to them how they got it.

One day they were sitting by the fire, watching some chestnuts roasting in the fireplace. How to get them was the question.

"I would gladly get them," said the clever monkey, "but you are much more skillful at such things than I am. Pull them out and I'll divide them between us."

Kitty stretched out her paw very carefully, pushed aside some cinders, and drew back her paw very quickly. Then she tried it again, this time pulling a chestnut half out of the fire. The third time she drew out a whole chestnut. She did this several times, each time burning her paw severely. As fast as she pulled the chestnuts out of the fire, the monkey ate them up.

Now the master came in, and away ran the trouble makers, the cat with a burnt paw and no chestnuts. From that time on, they say, she contented herself with mice and rats and had little to do with the monkey.

Moral: Never trust a flatterer.

Definite Articles

The definite article *the* is pronounced "tha" before consonant sounds (*"tha" wife*) and "thee" before vowel sounds (*"thee" eggs*). It commonly occurs in three situations.

- If a person, place, or thing is known to both the reader and the writer (or the speaker and the listener), the article *the* precedes it. Once a noun has been introduced, *the* is used with it, as in the second and third sentences.

> *A* man and woman woke up one sunny morning. *The* man went downstairs. *The* wife stayed in bed for a while.

The reader knows *which* man and woman are being discussed because they were introduced in the first sentence.

- The definite article is used when there is no confusion about the identity of the person, place, or thing because (a) it is the only one known to the speaker and listener or (b) it is familiar to them.

> He looked out at *the* garden.
>
> She telephoned *the* police department.
>
> *The* mailman comes at noon.

- *The* is used with nouns that are made definite in context, usually by a following phrase or clause, even if they haven't been mentioned before.

> *The* unicorn *in the garden* is not the same as *the* unicorn *that the man saw in the woods last week.*

With plural nouns, *the* is used only if the noun is familiar or made definite by the context or the situation in which it is used. Otherwise, no article is necessary.

> The man had pancakes with his eggs.
>
> *The* pancakes *that the man was eating* had blueberries in them.

In the second sentence, the context requires the use of *the.*

Article Usage

Review the following rules of article usage.

Some Rules of Article Usage	
a/an	• Used with indefinite, singular nouns mentioned for the *first* time: He saw *a unicorn* and *an orange rose.* • Used when a noun is *unknown* to 1) the listener and speaker, or 2) the speaker only: Paul says his mother has *a pet giraffe.* I saw *a giraffe* in Paul's back yard.
the	• Used with definite, singular nouns after they have been introduced: (He saw a unicorn and an orange rose.) *The unicorn* was eating *the orange rose.* • Used with *familiar* nouns: She picked up *the telephone* and called the *doctor.* • Used with singular *or* plural nouns if the context makes them definite: He enjoyed playing with *the beast(s)* in his garden.

✔ Checkpoint 8

Fill in the blanks with *a/an*, *the*, or ✘ (no article). Remember that no article is necessary if another determiner is used before a noun.

______ institution of marriage is not the same in all ______ countries. In the United States and many other countries, ______ people usually marry for ______ special reason: love. In some other countries, ______ family alliances or ______ social arrangements may be more important, and sometimes ______ match is arranged between ______ man and ______ woman by ______ outside person. ______ woman's family sometimes finds ______ relative to locate ______several possible husbands for ______ daughter who is to be married. ______ arrangement can also be made by ______ matchmaker or by someone hired to do ______ job.

In ______ some cases, especially in "love" matches, ______ mistake is made, and ______ married couple needs ______ counselor or psychiatrist, as in ______ case of ______ husband and wife in "The Unicorn in the Garden."

III Focus on Countable/Uncountable Nouns

Countable and Uncountable Nouns

A special category of nouns is called "uncountable" nouns. They are not used with *a/an*, and they do not have plural forms. (INCORRECT: *a furniture*, *informations*).

The psychiatrist gave Mary some excellent *advice.*

Sam has given Mary a great deal of *jewelry.*

They have a lot of *work* to do to save their marriage.

One common type of uncountable noun is the general name of a category or a group of items (*furniture*, *hardware*). Many refer to foods; to solids, liquids, or gases; and to the weather. Some fit into more than one group; for example, *coffee* can be a food item, a liquid, or a solid.

Here are some common uncountable nouns. A more complete list is given in the Appendix, page 388.

Some Uncountable Nouns

General	Food	Solids	Liquids	Weather	Emotions/ Abstractions	Languages/ School Subjects
equipment	bread	chalk	beer	fog	advice	Chinese
jewelry	butter	cotton	gasoline	heat	beauty	English
luggage	cheese	glass	milk	humidity	freedom	Engineering
machinery	meat	iron	water	rain	happiness	Geography
money	rice	sand	wine	thunder	insanity	History

Sometimes a noun can be used in both a countable and uncountable way; uncountable nouns are often more general than countable ones. The countable nouns in these examples refer to *specific*, individual items, while the uncountable nouns refer to a *general* amount or quantity.

Countable	Uncountable
six *cakes*	too much *cake*
two *chickens*	some *chicken*
the *wines* of France	a glass of *wine*
several new *interests*	little *interest* in music

✔ **CHECKPOINT 9** 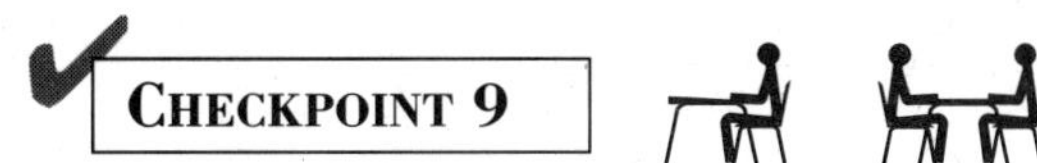

In each pair of sentences, one noun is uncountable. Put ✘ before the uncountable nouns and *a* or *an* or before the countable ones.

1. Sam has ______ homework tonight.
   He has ______ assignment on Will Rogers.
2. Please give me ______ suggestion.
   I need ______ advice.
3. They went to buy ______ toothbrush.
   They also need ______ toothpaste.
4. Do you have ______ equipment in your office?
   For example, do you have ______ typewriter?
5. Mary is looking at ______ chair.
   She loves to buy ______ furniture.

ARTICLES WITH UNCOUNTABLE NOUNS

Since uncountable nouns have no plural forms, they are always considered singular. However, they never appear with the articles *a* or *an*. They are often preceded by the word *some*. Compare these countable and uncountable expressions.

COUNTABLE: a meal, a dessert, a lesson

UNCOUNTABLE: (some) dinner, (some) ice cream, (some) homework

The definite article is used with an uncountable noun when the context or situation makes it specific, as in these two examples.

Put *the meat* on the table. (The listener knows which meat is being referred to.)

The pleasure of the woman disappeared quickly. (The phrase after *pleasure* shows that this is a *particular* person's feeling; it is not a general usage of the noun, as in "*Pleasure* is better than pain.")

COUNTING UNCOUNTABLE NOUNS

The only way to count uncountable nouns is to use a countable noun with them; the countable noun is usually an amount or container.

a *slice* of *bread* (*bacon*, *cheese*)

two *bottles* of *wine* (*soda pop*, *water*)

a *piece* of *chalk* (*advice*, *information*)

three *cartons* of *milk* (*juice*, *cream*)

Articles with Uncountable Nouns	
a/an	Used <u>only</u> with countable nouns that indicate a portion or container of an uncountable noun INCORRECT: an advice, a water CORRECT: a *piece* of advice, a *glass* of water
the	Used with uncountable nouns that are made specific in context The woman likes to repair and refinish *furniture.* She is proud of *the furniture she has restored.*

✔ **Checkpoint 10** 

Fill in the blanks with *a/an*, *the*, or ✘ (no article). Discuss your answers with other students.

______ unicorn is ______ mythical animal that has ______ single horn growing from ______ middle of its forehead. In ______ ancient Greek and Roman stories, it was described as ______ inhabitant of India. ______ people said it was ______ size of ______ horse, with ______ white body, ______ red head, and ______ blue eyes. This fantasy may have come from viewing ______ antelope with ______ horn broken off. Also in Nepal there are ______ sheep with ______ horns that may have been mistakenly identified as ______ unicorns. Throughout ______ history the unicorn has been a symbol of ______ purity and ______ strength. Supposedly, ______ unicorn could only be seen by ______ innocent young girl.

IV Focus on Pronouns

Pronouns are words that can substitute for nouns. Two groups of pronouns are **personal pronouns** and **demonstrative pronouns.**

Personal Pronouns

Personal pronouns can be singular or plural, and they can substitute for nouns used as subjects, objects, or possessives.

Personal Pronouns			
Person	**First**	**Second**	**Third**
SINGULAR			
Subjects	I	you	he, she, it
Objects	me	you	him, her, it
Possessives	mine	yours	his, hers, its
PLURAL			
Subject	we	you	they
Objects	us	you	them
Possessives	ours	yours	their

NOTE: Apostrophes are not used with possessive pronouns.

The following examples show nouns and pronouns used as *subjects.*

	Subject	
Noun:	*The man*	saw a unicorn in his garden.
Pronoun:	*He*	fed it a lily.
Noun:	*The unicorn*	cropped the roses.
Pronoun:	*It*	enjoyed eating flowers.
Noun:	*The police*	helped the psychiatrist.
Pronoun:	*They*	put the woman in a strait-jacket.

Nouns or pronouns used as *objects* usually "receive" the action of the verb; they are different from subjects in that subjects act, but objects are acted upon.

Subject & Verb	**Object**	
The wife didn't respect	*the husband.*	(noun)
The wife didn't understand	*him.*	(pronoun)
Did the husband understand	*the wife?*	(noun)
Did the husband respect	*her?*	(pronoun)
The unicorn ate	*the lilies.*	(noun)
The unicorn enjoyed	*them.*	(pronoun)

Pronouns, like nouns, are also used after prepositions. Pronouns that follow prepositions occur in the object form.

The police put a strait-jacket *on her.*

Officer Sanchez took a tulip *with him.*

The subject forms of pronouns can be used as *complements* after the verb *be* and other linking verbs.

It was *the police* who seized the woman.

It was *they* who seized her.

Possessive personal pronouns substitute for possessive nouns.

We didn't see *the man's* unicorn.

We didn't see *his* unicorn.

We admired *the woman's* roses.

We admired *her* roses.

The unicorn was *the man's*. It was *his*.

The roses were *the woman's*. They were *hers*.

Demonstrative Pronouns

The demonstrative pronouns are *this, that, these*, and *those*. *This* and *that* refer to singular nouns, and *these* and *those* refer to plural nouns. All four of the demonstratives can also be used as adjectives.

Pronouns	**Adjectives**
This is a funny story.	*That* story makes me laugh.
These aren't funny jokes.	*Those* people seem crazy.

Fill in the blanks with the appropriate pronouns. Pay attention to the way the pronoun is used in the sentence (as subject, object, possessive, or demonstrative).

1. The man told ___his___ wife about the unicorn in the garden.
2. However, ________ made fun of ___her___ husband. She told ________ that a unicorn is a mythical beast.
3. "________ couldn't have seen a unicorn," she said. "Unicorns don't exist. ________ are imaginary animals."
4. "________ (*Use a demonstrative*) is serious. ________'m calling the police."
5. ________ husband smiled because ________ was what ________ wanted to hear.

PART THREE. Review and Integration

Thurber Anecdotes: Noun Recognition

Read the paragraphs about James Thurber and circle all the nouns. Then answer the questions that follow each paragraph.

A. One of Thurber's favorite stories concerned a conversation he had with a nurse when he was in the hospital. "What seven-letter word has three ***u's*** in it?" he asked her. The nurse pondered and then said, "I don't know, but it must be unusual."

1. How many nouns are there in the passage? Which are singular? Which are plural? Which are possessive? What characteristics allow you to identify the nouns?
2. Underline the articles in the passage and discuss with your partner or group why each is used. Why are some of the nouns not preceded by any article?
3. The noun *letter* in the phrase "seven-letter word" is singular even though it is preceded by a number. Similar phrases are *five-story building* and *three-year-old child.* Can you think of other expressions using numbers and singular nouns to modify other nouns?

B. Having overdrawn his bank account, Thurber was summoned to a meeting with a bank manager. The humorist* freely admitted that he kept no record of the checks he wrote. "Then how do you know how much money is in your account?" asked the manager.

"I thought that was ***your*** business," retorted Thurber.

1. The word *bank* in the first sentence is a noun used to modify another noun (*account*). Look for another example of a noun modifier in the paragraph.
2. Make two lists of the nouns in the passage: those preceded by articles and those preceded by other determiners, such as possessives. (Leave out the proper noun *Thurber*, which is not preceded by any determiner.) Discuss the determiners with your partner or group. How many nouns are in each group? Can you draw any conclusions about the types of words used as determiners?
3. Divide your list of nouns preceded by articles into two groups: definite and indefinite. Discuss their differences.

---

* **humorist** writer of comic material

C. Thurber attended a friend's party after he had lost his sight.* As a certain couple departed, he remarked to his host, "They're going to break up."

"That's not possible!" exclaimed his friend. "I've never seen such friendliness and smiling."

"Yes," said Thurber, "you ***saw*** them. I ***heard*** them."

Six months later, the couple separated.

1. How many nouns are in the passage? How many are uncountable? How did you recognize them?
2. Underline all the personal pronouns in the passage. How many personal pronouns are subjects? Objects? How many are possessive?
3. What demonstrative pronoun is used in the passage?

Imaginings and Dreams: Regular and Irregular Plural Nouns

A. Situation: It's Sunday afternoon, and the husband and wife are enjoying their hobbies in the kitchen. Mary is listening to music in the breakfast nook, while Sam is preparing some delicious food. In their conversation, they use many plural nouns, some of which are irregular. Fill in the blanks with the plural forms of the nouns in parentheses.

Sam: You're going to love this vegetable omelet I'm making. I'm putting in (*onion*) ______________ and (*potato*) ______________. Should I add a few (*tomato*) ______________?

Mary: (*tomato*) ______________ sound good. But if you expect to get any (*kiss*) ______________ later, leave out the (*onion*) ______________. What are you doing? What's all that noise?

Sam: I'm chasing some (*mosquito*) ______________ that came in from the garden. Maybe they were on the (*lily*) ______________ that I brought in this morning. What are you doing?

Mary: I have both (*radio*) ______________ on to listen to the program of Irish tenor (*solo*) ______________. They're so romantic. The last song was about (*wish*) ______________ that come true.

Sam: Well, if you had four wishes, what would you wish for?

Mary: Hmmm. . . . I guess they'd be that our (*baby*) ______________ hadn't grown up and left us, that I could look more like those (*lady*)

---

* **lost his sight** became blind

____________ in the fashion magazines, that I never had to do the (*dish*) ____________ again, and that you were more like the (*hero*) ____________ in these romantic songs.

B. Fill in the blanks with the correct form of the noun in parentheses. Pay attention to whether it should be singular or plural. Look up any irregular plural forms you don't know in the Appendix on Irregular Noun Plurals (pages 383–385).

Maria: I had the strangest (*dream*) ____________ last (*night*) ____________. It was a (*nightmare*) ____________ about (*creature*) ____________ from another (*planet*) ____________ who came to carry me away with them.

Jeannie: How horrible! But I love to hear about (*dream*) ____________. Tell me about your (*monster*) ____________. Did they look at all like (*man*) ____________?

Maria: Not at all. They were smaller, the size of (*child*) ____________. They were awful. The first (*thing*) ____________ I noticed was their big square (*head*) ____________. Their (*face*) ____________ were dark green, with red (*eye*) ____________ and long sharp (*tooth*) ____________. They had (*foot*) ____________ like (*duck*) ____________ or (*goose*) ____________, but they were running toward me like (*deer*) ____________. Scales like those on (*fish*) ____________ covered their (*body*) ____________.

Jeannie: They sound really ugly. Were they making any (*noise*) ____________? Did they roar like (*lion*) ____________ or bleat like (*sheep*) ____________? Maybe they cooed like (*dove*) ____________ or (*quail*) ____________?

Maria: Actually, they made squeaking (*sound*) ____________ like (*mouse*) ____________, but softer, like (*mosquito*) ____________. What a weird (*experience*) ____________. What do you think it means?

Jeannie: Well, I have several (*hypothesis*) ______________. Are you nervous about your blind date* tonight?

Marie: Maybe I am. What if he looks like THEM!

Jeannie: Take my (*advice*) ______________. Stay home with a good (*book*) ______________ tonight.

The Unicorn Again: Article Practice

The third paragraph of "A Unicorn in the Garden" is reprinted here without articles before the nouns. Fill in each blank with *a*, *an*, *the*, or ✘ (no article). When you have finished, go back to the story on pages 43 and 44 to check your work. Discuss any differences in your answers with a partner or group.

As soon as ______ husband had gone out of ______ house, ______ wife got up and dressed as fast as she could. She was very excited and there was ______ gloat in her eye. She telephoned ______ police and she telephoned ______ psychiatrist; she told them to hurry to her house and bring ______ strait-jacket. When ______ police and ______ psychiatrist arrived they sat down in ______ chairs and looked at her with ______ great interest. "My husband," she said, " saw ______ unicorn this morning." ______ police looked at ______ psychiatrist and ______ psychiatrist looked at ______ police. "He told me it had ______ golden horn in ______ middle of its forehead," she said. At ______ solemn signal from ______ psychiatrist, ______ police leaped from their chairs and seized ______ wife. They had ______ hard time subduing her, for she put up ______ terrific struggle, but they finally subdued her. Just as they got her into ______ strait-jacket, ______ husband came back into ______ house.

Sam and Mary in the Kitchen: Noun Forms

Sam and Mary sometimes mix up nouns, including those that indicate portions or containers used to count uncountable nouns. For example, Sam might say "two pats of milk and a carton of butter" instead of "a carton of milk and two pats of butter." They also mix up the nouns in comparisons like "fat as a pig" and "hungry as a horse."

---

* **blind date** — arranged meeting with someone of the opposite sex whom one has never met before

The following conversation takes place between Sam and Mary at the breakfast table. Read the conversation and then try to unscramble or replace the misused nouns. Look up any unfamiliar words, like *pat* or *bagel*, or ask your teacher about them.

Sam: Susan, I'd love a bottle of coffee as soon as it's perked.

Mary: Susan was your first wife, Sam. I'm Mary. Are you sure you want a whole bottle, or will a box do?

Sam: Oh, there I go again . . . But really, dear, you make little ears yourself.

Mary: Errors, Sam, not ears. There's nothing wrong with my ears. Do you want a big breakfast or just a slice of cereal?

Sam: I think I'll have a bowl of bacon and some flies' legs—I mean fried eggs. I'd like a couple of pats of toast too, with a piece of butter and a cupful of that nice jackberry belly—er, blackberry jelly—on each. I'm as hungry as a pig.

Mary: No wonder you're as fat as a horse. You eat too much.

Sam: What are you going to have, dear? Just a piece of juice and a glass of toast?

Mary: I think I'll have a dish of tea and a bag of toast—I mean a toasted bagel.

Sam: What have you planned for lunch today?

Mary: I thought we could have a carton of that vegetable soup I made yesterday.

Sam: That sounds good. We could also warm up a couple of bottles of the pizza in the freezer. And I'd really like a slice of lemonade.

Mary: It's too cold for lemonade. I'd rather have a stick of milk. And I'm going to get a bowl of peanut butter for a sandwich when I go shopping. I'd prefer that to pizza.

Sam: Well, if we're going shopping, maybe we should eat lunch at a restaurant.

Mary: I'll never eat out with you again after you embarrassed me by ordering a dozen chickens on the halfshell.

Sam: Oh, well. I'm full now anyway. I can't think about food. I guess I'll feed the bat and take the hog for a walk.

Correspondence: Nouns and Articles

The wife in the institution has written a note asking her husband to pack some of her belongings to bring to her during visitors' hours. Read the note and do the exercise that follows.

> *Dear Sam,*
>
> *I'm very unhappy here in the hospital. I'm bored all day long because there is nothing to do. I don't have the right clothes with me; I'm freezing day and night, and I only have the dress I was wearing the day I was brought here. The nightgown the nurse gave me is too thin to keep me warm at night, and I have nothing to exercise in. I feel terrible about my appearance too, and you know how I like to look my best. Please bring the things I need when you come to visit on Sunday.*
>
> *Your wife,*
> *Mary*
>
> *P.S. The food here is terrible.*

Help Sam pack Mary's belongings. What should he bring? Be sure to use the appropriate singular and plural forms of nouns. Include articles where needed. The following are some categories of items Sam might bring.

Clothes: a jogging suit, etc.

Entertainment: magazines, a portable radio, etc.

Make-up:

Food:

Other:

Categories Game: Noun Types

Form teams of four or five students. Choose one student as the first speaker, and decide on the order in which each of the other team members will speak. Your instructor will give the speaker a card that contains a category and a list of five items, like this one.

Nouns That End in -Y
jelly
penny
city
gravy
morality

While the other teams listen silently, the speaker has two minutes to give hints to his or her team members, who try to guess the word. For example, the speaker might say, "This is something you put on toast," hoping the group will guess *jelly*. No body language is allowed; all clues must be spoken. The speaker is timed by the instructor or a student in another group. At the end of two minutes, the number guessed correctly is recorded on the board under the team's name. Then another speaker from a different team is chosen, and so on until each student on every team has had a turn. The team with the most correct guesses wins.

Suggestions for Writing

1. If you are keeping a journal, write an entry on one of the following topics: why people need psychiatrists, the value of daydreaming, or stories about husbands and wives in your culture.
2. Write a paragraph in which you describe an imaginary animal you have read about. Exchange your paragraph with another student. Circle all the nouns in each other's paragraphs and discuss their correctness. Check the use of articles as well.
3. Write a composition in which you compare and contrast two fairy tales; one of them might be a fairy tale from your native culture. Discuss how the stories are similar and how they are different. Be sure to explain the "morals" of the tales.
4. Write a humorous or frightening description of some visitors from another planet. Give a clear and very detailed description so that a reader can form a mental picture of the creatures. Change papers with another student; read each other's descriptions. Ask questions if some part of the paragraph is unclear or if you want more information.
5. Write a description entitled "My Most Interesting Relative(s)."

Unit Three

Adjectives, Adverbs, and Comparisons

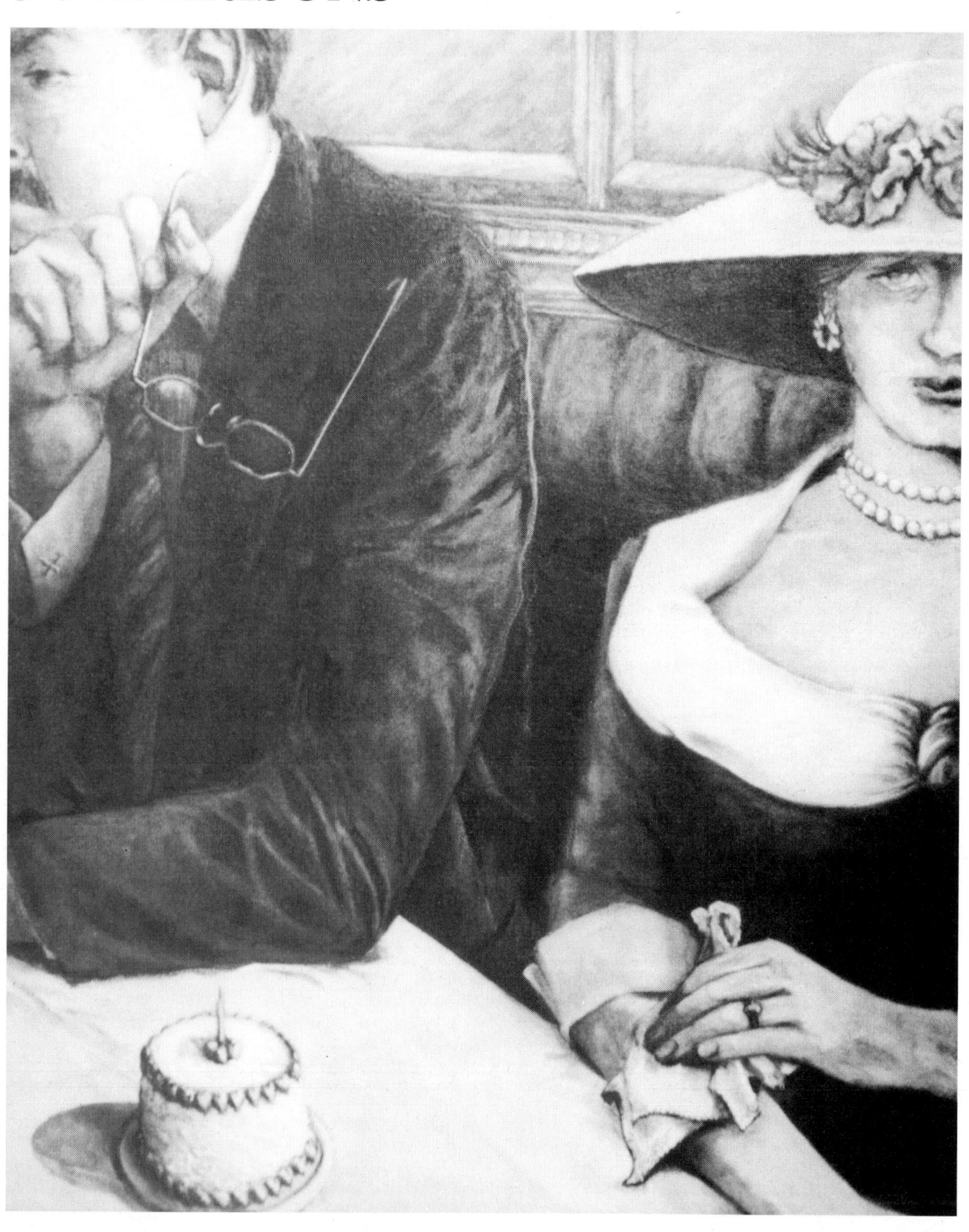

READING: "Birthday Party" by Katharine Brush

THEME: Holidays and Celebrations

PART ONE: The Context

Katharine Brush (1900–1952) was a novelist and short story writer. Her story "Birthday Party," originally published in *The New Yorker* in 1946, reveals a great deal about the relationship between a husband and wife through their reactions to a birthday surprise.

Pre-Reading Questions

1. In the United States, it is customary on birthdays to serve a cake decorated with lighted candles; the number of candles usually matches the person's age, especially if he or she is a child. The person whose birthday is being celebrated makes a wish and blows out the candles. Then friends and relatives sing "Happy Birthday" and give presents to him or her. How are birthdays celebrated in your culture? What special food, songs, dances, or other activities are associated with these celebrations?
2. Are birthdays always happy occasions? Do some people get embarrassed or depressed about birthdays? Discuss the reasons for their reactions.
3. Do adults and children react differently to birthdays? If so, why do you think this is true?

Reading: "Birthday Party" by Katharine Brush

(1) They were a couple in their late thirties, and they looked unmistakably* married. They sat on the banquette* opposite us in a little narrow restaurant, having dinner. The man had a round, self-satisfied face, with glasses on it; the woman was fadingly* pretty, in a big hat. There was nothing conspicuous* about them, nothing particularly noticeable, until the end of the meal, when it suddenly became obvious that this was an Occasion—in fact, the husband's birthday, and the wife had planned a little surprise for him.

(2) It arrived in the form of a small but glossy* birthday cake, with one pink candle burning in the center. The headwaiter brought it in and placed it before the husband, and meanwhile the violin-and-piano orchestra played "Happy Birthday to You" and the wife beamed* with shy pride over her little surprise, and such few people as there were in the restaurant tried to help out with a pattering* of applause. It became clear at once that help was needed, because

---

* **unmistakably**	clearly, without a doubt
banquette	bench with a back
fadingly	not as clearly as before (from fade, v, to lose brightness)
conspicuous	obvious, apparent
glossy	shiny, bright
beamed	smiled very brightly
pattering	faint tapping sounds

the husband was not pleased. Instead he was hotly embarrassed and indignant* at his wife for embarrassing him.

(3) You looked at him and you saw this and you thought, "Oh, now, don't *be* like that!" But he was like that, and as soon as the little cake had been deposited* on the table, and the orchestra had finished the birthday piece, and the general attention had shifted* from the man and the woman, I saw him say something to her under his breath—some punishing thing, quick and curt* and unkind. I couldn't bear to look at the woman then so I stared* at my plate and waited for quite a long time. Not long enough, though. She was still crying when I finally glanced* over there again. Crying quietly and heartbrokenly and hopelessly, all to herself, under the gay big brim of her best hat.

Comprehension Questions

1. What did the couple look like?
2. What surprises had the wife planned for the husband?
3. How did the wife feel about the celebration? How did the husband feel? How did he express his feelings to his wife?
4. Who is telling the story? How does he or she react to the scene?
5. How do you feel about the characters in the story?

Discussion Questions

1. Often birthdays become much less important to people in the United States as they get older. What does this reveal about the attitude of people in the United States toward getting older? Is the attitude toward older citizens different in other cultures? If so, explain.
2. The relationship portrayed in "Birthday Party" is not a happy one. What can a couple do about an unsatisfying relationship? When is a divorce the best solution? What factors usually lead to divorce?
3. The story was written late in the 1940s. Do you think the behavior of the woman was typical of that time period? Would the average woman react differently today?

---

* **indignant**	angry, insulted
deposited	put, placed
shifted	changed, moved away from
curt	brief and rude
stared	looked at continuously
glanced	looked at quickly

PART TWO. The Target Structures: Adjectives, Adverbs, and Comparisons

I Focus on the Position of Adjectives

Preview of Adjectives

Fill in the blanks in the following sentences with any words that fit.

The ____________ woman wore a ____________ hat.

The man was very ____________ to his wife.

Since you have just read "The Birthday Party," you might have filled in the blanks in the first sentence with words like *pretty* or *kind* and *big* or *gay*. You might have filled the blank in the second sentence with *cruel* or *unkind*. These words are adjectives, which are used to modify (describe, explain, or qualify) nouns or pronouns.

Position of Adjectives

The normal positions of adjectives are (a) *before* a noun and (b) *after* the verb *be* and other linking verbs such as *feel, look, seem,* or *become*.

A *glossy* **cake** arrived.	(adjective before noun)
The cake **looked** *glossy*.	(adjective after linking verb)

Checkpoint 1

Circle the adjectives in the first paragraph of "The Birthday Party" below and discuss them with other students. Then answer the questions that follow the paragraph.

They were a couple in their late thirties, and they looked unmistakably married. They sat on the banquette opposite us in a little narrow restaurant, having dinner. The man had a round self-satisfied face, with glasses on it; the woman was fadingly pretty, in a big hat. There was nothing conspicuous about them, nothing particularly noticeable, until the end of the meal, when it suddenly became obvious that this was an Occasion—in fact, the husband's birthday, and the wife had planned a little surprise for him.

1. How many adjectives are there in the passage?
2. How many precede nouns? How many follow linking verbs?

3. Can you find any phrases in which the adjective comes *after* the noun or pronoun it modifies?
4. Write down the two noun phrases that contain more than one adjective. Could the adjectives be reversed, or is the order fixed? What conclusions can you draw about the order of adjectives used together to modify nouns? For example, which goes first—an adjective that describes size or one that describes shape?

Order of Adjectives Before Nouns

When two or more adjectives precede a noun, the order in which they appear depends on the kind of information they provide about the noun. The following chart illustrates the usual order of adjectives before nouns.

Order of Adjectives Before Nouns

Determiner (article, possessive, etc.)	General Qualities	Physical Attributes (size, age, etc.)	Proper Adjective (nationality, etc.)	Noun Modifier	Noun
the					brim
their		late			thirties
one		pink			candle
the	pretty	young	American		woman
his	favorite			card	game
some	delicious			birthday	cake
a	famous		Italian	movie	star
two		tall	Jewish		men

Determiners also include demonstratives (*this, that, these, those*), numerals (*one, first*, etc.), and adjectives of indefinite quantity (*some, few, all*, etc.).

Nouns used as modifiers of other nouns are common in English. The word *birthday,* itself a combination of two nouns, becomes a noun modifier in the phrase "birthday party." Others are *air conditioner, television station, computer programmer, kitchen sink.* Notice that some of these phrases are written as one word.

The following phrases illustrate the usual order of adjectives in English.

a famous old French dessert
his beautiful little baby girl
a nice medium-sized green house
some shiny new Christmas tree ornaments

When adjectives that precede nouns follow the normal sequence, commas are not used between them. But when all the adjectives in a series are *general,* they are separated by commas, and the conjunctions *and* or *but* may be used before the last one.

an interesting, amusing, (and) meaningful story

some sophisticated, expensive, (but) dangerous weapons

When two adjectives are used, they may be separated by a comma or joined with *and* or *but.*

a clean, well-lighted place

some remarkable and fascinating news

the small but valuable diamond

Adjectives that describe the *physical appearance* of a noun usually occur in the following order.

Order of Adjectives That Describe Physical Appearance

Size	Shape	Age	Color	Noun
little	narrow			restaurant
big		old	blue	car
huge	round		red	apple
tiny	oval		black	stone
large	square		brown	box

The ordering of adjectives is flexible; these charts give guidelines rather than rules. In fact, all writers of English, especially creative writers, may vary the order of adjectives to add interest or emphasis to their style. For example, Katharine Brush used three adjectives connected by two *ands* (not separated by commas) **after** a noun in the following sentence.

I saw him say something to her under his breath—some punishing thing, *quick and curt and unkind.*

Checkpoint 2

A. 

A teenage girl is writing an entry in her diary about her birthday, which she has just celebrated. The adjective-plus-noun phrases have been left out of her sentences. Arrange groups 2–7 correctly, using the chart above and the one on page 72. Then complete sentences a–g with the appropriate phrases. After you finish, put the sentences in order to describe the party.

1. wonderful, party, my, sixteenth, birthday
   my wonderful sixteenth birthday party

2. roses, dozen, red, two, American
3. comfortable, Victorian, restaurant, the, seafood
4. tall, a, headwaiter, friendly, Indian
5. round, hat, dress, her, beautiful
6. chocolate, rich, layer, cake, my
7. necklace, this, fabulous, emerald

a. ______________________ were sent by my boyfriend.
b. We ate at ______________________ in town.
c. My mother wore ______________________.
d. My wonderful sixteenth birthday party was held last night.
e. My father gave me ______________________.
f. ______________________ was brought to the table after the meal.
g. ______________________ served us dinner.

B.

Make noun phrases by matching the modifiers on the left with the appropriate nouns on the right. Two of the modifier-noun combinations make one word. When you finish, group the words and noun phrases you have made under the names of the American holidays they are associated with.

Modifier	***Noun***
1. hot _f_	a. wreath
2. chocolate ___	b. melon
3. Plymouth ___	c. beans
4. roast ___	d. pie
5. red-nosed ___	e. crackers
6. water ___	f. dogs
7. pumpkin ___	g. reindeer
8. fire ___	h. eggs
9. jelly ___	i. turkey
10. holly ___	j. bunnies
11. painted ___	k. Rock

Holidays

Easter	*Fourth of July*	*Thanksgiving*	*Christmas*
	hot dogs		

ADJECTIVES AFTER *BE* AND LINKING VERBS

Adjectives can follow linking verbs, including the verb *be* and verbs of perception such as *taste, feel, seem, look, appear, sound,* and *become.* Adjectives that follow linking verbs or verbs of perception are called "predicate adjectives"; they complete the meaning of the verb, and they describe the noun or pronoun that is the subject of the sentence. For example, the adjectives *embarrassed* and *indignant* in the third sentence in the chart below modify the pronoun-subject *he*; they are connected to the subject by the linking verb *was* (a past form of *be*).

Adjective After Linking Verbs

Subject	Linking Verb	Predicate Adjective + Modifiers
They	*looked*	unmistakably *married.*
It	*became*	*obvious* that this was an Occasion.
He	*was*	hotly *embarrassed* and *indignant.*
The food	*smelled*	*delicious.*
The music	*seemed*	*romantic.*
The writer	*felt*	*sorry* for the wife.

CHECKPOINT 3  

The words in the following sentences containing linking verbs and predicate adjectives are scrambled or mixed up. Put the words in order so that they make a sentence.

1. baths feel good warm
2. man angry looks and the cruel
3. birthday tastes cake delicious chocolate
4. is popular children cream among ice
5. birthday chocolate tastes cake delicious
6. people other upset felt the
7. music sounds sad violin
8. pretty appears friend unhappy your
9. are children angry their
10. soda sweet tastes strawberry

II Focus on the Forms of Adjectives

SUFFIXES

Many English adjectives can be recognized by endings called *suffixes* that have been added to nouns or verbs.

Suffixes	Adjectives
-able or *-ible*	comfortable, enjoyable, responsible
-ful	plentiful, wonderful, joyful
-ic(al)	alphabetical, geographic(al), philosophical
-ish	childish, selfish
-ive	attentive, attractive, active
-less	penniless, useless
-ous	conspicuous, nervous, obvious
-some	awesome, bothersome, cumbersome
-y	wealthy, shiny

✔ CHECKPOINT 4

Write the adjectives that are formed from the following nouns and verbs. Use a dictionary if necessary. When you finish, use the adjectives (1–18) to complete the descriptions for nouns (A–H). You may use an adjective more than once. For example, *noisy* could be used to describe A, B, D, G, or H.

Noun	Adjective
1. music	________
2. child	________
3. noise	________
4. joy	________
5. energy	________
6. beauty	________
7. majesty	________
8. humor	________
9. fool	________
10. awe	________
11. grace	________
12. peace	________
13. nerve	________

Verb	Adjective
14. act	________
15. attract	________
16. like	________
17. hurt	________
18. jump	________

A. Birthdays can be ____________________.
B. A teenager is usually ____________________.
C. Lakes appear to be ____________________.
D. A two year old is often ____________________.
E. Mountains look ____________________.
F. A dancer is ____________________.
G. A puppy is ____________________.
H. Most clowns are ____________________.

-Ing and *-ed/-en* Forms

Many adjectives are formed from the *-ing* and *-ed/-en* forms of verbs,* which are called *participles*. The *-ing* form sometimes indicates *ongoing* action (*shocking* news, a *surprising* event) and usually expresses the cause of something. The *-ed/-en* form can indicate *completed* action (a *revised* composition, the *finished* product) and usually expresses a *result* or *reaction* to something. The following sentences show the difference between the two forms.

-Ing and *-ed/-en* Forms	
-ing	The man thought his cake was *humiliating.* (The cake *caused* his humiliation.)
-ed	He spoke cruelly because he felt *humiliated.* (His *reaction* to the cake was humiliation.)

Not all the *-ing* forms of verbs can be used as adjectives. For example, the *-ing* form of the verb *bother* is not used as an adjective; instead the adjective *bothersome* is used. Other exceptions are *delightful* (not *delighting*) and *scary* (not *scaring*). the *-ing* and *-ed/-en* forms of verbs will be discussed further in Unit 6.

Compounds

Some adjectives are formed by combining an *-ing* or *-ed/-en* form with another word; these are called compound adjectives.

He had a round, *self-satisfied* face.

The drug had *long-lasting* effects.

The discovery was *earth-shattering.*

---

* The *-ing* form has traditionally been called the *present* participle, and the *-ed/-en* form has been called the *past* participle. Although most verbs have past participles that end in *-ed* or *-en*, there are many irregular forms. See the list in the Appendix on pages 390–392.

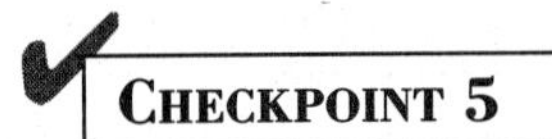

Circle the correct form.

1. The delicious meal was (satisfying, satisfied).
2. The smoke- (filling, filled) room looked stuffy.
3. The woman was prepared for a (delighting, delightful, delighted) evening.
4. Her (beating, beaten) expression showed her disappointment.
5. There were so many unusual foods on the menu that we found it (fascinating, fascinated).
6. After the long, unhappy evening, the (exhausting, exhausted) woman went to bed.
7. She had a (disturbing, disturbed) dream about her husband.
8. The (screaming, screamed) voices of her children woke her up.
9. They were (interesting, interested) in hearing about their father's birthday surprise.
10. Later she received a telegram, which was (scary, scaring, scared).

III Focus on the Forms of *Other*

One group of words that modify or replace nouns is sometimes a problem for non-native speakers. These words are *another*, *other*, *others*, *the other*, and *the others*.

Another and *The Other*

Another and *the other* can modify *or* replace a noun—that is, these words can be used as adjectives or pronouns. Study these examples.

a. Please have *another* piece of cake.

   Please have *another*.

b. We are going to two birthday parties today. One is at a restaurant.

   The other party is at my friend's house.

   The other is at my friend's house.

Another is always singular. In (a), it means one additional item or one more. In (b), *the other* is also singular. It refers to the only one that remains or the last of a group of two or more.

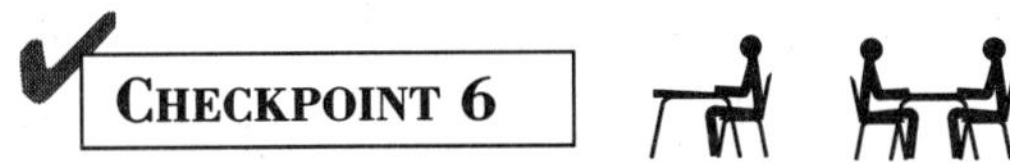

Fill in the blanks with *another* or *the other*.

One of my next-door neighbors has a wonderful garden filled with roses and ________________ type of flower. ________________ next-door neighbor isn't at

all interested in plants. ______________ neighbor down the street has some large trees in his yard. ______________, not far from him, poured concrete all over his lawn. His wife said he hated to cut the grass! This is her second husband; ______________ was a great gardener.

Other occurs with plural nouns unless it is preceded by *the, this,* an indefinite pronoun (*some, any, each*), or a possessive (*his, John's, my*).

> Occasionally people have eyes of different colors. For example, John has one brown eye. His *other eye* is blue.
>
> (John's *other* eye is blue. *The other* eye is blue.)

Other/Others and *The Others*

Other can be used with a singular or plural noun. It is an adjective that refers to an additional item or items in a group.

> Many people have brown eyes. *Other people* have blue eyes.
> (Still other people have additional eye colors, such as green and gray.)

Others is used in place of a noun. Like *other + noun, others* refers to additional or more items, but not all the items that remain.

> Some people have perfect vision. *Others* are near-sighted.
> (Still others have different vision problems. In other words, this does not refer to everyone else who has less-than-perfect vision.)

The others is used to replace a plural noun. It means all the remaining members of a group.

> The most common eye colors are blue, brown, gray, green, and hazel. *The others* are unusual.
> (*The others* refers to all the remaining eye colors, all that are left in the group.)

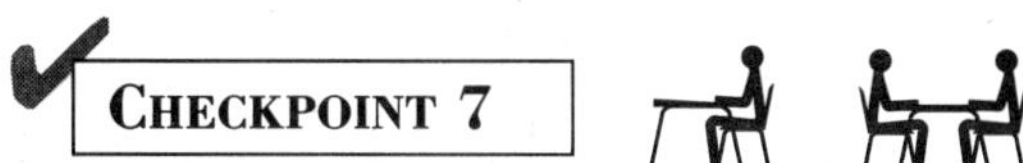

Complete the sentences with *other*, *others*, or *the others*.

A. Americans celebrate many holidays. Some of them, like Christmas and Thanksgiving, are celebrated nationally. __________ are Independence Day in July and Labor Day in September. Most people have the day off on these important holidays, and those who have to work are often paid extra, sometimes double or triple their usual wages. __________ holidays, like Presidents' Day in February and Veterans Day in November, are federal holidays; the offices of the federal government are closed on those days, but most other workers do not have the day off. Two holidays are celebrated in some cities or states but not in __________. One is Columbus Day; __________ is Saint Patrick's Day.

B. Throughout history, many mythical beasts have been described in art and literature. Some, like fire-breathing dragons, were harmful to mankind. __________ dangerous mythical beasts were griffins, which had the head of a bird and the body of a lion. __________, like the gorgons, had terrible snakes on their heads. __________ monsters had a combination of human and animal features; for example, the centaur was half horse, and the satyr was half goat. Of all __________, probably the most gentle were the unicorns.

Summary of the Forms of *Other*

The chart shows the forms of *other* used as adjectives and pronouns.

Forms of Other		
	Singular	**Plural**
Adjective	*another* + noun	*other* + noun
	the other + noun	
	He's having *another* party.	I have enjoyed *other* parties more.
	The other party at his house was fun.	
Pronoun	*another*	*others*
	the other	*the others*
	The cookies are delicious. I'd love *another.*	Oatmeal cookies and fruit are healthful desserts, but many *others* are rich and fattening.
	I ate one of the two cookies; please eat *the other.*	I don't care for peanut butter cookies, but I like *the others.*

Complete the sentences with the correct form of *other*. Look at the chart above for help.

Our neighborhood looks wonderful during the Christmas holidays. On the first of December, one of my next-door neighbors puts up a spectacular display of lights and __________ decorations. For example, Rudolph with his red nose prances across the roof with all the __________ reindeer.

_____________ next-door neighbor isn't at all interested in decorations, however. He's the only person on our block who doesn't make an effort. _____________ all do something special to their houses and lawns. I always put up a few lights outside and of course decorate a large pine tree for the house. It can be seen from the front and through _____________window on the side of the house. _____________ neighbor down the street decorates all the trees in his yard, including oaks, maples, and _____________ large trees. He really appreciates the assistance of his wife in putting up all the lights. (This is her second husband; _____________ was an electrician.)

IV Focus on Adjectives with Countable and Uncountable Nouns

Adjectives That Change with Countable and Uncountable Nouns

Three pairs of adjectives that change according to whether they precede countable or uncountable nouns are *much/many*, *(a) little/(a) few*, and *less/fewer*.

- **Much/Many**. The adjective *much* precedes uncountable nouns, while *many* precedes plural countable nouns.

Much and *Many*			
Uncountable		**Countable (Plural)**	
much	furniture	*many*	chairs
	money		dollars
	homework		lessons
	mail		letters

Much is used in **negative** statements and in questions, but usually not in affirmative statements. Examples:

He doesn't have *much* money.
I haven't received *much* mail.
Does he have *much* imagination?

Complete the sentences with *much* or *many*.

1. The family has __________ holiday meals at home.

2. The Allens have a large family, so they don't have __________ space for guests.
3. Mrs. Allen spends __________ days cooking special traditional dishes for holidays.
4. She chooses from the __________ hors d'oeuvres recipes she has collected over the years.
5. But there isn't __________ variation in the dinner menu from year to year.

- **Little/Few**. *Little* precedes uncountable nouns, and *few* precedes plural countable nouns. The intensifier *very* is often used with *little* and *few*:

Little* and *Few			
Uncountable		**Countable (plural)**	
(very) *little*	vocabulary	(very) *few*	words
	food		vegetables
	water		glasses (of water)

When the article *a* precedes *little* or *few*, the adjective has a positive meaning. When the article is not used, *few* and *little* have a negative meaning. Consider the differences in meaning between the following pairs of sentences.

(A) *Few* and (A) *Little*

John has (–) *few* friends. (He does not have many friends.)
John has (+) *a few* friends. (He does have some friends.)
Mary has (–) *little* money. (She does not have much money.)
Mary has (+) *a little* money. (She does have some money.)
In the sentences above, the adjectives have these meanings:

(–) *few*	not many
(+) *a few*	some (a small number)
(–) *little*	not much
(+) *a little*	some (a small amount)

NOTE: The adjective *little* can also be used with countable nouns when it means "small," as in "a little surprise."

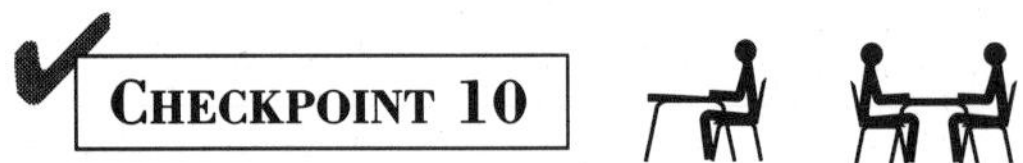

Complete the sentences with *little*, *a little*, *few*, or *a few*.

1. The couple getting a divorce felt __________ love for each other.

2. They had more than __________ problems with their marriage.
3. For one thing, the husband had __________ girlfriends.
4. Also, they were able to save very __________ money.
5. Every month there were __________ more bills that they couldn't pay because of the shortage of money.
6. The woman had __________ friends, so she was often lonely.
7. She had always wanted __________ children, but her husband wanted only one.
8. Because they spent __________ time together, they grew apart.
9. They liked different activities; they had __________ hobbies together.
10. In fact, some people had been __________ surprised when they got married.

- **Less/Fewer**. Like the preceding pairs of adjectives, *less* is used with uncountable nouns, and *fewer* is used with countable nouns.

Less* and *Fewer	
Uncountable	**Countable (plural)**
less fruit	*fewer* bananas, oranges
clothing	shirts, skirts
knowledge	facts

The following paragraph gives information about public celebrations on the Fourth of July. Complete it with *less* or *fewer*.

Until early in the twentieth century, every community in the United States celebrated the nation's independence on July fourth with grand public ceremonies consisting of fireworks displays, band performances of patriotic songs, and parades. Now __________ celebrations of this kind are held. For one thing, __________ money is set aside in town budgets for holidays. Also, there is __________ open space in many communities for large gatherings to listen to music or watch fireworks. __________ bands and orchestras specialize in patriotic songs because there is __________ enthusiasm for this kind of music nowadays. Parades used to be organized by the Veterans of Foreign Wars and other civic groups; at present, __________ of these groups exist. Some critics

of U.S. society feel there is ________ patriotism now, but if this were true, ________ citizens would have private celebrations as well.

- **Some/Any**. Two other adjectives that can cause problems for non-native speakers of English are *some* and *any*. *Some* is used in affirmative, or positive, statements, and *any* is usually used with negative statements.

Some* and *Any	
They have *some* friends.	(positive)
They don't have *any* friends.	(negative)

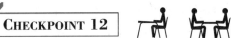

CHECKPOINT 12 

The following paragraph describes Christmas in the United States. Complete it with *some* or *any*.

Regardless of religion, everyone who is in the United States during December is affected by Christmas in ________ way. For example, most elementary schools don't have ________ students who don't learn at least a few Christmas songs. ________ towns and cities put up ________ colored lights or ________ angels. Statues of the reindeer who pull Santa's sleigh sometimes appear on Main Street, even in ________ southern states that never get ________ snow.

V Focus on Additional Rules About Adjectives

FORMS OF ADJECTIVES

In English, adjectives do not agree with nouns, although they do in many other languages. It is not correct in English to make an adjective plural.

INCORRECT: two attractives women

CORRECT: two attractive women

Only the demonstrative adjectives (*this that*, *these*, and *those*) change form according to the noun they are used with. *This* and *that* are singular; *these* and *those* are plural.

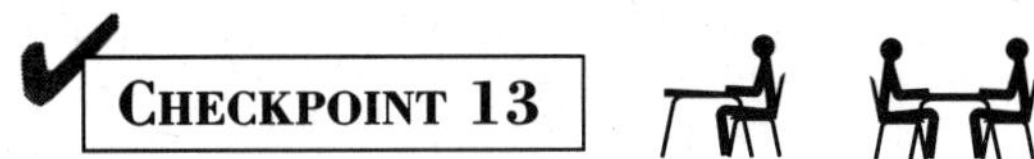

CHECKPOINT 13

In this paragraph about a Thanksgiving feast, circle the correct demonstrative adjectives.

(*This, These*) days, one must serve only (*that, those*) dishes that guests consider traditional. For example, turkey should be the main course because (*this, these*) bird is a symbol of the holiday. Pies made from pumpkin, pecans, and mincemeat can also be enjoyed by everyone; (*this, these*) desserts have been accepted as part of Thanksgiving for years. (*This, These*) special meal requires squash, of course. In some households, onions and yams are served, but (*that, those*) are less popular.

VI Focus on the Position of Adverbs

PREVIEW OF ADVERBS

With a partner, complete each sentence by filling in the blanks with any words that fit.

1. She was crying __________ and __________ and __________. (Answer the question "How was she crying?")
2. They looked __________ married. (Answer the question "*How* married did they look?")
3. I __________ glanced at her. (Answer the question "*When* did I glance at her?")
4. The couple sat at the table __________. (Answer the question "*Where* did they sit?")

If you had just read "Birthday Party," you might have filled in the blanks this way:

She was crying *quietly* and *heartbrokenly* and *hopelessly.*

They looked *unmistakably* married.

I *finally* glanced at her.

The couple sat at the table *nearby.*

The words you filled in are adverbs, which modify verbs, adjectives, or other adverbs. Most adverbs, but not all, end in *-ly*. Adverbs generally answer the questions "How?" "When?" or "Where?"

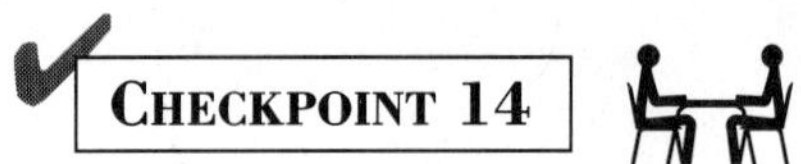

The following passage describes the U. S. holiday Presidents' Day. Read the passage and circle all the adverbs that you find. With your partner, determine which question (How? When? Where?) is answered by each adverb.

Presidents' Day commemorates the birthdays of two very famous U. S. presidents: George Washington and Abraham Lincoln.

George Washington, born on February 22, 1739, was the first president of the United States (1789–97) and is frequently characterized as the "Father of His Country." During the Revolutionary War, he was commander-in-chief of the Continental Army from 1775 to the ultimate defeat of the British in 1781. "First in war, first in peace, first in the hearts of his countrymen," Washington was greatly honored and almost universally admired during his lifetime. The record of a celebration of Washington's birthday first appeared in the Virginia *Gazette* in 1782. This holiday was first celebrated locally and then became quite widespread by 1800.

Abraham Lincoln, born on February 12, 1809, was the sixteenth president of the United States (1861–1865). His administration was a notably stormy one: through it raged the Civil War, or the War Between the States. Lincoln was brutally assassinated in April, 1865, shortly after the end of the war.

Position of Adverbs

Adverbs can appear in three positions in a sentence: beginning, middle, and end.

- **Beginning Position**. Some adverbs that appear at the beginning of a sentence are called "sentence modifiers" because they seem to modify the whole sentence rather than a single word. Common sentence modifiers are *obviously, (un)fortunately*, and *actually*.

  Unfortunately, the husband didn't like surprises.

  Obviously, the wife was heartbroken.

Some adverbs of time appear at the beginning of sentences, especially those that indicate sequence (*first, next,* etc.).

First, the headwaiter brought the birthday cake.

Next, the orchestra played "Happy Birthday."

Checkpoint 15

The following paragraph describes the U.S. holiday Labor Day. Read the passage and circle any adverbs you find. What is the position in the sentence of each adverb? Discuss your answers with a partner or small group.

Labor Day, celebrated on the first Monday in September, is a legal holiday in most U.S. states. Essentially, it honors the accomplishments of workers in this country. Picnics, outings, parades, and weekend vacations are featured. Unofficially, Labor Day marks the end of summer vacation time.

- **Middle Position.** Adverbs that modify verbs usually appear in the middle of a sentence. The exact position of the adverb varies according to the type of verb used. Adverbs appear after the verb *be* when they are followed by an adjective. They occur before other verbs. In this middle position, adverbs often express frequency, or *how often* something occurs. Examples are *sometimes, often, usually, rarely*, and *never.*

  The husband *is often* angry.

  The husband *often gets* angry.

  If the verb has one or more auxiliaries, the adverb appears *after* the **first** auxiliary.

  The husband *has often gotten* angry.

  The husband *was often seen* scolding his wife.

  NOTE: Do not place an adverb between a verb and its object.

  INCORRECT: The wife wears *usually* a hat.

  CORRECT: The wife *usually* wears a hat.

Checkpoint 16

A. The following paragraph describes the U. S. holiday Columbus Day. Read the passage and circle all the adverbs. Where in the sentence does each occur? What part of the sentence does the adverb modify? Discuss your answers with your partner or small group.

Columbus Day, October 12 or the second Monday in October, is a legal holiday in most states. (This day is recognized unofficially in a few other states.) This holiday commemorates the discovery of America by Columbus in 1492. Schools sometimes hold ceremonies or reenactments of Columbus's discovery. The holiday is always observed in South America and often in some cities in Italy and Spain.

B. Read the following percentages, which indicate the approximate frequency represented by the adverbs. Then do the exercise that follows.

100%	always
80%	usually
70%	often, frequently
40%	sometimes
20%	seldom, rarely, hardly ever
0%	never

With a partner or group, make sentences about what you do on your favorite holidays. Share your sentences with the whole class. Example:

On Chinese New Year, I *usually* join the parade.

On July Fourth, I *always* watch fireworks with my family.

- **Final Position**. Adverbs can also appear in the final position in a sentence; these adverbs often refer to a definite time.

We went to the beach *yesterday*.

I'm going to a restaurant with Francis *tonight*.

Adverbs of manner usually appear at the end of a sentence. These adverbs answer the question "In what way?"

They ate their meal *fast* and *hungrily*.

She drives *slowly* and *cautiously*.

He does his job *quickly* but *well*.

NOTE: Some adverbs can occupy all three positions (beginning, middle, and end), and many can occupy two positions. Writers often vary the position of adverbs to provide interest or emphasis to their work. For example, all three of the following sentences are correct, although the first is the most usual.

She opened the door *slowly* and *quietly*.

She *slowly* and *quietly* opened the door.

Slowly and *quietly*, she opened the door.

The following passage describes New Year's Day in the United States. Find and circle the adverbs in the passage. Which are adverbs of manner? Which is not?

New Year's Day on January 1 marks the beginning of the calendar year and is celebrated very widely around the world. In the United States, New Year's is the occasion for merry celebrations while the people wait for midnight, when church bells ring and whistles and horns blow wildly. New Year's Day is the time for making resolutions, or goals, about one's behavior in the coming year.

VII Focus on the Forms of Adverbs

ADVERBS WITH *-LY*

Many adverbs are formed simply by adding *-ly* to an adjective; some common examples are *clearly*, *fairly*, *fortunately*, *stupidly*, *wrongly*. Others require slight spelling changes. For example, to change adjectives that end in *y* to adverbs, you must change the *y* to *i*.

Adjective	**Adverb**
happy	happily
funny	funnily
jumpy	jumpily
merry	merrily

When adjectives that end in *-ic* or *-ical* are changed to adverbs, the adverb ends in *-ically*.

Adjective	**Adverb**
basic	basically
musical	musically
geographic	geographically
mechanical	mechanically

An exception to this rule is *public/publicly*.

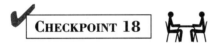

A. Go back to the passages in Checkpoints 14 through 17 on pages 86–88. Which of the adverbs are formed by adding *-ly* to adjectives? Which are not formed from adjectives? Discuss your answers with a partner.

B. Write five sentences about U. S. holidays. Exchange papers with a partner. (a) Mark any adverbs and discuss their usage. (b) Add adverbs where possible.

ADVERBS WITHOUT *-LY*

Many common adverbs do not end in *-ly*. Some examples are *too*, *fast*, *hard*, *often*, *soon*, and *late*. Others have two forms: *cheap/cheaply*, *loud/loudly*, *slow/slowly*. In these cases, the *-ly* form is more formal.

Jim *often* studies in the library.

The teacher will be here *soon*.

Please don't come to class *late*.

Some words can be both adjectives and adverbs, depending on the way they are used; examples are *hard*, *late*, and *fast*.

A few words that end in *-ly* are adjectives, not adverbs. These include *friendly*, *homely*, *ugly*, *leisurely*, *deadly*, *lowly*, and *lonely*. The word *kindly* can be used as an adjective *or* an adverb.

> They are very *friendly*, honest people.
>
> Although he is *homely*, he has many friends. He is never *lonely*.
>
> We took a *leisurely* walk through the downtown area.
>
> The *kindly* waiter treated the woman courteously. (adjective)
>
> Would you *kindly* reply to my letter as soon as possible? (adverb)

Two other suffixes that are used to form adverbs are *-ward* and *-wise*. Common adverbs with these suffixes are *backward*, *forward*, *lengthwise*, *clockwise*, and *counterclockwise*.

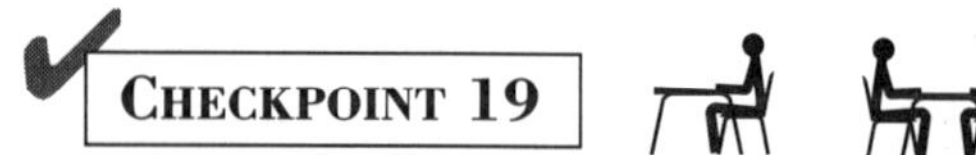

Checkpoint 19

Write the adverb form beside the adjectives listed below. Remember that not all adverbs end in *-ly* and that some adverb formations require spelling changes. When you finish, write five sentences with a partner, using at least one of the adverbs you have formed in each sentence. Example:

> We expected the Williamses to attend the graduation party, but they were *conspicuously* absent.

	Adjective	**Adverb**
1.	conspicuous	____________
2.	slow	____________ or ____________
3.	unhappy	____________
4.	public	____________
5.	long	____________
6.	quiet	____________
7.	solemn	____________
8.	grave	____________
9.	cold	____________
10.	back	____________

VIII Focus on Special Rules About Adverbs

FORMS WITH *BE* AND *FEEL*

It is incorrect in formal English to use only an adverb after the verb *be* or after verbs of perception like *feel, taste, look, appear,* and *sound.* These verbs are followed by adjectives.

INCORRECT: That music sounds *terribly.*

CORRECT: That music sounds *terrible.*

INCORRECT: She feels *badly.*

CORRECT: She feels *bad.*

The expression *feel bad* can refer to both mental and physical feelings. Both of the following sentences are correct.

She feels *bad* because she failed the test.

She feels *bad* because she has a cold.

USING *ENOUGH, HARD, HARDLY, WELL*

The common adverbs *enough, hard, hardly,* and *well* have special rules for usage. When *enough* is used as an adverb, it usually comes after the word it modifies.

This job is easy *enough* for a child to do.

He's feeling well *enough* to go to school.

(*Enough* can also be used as an adjective, as in the sentence "We have *enough* money.")

The adverbs *hard* and *hardly* have different uses. The following sentences show their differences.

The carpenter hit the nail *hard.*

We had *hardly* any money.

The adverb *hardly* carries negative meaning; in the second example sentence it means "not much money." *Hard* is an adverb of manner that modifies the verb *hit.* Here are some further examples of the use of *hard.*

We studied *hard* for the test.

The bad news hit him very *hard.*

Hard can also be used as an adjective.

Diamonds are very *hard.*

It was a very *hard* test.

In formal English, the adverb *well* is used differently from the adjective *good. Well* is an adverb of manner in the following sentences.

He did his job *well.*

It was a job *well* done.

Well can also be used as an adjective referring to a person's health.

She doesn't feel *well.*

It is incorrect in formal English to use *good* as an adverb.

INCORRECT: She did *good* on the test.

CORRECT: She did *well* on the test.

CHECKPOINT 20

Circle the correct word in the following sentences.

1. The birthday cake tasted (delicious, deliciously).
2. Mary felt (bad, badly) when she missed the birthday party.
3. John had (hard, hardly) any money to buy his friend a birthday present.
4. He tried (hard, hardly) to find an inexpensive but useful present.
5. He did (good, well); he found an appropriate gift.
6. The orchestra leader moved (slow, slowly).
7. The husband looked (ferocious, ferociously).
8. She fought (brave, bravely) to hold back the tears.
9. The musicians played the songs (loud, loudly).
10. The man felt (good, well) after he scolded his wife.

IX Focus on Adjectives and Adverbs in Comparisons of Equality and Inequality

PREVIEW OF COMPARISONS

The following poem by Judith Viorst offers a new ending to the "Cinderella" fairy tale, well known in many countries. It contains some comparisons. Working with a partner, find as many comparisons as you can.

. . . And Then the Prince Knelt Down and Tried to Put the Glass Slipper on Cinderella's Foot

I really didn't notice that he had a funny nose.
And he certainly looked better all dressed up in fancy clothes.
He's not nearly as attractive as he seemed the other night.
So I think I'll just pretend that this glass slipper feels too tight.

Expressing Equality

To make comparisons about two persons or things, use *as* + adjective + *as* to express equality.

> That woman is *as intelligent as* her sister. (Their intelligence is equal.)
>
> That pink cake looks *as rich as* the other dessert. (The desserts are equally rich.)

The same structure occurs with adverbs of manner.

> The violinist plays *as well as* the pianist.
>
> We ate our dinner *as fast as* the other couple did.

To express inequality, use *not as . . . as.*

> The husband is *not as* kind *as* his wife.

✔ Checkpoint 21

A. Write comparisons of equality or inequality about your classmates, using adjectives or adverbs of manner and *as . . . as.* Working with other students, write ten or more sentences. Examples:

> Kim speaks *as softly as* Anna.
>
> Francisco is not *as funny as* Toshi.

B. Match the nouns on the left with the adjectives on the right. Then work with a partner or small group to make comparisons of equality. Use one of the following two patterns.

1. He/She is (not) as ________ as (a) ________.
2. It is (not) as ________ as (a) ________.

1. pretty	a. lightning
2. cold	b. mule
3. green	c. turtle
4. slow	d. rock
5. soft	e. sugar
6. busy	f. silk
7. strong	g. bee
8. light	h. snow
9. stubborn	i. ox
10. hard	j. ice
11. sweet	k. feather
12. white	l. grass
13. quick	m. picture

Examples:

He is as *stubborn* as *a mule.*

It is as *quick* as *lightning.*

Comparisons of Inequality

The comparative degree can be used to show inequality between two things or two people. To form the comparative of adjectives and adverbs of one syllable, add *-er*, which means *more* (of the two).

Adjectives:

The dining room is small. The kitchen is *smaller.*

Her face is long. His face is *longer.*

My remark was quick. His remark was *quicker.*

Adverbs:

The violinist played low. The pianist played *lower.*

The orchestra leader tried hard to be kind. The headwaiter tried *harder.*

The woman spoke fast. The man spoke *faster.*

Spelling Rules for the Comparative Degree

For one-syllable adjectives that end in a single vowel followed by a single consonant, double the consonant before adding *-er.*

Their hats were big. Her hat was *bigger.*

The headwaiter looks fat. The orchestra leader looks *fatter.*

For adjectives of two syllables that end in *-y*, change the *y* to *i* before adding *-er.*

I'm hungry. You're *hungrier.*

The woman is pretty. Her mother is *prettier.*

The cake is heavy. The bottle of wine is *heavier.*

The word *than* often occurs after the comparative adjective or adverb in order to complete the comparison.

Hamburger is *cheaper than* steak.

I ate my dinner *faster than* you did.

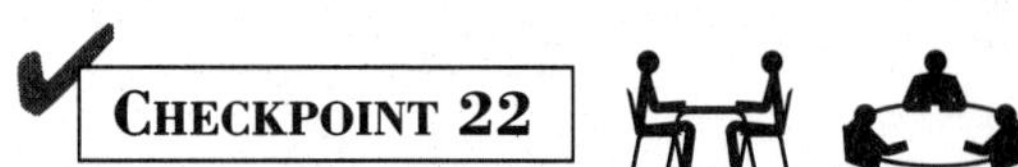

Checkpoint 22

A. Rearrange the words to make correct sentences with comparisons.

1. airplane than an higher a flies kite
2. a louder kitten a than cries baby

3. student excellent poor an a harder works student than
4. knives smaller are spoons than usually
5. fathers faster cars drive teenagers than

B. Complete the sentences with the comparative form of the adjective in parentheses. Be sure to make necessary spelling changes.

1. Yogurt is (*healthy*) ____________ than ice cream.
2. Birthday cake is (*rich*) ____________ than fruit.
3. Halloween occurs (*early*) ____________ in the fall than Thanksgiving.
4. A basketball player is usually (*tall*) ____________ than a baseball player.
5. Turkeys are (*heavy*) ____________ than chickens.

X Focus on Superlatives and Other Rules for Comparisons

Superlatives

To compare three or more people or things, use the superlative degree. For adjectives and adverbs of one syllable, add *-est* to form the superlative. The superlative form is usually preceded by *the*.

Adjectives:

I am sad. The man is sadder. The woman is *the saddest.*

The waiters at Sam's are friendly. The waiters at the Blue Rose are friendlier. The waiters at the narrow little restaurant are *the friendliest.*

Adverbs:

We waited a long time for the soup and longer for the chicken. We waited *the longest* for the dessert and coffee.

I stared hard at my plate, harder at the orchestra. But I stared at the man *the hardest.*

Sometimes a prepositional phrase or an adjective clause follows the superlative form to show what group is being compared or to complete the idea of the comparison.

She was *the loveliest* woman *in the restaurant.*

He was *the cruelest* person *in the world.*

That experience was *the worst* one *that I can remember.*

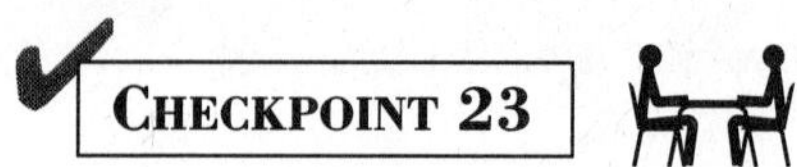

CHECKPOINT 23

A. Read the following passage about Independence Day and circle all the superlatives.

Independence Day, or the Fourth of July, commemorates the adoption by the Continental Congress of the Declaration of Independence in 1776 at the State House in Philadelphia, Pennsylvania. The "Glorious Fourth" is the occasion for the longest parades and the noisiest fireworks of the year.

In 1776, the greatest event in American history, the adoption of the Declaration of Independence, was greeted by the ringing of the Liberty Bell, which is now perhaps the most famous tourist attraction in Philadelphia. Inscribed on the bell is the saying "Proclaim liberty throughout all the land, to all the inhabitants thereof." The crack in the bell makes it impossible for it to ring again, but each year it is lightly struck with a mallet to commemorate the great day. Thomas Jefferson, the author of the declaration, and John Adams, one of the most important signers, both died on July 4, 1826.

B. Ask a partner's opinion about which classmate's name to put in each blank. Fill in the name and the superlative form of the adjective or adverb in parentheses. Remember to use *the*. Example:

<u>Roberto</u> speaks (loudly) <u>the loudest</u>.

1. ____________ usually arrives (late) ____________.
2. ____________ works (hard) ____________.
3. ____________ is (happy) ____________.
4. ____________ speaks (soft) ____________.
5. ____________ arrives (early) ____________.
6. ____________ is (wise) ____________.
7. ____________ tells (funny) ____________ jokes.
8. ____________ is (tall) ____________.
9. ____________ drives (new) ____________ car.
10. ____________ lives (close) ____________ to school.

IRREGULAR FORMS

Some adjectives and adverbs have irregular forms in the comparative and superlative.

Comparatives of Irregular Adjectives and Adverbs

good	better	(the) best
bad	worse	(the) worst
far	farther	(the) farthest (for distance)
far	further	(the) furthest (for degree)
little	less	(the) least
much	more	(the) most
many	more	(the) most

Special Rules for Adjectives of Two or More Syllables

Special rules for forming the comparative and superlative apply to adjectives of two or more syllables that don't end in *-y* and to adverbs that end in *-ly*. In these cases, the word *more* precedes the adjective or adverb in the comparative; the superlative is formed with *most* or *the most.*

We were *more comfortable* at the big table.

We were *the most comfortable* outside the restaurant.

The headwaiter handled the cake *more carefully* than the husband.

The woman handled the cake *the most carefully* of all.

The woman is *more cheerful* than her husband. Their daughter is *the most cheerful* member of the family.

Write sentences about yourself. In Part A, compare yourself now with the way you were five years ago by writing five sentences in the comparative degree. Examples:

I run *faster* now *than* I did five years ago.

I am *more mature* now.

Part A

1.
2.
3.
4.
5.

In Part B, answer the questions with sentences in the superlative degree.

When were you the most nervous
the happiest
the most excited
the most uncomfortable
the most relaxed in your life?

Examples:

I was the most nervous when I got married.
before my driver's test.
at my graduation.
in a high-school play.

Part B

1.
2.
3.
4.
5.

Other Forms of Comparison

To compare two people or things, the expressions *not as . . . as* or *less . . . than* are used to express inequality with adjectives and adverbs of manner.

This little restaurant is *less expensive than* that one. (In other words, it is cheaper.)

This seafood restaurant is *not as good as* the French café. (The French café is better.)

Checkpoint 25

Express each comparison in two other ways. Example:

A birthday is more enjoyable than Thanksgiving.

Thanksgiving is *less enjoyable than* a birthday.

Thanksgiving is *not as enjoyable as* a birthday.

1. The Fourth of July is not as popular as Halloween.
2. The weather at Christmas is usually colder than the weather at Easter.
3. Memorial Day is not as famous as the Fourth of July.
4. Many people feel that Christmas is less important as a religious holiday than Easter.
5. Memorial Day is not as festive a holiday as Halloween.

The Least

The superlative degree can sometimes be expressed with *the least . . .* for three or more people or things. This structure occurs with adjectives and adverbs of manner.

> This birthday celebration was *the least festive* of any that I'd seen.
>
> His wife is *the least confident* of all the women in the family.
>
> Of all the musical groups in the concert, the violin-and-piano group played *the least enthusiastically.*

Checkpoint 26 

Express the same meaning of each sentence with a different expression using *the least, the most,* or *the . . . -est.* Example:

> This was *the saddest* occasion of all.
>
> This was *the least happy* (*the most depressing*) occasion of all.

1. My dinner was *the cheapest* I had had in a while.
2. His face was *the least friendly* in the room.
3. It was also *the least attractive face* I had ever seen.
4. The waiter was *the laziest* person there.
5. The woman wore *the most unusual hat* in the place.

PART THREE. Review and Integration

Job Descriptions: Using Modifiers

Write a paragraph-long job description for each of the jobs listed below. Use as many modifiers as possible to describe the person who would be ideal for each job. Be sure you identify the main character traits for each position. For example, for the position "art director," you might explain that an applicant should be *creative, personable*, and *dynamic*.

elementary school teacher
librarian
research physicist
newspaper reporter
department store manager

Game: Adjective and Adverb Forms

In teams of three to five, complete the chart. The adjectives and adverbs on the chart should begin with the letters on the left. Your teacher will give you a time limit. When the time is up, exchange charts with another team. One speaker from each team will call out the other team's answers. An incorrect answer receives no points. A correct answer that was used by more than one team receives five points. An original answer (one chosen by only one team) receives ten points. Take off one point for a misspelling.

Adjective Forms

	able or *-ible*	*-ous*	*-ful*	*-ive*	*-ic(al)*
S					
A					
C or B					
M or L					
P or N					

Adverbs

	Manner	Time	Place	Degree	no *-ly*
T					
A or O					
L or H					
P or R					
S or D					

Images of Women: Adverb Review

Rewrite the following sentences, inserting the adverbs in parentheses in appropriate places. Some of the adverbs can be placed in more than one position in the sentence. Discuss with your partner or group the best positions for each one and the question each adverb answers.

1. In the United States, the attitude toward women who are celebrating their fortieth or fiftieth birthdays has become quite topical. (recently, quite)
2. Men and women have to change their ways of thinking at "middle age." (often, substantially)
3. These women want to be viewed. (romantically, more)

4. The accepted view that older women cannot be attractive is being challenged. (traditionally, nowadays)
5. Many women keep busy exercising and eating right; thus, they have slowed the aging process. (very, considerably)
6. In the past, a woman turning fifty could be considered more than pretty. (never, fadingly)
7. Not only Hollywood stars of that age are beautiful. (now, exceedingly)

Halloween: Comparisons

A group of neighborhood children are discussing Halloween before they go out "trick-or-treating." Complete each sentence with the appropriate comparative or superlative form of the adjective in parentheses.

Susie: Halloween is (*good*) ____________ holiday of all. It's a chance to be something else for one night. You can be (*beautiful*) ____________ or (*ugly*) ____________ creature in the world.

Jon: This year I want to look (*horrible*) ____________ and (*scary*) ____________ than I did last year. Maybe I'll be Dracula.

Ben: I'd rather be Batman. He's (*brave*) ____________ and (*strong*) ____________ than Dracula.

Sam: Last year I had (*bad*) ____________ costume I've ever worn. I was a ghost, and I couldn't see anything.

Tom: How about Frankenstein this year? It would be easy to make a costume, and I think he's (*frightening*) ____________ monster of all.

Susie: Who want to frighten people? I'll be a pumpkin! Pumpkins are (*happy*) ____________ and (*funny*) ____________ than those creepy creatures.

Jon: Come on, Susie. That's (*boring*) ____________ idea you've ever had. At least be an alien. That's (*interesting*) ____________ than a stupid pumpkin.

Dialogue: Review of Word Forms in Units Two and Three

The following imaginary dialogue takes place between Mary, a thirty-five-year-old woman from the 1950s, and Susan, a thirty-five-year-old woman from the 1990s. As you read the dialogue, look at the underlined words. Write the abbreviations of the parts of speech (*n* for noun, *adj* for adjective, and *adv* for adverb) on the lines to the right. Some lines have more than one underlined word.

Part of Speech

Mary: I need to talk to somebody about the *miserable* birthday *party* I ________ had for my husband last night. I am very *depressed.* ________

Susan: What happened that was *so* terrible? George probably *really* ________ appreciated the *effort* you made. *Where* were you, anyway?

Mary: We went to a *little* restaurant we have been going to for years. _____ I surprised *George* with a *cake*, and he hated it. He called me "stupid" and *other* names.

Susan: I hope you walked out. What a *cruel* thing for him to do! Did you at least throw a *drink* at him?

Mary: I didn't do anything. I cried through the *rest* of the meal and sat _____ *quietly* in the car on the way home. _____

Susan: Mary! You have to be *assertive*! You must discuss your *feelings*! _____ Nobody has the right to treat you *badly*.

Mary: I prefer to punish George in my *own* way. I won't be speaking to him _____ for *days*._____

Susan: This is exactly what was wrong with *marriages* in your day. People _____ should speak out about problems.

More Word Forms

The following exercise is adapted from James Thurber's "My Own Ten Rules for a Happy Marriage." Circle the correct word forms inside the parentheses.

1. An (intelligent, intelligently) husband does not criticize (former, formerly) boyfriends of his wife.
2. A (man, men) should make an effort to learn the (name, names) of his (wife, wife's) friends.
3. A husband should (never insult, insult never) his wife (public, publicly).
4. A (good, well) (husband, husbands) doesn't say, "Oh, well, you know how women are."
5. A husband sits (quiet, quietly) in his chair when his (wife, wives) is reading aloud; he must look (relax, relaxed) but (attentive, attentively).
6. A husband should try to remember where his (thing, things) are around the house.
7. If a husband is not (listening really, really listening) to what his wife is saying, he should not say "Okay" or "Yeah, sure."
8. When a wife stops calling her husband "(Sweet, Sweetly) Lips" or "Cutie Pie" during the first year of marriage, he should not worry.
9. A husband should not join the baseball team of (marry, married) men to play against the (single, singly) men at the Fourth of July picnic. He will get hurt.

10. A husband should stay away from his (spouse, spouse's) possessions. He would probably drop something (terrible, terribly) wet, oily, or sticky on them.

Suggestions for Writing

1. If you are keeping a journal, write an entry on one of the following subjects: how birthdays are celebrated in your culture, how you react to surprises, why some people lie about their age, your feelings about the characters in "Birthday Party."
2. Write a composition describing the ideal husband or wife. Give at least three examples of the qualities or characteristics that you believe the ideal mate should have.
3. Write a composition about one of the most interesting holidays celebrated in your culture. Describe the significance of the holiday and some of the customs, foods, or celebrations connected with it.
4. Use your imagination to write about the feelings of the husband or wife in "Birthday Party" *after* their dinner in the restaurant. Pretend that you are one of the characters writing in a diary or journal. For example, if you pretend to be the husband, you might write things like the following: "I hate eating in restaurants. Why didn't she cook my favorite meal on my birthday?" The wife might write, "I was so excited when I planned his birthday surprise. Why doesn't he appreciate me?"

   Before you write, you may want to discuss the husband's and wife's feelings with a partner. After you write, read each other's writings.

Unit Four

VERB TENSES

READING: "My Name" from *The House on Mango Street* by Sandra Cisneros

THEME: Hispanic Voices

PART ONE: The Context

The following reading, "My Name," is from *The House on Mango Street* by Sandra Cisneros. In the book, Cisneros describes the experiences and observations of a Mexican–American girl growing up in Chicago. Cisneros writes with sensitivity, simplicity, and humor about the adjustments that newcomers to the United States must make. Like Cisneros, millions of Hispanics have immigrated to the United States from many countries, especially Mexico, Central America, and South American countries.

PRE-READING QUESTIONS

1. The narrator of the following selection explains the meaning of her given name. Does your name have any special meaning? If so, how could it be translated into English? Do you have a nickname? How did you get it?
2. Various cultures have their own systems for explaining people's personalities. For example, the Chinese have a system that attributes characteristics to people according to the year of their birth (The Year of the Horse, Rat, Rooster, and so on). Another system, based on an unscientific but popular system of observing the planets (astrology), places people into "signs" according to the time and place of their birth. Some signs include Aries (the ram), Taurus (the bull), and Gemini (the twins). (A description of this system appears on pages 149–150.) What is your birth sign? What are its characteristics? Do you think it gives an accurate description of your personality? Explain.
3. The narrator's father sings Mexican songs when he is shaving. In addition to music, what aspects of their cultures do most people preserve when they move to another country?

PREVIEW OF KEY TERMS AND CONCEPTS

The following key words and ideas appear in the readings in this chapter. Guess the meaning of the terms on the left by matching them to the definitions on the right. Put the correct letter after each term. Discuss your answers with a partner or group, and ask your teacher about any terms you're not sure of.

1. chandelier ____
2. muddy ____
3. elbow ____
4. to baptize ____
5. sack ____

a. to christen and give a name to; to admit to the Christian church
b. fixture that hangs from a ceiling and has branches for lights
c. large bag, usually made of cloth
d. outer angle of the joint between a person's upper and lower arm
e. unclear or thick, like soft wet earth

READING: "My Name" by Sandra Cisneros

(1) In English my name means hope. In Spanish it means too many letters. It means sadness, it means waiting. It is like the number nine. A muddy color. It is the Mexican records my father plays on Sunday mornings when he is shaving, songs like sobbing.*

(2) It was my great-grandmother's name and now it is mine. She was a horse-woman too, born like me in the Chinese year of the horse—which is supposed to be bad luck if you're born female—but I think this is a Chinese lie because the Chinese, like the Mexicans, don't like their women strong.

(3) My great-grandmother. I would've liked to have known her, a wild horse of a woman, so wild she wouldn't marry. Until my great-grandfather threw a sack over her head and carried her off. Just like that, as if she were a fancy chandelier. That's the way he did it.

(4) And the story goes she never forgave him. She looked out the window her whole life, the way so many women sit their sadness on an elbow. I wonder if she made the best with what she got or was she sorry because she couldn't be all the things she wanted to be. Esperanza. I have inherited her name, but I don't want her place by the window.

(5) At school they say my name funny as if the syllables were made out of tin and hurt the roof of your mouth. But in Spanish my name is made out of a softer something, like silver, not quite as thick as my sister's name—Magdalena—which is uglier than mine. Magdalena who at least can come home and become Nenny. But I am always Esperanza.

(6) I would like to baptize myself under a new name, a name more like the real me, the one nobody sees. Esperanza as Lisandra or Maritza or Zeze the X. Yes. Something like Zeze the X will do.

Comprehension Questions

1. Why does Esperanza dislike her name? What problems does it cause her at school?
2. How does she feel about her great-grandmother? Why doesn't she want to inherit "her place by the window"?
3. What is her sister's nickname? What nicknames does Esperanza consider for herself?

Discussion Questions

1. Hispanics are sometimes considered one group, but the term "Hispanic" refers to people of vastly different cultures and customs. The one characteristic they have in common is the Spanish language, yet the dialects they speak are sometimes very dissimilar. What are some of the countries and/or regions where Spanish is the first language?

---

* sobbing crying, weeping

2. Should English be the only language used in U.S. public schools? Should some classes be taught in another language where a minority is very large? Under what circumstances, if any, should bilingual education exist?
3. Hispanic families tend to be "extended" rather than "nuclear." In extended families, different generations and branches of one family live together or near each other, whereas the typical nuclear family includes only parents and children. What are the advantages and disadvantages of each type of family? Which type do you prefer?

PART TWO: The Target Structure: Verb Tenses

I Focus on the Simple Present: General Rules

Preview of the Simple Present

The first paragraph of "My Name" is reprinted below. In each clause, draw a line separating the subject from the predicate and underline the predicate. (See page 9 if you need to review subjects and predicates.) Then find (a) one verb that expresses a permanent state; (b) one that expresses a habit or repeated action; and (c) one that expresses a temporary action. Discuss them with your group or partner.

In English my name means hope. In Spanish it means too many letters. It means sadness, it means waiting. It is like the number nine. A muddy color. It is the Mexican records my father plays on Sunday mornings when he is shaving, songs like sobbing.

All but one of the verbs in the first paragraph of "My Name" (*is shaving*) are in the simple present. Although it is called the present, this verb form is really general or "timeless." Its two most common uses are to express (a) generalizations or permanent states and (b) habitual or repeated actions.

Permanent	I *am* always Esperanza.
or	
General	Many women *sit* their sadness on an elbow.
Habitual	My father *plays* Mexican songs on Sundays.
or	
Repeated	At school they *say* my name funny.

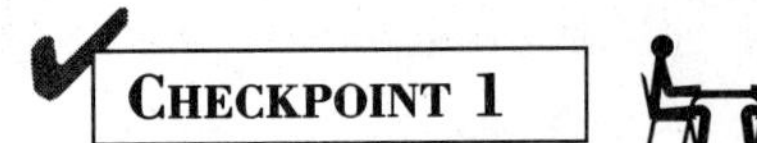

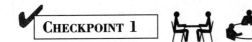

Read the following passage and underline the verbs. Decide which verbs are permanent or general and which are habitual or repeated. (The last verb in the passage, *is declining*, does not belong in either group.)

Most children of newcomers to the United States prefer English to the languages of their parents, a major new study claims. The study of children in South Florida and San Diego, the majority of whom are Hispanic, shows that the children use English more than their parents' languages. Ninety-nine percent of immigrant students in Miami like to speak English more than their parents' language. One Hispanic girl actually stutters when she speaks Spanish because she feels uncomfortable with it. The study concludes that the use of English in the U.S. is not declining, despite recent increases in immigration.

Forms of the Simple Present

The simple present consists of the base form of the verb except when the subject is a singular noun or one of the pronouns *he, she,* and *it.* With these subjects, an *-s* ending is added to the base form. Given below are the forms of *play* in the simple present.

Singular	Plural
I *play*	we *play*
you *play*	you *play*
he, she, it *plays*	they *play*

Unlike other verbs, *be* has three different forms in the simple present (*am, is,* and *are*).

Singular	Plural
I *am*	we *are*
you *are*	you *are*
he, she, it *is*	they *are*

In general, a present verb form ending in *-s* occurs with a subject without *-s* (a singular noun). Conversely, a verb without *-s* occurs with a subject ending in *-s* (a plural noun). In short, if the noun ends in *-s*, the verb doesn't, and vice versa.

The *house needs* repairs. (singular subject)

The *houses need* repairs. (plural subject)

Even the irregular verbs *be* and *have* follow this rule because their third-person singular forms end in *-s*.

Linda ha*s* a brother who i*s* in college.

CHECKPOINT 2

A.. 

Look at the picture of Maria's room. Make up at least five sentences about Maria based on your observations. Discuss the meaning of each simple present verb. Is it general or habitual? Examples:

She plays tennis. (habitual)

She likes music. (general)

B.

The following paragraph contains several errors in subject–verb agreement. Make the necessary corrections.

Maria and her family lives in a yellow house. The house is on King Street. Papa like the house, but Maria and her brother Julio wants to move. They has many neighbors on King Street. Many of them come from Mexico, but others are from Central American countries, such as Honduras and El Salvador.

Contractions, Negatives, and Questions

- **Contractions.** The simple present forms of the verb *to be* are often contracted (shortened) and combined with the subject.
- **Negatives.** To form the negative of the simple present, put *do* + *not* (or the contraction *don't*) before the base form. Use *does* + *not* (or *doesn't*) for the third person singular (*he*, *she*, *it*), and do not add *-s* to the main verb.

  Esperanza *does not (doesn't)* want to be like her great-grandmother.

  I *do not (don't)* like my nickname.

- **Questions and Short Answers.** To form questions in the simple present, move the auxiliary verb to the front of the subject. In information questions, a question word precedes the auxiliary. (Present-tense questions are also discussed in Unit One.) Short answers are formed with the auxiliary *do/does.*

  Does Esperanza *go* to school? Yes, she *does.*

  Do her parents *speak* Spanish? Yes, they *do.*

  Does Esperanza *like* her name? No, she *doesn't.*

  Do they *like* Mango Street? No they *don't.*

  Where *does* Esperanza *study*? In school.

  Why *do* the children *say* her name funny? They *don't speak* Spanish.

  Who *has* a nickname? Nenny *does.*

  What *sounds* like tin? The syllables of Nenny's name.

Checkpoint 3

A. Take turns making up sentences that describe Esperanza's habits and then Nenny's based on the situation and information provided. Add information about your own habits as well.

Situation: Esperanza and Nenny are sisters, but they have different interests. In general, Esperanza is very concerned about health and tries to maintain good health habits. Nenny is not interested in following a healthful routine. Example:

coffee/water/tea/soda

Esperanza doesn't drink coffee or soda. She drinks tea and water.

Nenny drinks whatever she wants, but she especially likes soda.

I drink coffee, but I don't drink soda or tea.

1. eat fruit/vegetables/fast food
2. skip meals/eat three meals a day
3. get to bed early/late
4. take naps
5. play sports
6. smoke
7. take vitamins
8. sleep late
9. exercise regularly
10. watch TV

B. Make up questions and short answers about the statements you composed for Part A. Give one YES/NO question and one information question for each. Examples:

Does Esperanza drink coffee or soda? No, she doesn't.

Why doesn't she drink them? Because they contain caffeine.

II Focus on Agreement

Special Rules About Subjects

Choosing the correct form of the simple present requires first determining whether a subject is singular or plural. The following are special rules regarding singular and plural subjects.

1. Subjects joined by *and* take a plural verb.

   The house and the street *need* repairs.

2. **Head words.** A verb must agree with the head word or words of the subject. For example, prepositional phrases that follow subjects do not affect agreement.

   The *design* of those buildings *reminds* me of Mango Street.
   (singular subject, *-s* on the verb)

   The *houses* on that street *look* very similar to the ones on Mango Street.
   (plural subject, no *-s* on the verb)

3. **Indefinite pronouns.** Some words, even though they may suggest plural meaning, always require a singular verb. These words include the indefinite pronouns *every*, *each*, *everybody*, *everyone*, *no one*, *nobody*, *none*, and *one*.

   None of the mothers *stays* home all day.

   Everyone attends P.T.A. meetings quite regularly.

4. **Irregular plurals.** The plural forms of many nouns do not end in *-s*. (See pages 60–62 on noun plurals and the Appendix on page 383 for irregular plurals.)

   Children love parties.

   Most *people* live in cities.

5. **Expressions of quantity.** Expressions such as *all of*, *some of*, *the majority of*, *most of*, and *a lot of*, as well as fractions and percentages, can be used with either singular or plural nouns. The verb agrees with the noun that follows the expression of quantity.

   Half of the *girls take* French.

   Half of the *class is* in the gym.

✔ CHECKPOINT 4

Take turns answering as your instructor calls out subjects from the list. Say *is* if the subject is singular and *are* if it is plural. Example:

Mango Street . . .

Mango Street *is* . . .

1. Esperanza
2. Papa
3. Papa and Nenny
4. The neighbor
5. The neighbors
6. Everyone
7. Uncle Tito and I
8. Each of the girls
9. One of the classes
10. Her sadness
11. She
12. The chandelier
13. The chandeliers
14. The streets of Chicago
15. Chicago
16. A city
17. Two cities
18. None of the parents
19. All of the parents
20. Nenny and her grandmother

ADDITIONAL RULES ABOUT SUBJECTS

6. **Languages/nationalities.** The names of languages ending in *-ese*, *-sh*, and *-ch* are singular, but the same words, preceded by *the*, are plural when they refer to a nationality.

Languages (singular):

English is spoken by many people.

Spanish is a Romance language.

Nationalities (plural):

The English usually drink tea in the afternoon.

The Spanish eat dinner very late.

7. **Adjectives used as nouns.** When an adjective describing a group of people is used as a noun preceded by *the*, it is plural.

   The hearing impaired need closed captioning, or subtitles, to be able to understand television programs.

   The old pass along their knowledge to *the young*.

8. **Words ending in *-ics*.** Fields of study and academic courses ending in *-ics* are singular.

   Statistics is a required course for many college majors.

   Physics is Maria's favorite course.

   Some *-ics* nouns, however, can be plural in other contexts.

   The statistics in the census report *show* new population trends.

9. **Measurements.** Expressions of distance, weight, time, or money are considered singular, even if they contain plurals, because they are thought of as single amounts.

   Five miles is a long way to run.

   Two hundred pounds seems to be a good weight for him.

   Twenty-six thousand dollars is the average income of people in that city.

10. **Singular nouns ending in *-s*.** Some nouns are singular even though they end in *-s*. This group includes the names of some countries, including the United States, the Netherlands, and the Philippines.

    The *news is* on television.

    The United States is sending a representative to the conference.

11. **Sentences with *there is* and *there are*.** The verb agrees with the noun that follows it.

    There are many old *houses* on Mango Street.

    There is a big *church* two blocks away.

12. ***A/the number of.*** The quantity expression *a number of* followed by a plural noun is considered plural, but *the number of* plus a plural noun is singular because it refers to a single quantity.

A number of students in our class *speak* Spanish.

The number of Japanese *speakers is* smaller.

CHECKPOINT 5

Complete the paragraphs with the correct form of the verb in parentheses. If one of the special agreement rules applies, write the number of that rule (1–12) after the verb.

A. There (*be*) __is (11)__ a race question on the U.S. census form that a number of people (*have*) __________ trouble filling out. Advocacy groups (*suggest*) __________ that the form be changed, but no one (*know*) __________ how to improve it. Race (*be*) __________ the basis for identifying minority groups now. According to some experts, however, perhaps language and immigration from a certain geographic area (*be*) __________ more important factors.

B. Most of the Hispanic respondents (*feel*) __________ they don't fit into any racial category. There (*be*) __________ no specific answer for "Hispanic" as a race; instead, a separate question (*ask*) __________ about "Hispanic origin." Everyone of Hispanic origin (*have*) __________ to answer "other" in the race category, even though statistics (*show*) __________ that this group (*be*) __________ a very fast-growing one. Nine and eight-tenths million (*be*) __________ the most recent number of Hispanic Americans in the U.S. available from the U.S. Census Bureau.

Choices on the census form (*consist*) __________ of white; black or Negro; Indian (American), Eskimo, Aleut; and Asian or Pacific Islander. The last group (*choose*) __________ from nine other sub-categories, including Chinese and Samoan. The Chinese (*be*) __________ another fast-growing minority in the United States.

III Focus on Uses of the Simple Present

Facts and General Information

One use of the simple present, as you have seen, is to express facts and general information. The simple present often expresses scientific generalizations.

Mammals *feed* their babies milk.

A triangle *has* three sides, and a square *has* four.

Sixteen ounces *make* a pound.

Proverbs and other sayings are usually in the simple present form because they express timeless information.

Haste *makes* waste.

A stitch in time *saves* nine.

The grass *is* always greener on the other side of the fence.

A. Write three common proverbs from your native language and translate them into English using the simple present. Be sure to check the subject-verb agreement. Exchange papers with a partner (one from a different language background, if possible). Explain your proverbs to each other. Are there any similarities between proverbs in your language and those in English or in your partner's language? Explain.

B. With a partner, make up sentences about general or scientific information, using the cues. Use the simple present. Example:

sun—east, west

The sun *rises* in the east and *sets* in the west.

1. earth—round
2. birds—south, north
3. stars—night
4. planets—sun
5. snow—winter

Habits and Routines: Adverbs of Frequency

When the simple present is used to express a habit or routine, adverbs of frequency, such as *often*, *usually*, and *always*, and other time expressions may accompany it. Adverbs of frequency occur *after* the verb *be* but *before* other verbs.

Magdalena *is* **usually** cheerful.

My father **often** *plays* records **on Sunday mornings.**

Esperanza and her sister **always** *go* to school **on week days.**

CHECKPOINT 7

A. Yolanda's and Maria's school schedule is printed below. With a partner or group, write sentences about their activities. Practice using time expressions, such as *every day, twice a week, at (9 A.M., noon*, etc.), *in the afternoon*, and so on. Use the simple present. Examples:

Yolanda and Maria *have* gym class every day.

They *go* to gym at 12:50 four times a week.

On Wednesday, they *have* gym at 12:40.

When you finish, exchange papers with another pair or group and check their work.

MONDAY	TUESDAY	WEDNESDAY	THURSDAY	FRIDAY
8:05–9:05 Class Meeting	8:05–9:15 Language Arts	8:05–9:00 Assembly	8:05–8:55 Math	8:05–8:55 Science
9:10–10:05 Science	9:20–10:00 Science	9:10–10:55 Language Arts	9:00–10:10 Language Arts	9:00–10:55 Language Arts
10:15–10:55 Library	10:10–11:00 Math		10:15–11:00 Music	
11:00–12:00 Lunch	11:15–11:35 Lunch	11:00–11:30 Lunch	11:00–11:30 Lunch	11:00–11:30 Lunch
12:05–12:45 Math	11:45–12:45 Language Arts Computer	11:50–12:35 Math	11:35–12:40 Class Meeting	11:35–12:45 History
12:50–1:40 Gym	12:50–1:40 Gym	12:50–1:20 Gym	12:50–1:40 Gym	12:50–1:40 Gym
1:40–1:50 Recess	1:40–1:50 Recess	1:20–1:35 Recess	1:40–1:50 Recess	1:40–1:50 Recess
1:55–2:40 Art	1:55–3:30 History	1:40–2:30 Science	1:55–2:40 History	1:55–2:40 Math
2:45–3:30 Study		2:35–2:45 Pack up	2:45–3:30 Art	2:45–3:30 Study

B. Using adverbs of frequency, rewrite your sentences from Part A, above. Substitute the single-word adverb for the time expression, as shown in the example below. Refer to the list for adverbs of frequency. Example:

100%	always
80%	usually
70%	frequently, often
40%	sometimes
20%	seldom, rarely, hardly ever
0%	never

Yolanda and Maria have gym class *every day* at 12:50.

every day = *always*

Yolanda and Maria *always* have gym class at 12:50.

IV Focus on the Present Progressive

Preview of the Present Progressive

With a partner, discuss the differences between the following pairs of sentences.

Esperanza's father *plays* records every Sunday.

Today is Sunday. He *is playing* a record.

Immigrants to the U.S. *experience* many difficulties in adjusting to the new culture.

Right now Esperanza's family *is experiencing* many difficulties in adjusting to the new culture.

The Present Progressive

Unlike the simple present, the present progressive expresses a *temporary* action taking place in present time. The progressive also emphasizes the *duration* (length of time) of an action. The last example sentence in the preview shows that the present progressive may express an action that takes place over a relatively long duration, and the action does not always include the present moment.

She *is writing* a book.

They *are studying* English at school.

In these examples, the action is in progress, but may not be taking place at the present moment. The verbs *is writing* and *are studying* refer to actions that have not yet been completed.

A few verbs, such as *hope*, *plan*, *live*, and *feel*, have almost the same meaning in the simple present and the present progressive. The progressive form emphasizes the duration or progress of an event or state.

Her family *lives/is living* on Mango Street.

He *feels/is feeling* depressed.

Forms of the Present Progressive

The present progressive includes a simple present form of the verb *be* and the *-ing* form of the main verb. In the present progressive, *be* is an auxiliary verb. The form of *be* must agree with its subject. The chart shows the forms of the present progressive including contractions.

Present Progressive	
Singular	**Plural**
I am (I'm) playing	We are (We're) playing
You are (You're) playing	You are (You're) playing
He, She, It is (He's, She's, It's) playing	They are (They're) playing

Checkpoint 8

A. 

Your teacher will write the base forms of verbs from "My Name" or other material you are studying on cards, one verb on each card. The teacher will give a card to each partner or team member, who will take turns performing the action of the verbs written on the cards. Guess what the verb is, using the present progressive in your answer. Example:

shave (A student pantomimes the action of shaving.)

His/her partner or teammates respond: She *is shaving*.

B. 

With a partner, look at the picture of the *Market in Tenochtitlan* by Diego Rivera on page 121. Use the present progressive to make up sentences about the various people in the picture. What are different people doing? Example:

A woman with a fan *is sitting* in a large chair.

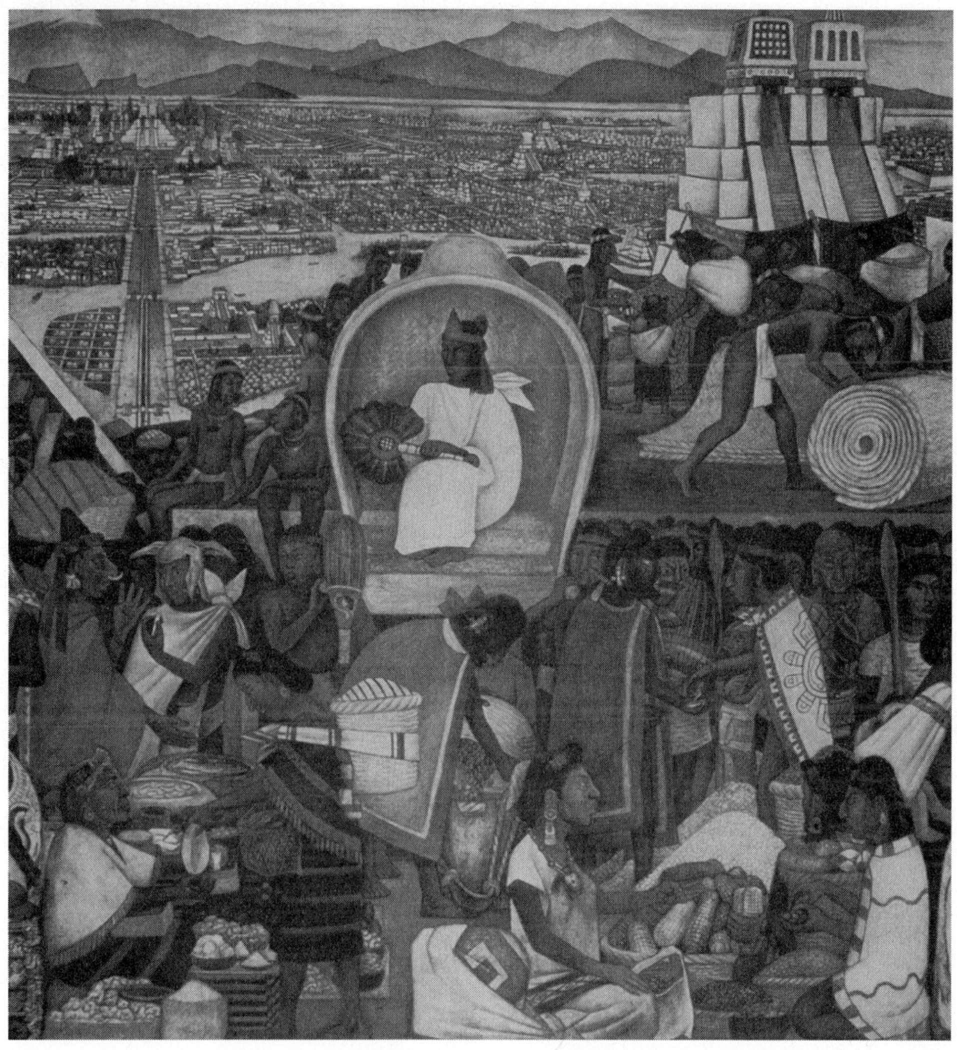

Negatives and Questions in the Present Progressive

- **Negatives.** To form the negative of the present progressive, put *not* between the form of *be* and the *-ing* form of the main verb. The negative can be contracted in two ways: the subject can contract with the *be* form, or the *be* form can contract with *not*. (Note that *am* does not contract with *not*.)

  He *is not playing* happy music.
  (He'*s not playing*, He *isn't playing*)

  They *are not enjoying* their American school.
  (They'*re not enjoying*, They *aren't enjoying*)

  I am not going to school today.
  (I'*m not going*)

- **Questions and Short Answers.** Questions are formed by moving the auxiliary in front of the subject. (See Unit One for more information on questions in the present progressive.)

Is her father *shaving* now? No, he *isn't*.

Are the girls listening to music? Yes, they *are*.

Where *are* the girls *going*? To school.

Why *is* Esperanza *running*? She's late.

What *is hurting* Esperanza's ears? The sound of her name.

Verbs Not Used in the Progressive

The progressive form is not used with certain verbs even when they express a temporary condition or a present occurrence. These verbs, often called *stative*, express little or no action and include (a) "linking" verbs, (b) mental state verbs, (c) emotional state verbs, (d) verbs of perception, and (e) a few other verbs, among them those that express possession, including *have*, *possess*, and *own*.

Some Stative Verbs

Linking	Mental State	Emotional State	Perception	Others
be	believe	admire	see	belong
appear	forget	like	hear	contain
seem	imagine	love	smell	depend
remain	know	regret	taste	have
stay	remember	trust	feel	mean
look	think	care	sound	need
become	understand			own
	wonder			possess

She *is* ill now. (INCORRECT: She *is being* ill now.)

I *believe* Esperanza is singing with her father.

She *knows* about her great-grandmother.

Esperanza *admires* her great-grandmother's spirit.

She *loves* her father very much.

I *see* Esperanza by the window.

She *hears* her father singing.

Magdalena *has* a nickname.

Esperanza *means* "hope."

When linking verbs, stative verbs, or verbs of perception express *action*, often in idiomatic expressions, the progressive may be used. Compare the following sentences:

Possession:	She *has* some friends.
Action:	She *is having* fun with her friends.
Linking:	She *looks* thoughtful.
Action:	She *is looking* at her father.
Mental state:	She *thinks* her great-grandmother was strong.
Action:	She *is thinking* about her great-grandmother.
Perception:	Her recipes always *taste* wonderful.
Action:	She *is tasting* the soup to find out if it needs more garlic.

CHECKPOINT 9

A. In groups of four or five, choose a planet other than Earth and imagine that you live on that planet. Write a description of yourselves, including your appearance, your values and beliefs, your economy, your system of government, your family unit, and other information you want to include. Use the simple present or present progressive. Exchange your descriptions with another group. Identify which present verbs are stative. Example:

We have green hair.

B. Complete the following sentences with the correct present form of the verb in parentheses.

1. Maria's aunt and uncle (*have*) <u>are having</u> a party at their church.
2. The church (*have*) ________________ a basement big enough for dancing.
3. Everyone (*have*) ________________ a good time at the party.
4. Mama (*taste*) ________________ the tamales.
5. She (*think*) ________________ they (*taste*) ________________ delicious.
6. Maria (*think*) ________________ about the brown school dress she (*wear*) ________________. She (*think*) ________________ it (*be*) ________________ ugly.
7. But now she (*dance*) ________________ with Uncle Tito, and all her friends and family (*look*) ________________ at her.
8. She (*know*) ________________ she and her uncle (*look*) ________________ wonderful dancing together, so she (*forget*) ________________ about her dress.

V Focus on Future Time

PREVIEW OF THE FUTURE TENSE

In "Papa Who Wakes Up Tired in the Dark," a chapter from *The House on Mango Street*, Esperanza's father returns to Mexico for his father's funeral. Read the following passage describing his trip and then underline all the verb phrases. (The first two have been done for you.) Discuss them with other students. Which ones have future meaning?

I <u>know</u> he <u>will have to go</u> away, that he will take a plane to Mexico, all the uncles and aunts will be there, and they will have a black and white photo taken in front of the tomb with flowers shaped like spears because this is how they send the dead away in that country.

WILL AND *BE GOING TO*

Future time in English is often expressed with the helping verbs *will* and *be going to* followed by the base form of the verb.

Tomorrow we *will leave* for Mexico.

Esperanza *is going to become* a writer when she grows up.

With *be going to,* the rules for subject-verb agreement must be followed.

I *am* going to . . .

He/she/it *is* going to . . .

You/we/they *are* going to . . .

These forms are often contracted.

I'm going to read Esperanza's books.

She's going to be famous.

We're going to enjoy her fame.

Will is used with all subjects. It does not change forms.

Papa *will* go home.

His friends *will* be there.

- *Negatives.* To form the negative of *will,* use *will not* or *won't* before the base form of the main verb.

Esperanza *will not/won't* live on Mango Street all her life.

To form the negative of *be going to,* insert *not* after the form of *be.*

She *is not/isn't going to live* there forever.

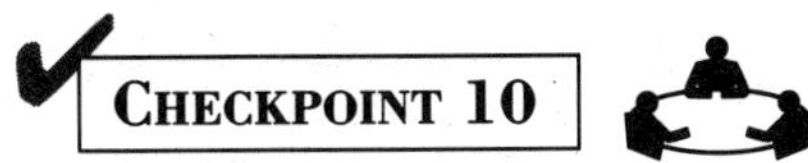

CHECKPOINT 10

A. With a group, make five or more predictions about Esperanza's future using *will* or *won't.* Discuss your ideas about her future with verbs or verb phrases from the reading, or use your own verbs. Have one person write the sentences. When you have finished, rewrite the sentences using *be (not) going to.* Possible verbs or verb phrases include *live on Mango Street forever, move away from Mango Street, get married, marry a man like/different from her great-grandfather, sit by the window, be happy, change her name, find a nickname.* Examples:

Esperanza *will change* her name to Zeze the X.

Esperanza *is going to change* her name to Zeze the X.

B. Write five sentences about your future plans. Use *will, won't,* or *be (not) going to.*

The Future Progressive

The future progressive has two major uses: to emphasize the duration of a future event and to express an action that will continue from the present into the future.

Duration:

They *will be driving* to Mexico for several days.

They *won't be staying* there for very long.

Present to future:

She *will be writing* that book for at least another year.

She *won't be traveling* much until she finishes the book.

Questions and Short Answers in the Future and the Future Progressive

Questions are formed by moving the auxiliary before the subject.

Will her father *come* back from Mexico soon? No, he *won't.*

Is he *going to stay* for a few days? Yes, he *is.*

Will all the relatives *be going* to the funeral? Yes, they *will.*

Are they *going* to send flowers? No, they *aren't.* (No, *they're not.*)

Who *will* the father *stay* with? His brother.

Why *will* everyone *be crying*? *They'll be* sad.

What *are* the women *going to wear*? Black dresses, probably.

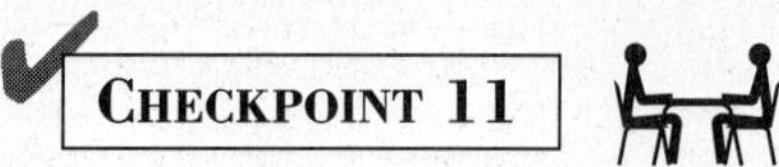

A. Write a paragraph with at least four sentences about what you *will* or *won't* be doing five years from now. When you finish, exchange your paragraph with a partner. Underline and discuss all the future-tense verbs. Examples:

Five years from now, I *will be* out of school.

I *will be working* as an accountant somewhere, probably for a company in New Orleans.

B. Use the cues to form sentences in the future or future progressive two ways, with *will be* + *-ing* form and *be going to*, about the funeral of Esperanza's *abuelito* (grandfather), which will take place in Mexico tomorrow at 4 o'clock. Example:

Papa/feel sad

Papa will be feeling sad.

Papa is going to be feeling sad.

1. Many people/attend the funeral
2. Papa/see many old friends
3. At 4:30, musicians/play Abuelito's favorite songs
4. At 5:00, Esperanza's uncle/make a speech
5. All afternoon, many of the relatives/cry
6. At 5:30, everyone/leave/church

Using the Present to Express the Future

The present tense (simple or progressive) may also be used to express future time with verbs that refer to schedules and plans, such as *come, go, begin, start, finish, leave, bring, take*, and *be*. A future time expression almost always occurs with the present tense verb.

Papa's plane *departs* (or *will depart*) at 3:20 P.M.

The test *is* (or *will be*) tomorrow.

He *leaves* (or *will leave*) for Mexico later today.

Her father *is flying* (or *will be flying*) to Mexico for a funeral.

He *is returning* (or *will be returning*) next Monday.

The present tense is also used to express the future in time clauses beginning with words like *before, after, when*, and *until*, and in *if-* and *unless*-clauses expressing real conditions. (Conditional clauses are discussed in detail in Unit 9.) In time clauses and clauses that express real conditions, it is incorrect to use *will* or *be going to*.

INCORRECT: When she will graduate from high school, she will go to college.

CORRECT: When she *graduates* from high school, she will go to college.

INCORRECT: If she is going to study hard, she will probably receive a scholarship.

CORRECT: If she *studies* hard, she will probably receive a scholarship.

INCORRECT: Unless she will/is going to study hard, she will not (won't) receive a scholarship.

CORRECT: Unless she *studies* hard, she will not (won't) receive a scholarship.

CHECKPOINT 12

Read the situation and fill in the blanks with appropriate verbs to express future meaning. Use the simple present or present progressive forms where possible to refer to scheduled events and future plans.

Situation: Maria and her cousin Carlos are making plans on the telephone for Carlos's visit tomorrow. He's flying in for Maria's graduation from high school.

Maria: I can't wait until tomorrow! Your plane (*arrive*) ________________ at 2, right? That (*not, give*) ________________ you much time to get ready for Tito's party, which (*start*) ________________ at 3. If your plane (*be*) ________________ late, we'll go directly to Tito's from the airport.

Carlos: I (*wear*) ________________ blue jeans on the plane. (*be*) ________________ that okay for the party?

Maria: I guess so. The graduation ceremony (*not, begin*) ________________ until 8, so you (*have*) ________________ time to get dressed for that. Of course, I (*take*) ________________ my graduation gown to the party. We all (*change*) ________________ our clothes there.

Carlos: Sounds good. I (*not, believe*) ________________ you're graduating until I (*see*) ________________ you in your gown. See you tomorrow.

Maria: See you. I (*not, talk*) ________________ to you before then unless there (*be*) ________________ a change in the plan.

VI Focus on the Simple Past

PREVIEW OF THE SIMPLE PAST

- Esperanza compares herself with her great-grandmother in "My Name," and she discusses her great-grandmother's life. Reread paragraph 4 reprinted below and underline all the verb phrases. Which ones express past time? Discuss your answers with other students.

- The simple past is often formed by adding the ending *-d* or *-ed* to the base form of the verb. Find the two verbs in the paragraph that have been formed this way. (Do not include *inherited*, which is part of a present perfect verb.)
- Many verbs have irregular past forms. In the paragraph, find three irregular past forms besides the verb **be**.

And the story goes she never forgave him. She looked out the window her whole life, the way so many women sit their sadness on an elbow. I wonder if she made the best with what she got or was she sorry because she couldn't be all the things she wanted to be. Esperanza. I have inherited her name, but I don't want her place by the window.

The Simple Past

The simple past is used to express a definite time in the past. It can be used for repeated or single events as well as for periods of long duration. It can also express consecutive actions (those that occur one after the other in chronological order). The event or period must have occurred in the past, however, and have no connection to the present moment. The following sentences about Esperanza's great-grandmother illustrate uses of the simple past.

Esperanza's great-grandfather *carried* her off. (single event)

He *carried* her off and *married* her. (consecutive actions)

She *looked* out the window many times. (repeated event)

She *lived* in Mexico all her life. (period of long duration)

The simple past is generally used for historical events, as in the following examples.

Simon Bolivar *freed* the slaves in Honduras, El Salvador, and Nicaragua.

The Incas *dominated* Peru before the Spanish *arrived* in the New World.

Jose Cecilio del Valle *wrote* the national anthem of Honduras.

Most people think that Christopher Columbus *discovered* America.

Negatives in the Simple Past

To form the negative of the simple past, put *did* + *not* (or the contraction *didn't*) before the base form of the main verb. No ending is used on the base form.

Columbus *did not/didn't realize* that America wasn't India.

Bolivar *did not/didn't stay* in his native South America.

Special care must be taken to use the correct past forms of irregular verbs.

Maria *bought* some candy, but she *didn't buy* any popcorn.

Questions and Short Answers

To form questions, move the auxiliary *did* in front of the subject. Negative short answers are usually contracted.

Did Columbus *know* America wasn't India? No, he *didn't.*

Did the Spanish *explore* the new continent? Yes, they *did.*

Where *did* Columbus *think* he had landed? In India.

How many ships *did* he *have*? Three.

Who *went* on the voyage with him? European sailors.

Why *did* they *make* the trip? Adventure and economic gain.

✔ Checkpoint 13

Your teacher will give each pair of students a card with one of the expressions from the list below on it. Pretend you are detectives, and ask and answer questions using words from the list until you guess which expression your partner has. Use the past tense. Example:

stole the wallet

Student A: *Did* you *steal* the wallet?

Student B: No, I *didn't steal* it. OR
Yes, I *stole* it.

saw the robbery	broke the window	wrote the teller a note
heard the gunshot	ran out of the bank	put a mask on
drove the getaway car	found the gun	said "Give me the money"
lost some money	hid the evidence	made a threat
shot the gun		hit a customer

Adverbial Expressions with the Simple Past

Adverbial expressions typically used with the simple past name a specific time in the past. These expressions make clear that an event or state was completed before the present moment.

Cecilia *moved away* from Mango Street *last week.*

Two years ago, the family *lived* on Linden Street.

At one time, Uncle Tito *worked* in a factory.

Other examples of past time expressions include *a minute ago, this morning* (if it is now afternoon or night), *last night, yesterday,* and *two weeks ago.*

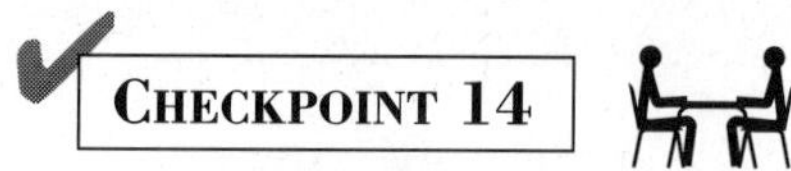

A. Pretend that Esperanza is an old woman. Underline all the verbs in the following paragraph. Then rewrite it, changing all the present verb forms to simple past. (Change the verb *can* to *could* and leave the verbs that directly follow it in the base form.) Exchange paragraphs with a partner and check each other's work. Begin this way:

At school they *said* my name funny . . .

At school they say my name funny as if the syllables were made out of tin and hurt the roof of your mouth. But in Spanish my name is made out of a softer something, like silver, not quite as thick as my sister's name—Magdalena—which is uglier than mine. Magdalena who at least can come home and become Nenny. But I am always Esperanza.

B. In the following passage about the discovery of America, write the correct form (present or past) of the verbs in parentheses. (Look in the Appendix on page 392 if necessary to find irregular forms.) The first two verbs have been filled in for you.

In 1492, educated people actually (*know*) ___knew___ a great deal about science. They (*think, not*) ___didn't think___ the earth was flat, for example. The year 1992 (*be*) ______________ the 500th anniversary of Columbus's "discovery" of America. However, in 1991, Scandinavians (*celebrate*) ______________ the 1000th anniversary of Leif Ericsson's voyage to New Foundland in Canada. Many people (*consider*) ______________ Ericsson the discoverer of the "New World," which (*be*) ______________ actually not a good name for a land where millions of people already (*live*) ______________. So, both Columbus and Ericsson really (*find*) ______________ another "old" world.

VII Focus on the Past Progressive

Preview of the Past Progressive

Read the following passage about Latin American art. With a partner, circle the verbs in the simple past. Then find the verbs that begin with *was* or *were* followed by the *-ing* form of the main verb; underline them. Decide whether these verbs indicate longer or shorter duration than those in the simple past.

Before the twentieth century, most Latin American artists were painting in styles that showed the influence of European traditions. For example, in Brazil, the influences of Neo-classicism and Romanticism were evident in the work of Nicolas-Antoine Taunay. In Bolivia, most painters favored the Baroque school. The Chilean artist Juan Francisco Gonzalez followed the example of French Impressionists, whereas the Uruguayan Pedro Figari's work echoed that of the Post-Impressionists.

In Mexico, following the agrarian revolution of 1910, a new style of painting called Naturalism emerged and gradually changed the direction of Latin American visual art. During these years, the social order was changing; the middle class was growing. To reflect these changes, artists were looking for ways to express historical and social themes unique to their countries.

The Past Progressive

Like the present progressive, the past progressive indicates duration, or action occurring over a period of time. It expresses ongoing action rather than a single event. Like the simple past, however, the past progressive refers to an action completed in the past.

> Esperanza *was sitting* by the window all afternoon.
>
> (She is no longer doing this.)
>
> Papa and his friends *were singing* Mexican songs at parties during those years.
>
> (The activity occurred over a period of time in the past.)

In the past progressive, appropriate forms of *be* must agree with subjects: *was* is used with *I*, *he* , *she*, and *it*. *Were* is used with *you*, *we*, and *they*. The negative is formed by inserting *not* between the form of *be* and the *-ing* form of the main verb.

Forms of the Past Progressive	
I was (not) singing	We were (not) singing
You were (not) singing	You were (not) singing
He/She was (not) singing	They were (not) singing

Contractions and Questions

- **Contractions.** Negative forms in the past progressive are often contracted: I *wasn't singing*, you *weren't singing*, she *wasn't singing*, etc.
- **Questions.** Questions in the past progressive are formed by moving the auxiliary in front of the subject.

  Was she *singing*? Yes, she *was*. (No, she *wasn't*.)

  Where *was* she *singing*? In the shower.

  How *was* she *singing*? Beautifully.

Contrasting the Simple Past and the Past Progressive

Like the two present forms, the simple and progressive forms of the past are often used in contrast in the same sentence.

> When her mother *called* her, Esperanza *was thinking* about her great-grandmother.

(The verb *called* describes a single event, while *was thinking* expresses the duration of an activity that occurred over a longer period of time.)

The past progressive can be used to express two actions that were in progress simultaneously.

> While she *was looking* out the window, she *was thinking* about how her life could have been different.

Checkpoint 15

A. Complete the paragraph with the past progressive forms of the verbs in parentheses.

Diego Rivera became the most famous of the Mexican naturalists; in his huge paintings he told the story of Mexico from its earliest beginnings. Rivera's wife Frida Kahlo is also a prominent figure in the history of Latin American art. Throughout their twenty-five years of marriage, both artists (*work*) ____________________ on their own styles. While Rivera (*develop*) ____________________ his muralist technique, Frida Kahlo (*discover*) ____________________ her symbolic, almost surreal, form of personal expression. When Kahlo died in 1954, she was not well-known. Today, however, her paintings are famous and extremely valuable.

B. The Legend of "La Llorona," the weeping woman of Mexican-American folklore in southern Arizona, is told below in the narrative present tense. Imagine that you are retelling the story in the year 3000, when the legend is no longer known. Change the verbs from present to past.

The legend of La Llorona is probably based on Aztec Indian stories about female spirits heard by the Spanish who conquered the territory that became Mexico. The weeping woman is always wearing white and has long black hair. She comes out on moonlit nights and walks through the streets crying and moaning as if in pain. Some say she is mourning the death of her children. Others think she is suffering from grief following her husband's death. Sometimes when people see her, she is walking into a lake; some people hear terrible screams. While people are running away from her, they feel the icy cold breath of La Llorona on their necks.

VIII Focus on the Present Perfect: Forms and Meanings

Preview of the Present Perfect

With a partner, read the excerpt from "Papa Who Wakes Up Tired in the Dark" from *The House on Mango Street* and answer the questions that follow.

Your *abuelito* is dead, Papa says early one morning in my room. *Esta muerto*, and then as if he just heard the news himself, crumples like a coat and cries, my brave papa cries. I have never seen my papa cry and don't know what to do . . . .

Because I am the oldest, my father has told me first, and now it is my turn to tell the others.

Find the two verbs that begin with *have* or *has*. They are are called *present perfect* tense verbs, even though they include time before the present. What is their relationship to the past? to the present?

Formation of the Present Perfect

The present perfect is formed with *have* or *has* and the *-ed/-en* form of the main verb. *Have* agrees with the subjects *I*, *you*, *we*, and *they*. *Has* agrees with *he*, *she*, and *it*.

I *have* never *seen* my father cry.

My father *has told* me first.

The *-ed/-en* form (sometimes called the past participle) of a verb is most commonly formed by adding *-ed* or *-d* to the base form. Many past participles, however, are irregular. (See the list in the Appendix on page 390.)

- **Negatives.** To form the negative of the present perfect tense, use *not* or the contraction *-n't* after *have* or *has*.

  Esperanza *has not* (*hasn't*) visited Mexico yet.

  Some of her relatives *have not* (*haven't*) ever visited the United States.

- **Questions and Short Answers.** To form questions, the auxiliaries *have* and *has* are moved before the subject. Negative short answers are usually contracted.

  Has Esperanza *visited* Mexico? No, she *hasn't.* (Yes, she *has.*)

  Have some family members in Mexico *visited* the United States?
  Yes, they *have.*

  (No, they *haven't.*)

  Which ones *have visited* the United States? Some of her cousins.

  Where *has* Angela *traveled*? To a few states in the United States.

  With whom *has* she *traveled*? Her family.

  How many states *have* they *toured*? Three or four.

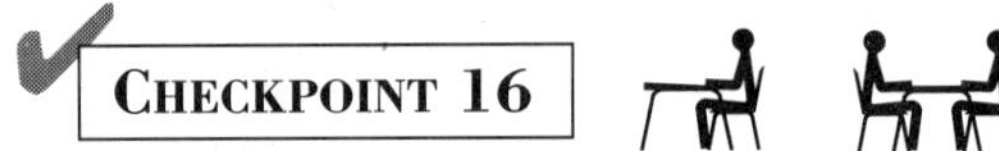

Circle the auxiliary in parentheses that matches the subject and completes the sentence correctly.

1. Papa (has, have) told me first.
2. The other children (hasn't, haven't) heard the news.
3. Esperanza's grandfather (has, have) died.
4. Mama and Papa (hasn't, haven't) been in Mexico for several years.
5. We (has, have) seen Papa's plane take off.

IX Focus on Uses of the Present Perfect

MEANINGS OF THE PRESENT PERFECT

The present perfect has two basic meanings: (a) to describe a time period that began in the past and includes the present; and (b) to express an indefinite time in the past.

Adverbial phrases expressing duration commonly occur in sentences that express past-to-present meaning.

Esperanza *has never liked* Mango Street.
(She didn't in the past and still doesn't.)

Esperanza and Nenny *have had* a close relationship *for many years.*
(They were close in the past and still are now.)

The second common use of the present perfect is to express an *indefinite* time in the past. The action or state expressed may be a repeated one.

I *have been* to Mexico several times.
(The specific times are not indicated.)

Papa *has told* Esperanza about his father's death.
(The exact time when he told her is not indicated.)

✔ CHECKPOINT 17

A. Underline the present perfect tense verbs in the following dialogue. Decide which meaning each one expresses: (a) past-to-present or (b) indefinite past.

Esperanza: I was thinking about the story called "The Three Brothers." Have you heard it?

Nenny: Yes. Several of my friends from Puerto Rico have mentioned it. How did you learn about it?

Esperanza: Luis told me at the doctor's office yesterday. It's the most fantastic story I've ever heard.

Nenny: It is a good story. Why was Luis at the doctor's again? He has been there three or four times this month.

Esperanza: He hasn't felt well lately.

B. Write the appropriate form of the verbs in parentheses. In most cases, the present perfect tense is required.

1. Since the 1950s, many people of Hispanic descent (*move*) ______________ to the United States.
2. Most of the Mexicans who (*live*) ______________ in the United States (*settle*) ______________ in the Southwest, including Texas and California.
3. Since the 1950s and 1960s especially, thousands of residents of Cuba (*migrate*) ______________ to Miami in southern Florida.
4. New York City (*be, always*) ______________ a favorite place for Puerto Rican immigrants to live in.
5. Many Latin Americans from Central American countries such as Honduras, Guatemala, and Nicaragua (*make, now*) ______________ their home in Louisiana.
6. Studies (*show*) ______________ that most of the Hispanic residents of the United States (*enjoy*) ______________ living there.

Using *Ever* and *Never* with the Present Perfect

The adverb *ever* is often used with the present perfect in questions about experiences.

Have you *ever been* to Mexico? *Has* your father *ever been* there?

If the answer to these questions is negative, *never* or *not ever* is used.

I *have* (I'*ve*) *never been* there.

I *have not (haven't) ever been* there.

Checkpoint 18

With a partner, practice forming present perfect verbs by making questions and answers about things you have or haven't done. Use irregular past participles from the list below. Examples:

ever eat/frog legs?

Have you ever eaten frog legs?

Yes, I have eaten them several times.

No, I have never eaten frog legs.

No, I haven't ever eaten them.

fall in love

Have you ever fallen in love?

Yes, I have fallen in love several times.

be to/ France?	eat/alligator	see/mountain
Italy	rabbit	forest fire
Japan	paella	ocean
Australia	cotton candy	iceberg
Egypt	couscous	geyser

Using *For* and *Since* with the Present Perfect

For and *since* are often used with present perfect verbs; *for* precedes a period of time (*many years, six weeks, three hours*, etc.), and *since* precedes a phrase referring to the beginning of the period of time, often a day, date, month, or year.

They have lived on Mango Street *for* several years.
(*for* + period of time)

They have lived there *since* April, 1990.
(*since* + beginning of time period)

Since can also be used as a conjunction introducing a time clause. Usually the verb in the time clause is in the simple past.

They have lived on Mango Street *since* they first moved to the city.

Patterns with *Since* and *For*		
Clause with Present Perfect +	**For/Since +**	**Rest of Sentence**
We have known Esperanza	for	three months.
She has lived in Chicago	for	six years.
Her parents have been here	since	April 1980.
Her father hasn't worked in a factory	since	the mid-eighties.
They have lived on Mango Street	since	they moved to the city.

Checkpoint 19

Complete the sentences in the following paragraph about the Rio Grande river by filling in the blanks with *since* or *for*.

The Rio Grande has had at least ten names ____________ Alonzo Alvarez de Pineda sailed into it in 1519. It has been the Rio Bravo del Norte on Mexican maps ____________ 1598, when scouts of Don Juan de Onate first saw it. This river has irrigated crops of farmers ____________ almost a thousand years. At its source, in the cold and windy San Juan Mountains in Colorado, very few plants or animals have been able to survive ____________ as long as anyone can remember. The river has marked the border between Texas and Mexico ____________ the treaty of Guadalupe–Hidalgo was signed in 1848.

Using *Yet, Still, Already,* and *So Far*

Read the following conversation between Esperanza and Nenny. They are planning a party for Saturday. Today is Wednesday.

Esperanza: *Have* you *invited* any of your friends at school *yet*?

Nenny: A few of them.

Esperanza: How many *have* you *invited so far*?

Nenny: I've invited three or four, but two were absent today. I *still haven't told* them about the party, but I will.

Esperanza: I'*ve already invited* my best school friends, four girls and three boys.

The adverbs *yet*, *still*, *already*, and *so far* often accompany the present perfect. They express actions that have occurred before the present during a period of time that is not yet complete. *Yet* occurs in YES/NO questions and negative sentences.

Have you invited Linda *yet*?

No, I haven't seen her *yet*.

Yet usually goes at the end of a sentence, but it appears *before* a time period in a question or negative statement.

I haven't seen her *yet* this week.

So far is used in affirmative statements and indicates that an action has occurred before now. It usually goes at the end of the sentence, but it can also go at the beginning.

Nenny has invited four friends *so far*.

So far, they *have invited* eighteen friends and neighbors.

Already occurs in affirmative statements and often emphasizes that something happened sooner than expected.

She *has already finished* calling her friends, but it's going to take me another hour to finish.

Already usually occurs in the middle position after the auxiliary *have* or *has*.

Still, which usually occurs in negative sentences, emphasizes that something hasn't happened as of the present moment.

Linda *still hasn't returned* to school.

CHECKPOINT 20

A. Using the expressions in parentheses, rephrase each of the following sentences by using a different adverb. Examples:

I've already been to three of Nenny's parties. (*so far*)

I'*ve been* to three of Nenny's parties *so far*.

1. We still haven't tried any Mexican food. (*yet*)
2. My sister hasn't heard guitar music yet. (*still*)
3. Carlos has already introduced me to several interesting people. (*so far*)
4. I still haven't been to a better party. (*yet*)

B. Maria is angry at her brother Carlos. Make sentences using *yet*, *still*, or *already* and the present perfect from the following cues explaining why she is angry. Example:

still/not repay the money he borrowed

He *still hasn't repaid* the money he borrowed.

1. still/not find her guitar, which he lost
2. already/break the tape player their parents gave them last week
3. yet/not clean up his room
4. already/ruin his new shirt
5. yet/not start doing his homework

X Focus on Additional Uses of the Present Perfect

Using *Just* with the Present Perfect

The adverb *just* is commonly used with the present perfect. It shows that an event occurred very recently or a short time before the present moment.

Look! There's Papa! He *has just stepped* off the plane.

The children are happy because they'*ve just seen* him.

When the simple past is used with *just*, it has almost the same meaning as the present perfect.

Papa *just stepped* off the plane.

The children *just saw* him.

Read the situation and use the cues to form sentences using *just* and the present perfect.

Situation: It's recess time at Esperanza's school. All the children are on the playground and there's a lot of activity.

Example:

Why is Pedro laughing? (*hear a joke*)

He *has just heard* a joke.

1. Why is Nenny crying? (*fall down*)
2. Why are the boys smiling? (*won a soccer game*)
3. Why aren't Nina and Maria hungry? (*eat a snack*)
4. Why is the teacher punishing Jose? (*hit a classmate*)
5. Why are some of the children going inside? (*hear the bell*)

Contrasting the Simple Past and the Present Perfect

With a partner or small group, discuss the differences in meaning between the verbs in each pair of sentences.

I *went* to Mexico last summer.

I *have been* to Mexico many times.

Papa *has told* Esperanza about his father's death.

He *told* her yesterday about his father's death.

The simple past refers to a definite past time with no relation to the present moment; often a specific past time (*last summer, yesterday*) is mentioned. On the other hand, the present perfect in the sentences above refers to an indefinite time before the present. If a definite time or period of time is mentioned with the present perfect, the expressions *since* or *for* are usually used.

I *haven't been* to Mexico *for* six months/ *since* last summer.

Checkpoint 22

A. Complete the paragraph with the simple past or present perfect form of the verb in parentheses. Use the simple past to show definite past time and the present perfect to indicate indefinite past time or past-to-present meaning.

Maria's family (*not, always, live*) ____________________ on King Street. Ten years ago, they (*have*) ______________ a house on Homestead Avenue. Papa (*look*) ______________ at several other houses since then, but he (*not, find*) ______________ one to move into. Kids (*break*) ______________ some of the windows of their house from time to time, and most of the other residents of King Street (*put*) ______________ boards on their windows. Last year someone (*rob*) ______________ the laundromat, and ever since, Maria and her brother Julio (*be*) ______________ afraid to go out at night.

B. Change indefinite situations into definite ones by writing sentences with verbs in the simple past after the ones in the present perfect. Use a time expression with the simple past. Example:

INDEFINITE:	Esperanza's father has returned to Mexico several times since he moved to the United States.
DEFINITE:	He went there last month for his father's funeral.

1. INDEFINITE: Nenny has gone to the doctor three times recently.
   DEFINITE:

2. INDEFINITE: Esperanza has written quite a few stories so far this year.
   DEFINITE:

3. INDEFINITE: Papa has often come home late since he began working as a gardener.
   DEFINITE:

4. INDEFINITE: Mama has complained several times recently about the noise on Mango Street.
   DEFINITE:

Preview of the Present Perfect Progressive

Read the passage and underline the verb phrases. With a partner discuss the differences in meaning between the present perfect (*have/has [not]* + the *-ed/-en* form of the main verb) and the present perfect progressive (*have/has [not] been* + *-ing* form). Which one emphasizes the *duration* of an action?

Yolanda's family has lived in the United States since 1990. She has been studying English as part of her curriculum since she entered junior high school that year. She has improved so much in the time that she has been speaking English regularly that she has become almost as fluent as a native speaker.

The Present Perfect Progressive

Like other progressive forms, the present perfect progressive emphasizes the duration of an action or state, in this case the duration *before now* or *up to now.*

> Yolanda *has been studying* English for several years.
> (time up to and including now)

As the preceding sentence shows, the present perfect progressive is frequently used to express habit or routine; often it implies that these routines will continue in the future.

> We *have been working* on verbs, but we haven't finished our work yet.

Sometimes, particularly with the verbs *live* and *work*, there is very little difference in meaning between the present perfect and the present perfect progressive used with *since* and *for.*

> Yolanda's family *has lived/has been living* in Esperanza's neighborhood for three years.

The words *just, already, ever,* and *never* are <u>not</u> used with the present perfect progressive.

Questions and Short Answers

To form questions, move the auxiliary, *have* or *has*, before the subject. Negative short answers are usually contracted. The following examples illustrate the forms of the present perfect progressive in questions and short answers.

Has Yolanda *been studying* English at school? Yes, she *has.*

Have her sisters *been studying* it too? Yes, they *have.*

Have her parents *been studying* it? No, they *haven't.*

When *have* they *been studying*? In the evening after work.

How long *have* they *been studying* it? For about three years.

Checkpoint 23

With a partner, use the present perfect progressive to form sentences from the cues. Try to give additional information.

Situation: The Martinez family, originally from Honduras, has just moved to Mango Street. Mr. and Mrs. Martinez have three children: Maria (nine), Eduardo (seven), and Jose (three). What *have they been doing* since they moved to the neighborhood?

Example:

Mrs. Martinez/look for/a good job

Mrs. Martinez has been looking for a good job as an accountant.

1. Mr. and Mrs. Martinez/visit/day care centers for Jose
2. Maria and Eduardo/meet/children on Mango Street
3. The family/explore/neighborhood
4. They/look for/furniture for the house
5. Mrs. Martinez/shop/different stores

XI Focus on the Past Perfect

Preview of the Past Perfect

With a partner, read the following sentences and underline the verb phrases. Decide which action happened first; put "1" above that verb phrase and "2" above the verb that expresses the second action. If a third verb is used, put a "3" above it. The first sentence has been done for you.

1. Esperanza's grandmother resented (2) her husband because he had carried (1) her off against her will.
2. Esperanza's father loved Mexican music, which he had listened to all his life.

3. When he had shaved, he got dressed and went to work.
4. The girls admired the beautiful cake they had made and then ate some of it.

The Past Perfect

Just as the present perfect expresses time before the present, the past perfect expresses time before a given point in the past. ("Perfect" means completed before another time.) The past perfect is formed in the following way.

Subject + *had* (*not*) + *-ed/-en* form of verb + rest of sentence

Nenny *hadn't finished* her homework before she went to bed.

There is only one form; the auxiliary *had* doesn't change, regardless of the subject.

The context in which the past perfect is used always makes clear that the time referred to is before the past, not before the present. Very often the simple past will be used in the same sentence. The following sentences illustrate the use of the past perfect to express "past-before-the-past."

Papa *had brushed* his hair before he *left* for work.

Nenny *was* sad because she *had heard* about her grandfather's death.

Questions and Short Answers

To form questions in the past perfect, move the auxiliary *had* in front of the subject.

Had Nenny *finished* her homework before bed? No, she *hadn't.*

Had she *done* her chores? Yes, she *had.*

What chores *had* she *done*? Washing the dishes and sweeping.

When *had* Papa *brushed* his hair? Before he left for work.

Checkpoint 24

Use the past perfect to form sentences about the following situation. Yesterday was Maria's birthday. Her family and friends wanted to surprise her. When Maria got home, ... Example:

Julio/plan/surprise party

Julio *had planned* a surprise party.

1. Julio/bake/cake
2. Papa/decorate/living room
3. Uncle Tito/bring/dance music
4. Mother/make/dinner
5. Friends/hide/(in) kitchen

6. Julio/turn off/lights

   When Maria arrived, they all shouted "Surprise!"

THE PAST PERFECT WITH TIME EXPRESSIONS

In informal usage, it is not always necessary to use the past perfect to express time before the past. When time words like *before, after, when,* or *as soon as* are used, the relationship between the two past times is clear without the use of the past perfect. It is not incorrect, however, to use the past perfect when the time words occur in the sentence; in fact, the past perfect should be used in formal writing, even with the time words.

INFORMAL: The family *cleaned up* the house when all the guests *left.*

FORMAL: The family *cleaned up* the house when all the guests *had left.*

INFORMAL: After Ana *finished* work, she *went* to dinner with some co-workers.

FORMAL: After Ana *had finished* work, she *went* to dinner with some co-workers.

✔ CHECKPOINT 25

A. Complete the following sentences about what Silvia *had expected* to be true versus what actually *happened* when she took her first job. Use the simple past or the past perfect of the verbs in parentheses; in some cases, either one may be correct. Look up the forms of irregular verbs in the Appendix on page 390 if you need to.

Before I (*start*) ______________ my first job, I (*want*) ______________ to be an office manager. I (*always, think*) ______________. that business women (*be*) ______________ smart and glamorous. However, on my first day of work, I (*find*) ______________ out the truth. The office work (*seem*) ______________ harder than I (*expect*) ______________. The other workers (*act*) ______________ very unfriendly and cold. I almost (*quit*) ______________ at the end of the first day. But the next day, my boss (*call*) ______________ me, and, after we (*talk*) ______________ for a long time, I (*decide*) ______________ to give it another chance. The second day (*be*) ____________ much better. Office work (*turn out*) ______________ to be good career choice after all.

B.

Write a paragraph describing your expectations about coming to the United States, starting school, or starting a new job, and how your expectations differed from the reality. Exchange paragraphs with a partner and discuss the forms of the verbs used.

Preview of the Past Perfect Progressive

The past perfect progressive is formed in the following way.

Subject + *had (not)* + *been* + the *-ing* form of main verb

Her father *had (not) been sleeping* well.

Underline the past perfect and past perfect progressive verbs in the following passage and discuss the differences between them.

When the Spanish *conquistadores* and other European explorers came to the New World, they found that Native Americans (whom they mistakenly named "Indians") had been living in the Americas for a long time. These ancient people had come from Asia to North America in prehistoric times, and some had migrated all the way to the tip of South America. For these tribes, whose cultures had been developing for many centuries before the Europeans arrived, the New World was very old.

The Past Perfect Progressive

The past perfect progressive expresses the duration of an event or activity occurring before the past. (The duration can sometimes be very long, as the passage on Native Americans demonstrates.) It can also express time right before the past. Examples:

By eight A.M., Esperanza *had been sleeping* for many hours.
(emphasis on duration)

She *had been dreaming* about school when her alarm clock rang.
(time just before the simple past)

Had she *been worrying* about school? Yes, she *had.*

What *had* she *been worrying* about? A chemistry test.

Working with a partner, use the past perfect progressive to form sentences from the cues. Try to provide additional information after the subject and verb.

Situation: Papa had the day off yesterday, and he wanted to rest. When Esperanza and Nenny got home from school, Papa was tired and angry. Why?

Example:

The neighbors/argue

The neighbors had been arguing loudly for hours.

1. He/not/rest
2. The telephone/ring
3. The dog/bark
4. The air conditioning/not/work
5. His back/hurt

XII Focus on the Future Perfect

Preview of the Future Perfect

With a partner, read the following sentences and underline the verb phrases. Decide which action will happen first. Put "1" above that verb phrase and "2" above the phrase the expresses the second action.

When Esperanza graduates, she will have taken three computer classes.

We will have spent six months planning our vacation in Costa Rica by the time we finally leave next week.

The Future Perfect

The future perfect is used to express time before a specific point in the future. The future perfect is formed in the following way:

Subject + *will* (*not*) + *have* + *-ed/-en* form.

Next December, I *will have known* Esperanza for five years.

Papa *will have* just *come* home when dinner is ready.

Will Esperanza *have helped* to prepare it? No, she *won't* (*have*), but Nenny *will* (*have*).

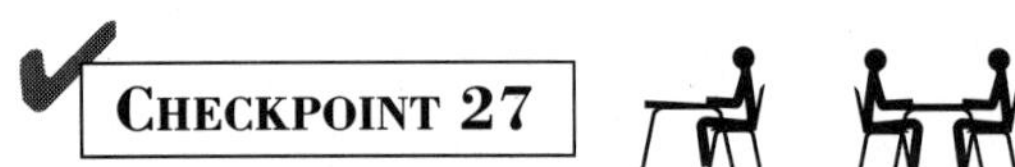

Use the cues to form sentences that include the future perfect.

Situation: Maria is writing down goals for herself about what she hopes to accomplish before graduation.

Before graduation, Maria hopes she . . .

Example:

learn/use/computer

She hopes she *will have learned* to use the computer.

1. improve/English
2. apply for/scholarships
3. do research about/some colleges
4. make/many new friends

The Future Perfect Progressive

The future perfect rarely occurs in the progressive form. It is only used (a) to express time right before a point in the future or (b) to emphasize the duration of an event or activity before a point in the future. It is formed in the following way.

Subject + *will* (*not*) + *have* + *been* + *-ing* form

Maria's family *will have been living* in the United States for several years when she finishes high school.

Will they *have been learning* English during that time? Yes, they *will* (*have*).

Checkpoint 28

Use the cues to make questions that include the future perfect progressive and then answer them.

Situation: Maria and her cousin Eduardo are expecting Papa to come home from work at 6 P.M. They have lots of work to do, and they won't be finished when he gets home.

Example:

She puts the dishes in the sink at 3:30.
soak/2½ hours

How long *will* the dishes *have been soaking* when Papa gets home?
The dishes *will have been soaking* for 2½ hours.

1. He puts the bread in the oven at 4 o'clock.
   bake/2 hours
2. She turns the radio on at 4:30.
   listen to/radio/an hour and a half.
3. He starts to chop onions and tomatoes at 5 P.M.
   chop/an hour
4. She turns the water on in the tub at 5:45.
   The water/run/fifteen minutes

PART THREE. Review and Integration

Memory Game: Facts and Proverbs

Your teacher will write fifteen facts and proverbs on cards, half of each proverb on one card and half on another. The cards are shuffled and placed on a table face down with the numbers 1 to 30 written on the backs of the cards. One team starts the game and chooses two numbers. If the two cards form the two halves of a sentence, they are a match and are removed from the arrangement. The team that made the match gets a point. If the two cards do not match, they are returned to the arrangement face down. The second team then chooses two numbers. The steps are repeated until all cards have been matched. Here are some examples of facts and proverbs.

Charity/begins at home.

Actions/speak louder than words.

All that glitters/is not gold.

Simple Present or Present Progressive?

A. In the following passage, underline the verbs, which are either simple present or present progressive. Then make three lists: Temporary, Habitual, and General.

Esperanza and her family are living on Mango Street. The girls go to school with Hispanic and non-Hispanic children. Most classes are in English, but the school offers some classes in Spanish for new immigrants.

The girls love their father very much. He works hard to support the family. Right now Esperanza is listening to his favorite song. It sounds sad. He likes Mexican songs, and so do his daughters. Although some Mexican songs sound like sobbing, many are cheerful and fun to dance to.

B. Fill in the blanks with either the simple present or the present progressive in the exercise about a party on Mango Street.

1. Right now Esperanza's friend Ruthie (*have*) ________________ a party for her friends on Mango Street.
2. Ruthie's family (*have*) ________________ a big room for dancing.
3. All the children on Mango Street (*have*) ________________ a good time at Ruthie's party.
4. The special foods (*taste*) ________________ delicious.
5. Ruthie (*taste*) ________________ the guacamole she is preparing.

6. The men and women (*listen*) ________________ to Mexican music.
7. The music is so loud that people on Pleasant Street (*hear*) ________________ it too.
8. All the neighbors (*look*) ________________ happy to be at the party.
9. Some women (*look*) ________________ at Ruthie's photographs.

Signs of the Zodiac: Agreement in the Simple Present

Read the descriptions of the birth signs of the Zodiac and then do the exercises that follow.

SIGNS OF THE ZODIAC

ARIES, THE RAM
(March 21–April 19)

Aries people are self-reliant and energetic. They like to meet and overcome obstacles. They have courage and great powers of persuasion. Aries people act immediately in a crisis. They sometimes use too much force. They need to think more before they act.

CANCER, THE CRAB
(June 22–July 22)

Cancer people feel deeply for others and love to take care of them. They often make decisions based on feelings rather than facts. Cancer people need security. They appear different on the outside than they are on the inside.

TAURUS, THE BULL
(April 20–May 20)

Taurus people love order and have great patience. They use energy wisely and pay attention to small but important details. They care about the practical side of life. Taurus people have great common sense. They are calm. They understand the value of their possessions.

LEO, THE LION
(July 23–August 22)

Leo people have dramatic and bold personalities that attract people to them. They enjoy cheering people up or entertaining them. They often lead or direct activities in the family or community. Leos are warm and strong. They also have great humor. They take chances willingly.

GEMINI, THE TWINS
(May 21–June 21)

Gemini people see both sides of an issue. They are intellectual, and they charm other people. They change quickly; they communicate well. Gemini people sometimes do too many things at once. They sometimes lack compassion for other people.

VIRGO, THE VIRGIN
(August 23–September 22)

Virgo people are practical and well ordered. They adapt to changes easily. Virgos observe themselves and the world around them carefully and think deeply about life. Virgos hate disorder and try to fix things that don't operate properly. They pay attention to details and solve problems quickly and efficiently. They are dependable.

LIBRA, THE SCALES
(September 23–October 23)

Libra people cooperate with others. They think through problems carefully by weighing factors. Libras' partners influence them greatly. Libras seek balance and harmony. As a result they resolve conflicts well. Libras are concerned with justice and equality.

CAPRICORN, THE GOAT
(December 22–January 19)

Capricorn people organize their world completely. They enjoy positions of authority and make good managers. They are responsible, serious, and ambitious. They often perform small boring tasks in order to get ahead. They look at the future with the eyes of the past.

SCORPIO, THE SCORPION
(October 24–November 23)

Scorpio people have great determination and intensity. They use powerful intelligence to solve problems or improve negative situations. Scorpios understand the forces of life and death. They keep secrets and hide their feelings. Scorpio people are serious and determined. Their magnetic personalities attract others.

AQUARIUS, THE WATER BEARER
(January20–February 19)

Aquarians are friendly and kind. They get along well with other people. They have original ideas that bring people closer together. In other words, they are creative in useful ways. Aquarians seldom work alone; they need partners and are strongly influenced by their associates. Aquarians represent hope to the world.

SAGGITARIUS, THE ARCHER
(November 22–December 21)

Sagittarius people love adventure. They combine idealism with practicality. They are honest and bold. Sagittarius people encourage and lead others. They use intuition to make decisions. Sagittarius people are athletic. They enjoy traveling. They often look at "the big picture" and ignore details. They love company and make friends easily.

PISCES, THE FISH
(February 19–March 20)

Pisces people are sympathetic to people and often make sacrifices for others. They have great powers of imagination and mystical ability. Pisces people understand the world of emotions and demonstrate sensitivity to emotional problems in others. They enjoy helping people, but they also need solitude and time for reflection.

1. **Group Discussion**: Find your astrological sign and take turns discussing the description with members of your group. Does the sign give an accurate description of your personality? Are the descriptions of your group members' signs accurate pictures of their personalities?
2. **Written Work**: Write a paragraph in response to the description of your sign. Agree or disagree with individual points, using the first person ("I") and simple present verbs. For example, a Pisces student might write, "I am sympathetic to other people, but I don't make sacrifices for them." Share your writing with a member of your group. Underline the verbs in each other's descriptions and check their forms.
3. Individually, rewrite the description of your sign, changing the description from plural to singular. Make sure subjects and verbs agree. For example, the description of Aries would begin this way.

   An Aries person is self-reliant and energetic.

   Exchange your description with another student and check the subject/verb agreement.

4. Without writing the person's name, write a description of the personality of someone in your group. Pass the papers around the group and decide whose personality is described.
5. Prepare a short report about your birth sign and share it with the class. Include information from the horoscope in your daily newspaper.

Future Time: The Crystal Ball

Choose a year in the future, for example, A.D. 2500. Take turns asking and answering questions that make predictions about this year. Use the cues to make up sentences in each of the following: simple future, future progressive, future perfect. Example:

What/life/be like?

What will life be like?

There *will be* no plants on earth.

People *will live* in shopping malls.

Men *will be wearing* skirts.

Researchers *will have discovered* a cure for cancer.

1. What/people/buildings/be like?
2. People/live/in families?/houses?
3. The same countries/cities/exist that exist now?
4. How/people/be dressing/working/traveling/relaxing?
5. People/solve/the problems of war/incurable diseases/ famine/homelessness?

Spelling Contest: Irregular Verbs

Make a circle of chairs for each group (or for the whole class). Each student should stand in front of his/her chair. Your instructor will give each student the simple form of an irregular verb. The student must spell the simple past form of the verb. If he/she is incorrect, he/she sits down. The teacher goes on to the next student and repeats the process with another verb. The last student who remains standing is the winner.

Claim to Fame Game: Simple Past

Divide into teams of 3 to 5 students. Your instructor will write the names of famous people on pieces of paper and place them in a container. Each student draws a name and prepares to tell the other members of his/her group what his/her person did. The other teams listen quietly as each student tells his/her teammates about the famous person. If the group guesses the name within the time limit, the team gets a point. Some examples of famous people: Shakespeare, Joan of Arc, Eleanor Roosevelt, Confucius, Einstein, Freud.

Story-Telling: Simple Past

With a partner, take turns telling each other a story on one or more of the following topics. Use simple past verbs.

How my mother met my father

How I met my wife/husband/girlfriend/boyfriend

My first day at school/work

The story of my great-grandmother's/grandmother's/great-grandfather's/grandfather's life

Identification Cards: Present Perfect

Your instructor will give each student a card like the one pictured below. Fill in your card, but don't write your name. Your group will then receive the cards from another group. Discuss the information and guess the identity of the students whose cards you have received. Each member of the group should then take a card and try to find the student whose information is on the card by asking questions like the following.

How long have you lived in this city?

How long have you been at the university?

What English courses have you taken so far?

1. Number of Years/months/weeks in __________ (city): __________
2. Years/semesters at __________ (name of college/university): __________
3. Years/months of speaking English: __________
4. Number of courses in English: __________
5. Other schools attended: __________
6. Countries you've lived in/visited: __________

Simple Past or Present Perfect?

Maria's Uncle Tito is a businessman who makes frequent trips to Latin American countries. Use the chart and cues to make up sentences that include either the present perfect or simple past tense. The chart shows where and when Uncle Tito took his business trips. Think of today's date as June 15, 19— (this year's date).

	Jan	Feb	Mar	Apr	May	June
19– (fill in this year)	1 Mex	2 Guat	2 Mex	3 Nic	1 Mex	2 Mex
	2 Nic	1 Hon	1 Hon		1 Guat	1 Hon
19– (fill in last year)	1 Nic	2 Hon		3 Nic	1 Nic	
Mex = Mexico	Hon = Honduras					
Guat = Guatemala	Nic = Nicaragua					

Example:

Uncle Tito . . .

Nic/April 19*94* (last year)

Uncle Tito took three trips to Nicaragua in April 19*94*.

a. Mex/19– (last year)
b. Hon/June 19– (this year)
c. Mex/this year
d. Hon/last year
e. Guat/Feb 19– (this year)
f. Nic/June 19– (this year)
g. Nic/19– (last year)
h. Guat/May 19– (this year)
i. trips/19– (this year)
j. trips/19– (last year)

It Was a Very Good Year: Review of the Simple Past and the Past Perfect

Choose a year from the past that all the students in your group remember. Take turns answering the following group of questions. Use the same tense in your answers.

Where were you in that year?

How long had you been there?

What were you doing?

How long had you been doing that?

Verb Tense Review

A. The information shows some important dates in Esperanza's family history. Use the information to complete the sentences with numbers or dates. Discuss the verb tenses used.

1970—Papa and Mama got married.

1972—Esperanza was born.

1977—Esperanza started school.

1980—The family moved to the United States.

1982—The family moved to Mango Street.

1986—Grandfather died in Mexico.

1. They *have lived* on Mango Street for ____________ years.
2. They *moved* to the United States ____________ years ago.
3. Papa and Mama *had gotten* married ____________ years before they moved to the United States.
4. After Esperanza's family *had lived* on another street for ____________ years, they moved to Mango Street.
5. Papa's father *died* ____________ years after his son had left Mexico.
6. When Esperanza came to the United States, she *had been attending* school since ____________.
7. Grandfather *died* ____________ years ago.
8. Esperanza *was* ____________ years old when she started school.
9. Esperanza's parents *had gotten* married ____________ years before she was born.
10. Esperanza's parents *have been* married for ____________ years.

B. Complete the sentences with appropriate forms of the verb in parentheses. In a few cases, more than one answer is possible.

1. The term "Hispanic" (*be*) ______________ difficult to define because it (*include*) ______________ groups as diverse as Mexicans, Cubans, Chileans, Argentines, and many others. These groups (*have*) ______________ completely different histories and cultural heritage. The common factor (*be, always*) ______________ language; in other words, Hispanics (*speak*) ______________ Spanish, or (*be*) ______________ descendants of Spanish-speaking people. Various sub-groups of Hispanics (*use*) ______________ other accepted terms for themselves, such as Latino, Chicano, or Cubano. Since the 1950s the loosely-connected minority called Hispanics (*grow*) ______________ faster than any other in the United States. When the Census Bureau (*find*) ______________ in 1986 that Hispanics in this country (*number*) ______________ eighteen million, the Bureau (*declare*) ______________ the 1980s "the decade of the Hispanics." And the Census Bureau (*project*) ______________ that Hispanics (*make up*) ______________ 23.4 percent of the population in the year 2010. By contrast, in that year, African-Americans (*be*) ______________ 14.7 percent and Asians and others

(*be*) ______________ 12.1 percent. It (*be*) ______________ possible that minorities in the United States (*outnumber*) ______________ Caucasians in the year 2010.

2. Many years ago, three brothers (*live*) ______________ with their father, whose wife (*die*) ______________ long before. They (*earn*) ______________ a living by selling apples. One year the apples (*begin*) ______________ to disappear before market day. The brothers (*not, know*) ______________ who (*steal*) ______________ them. The two older boys (*try*) ______________ to catch the robber, but they (*be, not*) ______________ successful.

The youngest son (*go*) ______________ up the apple tree with his violin and his cat. He (*play*) ______________ music all night until he (*notice*) ______________ that his cat (*hiss*) ______________. He (*know*) ______________ that someone (*come*) ______________ to steal apples. A giant (*approach*) ______________!

Then the cat (*attack*) ______________ the giant robber, who (*think*) ______________ a poisonous snake (*bite*) ______________ him. He (*run*) ______________ to his secret cave where he (*keep*) ______________ three princesses as prisoners. A lion, a tiger, and a witch (*guard*) ______________ the princesses. After the youngest son (*follow*) ______________ the giant into the cave, he (*kill*) ______________ the lion, the tiger, the witch, and the giant. The boy (*fall*) ______________ in love with the very beautiful princess.

Then the boy (*go*) ______________ home with a magic coin he (*take*) ______________ from the giant. His brothers (*plan*) ______________ an evil surprise and (*try*) ______________ to kill him. But the boy (*escape*) ______________ and, as he (*rub*) ______________ the coin, a magic eagle (*appear*) ______________. The eagle (*carry*) ______________ the boy to the home of an old couple, who (*like*) ______________ him and (*let*) ______________ him stay.

For a long time, the king (*look*) ______________ for husbands for his three daughters. He (*make*) ______________ a plan. "I (*think*)

__________ I (*bring*) __________ the three most dangerous bulls to the palace for a bullfight. If a man (*kill*) __________ a bull, he (*win*) __________ one of my daughters as a wife."

For days, many men (*fight*) __________ the bulls, and they all (*die*) __________. One very young bullfighter (*arrive*) __________ at the palace and (*say*) __________, "This time next month, I (*live*) __________ at the palace because I (*kill*) __________ the fiercest bull and (*marry*) __________ the beautiful princess, whom I (*love*) __________."

He (*enter*) __________ the bull ring and (*kill*) __________ the most dangerous bull. While the bullfighter (*look*) __________ around the bull ring, he (*see*) __________ his brothers. He (*take*) __________ out the magic coin, which (*break*) __________ into many pieces. The evil brothers (*drop*) __________ dead.

The princesses (*watch*) __________ the bullfight, and they (*recognize*) __________ the boy who (*save*) __________ them in the giant's cave. The youngest princess (*run*) __________ to her father and (*cry*) __________, "We (*know*) __________ the boy who (*fight*) __________ the bull. I (*love*) __________ him since he (*save*) __________ us from the giant, and I (*want*) __________ to be his wife."

The young bullfighter and his beautiful princess (*be*) __________ married the next week and (*live*) __________ happily in the palace for many, many years.

3. Over the last few decades, the demographic distribution of Hispanics in the U.S. (*change*) __________ dramatically. For example, in Dade County, Florida, which (*include*) __________ Miami, the Hispanic population (*grow*) __________ from 5 percent to a majority in just thirty years.

Hispanic residents of the U.S. (*identify*) __________ themselves by their cultural and linguistic heritage rather than by race. This fact (*create*)

_______________ conflicts among other minority groups that (*not, speak*) _______________ Spanish, which (*become*) _______________ the dominant language in south Florida right now.

When Cubans (*begin*) _______________ arriving in Miami thirty years ago, English (*be*) _______________ the only language used in schools and in business. But recently the Dade County Commission (*change*) _______________ the English-only rule for county business. In the future, business people (*conduct*) _______________ their affairs in Spanish if they (*want*) _______________ to compete successfully. Eduardo J. Padron, president of the Wolfson campus of Miami–Dade Community College, (*say*) _______________, "The situation we (*live*) _______________ in in Miami today (*be*) _______________ true of most major cities in America in the next 10 years."

According to U.S. Census Bureau projections, the Hispanic population (*increase*) _______________ more rapidly than any other by the year 2010. As a result, many more of the mainstream children (*learn*) _______________ Spanish in that year. And many more business people (*use*) _______________ Spanish to conduct their affairs.

Suggestions for Writing

1. If you are keeping a journal, write an entry about one or more of the following: the house you live in, the meaning of your name, how you feel about your name, your first job.
2. Write a composition about the ways your family or ethnic group maintains its culture (through food, music, religion, customs, holidays, and so on).
3. Write a letter to Esperanza as if she were a close friend of yours. Tell her your feelings about her, her family, her problems, the adjustments newcomers to the United States have to make, and any other topics that you think she might be interested in.
4. Compose an essay in which you describe your true self honestly. Discuss your main characteristics and give examples or illustrations. If you wish, refer to your horoscope or some other system that characterizes people's personalities according to the time of their birth.

Unit Five

Modal Auxiliaries

READING: From *I Know Why the Caged Bird Sings* by Maya Angelou

THEME: African-Americans

PART ONE. The Context

Maya Angelou is a well-known African-American author. In the following excerpt from her autobiography *I Know Why the Caged Bird Sings* (1969), she describes a difficult period in the life of Marguerite, her young self, after she is raped by her mother's boyfriend in St. Louis. She and her brother Bailey have been sent to live with their grandmother, Momma, in Stamps, Arkansas. Shaken and depressed by her experience, Marguerite has withdrawn to the point of not speaking at all. The story describes how forming a friendship with an older person, Mrs. Flowers, helps the girl to regain her self-confidence.

Pre-Reading Questions

1. What different kinds of friendships have you had with older or younger people? What can an older or younger friend provide that a friend of the same age cannot?
2. In the excerpt, Mrs. Flowers serves Marguerite cookies and lemonade. In the United States, people frequently develop relationships while sharing food—for example, at coffee breaks or lunch hours. What are some other social occasions when people share food? What similar rituals exist in another culture that you are familiar with?
3. Mrs. Flowers and Marguerite share a love of language and literature. What are some other common interests that cause people to become friends?

Preview of Key Terms and Concepts

The following words and ideas appear in this unit. Guess the meanings of the terms on the left by matching them to the definitions on the right. Put the correct letter after the term. Discuss your answers with a partner or group, and ask your teacher about any terms you're not sure of.

1. life line ____
2. denim overalls ____
3. bear in mind ____
4. mother wit ____
5. *A Tale of Two Cities* ____
6. single out ____
7. try one's hand at ____

a. novel by Charles Dickens about the French Revolution
b. choose from a group
c. rope used for saving people in danger
d. work clothing made of blue jeans fabric, consisting of loose pants with attached chest covering and shoulder straps
e. attempt
f. wisdom that one is born with, common sense
g. remember

READING: From *I Know Why the Caged Bird Sings* by Maya Angelou

(1) For nearly a year, I sopped* around the house, the Store, the school and the church, like an old biscuit,* dirty and inedible.* Then I met, or rather got to know, the lady who threw me my first life line.

(2) Mrs. Bertha Flowers was the aristocrat of Black Stamps. She had the grace of control to appear warm in the coldest weather, and on the Arkansas summer days it seemed she had a private breeze which swirled around, cooling her. She was thin without the taut* look of wiry people, and her printed voile* dresses and flowered hats were as right for her as denim overalls for a farmer. She was our side's answer to the richest white woman in town.

(3) Her skin was a rich black that would have peeled like a plum if snagged,* but then no one would have thought of getting close enough to Mrs. Flowers to ruffle* her dress, let alone snag her skin. She didn't encourage familiarity. She wore gloves too.

(4) I don't think I ever saw Mrs. Flowers laugh, but she smiled often. A slow widening of her thin black lips to show even, small white teeth, then the slow effortless closing. When she chose to smile on me, I always wanted to thank her. The action was so graceful and inclusively* benign.*

(5) She was one of the few gentlewomen I have ever known, and has remained throughout my life the measure of what a human being can be. . . .

(6) One summer afternoon, sweet-milk fresh in my memory, she stopped at the Store to buy provisions.* Another Negro woman of her health and age would have been expected to carry the paper sacks home in one hand, but Momma said, "Sister Flowers, I'll send Bailey up to your house with these things."

(7) She smiled that slow dragging smile, "Thank you, Mrs. Henderson. I'd prefer Marguerite, though." My name was beautiful when she said it. "I've been meaning to talk to her anyway." They gave each other age-group looks. . . .

(8) There was a little path beside the rocky road, and Mrs. Flowers walked in front swinging her arms and picking her way over the stones.

(9) She said without turning her head, to me, "I hear you're doing very good school work, Marguerite, but that it's all written. The teachers report that they have trouble getting you to talk in class." We passed the triangular farm on our

---

* **sopped**	acted sad
biscuit	small, usually circular, piece of baked dough
inedible	not eatable
taut	tight
voile	light fabric used for women's dresses and curtains
snagged	torn
ruffle	disturb, bother
inclusively	completely
benign	kind, good, gentle
provisions	items needed in a household, including food and supplies

left and the path widened to allow us to walk together. I hung back in the separate unasked and unanswerable questions.

(10) "Come along with me, Marguerite." I couldn't have refused if I wanted to. She pronounced my name so nicely. Or more correctly, she spoke each word with such clarity* that I was certain a foreigner who didn't understand English could have understood her.

(11) "Now no one is going to make you talk—possibly no one can. But bear in mind, language is man's way of communicating with his fellow man and it is language alone which separates him from the lower animals." That was a totally new idea to me, and I would need time to think about it.

(12) "Your grandmother says you read a lot. Every chance you get. That's good, but not good enough. Words mean more than what is set down on paper. It takes the human voice to infuse* them with the shades of deeper meaning."

(13) I memorized the part about the human voice infusing words. It seemed so valid and poetic.

(14) She said she was going to give me some books and that I not only must read them, I must read them aloud. She suggested that I try to make a sentence sound in as many different ways as possible.

(15) "I'll accept no excuse if you return a book to me that has been badly handled." My imagination boggled* at the punishment I would deserve if in fact I did abuse a book of Mrs. Flowers'. Death would be too kind and brief.

(16) The odors in the house surprised me. Somehow I had never connected Mrs. Flowers with food or eating or any other common experience of common people. There must have been an outhouse, too, but my mind never recorded it.

(17) The sweet scent of vanilla had met us as she opened the door.

(18) "I made cookies this morning. You see, I had planned to invite you for cookies and lemonade so we could have this little chat.* The lemonade is in the icebox."

(19) It followed that Mrs. Flowers would have ice on an ordinary day, when most families in our town bought ice late on Saturdays only a few times during the summer to be used in the wooden ice-cream freezers.

(20) She took the bags from me and disappeared through the kitchen door. I looked around the room that I had never in my wildest fantasies imagined I would see. Browned photographs leered* or threatened from the walls and the white, freshly done curtains pushed against themselves and against the wind. I wanted to gobble up* the room entire and take it to Bailey, who would help me analyze and enjoy it.

(21) "Have a seat, Marguerite. Over there by the table." She carried a platter covered with a tea towel. Although she warned that she hadn't tried her hand

---

*	
clarity	clearness
infuse	put into
boggled	was overwhelmed
chat	informal conversation
leered	looked at in a frightening way
gobble up	take in completely; also, eat quickly

at baking sweets for some time, I was certain that like everything else about her the cookies would be perfect.

(22) They were round wafers, slightly browned on the edges and butter-yellow in the center. With the cold lemonade they were sufficient for childhood's lifelong diet. Remembering my manners, I took nice little lady-like bites off the edges. She said she had made them expressly* for me and that she had a few in the kitchen that I could take home to my brother. So I jammed one whole cake in my mouth and the rough crumbs scratched the insides of my jaws, and if I hadn't had to swallow, it would have been a dream come true.

(23) As I ate she began the first of what we later called "my lessons in living." She said that I must always be intolerant* of ignorance but understanding of illiteracy.* That some people, unable to go to school, were more educated and even more intelligent than college professors. She encouraged me to listen carefully to what country people called mother wit. That in those homely* sayings was couched* the collective* wisdom of generations.

(24) When I finished the cookies she brushed off the table and brought a thick, small book from the bookcase. I had read *A Tale of Two Cities* and found it up to my standards as a romantic novel. She opened the first page and I heard poetry for the first time in my life. . . .

(25) "How do you like that?"

(26) It occurred to me that she expected a response. The sweet vanilla flavor was still on my tongue and her reading was a wonder in my ears. I had to speak.

(27) I said, "Yes, ma'am." It was the least I could do, but it was the most also.

(28) "There's one more thing. Take this book of poems and memorize one for me. Next time you visit, I want you to recite . . ."

(29) I was liked, and what a difference it made. I was respected not as Mrs. Henderson's grandchild or Bailey's sister but for just being Marguerite Johnson.

(30) Childhood's logic never asks to be proved (all conclusions are absolute.*) I didn't question why Mrs. Flowers had singled me out for attention, nor did it occur to me that Momma might have asked her to give me a little talking to. All I cared about was that she had made tea cookies for *me* and read to *me* from her favorite book. It was enough to prove that she liked me.

Comprehension Questions

1. How is Mrs. Flowers described? What effect does she have on people in Stamps and on Marguerite in particular?

---

*	
expressly	specifically, particularly
intolerant	not accepting
illiteracy	inability to read and write
homely	simple, plain
couched	contained
collective	belonging to a group
absolute	without doubt

2. How does Mrs. Flowers arrange to talk with Marguerite?
3. What are Marguerite's reactions to Mrs. Flowers' house and the food she is served?
4. What are Mrs. Flowers' "lessons in living"?
5. Why does Marguerite break her silence and speak to Mrs. Flowers?

Discussion Questions

1. What does Angelou mean by "our side" when she calls Mrs. Flowers "our side's answer to the richest white woman in town"?
2. Mrs. Flowers is referred to as an "aristocrat" and a "gentlewoman." The term "aristocrat" usually refers to a person with inherited power and wealth, and "gentlewoman" suggests nobility. Is Mrs. Flowers powerful and wealthy? What other qualities does Mrs. Flowers possess that make her an aristocrat?
3. Maya Angelou is one of the most famous and talented writers in the United States today. In fact, she read one of her poems at President Clinton's inauguration in 1993. How much influence do you think Mrs. Flowers has had on Angelou's life and career?
4. Mrs. Flowers gives her personal definition of language. Why is language so important? What makes speech different from the written word?

PART TWO. The Target Structure: Modal Auxiliaries

I Focus on Modals of Ability, Permission, and Polite Requests

Preview of Modal Auxiliaries

Complete the second sentence of each pair with a verb that means about the same thing as the underlined phrase in the first sentence.

Marguerite knows how to read.

Marguerite ____________ read.

Mrs. Flowers thinks it is advisable for Marguerite to read aloud.

Mrs. Flowers thinks Marguerite ____________ read aloud.

Did you write *can* in the first sentence and *should, ought to,* or *had better* in the second? If so, you used modal auxiliaries, verbs that express conditions or states such as ability, permission, advisability, possibility, probability, logical deduction, and necessity.

Frequently Used Modal Auxiliaries		
can	had better	could
may	must	might
should	have to	will
ought to	be able to	would

CHECKPOINT 1  

In paragraphs 11, 14, and 15 of the reading (page 163), find and circle the modal auxiliaries and the verbs that follow them, if any. Discuss these questions: What form of the main verb follows the modals? Do these modals change to agree with different subjects?

MODALS OF ABILITY: PRESENT/FUTURE AND PAST

- **Present/Future Ability**. The modal auxiliaries that express ability in the present and future are *can* and the appropriate forms of *be* + *able to*. These verbs mean that someone knows how to do something or has the ability to do something. *Can* is followed by the base form of the main verb and does not change to agree with its subject. *Be able to* is also followed by the base form of the verb, and the form of *be* must agree with its subject.
- **Inability**. Not knowing how to do something is expressed by *cannot, be + not able to*, or *be + unable to*. Again, the forms of *be* change to agree with the subject and to show tense.
- ***Be Able to*** **versus** **Can**. Whereas *be (not) able to* and *be unable to* emphasize ability, *can* often suggests possibility combined with ability. This difference in meaning is illustrated in the following sentences:

  Bailey *is able to find* Marguerite at Momma's store.
  (ability)

  Bailey *can find* Marguerite at Momma's store.
  (ability and possibility)

- **Past Ability**. Ability in the past is expressed by *could* or past tense forms of *be* + *able to* + the base form of the main verb.

Modal Auxiliaries of Ability

Present	***can, be able to***
Affirmative	Mrs. Flowers *can make* prose sound like poetry.
	She *is able to read* beautifully.
Negative	*cannot, can't, be not able to, be unable to*
	Marguerite *cannot/can't imagine* damaging Mrs. Flowers' books.
	Momma *isn't able/is unable to convince* Marguerite to talk.
Past	***could, was/were able to***
Affirmative	Marguerite *could read* at an early age.
	She *was able to get* good grades in school.
Negative	*couldn't, wasn't/weren't able to, was/were unable to*
	Marguerite *couldn't forget* what happened to her.
	She *wasn't able/was unable to stay* in St. Louis with her mother.

CHECKPOINT 2

A.

Return to paragraphs 5, 18, and 22 of the reading (pages 162–164) and find the modal auxiliaries that express ability. Underline them and the main verbs that follow. Write the modals and verbs with their subjects. Then rewrite each one substituting *be able to*. Example:

A human being *can be* A human being *is able to be*

B.

Take turns making up sentences using *can/can't* or *could/couldn't*. Use the cues provided below. Follow these models:

When I was a child, I ____________, but now I ____________.

I ____________, and I still ____________.

Examples: When I was a child, I *couldn't choose my own clothes, but now I can*. I *could ride* a bicycle, and I still *can*.

1. drive a car
2. ride a horse
3. stay out all night
4. use a computer

5. run fast
6. drink coffee
7. watch three movies in a row
8. sleep late

C. Make up sentences from the cues to express ability or inability using *can/can't/could/couldn't.* Then rewrite each sentence using *be (not) able to* or *be unable to.* Example:

Marguerite/stop looking/at the photographs on the wall (present inability)

Marguerite *can't stop looking* at the photographs on the wall.

1. Mrs. Flowers/inspire children (present ability)
2. People/get too close/to Mrs. Flowers (present inability)
3. Black residents of Stamps/shop/at all stores (past inability)
4. Bailey and Marguerite/lift/heavy bags of groceries (past ability)

D. Write a paragraph about the past experiences of a grandparent or an older friend. Describe what he or she could do and couldn't do. Example:

My grandfather *could run* as fast as a teenager until the day he died. He *couldn't* just *watch* my brother and his friends play football. He always wanted to play. One day . . . .

Present/Future Modals of Permission

There are a number of ways to ask for, give, and refuse permission. The most common modals that express this meaning are *may* and *can.* The expression *be allowed to* is also used for this purpose. These modals often have the same meaning. They are all followed by the base form of the main verb. The forms of *be* in *be allowed to* change according to the subject.

Modals of Permission

Ask for Permission: Polite Questions with "I" as Subject

May/Can I (please) go to Mrs. Flowers' house?

Am I *allowed to* go to Mrs. Flowers' house?

Give Permission

Marguerite *may/can* have some lemonade and cookies.

Marguerite *is allowed to* have some lemonade and cookies.

Deny Permission

You *may not* go to Momma's store after dark.

You *are not* allowed to run around in Mrs. Flowers' house.

The meaning of *may* and *can* is the same in these sentences, but *may* is more formal. *May* is usually used only with *I* and *we*; *can* is used with all persons. *Be allowed to* has a more "legal" meaning than the other modals in this group. For example, the following sentence means that it is legal to drive a car:

Teenagers *are allowed to* drive in this country.

Polite Requests with *You* as Subject

The modals *would, will, could,* and *can* and the expression *would you mind* are commonly used to make polite requests. The word *please* often accompanies the modals.

Polite Requests with *You* as Subject
Would/Will
Would you please read to me? Okay.
Will you please pass the cookies? Sure.
Could/Can
Could you give me a ride to Mrs. Flowers' house? Of course.
Can you help me carry my groceries, please? I'd be glad to.
Would you mind + -ing
Would you mind help*ing* me with my homework? Not at all.

An expression similar to *would you mind + -ing* is *would you mind if + I* + past tense verb. In the first expression, the speaker asks someone else to do something; in the second, the speaker asks permission to do something.

Would you mind driving me home now?

Would you mind if I drove home now?

Some responses used to refuse polite requests are listed below.

I'm sorry, but I can't do that right now.

I wish I could help you, but . . . (I'm too busy now, I really don't have time, I'm broke, I don't have any money, etc.)

Short answers are often given to polite questions. They consist of *Yes* or *No* + Pronoun Subject + modal (+ *not* in negative answers).

May I have another cookie? Yes, you *may*. No, you *may not.*

Can I go out? Yes, you *can*. No, you *cannot (can't).*

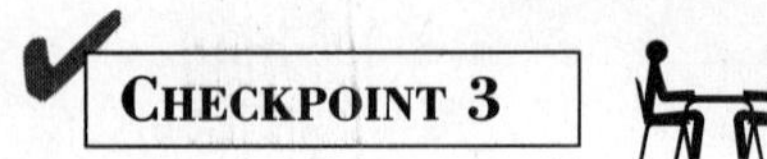

Practice making up polite questions that Mrs. Flowers asks Marguerite in as many ways as possible. Use the ideas expressed in the sentences. Example:

Carry my groceries.

Can you carry my groceries please, Marguerite?

1. Let me talk with you.
2. Answer my questions.
3. Come in.
4. Have a cookie.
5. Listen to me while I read aloud.
6. Remember what I say.
7. Let me be your friend.

B. In the following role play, each member of the group takes the role of a character, brainstorms some requests or statements that the character might make, and acts out his/her part for the class.

Situation: Marguerite and Bailey are visiting Mrs. Flowers. They ask permission to do a variety of things at her house. Mrs. Flowers gives or denies permission after each request.

Marguerite: *You ask permission to borrow a book, take down a photograph, have another cookie, read aloud, etc. Use* I *as the subject.*

Bailey: *You ask Mrs. Flowers to tell you a story, read a poem, pour some more lemonade, invite you back tomorrow, etc. Use* you *as the subject.*

Mrs. Flowers: *You want to show the children kindness but not let them do everything they want. Give a variety of responses, including short answers.*

II Focus on Modals of Advisability and Obligation

Present/Future Modals of Advisability and Obligation

Some modal auxiliaries that express advisability or obligation in the present and future are *should, ought to*, and *had better*. These are followed by the base form of the main verb, and they do not change form to agree with subjects. Another modal expression that shows obligation is *be supposed to*. This is also followed by the base form, but *be* does change form according to tense and person.

Modals of Advisability and Obligation

Present/Future

Affirmative	*should, ought to, be supposed to, had better*
	Marguerite *should* talk in class.
	She *ought to* express her ideas.
	A good student *is supposed to* participate in class discussions.
	She *had better* listen to Mrs. Flowers if she wants to be invited back.
Negative	*should not/n't, be not supposed to, had better not*
	Children *shouldn't* go with people they don't know.
	The little girl *is not supposed to* talk to strangers.
	She *had better not* stay at Mrs. Flowers' house too long.

Had better is stronger than the other modals of advisability and suggests a greater obligation or sense of urgency. Sometimes *had better* suggests a threat.

You *had/'d better not forget* to do your homework.

You *had better do* your chores if you want to go out with your friends this afternoon.

Ought not to is rarely used in everyday spoken language; when it is used, *to* is sometimes omitted.

Children *ought not/oughtn't speak* to strangers.

Be supposed to suggests the idea of rules or regulations and expected behavior.

Marguerite *is supposed to come* right home after school.

(That's Momma's rule.)

✔ Checkpoint 4

A. Use the cues to make up sentences that contain *should, ought to,* or *had better* to express advice Mrs. Flowers might have given to Marguerite. Example:

Listen to Momma.
You *had better* listen to Momma.

1. Study hard.
2. Participate in class.
3. Be kind to Bailey.
4. Let go of your bad memories.
5. Write down your thoughts and feelings.
6. [Make up your own.]

B. Brainstorm a few sentences to give advice in the following situations. Use *should/shouldn't, had better (not),* and *ought to.*

Situation 1: Marguerite's friend Angela has a math test tomorrow. She's failing math.

Situation 2: You are carrying groceries for one of Momma's customers. You drop the bags. The eggs and milk bottle break.

Situation 3: Marguerite is going to visit Mrs. Flowers. On the way she sees an unfamiliar man go into her neighbor's house. He's carrying a sack and looks very dangerous.

Situation 4: In her house, Mrs. Flowers has just discovered a library book that is ten years overdue.

C. Write two lists of at least five sentences each. In one list write what a person *should* do to stay healthy. In the second write what a person *should not* do to remain healthy. Examples:

A person *should drink* about a gallon of water daily.

A person *should not drink* more than two cups of coffee each day.

III Focus on Modals of Possibility and Impossibility

Present/Future Modals of Possibility

The modal auxiliaries most often used to express possibility are *may, might,* and *could* followed by the base form of the verb. They can be used interchangeably, but *could* usually indicates more doubt than *may* or *might. Could* often combines the ideas of possibility and ability.

Mrs. Flowers *could buy* ice every day if she really wanted to.

(It is possible for her to buy it, and she is able to buy it.)

Modals of Possibility	
May	Mrs. Flowers *may* bake some more cookies for the children.
Might	She *might* have ice even though it's Thursday.
Could	Momma *could* have ice on Thursday, but I doubt that she will.

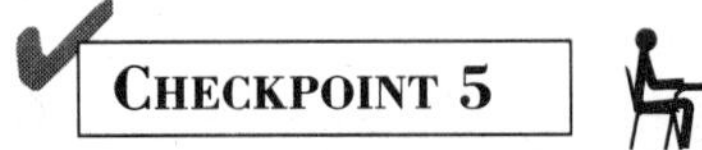

A. Take turns asking and answering questions based on the cues. Use *may* or *might* in your answers. Example:

What/do/next weekend

What are you going to do next weekend?

I don't know. I may go to ____________ (the movies, Houston, etc).

1. Where/go/next vacation
2. What/study/next year
3. Who/be/the next president of ____________
4. When/finish/studying English
5. Live/at your present address forever

B. Mrs. Flowers is asking Marguerite about the future. Marguerite is not certain about her answers. She tells Mrs. Flowers what *could/might/may* happen.

1. Where/you/go/college
2. What/plan to study/college
3. Bailey/graduate/high school
4. How many/children/you/have
5. You/leave/Stamps

C. Think of the names of a famous person alive today. Write down three questions about the person. Exchange your name and questions with another group and answer that group's questions. If you aren't sure of the answer to a question, write a sentence in which you take a guess. Use *may*, *might*, or *could*. Example:

Princess Diana of England

1. Where does Diana live?
2. How many necklaces does she have?
3. How old is she?

1. I'm not sure. She *may live* in England.
2. I don't know. She *could have* a hundred.
3. I don't know. She *might be* around thirty-five.

Asking for and Giving Suggestions

The modal auxiliaries *can*, *could*, and *should* are used in questions that ask for suggestions, which are less urgent questions than those that ask for advice.

What *could* we give her?

How *can* we help them?

Where *should* we go after school?

The modal *could* frequently occurs in suggestions, but other equivalent expressions are also commonly used.

You *could* give her a book, or you *could* give her some money.

You *could* offer them a ride.

Why don't we go to the library?

Let's go to the movies.

Possible Responses:

(Negative) No, thanks.
I'd rather not.
I don't think so.
Let's not.

(Affirmative) Okay.
Good idea.
Let's.
All right.

CHECKPOINT 6

Take turns making suggestions and giving responses based on the situations described below. Use modal auxiliaries where appropriate. Example:

You are lost in a strange city.

A. Why don't you ask directions?
B. I'*d rather* not.
A. You *could* get a map.
B. Good idea. I think I *will*.

1. You can't find your wallet.
2. The neighbor's dog is always barking.
3. You need to find an apartment.
4. You want to sell your car.
5. You want to take a bus to St. Louis, but the last one left thirty minutes ago.

IMPOSSIBILITY: *CAN'T* AND *COULDN'T*

The negative forms of *can* and *could* are used to express impossibility as well as inability. As in the affirmative, negative expressions with *can* and *could* often combine the ideas of impossibility and inability.

Modals of Impossibility	
Present/Future	
Can't	Is Mrs. Flowers older than Momma? She *can't* be! She looks twenty years younger.
Couldn't	Stamps is a very small town; it *couldn't* have a large business district.

CHECKPOINT 7 

Make up sentences that express impossible situations about your classmates, teacher, and school. Take turns reading the sentences to other groups. Students in the other groups respond to the sentences using *can't* or *couldn't* to express impossibility. Examples:

A. ________________ has two husbands.

B. ________________ can't have two husbands. That's illegal!

C. There's a lion in the restroom.

D. There couldn't be a lion in the restroom. The only lions we know of are in the zoo.

IV Focus on Modals of Logical Deduction, Assumption, and Expectation

Present/Future Modals of Logical Deduction and Assumption

The modal auxiliary *must* is stronger than *may* or *might* and is used to express assumption or logical deduction. *Must* is followed by the base form of the main verb. The negative form is *must not (mustn't)* + base form.

Have to expresses stronger possibility than *must* when it is used to mean logical deduction; it indicates that the speaker is almost certain that something is true. *Have to* is not used in the negative to express logical deduction or assumption.

Modals of Logical Deduction and Assumption

Present/Future

Must	Marguerite *must* love to read; she spends every spare moment reading. (We can assume she loves reading.)
	It's four o'clock and Marguerite isn't home from school yet. She *must* be at Mrs. Flowers' house. (She's probably there.)
	She *must not* realize how late it is.
Have/has to	It's four thirty and we've looked everywhere else for Marguerite. She *has to* be at Mrs. Flowers' house. (She 's almost certainly there.)

CHECKPOINT 8

A. Take turns asking and answering questions based on the cues. Use *must* or *must not* in the answers to express logical deduction. If you can be almost completely certain, use *has to/have to* in your answer. Example:

yawning

Why is he yawning?

He *must be* tired.

1. sneezing
2. frowning
3. smiling
4. scratching/arm
5. tapping/foot
6. drinking/water

B. Write reactions to each statement about a famous African-American. Use *must (not)* to express the idea of logical deduction. Example:

Toni Morrison won the Nobel Prize for Literature in 1993.

She *must write* very well.

She *must be* very intelligent.

1. Alice Walker's novel *The Color Purple* is recognized as a modern classic. It portrays the life of an African-American family in the United States and Africa.
2. Judith Jamison is the artistic director of the African-American dance group founded by Alvin Ailey. She trains young dancers and choreographs, or arranges, the dances.

3. Jesse Jackson is a famous African-American religious and political leader. He has participated in national and international affairs.
4. *Black Boy* and *Native Son* are two books by Richard Wright, a well-known African-American author who lived from 1908 to 1960. Although these books were written decades ago, they are still read and appreciated for the picture they provide of the experiences of the African-American in 20th-century U.S. society.
5. Reverend Martin Luther King, Jr.'s "I Have a Dream" speech about civil rights and racial equality still moves people to tears.

Modals of Expectation

Should and *ought to* can be used to express expectation about future events.

Maya Angelou is a gifted writer. You *should* find her books interesting.

Angelou has led a fascinating life. Her future *ought to be* just as interesting as her past.

Checkpoint 9

Fill in the modal that best completes each sentence. In some cases, more than one might be appropriate. Discuss differences in meaning that result from the use of various modals (*should/ought to, must, may/might*).

1. Let's go to some bookstores; we ____________________ find some books by Maya Angelou.
2. Maya Angelou has been successful as an actress and singer as well as in the field of writing; she ____________________ have a lot of talent.
3. When does the stage production of *I Know Why the Caged Bird Sings* begin? It ____________________ start any minute.
4. She likes music; she ____________________ enjoy listening to some of Mahalia Jackson's gospel songs.
5. A. Are we going to miss the bus?
   B. No, we ____________________ have plenty of time.
6. They don't really want to leave Stamps, but you never know. They ____________________ enjoy a vacation in Chicago.
7. Knowing she is liked for herself ____________________ make Marguerite feel good.
8. Her uncle doesn't answer the phone, and his car isn't in the usual place. He ____________________ be out somewhere.

V Focus on Modals of Necessity, Lack of Necessity, and Prohibition

Modals of Necessity

The modal auxiliaries used most often to express necessity are *must* and *have to.* (*Have got to* is used informally.) The expression *be to* also expresses necessity, but only to express rules and regulations. All of these expressions are followed by the base form of the verb. *Have to, have got to*, and *be to* change form according to the subject, but *must* does not.

Modals of Necessity	
Present/Future	
must	Children *must* show respect for their teachers.
have to/have got to	A teacher *has to* earn a certificate before s/he begins teaching.
	Bailey and Marguerite *have got to* help out at the store.
be to	The children *are to* arrive at school by eight o'clock each day.

Checkpoint 10

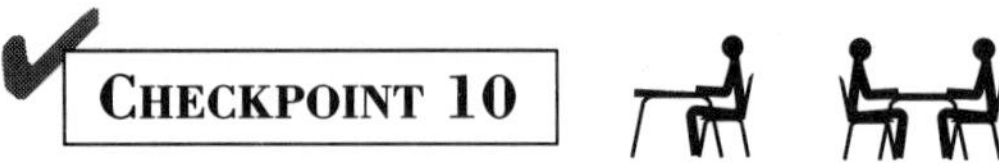

A. Practice the most common modals of necessity. Rewrite these sentences using *must* instead of *have to* or vice versa.

1. Marguerite *has to read* aloud, or she won't fully appreciate language.
2. Her grandmother *must learn* to communicate with the girl better.
3. The family members *have to understand* her reason for not speaking.
4. They *must listen* to their "mother wit."
5. Everyone *has to be* quiet so that she can practice reading aloud.

Other Uses of *Must*

Must is also used in polite statements to urge someone to do something, often a social activity.

We *must* get together soon.

These cookies are delicious. You *must* try some.

Be To

Be to is used in orders and commands to express necessity or absence of choice.

Bailey, you *are to* carry the groceries for the older customers.
(These are Momma's orders.)

The soldier *is to* report to headquarters.
(These are military orders.)

Be to also refers to a future event that has been arranged.

The children *are to* go to St Louis next week.

Maya Angelou *is to* speak at the university this evening.

CHECKPOINT 11

Write the letter corresponding to the meaning of the modal axuiliary on the line after each sentence.

a. necessity
b. orders
c. planned future event
d. logical conclusion

1. Someone *has to deliver* the groceries. ____________________
2. A friend in Stamps, a soldier, has been told that he *is to report* to his commanding officer immediately. ____________________
3. That *has to be* Bailey at the door. He's the only person who knows I'm home. ____________________
4. There's an emergency at the store. They *have to get* help immediately. ____________________
5. The accused man *is to face* trial next week. ____________________

B. Rewrite the following rules with *be (not) to*. Example:

No talking!

You *are not* to talk.

1. Do not touch the photographs.
2. No smoking in this section.
3. Proceed with caution.
4. Do not use a flash.

NEGATIVE FORMS: LACK OF NECESSITY AND PROHIBITION

Have to and *must* can be used interchangeably in the affirmative to express necessity. In the negative, however, they express different meanings. *Do/does not (don't/doesn't) have to* expresses lack of necessity. *Must not (mustn't)* expresses prohibition. The following pairs of sentences illustrate the differences between the affirmative and negative forms of *have to* and *must*.

Marguerite *must/has to practice* reading aloud. (necessity)

She *doesn't have to read* everything aloud. (lack of necessity)

The children *must go* to school. (necessity)

They *must not go* into town without permission. (prohibition)

CHECKPOINT 12 

A. Complete the sentences with the most logical modal expression. Use *must* for necessity, *don't/doesn't have to* for lack of necessity, and *must not* for prohibition.

1. Marguerite ________________________ get up early tomorrow. She can sleep late.
2. She ________________________ drink lemonade if the doctor says it might make her sick.
3. She ________________________ recover from her illness before she returns to school.
4. The children ________________________ work at the store today. There are plenty of sales clerks.
5. Mrs. Flowers ________________________ forget to buy butter and flour at the store because she has no more at home.

B. Read the situation and then use the cues to write sentences that contain modal auxiliaries to express necessity/obligation or prohibition. Practice using *must, has/have to, must not/mustn't.*

The well-known African-American author Richard Wright (1908–1960) grew up in the strict religious home of his grandmother.

Situation: Imagine that you are a member of Richard Wright's grandmother's household early in the twentieth century. There are many rules to follow. The sentences express Richard's grandmother's household rules. Example:

Boys/not play/games/like baseball

Boys *must not play* games like baseball.

1. Richard/pray/six times a day
2. People/not read/books on religious subjects
3. Richard/not eat/foods that are considered unclean
4. The family/attend/all-night prayer meetings
5. Children/be protected/from the world outside the home

PAST NECESSITY

Only one modal auxiliary—*had to*—expresses necessity in the past. Both *must* and *have to* become *had to* + base form. *Had to* does not change form when the subject changes. *Didn't have to* expresses lack of necessity in the past.

Modals of Past Necessity and Lack of Necessity

Had to

The girl *had to* return the books to Mrs. Flowers.

The children *had to* go to school Friday.

Didn't have to

As soon as she found a friend, she *didn't have to* think about being alone anymore.

CHECKPOINT 13

A. Change the following sentences to the past using *had to* and *didn't have to*. Make any other necessary changes. Examples:

Momma *doesn't have to* bake cookies today.

Momma *didn't have to* bake cookies yesterday.

1. She *must* cook a great deal of food for the family this week.
2. Marguerite and Bailey *had to* share household responsibilities *last* month because Momma *was* busy at the store.
3. They *don't have to* deliver groceries this month.
4. The hired man *must* work overtime today.

B. Working with a partner, rewrite the following sentences so that they include modal auxiliaries of past necessity and lack of necessity. Example:

At the beginning of the Civil War in 1861, thousands of African-American men felt that they needed to help the North under President Lincoln.

At the beginning of the Civil War in 1861, thousands of African-American men felt that they *had to* help the North under President Lincoln.

1. But the Union generals were not required to use African-Americans as soldiers.
2. Some Union commanders, such as Major General Butler, said that the black volunteers would be forced to work as laborers.
3. In 1864, Jefferson Davis, the president of the Southern states, declared that it was necessary for the Confederate Army to use African-American men in any way possible to win the war.

4. President Davis suggested a major change in Confederate military policy: an African-American was not be required to remain a slave if he fought as a soldier.

C. Complete the sentences with the appropriate modal expressions; clues are given at the end of each sentence. Use the verbs in parentheses.

1. The biographies of many famous African-Americans prove that people (*have*) ___don't have to have___ money, social position, or even education to become successful. (lack of necessity/present)
2. Richard Wright (*move around*) ______________ so often as a child that he never attended school or got a formal education. (necessity/past)
3. As a child, Jesse Jackson (*work*) ______________ as a shoeshine boy, a lumberyard worker, and a golf caddy to help out with finances at home. (necessity/past)
4. Today, Jesse Jackson tells young African-Americans that they (*get*) ______________ as good an education as possible in order to improve the conditions of their lives. (necessity/present)
5. In the 1960s, Jackson began working for Martin Luther King, Jr., a man who believed that African-Americans (*accept*) ______________ a position in U.S. society below that of other citizens. (lack of necessity/past)
6. Under King's leadership, Jackson headed "Operation Breadbasket" in 1966; this organization, formed to get more jobs and better services for African-Americans, was so powerful that government agencies and businesses (*pay*) ______________ close attention to its activities. (necessity/past)
7. In the seventies, Jackson continued these programs in Operation PUSH. During this time, he told African-Americans, "You (*believe*) ______________ in yourselves." (necessity/present)
8. Jackson became well known for his involvement in Middle Eastern politics late in the 1970s and for his involvement in U.S. national politics in 1984. He has shown young African-Americans that they (*feel*) ______________ powerless. (lack of necessity/present)
9. They (*work*) ______________ hard to change things, but with hope and effort, anything is possible. (necessity/present)
10. Young people (*have*) ______________ role models like Martin Luther King, Jr., and Jesse Jackson. (necessity/present)

VI Focus on the Uses of *Would*

THE USES OF *WOULD*

The modal auxiliary *would* has several different uses. *Would* is used to express actions that were repeated in the past. It is also used in the expression *would rather* to express preference. *Would* is frequently used to tone down statements that would otherwise sound impolite or abrupt; for example, *would like* is more polite than *want*.

I *want* to have Marguerite carry my groceries.

I *would like* to have Marguerite carry my groceries.

Would is commonly used this way with the verbs *prefer*, *appreciate*, and *be glad/happy*. *Would* is also used in polite questions.

Some Uses of *Would*

Repeated Past Actions

When I was in Stamps, I *would* visit Mrs. Flowers every day.

She *would* offer me cookies and lemonade.

Expressing Preference

I *would rather* deliver the groceries *than* work as a cashier.

I*'d rather not* work as a cashier.

Polite Requests and Statements

I *would* be glad to help you.

She *would* appreciate your help.

Polite Questions

Would you like some coffee?

Would you mind if I smoked?

Past Form of *Will* in Indirect Speech

Direct: "I *will* pour the lemonade.

Indirect: She says she *will* pour the lemonade.

She said she *would* pour the lemonade.

Wishes and Conditions

I wish you *would* speak up in class.

If you spoke in class, you *would* feel more a part of the group.

The uses of *would* in wishes and conditions is explained in detail in Units 9 and 10.

A. Return to the reading at the beginning of the chapter and find the modal expressions with *would* in paragraphs 7, 11, 15, 19, 20, 21 (pages 162–164). Underline the entire verb phrase. Discuss which of the uses described in the chart above applies to the verbs you have underlined.

B. Take turns asking and answering questions with *would you rather* following the example:

tell stories/read books

Would you rather tell stories or read books?

I'd rather tell stories [than read books].

1. see a movie/watch television
2. go shopping/play sports
3. watch ______________ (a sport)/play ______________ (a sport)
4. listen to classical music/listen to rock
5. have a big lunch/just have a salad

C. Write the letter of the correct use of *would* on the line after each sentence.

a. Repeated past action
b. Preference
c. Willingness (past of *will*)
d. Condition
e. Polite Question
f. Polite Request

1. When novelist Toni Morrison was a child, her parents and grandparents *would* tell her about African-American folklore, music, and cultural practices. ______
2. *Would* you like to read Toni Morrison's book *Beloved*? ______
3. Her fiction *wouldn't* be so typical of African American fiction if she hadn't had great exposure to the rituals and traditions of her people. ______
4. Morrison's first novel, *The Bluest Eye*, was about an African-American girl with brown eyes who *would* rather have had blue eyes. ______
5. Toni Morrison *would* like readers to consider the way African-American culture can be seen in many works of fiction. ______
6. If schools *would* re-think what literature should be taught, African-American writers might be more widely read and studied. ______

VII Focus on Perfect Modals and Progressive Modals

Perfect Forms of Modal Auxiliaries

The perfect forms of several modals follow this pattern:

modal + (*not*) + *have* + *-ed*/*-en* form of the main verb.

Most of these modals refer to past time, but a few have future meaning.

Perfect Modals Referring to the Past

The modals that refer to the past include *should/ought to have*, *may/might/could have*, *can't/couldn't have*, and *must/had to have*. In some cases, the past meanings are significantly different from the present meanings. For example, *should* and *ought to* in the present/future express advisability, but in the past they express regret or hindsight (understanding gained by the passage of time). *Can have* and *could have*, which express possibility in the affirmative, refer to impossibility in the negative.

Perfect Modals with Past Meaning

Hindsight or Regret: *should/ought to have + -ed/-en*

The civil rights movement *should have succeeded* sooner. (Unfortunately, it didn't.)

The Constitution *ought to have made* slavery illegal.

Unfulfilled Possibility: *may/might/could have -ed/-en*

These forms are often used to express conditional meaning.

Martin Luther King, Jr. *may have become* a political leader in the United States [*if he hadn't been assassinated*].

King *might have given* many speeches as inspiring as "I Have a Dream" [*if he had lived*].

He *could have accomplished* many of his goals. (*Could* = ability + possibility)

Past Impossibility: *can/couldn't have + -ed/-en*

You *can't have read* "I Have a Dream" in 1962! Martin Luther King, Jr., delivered it in 1968.

King *couldn't have been* in Washington, D.C., on February 5, 1965; he was in Birmingham, Alabama on that day.

Past Assumption/Logical Deduction: *must/had to have + -ed/-en*

People at Martin Luther King, Jr.'s, funeral *must have been* grief-stricken. (We assume this is true.)

They *had to have realized* that a great leader had been lost. (*Had to have* is stronger than *must have*.)

Perfect Modals Referring to the Future

The modals that express future possibility and expectation include *may/could have* and *should/ought to have*.

Perfect Modals with Future Meaning

<u>Future Possibility:</u> *may/could have*

By the year 2000, the U.S. Supreme Court *may have enforced* more rulings against racial discrimination.

Major U.S. cities *could have solved* many of their problems by then.

<u>Future Expectation:</u> *should/ought to have*

The United States *should have accomplished* racial equality by the end of the twentieth century.

We *ought to have learned* to live together by then.

Checkpoint 15

A. 

Complete the following sentences by using perfect modal verb phrases to express the meaning given at the end of the sentences. Example:

Maya Angelou (*be*) <u>had to have been</u> a strong woman to survive through such hard times. (strong probability past)

1. Her life (*turn*) ______________________ out differently if she had stayed in St. Louis. (possibility/past)
2. She (*become*) ______________________ a dancer or singer instead of a writer. (ability/past)
3. You (*see*) ______________________ her dance and sing in the United States from 1954–55; she was touring in Africa during those years. (impossibility/past)
4. Perhaps she (*continue*) ______________________ with her acting career; her role as the queen in Jean Genet's play *The Blacks* brought her a great deal of acclaim. (advisability/past)
5. The publication of the autobiographical *I Know why the Cage Bird Sings* (*be*) ______________________ a major event in this talented woman's life. (probability/past)
6. In recent years, she has published more books and been active in the arts; one of her most memorable appearances on television (*occur*) ______________________ when she read a poem at President Clinton's inauguration. (strong probability/past)
7. In any case, her readers (*never, get*) ______________________ such insight into the African-American experience if Angelou hadn't shared her observations in her books and interviews. (possibility/past)

B.

Read the descriptions of the contributions made by famous African-Americans who are no longer living. Write sentences that contain *must/have to* + *have* + *-ed/-en* to make logical deductions about past situations or events. The first one has been done for you. Example:

Mahalia Jackson was a great African-American singer of gospel music, songs that originated in African-American churches. Her music became extremely popular in Europe. She began singing in her father's church and then sang on the radio. She made numerous records, gave frequent recitals, and toured the world spreading the popularity of gospel music.

She had to have loved to sing.

She must have had a beautiful voice.

1. W.E.B. Du Bois (1868—1963) was an extremely important figure in American history. He was the first African-American in the United States to receive a Ph.D. in a secular (non-religious) subject. A historian, an academic, and a social critic, Du Bois devoted his life to eliminating racism in the United States.
2. Martin Luther King, Jr. (1929—1968) brought Gandhi's principles of non-violent protest to the African-American struggle for equal rights that began in the 1950s. His leadership and self-sacrifice, as well as his speaking skills, inspired millions.
3. Louis Armstrong (1900—1971), an African-American jazz musician who played the trumpet and sang vocals, introduced jazz to listeners around the world and made it a widely accepted form of music.

C. 

The following sentences express some of W.E.B. Du Bois' opinions about American history. Complete the sentences with perfect forms of the verbs in parentheses to express hindsight about what *should have been done* in the United States

1. Du Bois thought the U.S. Constitution (*give*) ______________________ all citizens, including women, equal rights from the beginning.
2. The Founding Fathers of the country (*make*) ______________________ slavery illegal.
3. In other words, the law (*guarantee*) ______________________ freedom for all.
4. He thought the Northern states (*not, tolerate*) ______________________ the growing slave trade in the South.
5. He also believed historians of that period (*be*) ______________________ more critical of the use of slaves in the South.

D.

Write the letter of the correct use of *should* on the line after each sentence.

a. Expectation
b. Advice
c. Asking for suggestions
d. Hindsight

1. We *should* have looked for some gospel music by Mahalia Jackson when we were in the music store. ______
2. There's almost always some gospel music on the radio on Sunday morning. It's Sunday morning, so we *should* find some on the radio now. ______
3. If you want to improve your voice, you *should* take singing lessons. ______
4. What *should* we do? *Should* we go to the gospel concert? ______
5. Gospel music has become so famous that most people in the U.S. *should* have heard it at some time. ______
6. Your friend *shouldn't* have quit the church choir. She might have become another Mahalia Jackson. ______

Progressive Forms of Modal Auxiliaries

Progressive forms that contain modal auxiliaries, like all progressive verbs, show continuing action or emphasize the length or duration of the main verb. They are often used in relationship to another verb. Progressive modals can express a present-future or perfect meaning.

- **Present-Future Progressive Modals.** The present or future progressive verb consists of a modal auxiliary + *be* + the *-ing* form of the main verb.

Progressive Modals
You look tired. You *may be working* too hard. (possibility)
A person *doesn't have to be living* in Arkansas in order to find out about that state. (lack of necessity)
Bailey is laughing in his sleep. He *must be dreaming*. (probability or logical deduction)
He *had better be sleeping* when Momma comes home. (strong advisability)

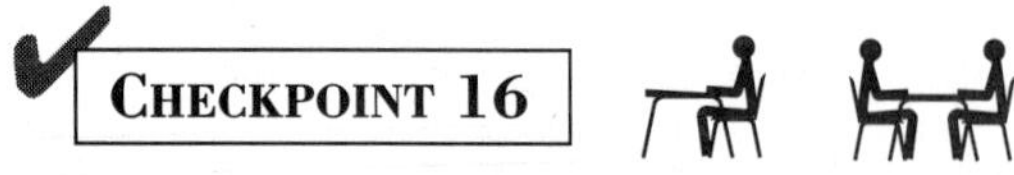

Using the modal auxiliaries that express the meanings given in at the end of the sentences, complete the sentences with the progressive forms of the verbs in parentheses. Example:

Mrs. Flowers isn't here. She (*visit*) ___may be visiting___ one of her other friends. (possibility)

1. You (*prepare*) ______________ dinner while I am reading aloud. (permission)
2. Momma isn't at the store. She (*walk*) ______________ home right now. (logical deduction)
3. Bailey (*do*) ______________ his homework when Momma gets home. (strong advisability)
4. The phone (*ring*) ______________. I took it off the hook. (impossibility)

- **Perfect Progressive Modals.** The perfect progressive verb phrase consists of modal auxiliary + *have been* + the *-ing* form of the main verb. The perfect progressive verb usually expresses past time, but in some cases it can express future time.

Perfect Progressive Modals

Past Meaning

She *should have been sleeping* instead of reading until midnight.

He ate ten cookies. She *must have been feeling* very hungry.

Future Meaning

Maya Angelou is going to appear on television next week. She *may have been working* on a new book that she will talk about.

The night before exams begin, she *had better not have been watching* television all day.

VIII Focus on the Uses of *Will*

THE USES OF WILL

On page 124, *will* and *won't* were discussed as auxiliaries that express future tense. These auxiliaries can express other meanings as well.

- **Promise**

  I *will* always remember your kindness.

  I *won't* ever forget you.

- **Offer of Help**

  I *will* carry your groceries, Mrs. Flowers.

  They *will* meet you at the bus station in Stamps.

- **Prediction**

  The U.S. *will* have an African-American president within 25 years.

- **Threat** (used with *I* and *we*)

  I *won't* speak to you again, not ever!

  We*'ll* show him who's in charge here.

- **Agreeing to a Request**

  We *will* gladly attend the party at Mrs. Flowers' house.

  They*'ll* be delighted to make a contribution to your church.

- **Polite Questions**

  Will you please have a seat? *Won't* you come in?

- **Refusal**

  Marguerite *won't* speak.

  I *won't* eat this cold food.

CHECKPOINT 17  

A. Read the following dialogue between a father and child. Underline all the uses of *will* and decide which of its meanings is being used.

Child: Dad, will you tell me a story?

Father: Sure, I will. But then you have to try to go to sleep.

Child: Okay, I will.

Father: I'll tell you a story from *Roots*. Remember, you saw part of it on television.

Child: Just one? Won't you tell me a few?

Father: No, I won't. It's getting too late.

Child: Okay, but will you please let me watch the rest of the television series?

Father: If you'll go to bed right now.

B. Underline the uses of *will* in the following description of a photography exhibit, and decide which meaning applies.

"Songs of My People: African-Americans: A Self-Portrait" included a group of 150 photographs of African-Americans that toured through many museums around the world in 1993–94. The work of 53 African-American photographers, the show will long be remembered for enlightening the public about the diversity

and strength of this minority group in the U.S. Perhaps stereotypes of African-Americans won't be as common as a result of the popularity of the exhibit, which includes portraits of African-Americans of many different backgrounds and lifestyles: old and young, rich and poor, cowboys, students, and doctors, among many others. The photographs are available in book form, so the revelations about the character of African-American life will be preserved.

IX Focus on Modal Auxiliaries in Questions

Modals in YES/NO Questions

Most modal auxiliaries are used in questions the same way as other auxiliaries. Some modals, including *might, must,* and *ought to,* are not commonly used in YES/NO questions, however.

Modals in YES/NO Questions and Short Answers

Modal	Subject	Rest of Verb	Rest of Sentence	Answer
Can	I	see	those photographs?	Yes, you can.
				No, you can't.
Should	we	buy	a program?	Yes, we should.
				No, we shouldn't.
Will	he	look	at the pictures?	Yes, he will.
				No, he won't.
Could	they	have arrived	on time?	Yes, they could have.
				No, they couldn't have.

Questions with *Must and Has to/Have to*

Must (with the meaning of necessity) and *has/have to* do not follow the usual pattern in YES/NO questions. In both present-future and past questions only one form, *have to,* is used with *do, does,* or *did.* YES/NO questions with *must* occur rarely in American usage. The following question sounds very formal or British to U.S. speakers of English: *Must we arrive early?*

Statement	*Question*
They *must* arrive early.	*Do* they *have to* arrive early?
They *have to* arrive early.	
He *has to* be on time.	*Does* he *have to* be on time?
He *must* be on time.	
They *had to* take the bus.	*Did* they *have to* take the bus?
He *had to* leave early.	*Did* he *have to* leave early?

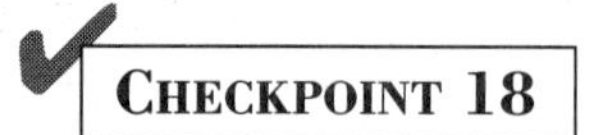

Change each statement to a YES/NO question. Example:

Photographers *are able to* record scenes that other artists can't.

Are photographers *able to* record scenes that other artists can't?

1. Photographers must pay attention to light and shadow contrasts.
2. In the past, photographers had to use sunlight for their work.
3. They couldn't take photographs at night.
4. Now, most photographers can use a flash attachment to work at night or indoors.

MODALS IN INFORMATION QUESTIONS

Information questions with modals are formed in the same way as questions with other auxiliaries. As in all information questions, the question word begins the question and determines the type of answer that is called for.

Information Questions and Short Answers with Modals

Question Word	Modal	Subject	Rest of Verb	Rest of Sentence	Possible Responses
Where	can	I	sit?		There. Over here.
When	would	you	like	to go to the museum?	Later. Right now.
Which road	will	they	be taking?		Main Street. The safest one.
What	can	a photographer	do?		Many things. Create a feeling. Capture a scene.

Write an appropriate question for each answer. Use the modal expression indicated. Example:

ANSWER: No, they don't (have to).
QUESTION: Do photographers have to take all their pictures in sunlight?

1. ANSWER: Maya Angelou is (able to).
   QUESTION:
2. ANSWER: Yes, you may.
   QUESTION:
3. ANSWER: Yes, they did. (They had to.)
   QUESTION:
4. ANSWER: Mrs. Flowers could.
   QUESTION:

PART THREE. Review and Integration

Classifying Modals: A Review

Return to the reading on pages 162–164 and find at least 20 verb phrases containing modal auxiliaries. Put the missing information into the columns below, noting the paragraph in which each modal appears. Some categories contain several modals. Compare your answers with those of other groups. Four verb phrases have been filled in.

Meaning	Present/Future	Past/Perfect
Ability	can (5)	
Advisability/ Obligation		
Possibility		
Probability/ Logical deduction		
Necessity		
Lack of necessity		
Prohibition		
Uses of *would*		
Preference	I'd prefer (7)	
Repeated past action		
Past of *will*	would need (11)	
Condition		would have been (22)

Cumulative Exercise: Modal Review

A. Use a modal auxiliary or equivalent expression to complete each sentence. In some cases more than one choice is possible.

Martin Luther King, Jr (*be*) ______________________ the best known African-American leader of the twentieth century. To this day, his ideas are widely known and respected. They include the idea that African-Americans (*use*) ______________________ non-violent means of protesting unfair treatment in the U.S. In other words, African Americans and their supporters (*hurt, not*) ______________________ others in their struggle for equal rights. While King was still a student, he began preaching in his father's church. He convinced church members that they (*help*) ______________________ the cause of equal rights by joining the NAACP, or the National Association for the Advancement of Colored People.

The fight for equal rights (*begin*) ______________________ in 1955. A historic moment occurred when Mrs. Rosa Parks, an African-American seamstress in Alabama, (*give up, not*) ______________________ her seat on a bus to a white person. She was asked many times, (*move*) "______________

you ________________ to the back of the bus?" But she refused. The police came and told her she (*do*) ________________________ as she was told. Then they arrested her.

African-American organizations, such as the Montgomery Improvement Association, of which Martin Luther King became the president, organized a boycott of buses. The organizations advised their members that they (*use, not*) ________________________ the buses in order to show that they (*accept, not*) ________________________ unfair treatment. They achieved success in 1956 when the U.S. Supreme court passed a law that declared that bus employees (*discriminate, not*) ________________________ against African-Americans. During this time, King emerged as an important leader of his people and received national attention.

By the early 1960s, his followers believed that he (*lead*) ________________ them to "The Promised Land." King's activities brought him more and more recognition. During the 1963 march on Washington, King delivered his famous "I Have a Dream" speech, which (*be*) ________________________ one of the classic addresses in American history. His greatest award (*be*) ________________ the Nobel Peace Prize, which he received in 1964. Biographers of King say that he (*have*) ________________________ special powers of prediction because he knew he (*kill*) ________________________ before his fortieth birthday.

B. Write appropriate modals or equivalent expressions. In some cases, more than one choice is appropriate.

1. Where is Marguerite? She (*arrive*) ________________________ an hour ago. She (*work, still*) ________________________ at the store.
2. Before Marguerite went to school, she (*already/read*) ________________________ very well
3. We don't know exactly where Mrs. Flowers lives. We (*ask*) ________________________ directions, or we (*get*) ________________________ lost.
4. That (*be*) ________________________ Mrs. Flowers' book! It's in terrible shape.
5. When you promise to keep a secret, you (*tell*) ________________________ anyone.

6. When Bailey and Marguerite were little, he (*play*) ______________________ in the store. Marguerite (*always, read*) ______________________.
7. If Mrs. Flowers lived now, she (*prepare*) ______________________ her food in a microwave.
8. She (*not, need*) ______________________ ice; now she (*probably, own*) ______________________ a refrigerator.
9. Marguerite doesn't miss school unless she's sick. She was absent from school yesterday. She (*be*) ______________________ sick.
10. Is a driver's license required in all countries? (*have*) ______________________ all drivers ______________________ a license?
11. One of the boys broke Momma's window. He (*tell*) ______________________ her about it before she finds out.
12. Momma is giving Marguerite a rest. She (*deliver*) ______________________ groceries if she doesn't want to.
13. What should I read next? Well, you (*try*) ______________________ this mystery. I'd also suggest a romance by this author.
14. When does the bus from St. Louis arrive? It (*get*) ______________________ in any minute now.
15. When I was a teenager, I (*stay*) ______________________ up all night. Now I (*keep*) ______________________ my eyes open past eleven.
16. (*spend*) ______________________ you like to ______________________ the summer in St. Louis? No, I (*stay*) ______________________ in Stamps.
17. Back in those days, girls (*wear*) ______________________ dresses to school. Now they (*wear*) ______________________ almost anything.
18. Marguerite has a big test tomorrow. She (*review*) ______________________ all the material she's learned so far.

C. Discuss the differences in meaning of the sentences in each group.

1. We were playing music last night.
   a. The neighbors might have heard it.
   b. The neighbors couldn't hear it.
   c. The neighbors couldn't have heard it.
2. a. You might enjoy going to the concert.
   b. You should enjoy going to the concert.
   c. You must have enjoyed going to the concert.
3. a. He is to play with the jazz band tomorrow.
   b. He can't play with the jazz band tomorrow.
   c. He won't play with the jazz band tomorrow.
4. a. She ought to practice the piano soon.
   b. She is supposed to practice the piano soon.
   c. She may practice the piano soon.

5. a. They aren't allowed to sing here.
   b. They don't have to sing here.
   c. They mustn't sing here.

An African-American Artist: Modal Review

Complete the sentences with the letter of the modal expression that *best* describes the painter Henry Ossawa Turner (1859–1937).

1. As a baby, Henry Turner was so weak that doctors thought he ______ live.
   a. shouldn't b. must not c. wouldn't
2. In 1873, Henry was walking with his father in Philadelphia when they saw an artist painting. The boy asked, "______ I do that?"
   a. would b. can c. must
3. The father answered that he ______ succeed at anything he tried.
   a. should b. had to c. could
4. The boy taught himself to paint because his father, a minister, ______ pay for art lessons.
   a. mustn't b. couldn't c. was able to
5. Henry ______ work as a salesman in a flour mill even though he didn't want to.
   a. had to b. should have c. might
6. In 1880, Henry went to study at the Pennsylvania Academy of Fine Arts with the great painter Thomas Eakins. Eakins advised Henry that he ______ paint what he observed around him.
   a. ought to b. would c. might
7. After his first show of paintings in Ohio, Henry went to Paris where he thought he ______ find great success.
   a. must b. might c. can
8. He loved Paris but became so sick with typhoid fever that he ______ return to the United States.
   a. might have b. was supposed to c. had to
9. Finally he developed his own style with which he ______ express his view of the world and his personal religion.
   a. should b. could c. might
10. Turner became very popular and successful. He painted in Europe until World War I broke out , but then he became so depressed that he ______ work.
    a. was unable to b. might have c. had to

Dear Gabby Letters: Asking for and Giving Advice

In groups of 3 to 4 students, discuss possible responses to each of the following letters to the advice column of a newspaper. Use as many appropriate modals as possible, and try to practice different forms. Take turns writing down your group's responses. Write at least five sentences with modals in response to each letter. When you finish, a member of your group will read your responses to the class.

Dear Gabby

Dear Gabby:

My daughter is sweet, but she's always in trouble. Two months ago she was convicted of armed robbery and sent to prison. Yesterday she came home to hide. Right now she's upstairs in her bedroom. I want to be a good father, but I'm afraid of getting in trouble with the law myself. Please tell me what to do.

Desperate Dad

Dear Gabby,

I am the grandfather of three wonderful kids who live with their parents across the street. I babysit for them while their parents are working. I love my grandchildren very much, and I hate to say "No" to them. I let them eat as much candy as they want and watch any program they want on television. My daughter-in-law says I am wrong to do this. I say grandparents are supposed to spoil their grandchildren. What do you say?

Old Softie

Dear Gabby,

I'm a pretty typical twelve-year-old seventh grader. I live in a nice house and have a dog. My parents are wonderful people, and everyone in town loves them. There's only one problem. They're gamblers. Every weekend they go to a racetrack or a casino. They spend the grocery money on gambling; they even try to borrow my allowance to play the lottery. I'm considering reporting them to the authorities. I'm scared and worried about them. Should I turn in my own parents? Please advise me.

Caught in the Middle

Role Play: Practicing Modals

Working in pairs, choose parts for each of the situations below. Practice a dialogue between the two characters, using as many modal auxiliaries as possible. Take turns acting out your role plays for the whole class.

Situation 1: "Landlord, you've got to fix this leak."

Mrs. Flowers: *Your roof leaks, and you have water on your floor. You want the landlord to fix the roof.*

Landlord: *You are apologetic but too busy to do the job right away.*

Situation 2: "What would Marguerite like?"

Bailey: *You are looking for a birthday gift for Marguerite at a department store. You have several ideas but would also like some suggestions.*

Salesclerk: *You make several suggestions about the gift. You want to please the customer and also make a big sale.*

Situation 3: "When can I get my ice?"

Mrs. Flowers: *The ice delivery man is late. It's 105 degrees outside and you want your ice right away.*

Ice man: *You have no more ice today. Mrs. Flowers is one of your best customers, so you want to keep her happy.*

Situation 4: "Would you mind explaining the card catalogue/ microfiche machine to me?"

Marguerite: *You are looking around the library for some materials to use in your report on* ____________________ *(fill in the blank). You explain exactly what you need to the librarian.*

Librarian: *You try to help her find what she needs.*

Role Play: Practicing Modals

Your teacher will give each group of three to five students a group of related modal auxiliaries to teach to the rest of the class. Plan the lesson. Decide how to explain and illustrate the grammar lesson; you might want to create a situation (at home, at school, at work, with a friend, at a hospital, police station, city hall, etc.) in which the particular group of modals might be used.

Each group should then take turns giving the "lessons" to the rest of the class, who may ask questions after each lesson.

ESL Memory Game: Match the Modals

This game is played with 30 cards numbered on the back from 1 to 30. Thirty modal auxiliaries (15 pairs of modals and/or equivalent expressions) are written on the cards. Each card must have a "match," a synonym or expression with the same meaning, such as *must/have to* or *can/be able to*. The index cards are shuffled and placed face down on a table in a rectangle. Teams take turns calling out two numbers that they hope will be a "match." If a matched pair is called, the two cards are removed from the rectangle and given to the team that made the match. If the two numbers called do not make a match, they are returned face down to the rectangle. The procedure is followed until all cards have been matched. The team that matches the most pairs wins.

Suggestions for Writing

1. If you are keeping a journal, write an entry on one or more of the following: an older/younger friend who has influenced your life; a famous African-American writer, educator, or politician; your observations or opinions of minorities in the United States, including African-Americans, Asian-Americans, and Hispanics.
2. Imagine that you are Mrs. Flowers or Momma. Write a journal or diary entry describing your feelings toward Marguerite, her inability to speak, her love of books and language, and the advice you would give her to achieve happiness and success.
3. Write a composition describing the accomplishments of two or three African-Americans who have worked in the same field (education, art, entertainment, politics, religion, sports). Consult an encyclopedia for help.
4. Write a composition describing three or four major qualities of a good friend. You may want to refer to Marguerite's friendship with Mrs. Flowers.
5. Write a letter to a friend in another country about a visit to the United States. Give your friend suggestions and advice about what to bring and what to expect. Use modal auxiliaries if appropriate.

Unit Six

The Passive Voice

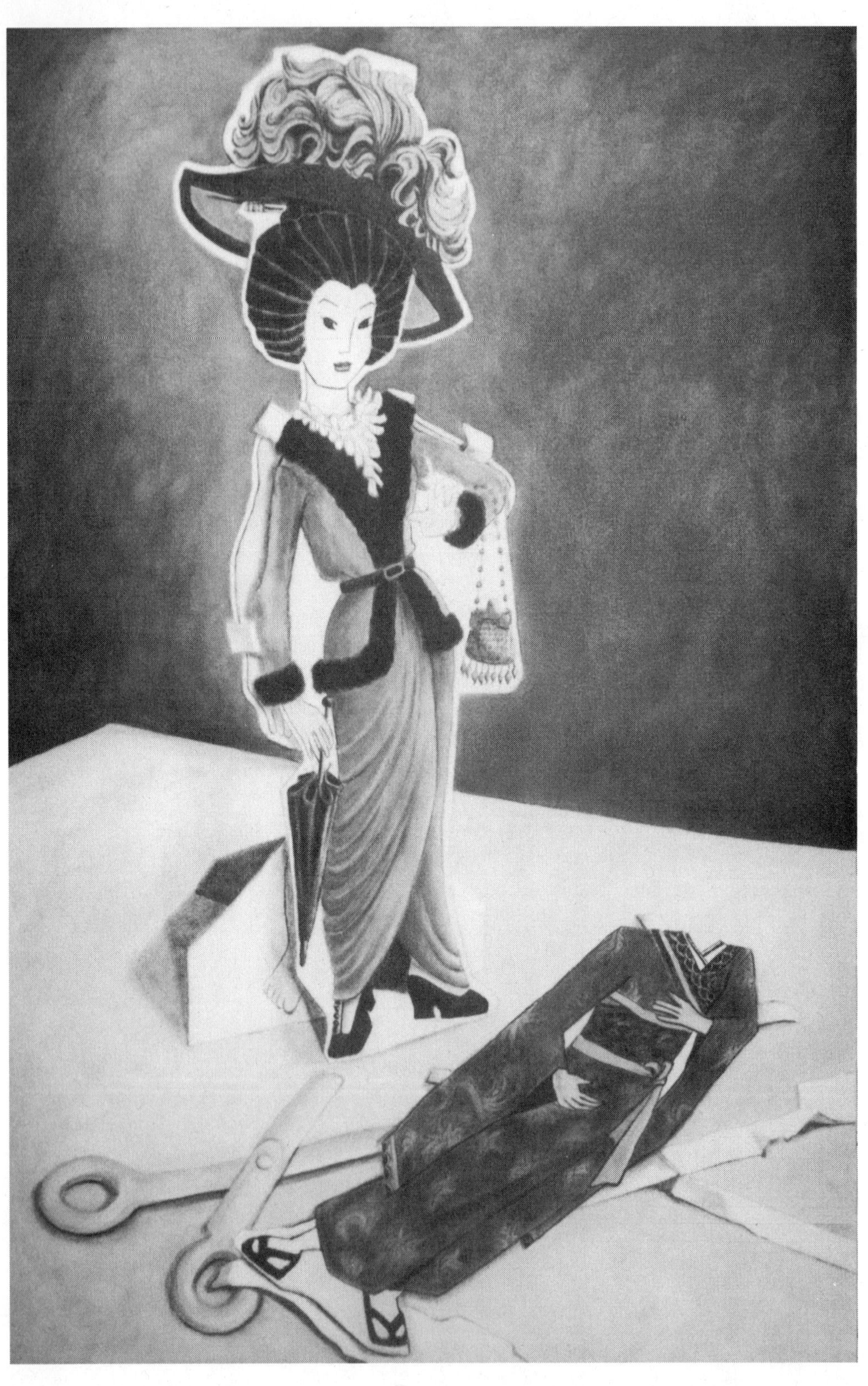

READINGS: From *Yokohama, California* by Toshio Mori

THEME: Asia and Asian-Americans

PART ONE. The Context

The reading passage for this chapter is an excerpt from *Yokohama, California* by Toshio Mori. It describes the experiences of an Asian couple who settled in the San Francisco area before World War II and raised a family there.

Pre-Reading Questions

1. Have you observed differences between parents from one country/culture and their children born or brought up in another? If so, what are some of the ways they are different?
2. Adults who move to a new country usually have many more problems learning the new language than their children do. Why do you think this is true?
3. In recent years, many immigrants and refugees from Asian countries like Vietnam, Korca, China, and Japan have arrived in the United States. What changes in their lives can people expect when they move to the United States? What effects does a large group of immigrants have on U.S. culture?

Preview of Key Terms and Concepts

The following key words and ideas appear in this unit. Guess the meaning of the terms on the left by matching them to the definitions on the right. Put the correct letter after each term. Discuss your answers with a partner or group, and ask your teacher about any terms you're not sure of.

1. fête ____
2. acrobat ____
3. headliners ____
4. missionary ____
5. kimono____

a. traditional Japanese dress for men and women
b. give a party or parties; celebrate (from the French noun for "festival" or "celebration")
c. person who does religious or charitable work, usually in foreign countries or among newcomers to a country
d. major performers; stars
e. person skilled in performing on the trapeze and tightrope or in gymnastics

READING: From *Yokohama, California* by Toshio Mori

The narrator of the following passage from Yokohama, California, a woman who came to San Francisco from Japan in her youth, tells her grandchildren about her early experiences in the United States.

"Tomorrow Is Coming, Children"

(1) Long ago, children, I lived in a country called Japan. Your grandpa was already in California earning money for my boat ticket. The village people rarely went out of Japan and were shocked when they heard I was following your grandpa as soon as the money came.

(2) "America!" they cried. "America is on the other side of the world! You will be in a strange country. You cannot read or write their language. What will you do?" I smiled, and in my dreams I saw the San Francisco your grandpa wrote about: San Francisco, the city with strange enticing* food; the city with gold coins; the city with many strange faces and music; the city with great buildings and ships.

(3) One day his letter came with the money. "Come at once," he wrote. "Don't delay." The neighbors rushed excitedly to the house. "Don't go! Live among us," they cried. "There will be war between America and Japan. You will be caught in mid-Pacific. You will never reach America." But I was determined. They painted the lonely lives of immigrants in a strange land. They cried on my shoulders and embraced me. "I have bought my ticket and my things are packed. I am going," I said.

(4) For thirty days and nights the village people invited me to their houses, and I was dined and feted. It was hard not to change my mind and put off the trip. They came to see me off at the station. They waved their hands cheerfully though their eyes were sad. But my spirits were not dampened.* I was looking ahead, thinking of your grandpa and San Francisco. . . .

(5) What was I wearing, Annabelle? My best kimono, a beautiful thing. But do you know what your grandpa did when he saw me come off the boat? He looked at it and shook his head. He hauled me around as if he were ashamed of me. I could not understand.

(6) "Never wear this thing again," he told me that night.

"Why?" I demanded. "It's a beautiful kimono."

"You look like a foreigner," he said. "You must dress like an American. You belong here."

(7) He gave me a dress, a coat, a hat, stockings, and shoes, my first American clothes. I stopped dozens of times in front of the mirror to see how I looked. Yes, I remember the big hats they used to wear then, and the long skirts that dusted the dirt off the streets. Some day I shall go up to the attic of our Oakland home and bring down the album* and show you the pictures of those days.

---

*	
enticing	attractive, appealing
dampened	depressed
album	a book to hold photographs

(8) I cannot find the street now where your grandpa and I lived that first year but it is somewhere in San Francisco. We had a small empty house and no money. We spread our blankets on the floor and slept. We used big boxes for tables and small ones for chairs. The city of my dreams began to frighten me. Rocks were thrown at the house and the windows smashed to bits. Loud cries and laughter followed each attack, and I cowered* in the corner waiting for the end.

(9) "Oh, why did I come? Whatever did we come for?" I asked your grandpa.

He only looked at me. "Just a little more time . . . a little more time," his eyes seemed to say.

(10) I could not refuse. But we moved out of San Francisco. We came across the bay, and after much saving your grandpa bought a bathhouse in Oakland. And that was where your daddy was born. We lived in the rear, and for four years it was our home. Ah, the year your daddy was born! That was when for the first time I began to feel at home.

(11) It was on account of a little neighbor, the white American wife of a Japanese acrobat. They were touring the country as headliners but had settled down in Oakland for some reason. They lived next door with their adopted Japanese children. "Mich-chan, Taka-chan! Come home! Mich-chan, Taka-chan!" Her cries used to ring across the yard like a caress.*

(12) The Japanese acrobat came often. "Please come and talk with my American wife. She is lonely and has no friend here," he told me.

(13) I shook my head ashamedly. "I am lonely, too, but I cannot speak English. When your American wife starts talking, I am in trouble," I explained.

(14) Then he would laugh and scold me. "Talk? You don't have to talk. My wife will understand. Please do not be afraid."

(15) One day the American lady came, and we had tea. We drank silently and smiled. All the time I was hoping she would not begin talking. She liked my tea and cakes, I could tell. She talked of simple things so that I would grasp a little of it. She would pick up her teacup and ask, "Satsuma? Satsuma,* Japan?"

(16) I would nod eagerly. "Yes, Satsuma."

(17) She came often. Every time we sat silently, sipped tea, and smiled. Every once in a while her Japanese husband came and thanked me. "She is happy. She has a friend."

(18) "I do not speak to her. I cannot express myself," I told him.

(19) "No, no. She understands. You do not have to talk."

(20) Ah, I can never forget her. She knitted baby clothes for your daddy. "I think it will be a girl," she said. But it was your daddy. I cried when she had to go away again. Yes, it was long ago. All your uncles and aunts came afterwards: Mamoru, Yuri, Willie, Mary Ann, Yoshio and Betty.

(21) Yes, time is your friend in America, children. See, my face and hands are wrinkled, my hair gray. My teeth are gone, my figure bent. These are of America. I still cannot speak English too well, but I live among all kinds of people

---

* cowered	to shrink or crouch in fear
caress	affectionate touch
Satsuma	cream-colored Japanese pottery

and come and go like the seasons, the bees, and the flowers. Ah, San Francisco, my dream city. My San Francisco is everywhere. I like the dirty brown hills, the black soil and the sandy beaches. I like the tall buildings, the bridges, the parks and the roar of city traffic. They are of me and I feel like humming.

(22) You don't understand, Johnny? Ah, you are too young. You will. Your grandma wants to be buried here in America. Yes, little ones. Once I had a brother and a sister in Japan. Long ago they wrote me a letter. Come back, sister, they said. We want to see you again. Hurry. Oh, it was long before you were born. But I did not return. I never saw them again. Now they are dead. I stayed in America; I belong here.

Comprehension Questions

1. How did the Japanese villagers feel about the narrator's departure for the United States? How did the villagers show their feelings?
2. Describe the Japanese couple's first house in San Francisco. What kinds of experiences did they have there?
3. How did the Japanese woman meet her first friend in the United States? How did they spend their time together?
4. When did the narrator of the story come to the United States? How did she travel?

Discussion Questions

1. The concept of the United States as a "melting pot" suggests that people of different backgrounds give up their native customs and languages and adopt the U.S. lifestyle. Why do you think people like the idea of a melting pot? How do you feel about it?
2. What unique cultural features have Asians introduced to the United States? How might misunderstandings arise because of cultural differences between Asian immigrants and the other U.S. groups?
3. Asian-American U.S. residents have been called "the model minority" because many people think that Asians have quickly adapted to the culture and become successful. Do you think this label is an accurate one? Could it lead to problems for those Asians who have not had an easy time adjusting to the U.S. culture?

PART TWO. The Target Structure: The Passive Voice

I Focus on Forming and Using Passives

Preview of the Passive Voice

Go back to paragraph 4 in *Yokohama, California* (page 205). Find the three verbs that consist of a form of the verb *be* + the *-ed/-en* form of the main verb. These are examples of verbs in passive voice. Underline the verbs and circle their subjects.

With a partner, discuss these questions: Does the subject of each of the passive verbs *perform* (*do*) the action of the verb, or does it *receive* the action? If the subject does not perform the action, can you identify who or what does? Why do you think the verb is called "passive"?

Forming Passive Verbs

A passive verb consists of a form of the verb *be* + the *-ed/-en* form of the main verb; the form of *be* must agree with its subject. The passive verbs in the fourth paragraph of the reading are in the past tense: *was dined*, [*was*] *feted*, and *were dampened*, but passives can occur in other tenses as well.

Passive Verbs in Different Tenses

Subject	Be	-ed/-en Form	Rest of Sentence
San Francisco	*is*	*called*	a city of many strange faces.
She	*was*	*feted*	by the villagers.
You	*will be*	*caught*	in mid-Pacific.
Kimonos	*have been*	*worn*	by Japanese women for centuries.
The Satsuma tea set	*had been*	*bought*	before the couple immigrated.
Asian languages	*are being*	*spoken*	by millions of people in the United States today.
Short stories	*were being*	*written*	by Toshio Mori in the 1930s and '40s.

CHECKPOINT 1

A.

Use the cues to form passive sentences that contain present verb forms. Remember that the form of *be* must agree with its subject. Then decide how to order the sentences so that they give instructions for making tea. Put the number of each sentence in the space provided. The first one has been done for you.

____ a. the tea/allow to sit

__1__ b water/heat
Water is heated.

____ c. hot tea/enjoy/by everyone

____ d. cups/fill

____ e. tea bags/place/in pot

B.

Use the cues to form passive sentences that contain simple past verbs.

Situation: The Japanese woman is on the boat headed for California. She is thinking about her departure from Japan and everything that was done to prepare for the trip. Example:

family members/tell

Family members were told.

1. house/sell
2. neighbors/inform
3. boat ticket/buy
4. my things/pack
5. I/send off/by family and friends

C.

Practice forming present and past forms of the passive by filling in the blanks with the correct tense of *be* and the *-en/-en* form of the main verb. Example:

Yokohama, California *was written* by Toshio Mori. (past, *write*)

1. It ______was published______ first in 1949 and again in paperback in 1985. (past, *publish*)
2. It ________________________ of short stories. (present, *compose*)
3. The lives of Japanese-Americans in San Francisco ____________________ by Mori in the stories. (present, *describe*)

4. Mori's humor and compassion ____________________ in such stories as "The Seventh Street Philosopher" and "The Eggs of the World." (present, *show*)
5. Mori's stories ____________ largely ____________________ during his lifetime, but they ____________________ better ____________ now. (past, *ignore*; present, *know*)

Passive Sentences

The subject of a passive verb does not perform the action of the verb; instead it *receives* the action, like the object of an active verb. When a subject is passive, its form does not change; instead, its passivity is shown by a change in the verb form. It is more accurate, therefore, to discuss passive *sentences* rather than passive verbs since both the subject and predicate are involved in the passive construction.

Sometimes the preposition *by* follows the passive verb; in that case, the object of *by* is the performer of the action. Often the performer of the action is not mentioned, and no *by*-phrase is used. None of the sentences with passive verbs in the reading passages contains a *by*-phrase, although the performers of the action can be inferred from the context.

I was feted *by the village people.*

My spirits were not dampened *by their sadness.*

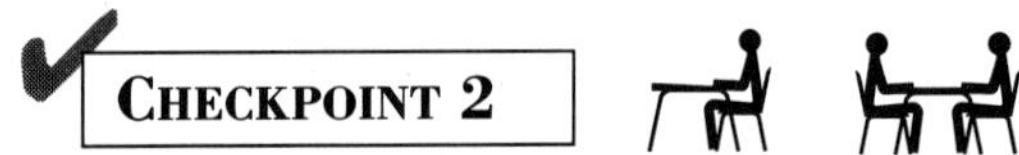

Checkpoint 2

After each of the following active sentences, write the tense of the verb. Then rewrite the sentences, changing the active verbs to passive. Use the same tense in the passive sentence. Example:

The husband *sent* the money for his wife's ticket. <u>Past</u>
The money for his wife's ticket *was sent* by the husband.

1. Her husband *told* the woman not to wear a kimono anymore. ____________
2. An American woman *helped* her. ____________
3. Immigrants to the United States *bring* customs and traditions from their native lands. ____________
4. The U. S. government *will take* a census in 1998 to analyze changes in the population. ____________
5. Newcomers *receive* help from different organizations. ____________
6. Readers *will enjoy* Mori's stories for years to come. ____________

When to Use the Passive

The passive verb emphasizes the receiver (subject) of the action and de-emphasizes the *agent* or performer of the action. Therefore, the passive is most appropriate when the agent is unimportant, unknown, or obvious. Often the agent, expressed in a *by*-phrase, is so insignificant that it is omitted.

The Satsuma teacup *was made* in Japan.
(Who made it is unimportant and unknown.)

The I Ching *was written* many centuries ago.
(The writers are unknown.)

Is Chinese still *spoken* in Hong Kong?
(It is obvious that people speak Chinese; the phrase "by people" is not necessary.)

CHECKPOINT 3 

A. Change the following sentences to the passive. If the performer of the action is obvious, unknown, or unimportant, do not include a by-phrase. Example:

Someone *threw* rocks at the house.
Rocks *were thrown* at the house.

1. People smashed the windows to bits.
2. Loud cries and laughter followed each attack.
3. The city of her dreams frightened her.
4. Someone knitted baby clothes for the children.
5. The family brought a trunk to the United States.
6. Someone introduced Mrs. Liao to mah jong when she was very young.
7. People drink tea daily in many Asian countries.

B. The grandmother is describing the experiences of her yout to her granddaughter, Annabelle. The ideas are expressed in the active voice. Change the sentences to the passive and delete the agent if possible.

Grandma and Grandpa . . .
spread blankets on the floor.

Their blankets *were spread* on the floor.

1. sipped tea.
2. bought American clothes.
3. made friends with their neighbor, a Japanese acrobat.
4. bought a bathhouse in Oakland.
5. ignored the objections of the Japanese villagers.
6. loved San Francisco's hills, black soil, tall buildings, and traffic.

VERBS NOT USED IN THE PASSIVE

The object in an active sentence becomes the subject in a passive one; therefore, only verbs that can take objects (transitive verbs) can be used in the passive. Because of their meanings, verbs like *happen*, *occur*, *come*, *seem*, *fall*, *live*, and *die* do not take objects; they cannot be used in passive sentences.

INCORRECT: The story *was happened* in San Francisco.

CORRECT: The story *happened* in San Francisco.

Some verbs, such as *change* and *develop*, can be transitive or intransitive depending on the way they are used. When these verbs have an intransitive meaning, they are not used in passive sentences.

TRANSITIVE: The move to the United States *changed* the family's lifestyle. (active)

The family's lifestyle *was changed* by the move to the United States. (passive)

INTRANSITIVE: The way they celebrated holidays *changed*, for example. (no passive)

CHECKPOINT 4 

A. Make up sentences using the given cues. If the verb is transitive, write an active and a passive sentence; if it is intransitive, write an active sentence. Use the tense given in parentheses. Examples:

Grandpa/send/the money (past)
Grandpa sent the money. The money was sent by Grandpa.

Grandma/come/when she was young (past)
Grandma came when she was young. (no passive form)

1. She/often serve/tea and cakes(past)
2. Annabelle/not alter/the story (future)
3. Annabelle's grandparents/come/to the United States/in 1949 (past)
4. Grandpa/give Grandma/new American clothes (past)
5. Immigrants' lifestyles/change/in their new countries (present)

B. Return to paragraph 8 of *Yokohama, California* (page 206) and underline the verbs, most of which are active. Rewrite at least three active sentences as passive ones.

II Focus on Progressive and Perfect Passives

Progressive Forms of the Passive

Transitive verbs cannot be used passively in all forms and tenses. For example, the progressive form of the future tense is not used in the passive. Only the present and past progressive forms can be made passive.

The passive progressive consists of a form of *be* + *being* + the *-ed/-en* form.

Tea *is being served* to the visitors.

Kimonos *were being worn* in Japan but not in the United States.

CHECKPOINT 5 

A. Use the cues to form passive sentences that contain verbs in the present progressive.

Situation: The Japanese woman and her husband are moving into the bathhouse in Oakland. They are working hard to get the house ready. Example:

> blankets/spread/floor
> Blankets *are being spread* on the floor.

1. boxes/move/living room
2. albums/place/bookshelves
3. furniture/arrange
4. bedroom/paint

B. Underline the progressive verbs in the following sentences and change them from active to passive. Make other necessary changes. Omit the *by*-phrase where possible. Pay attention to tense (present versus past) and subject–verb agreement. Example:

> In Hong Kong, developers are expanding residential and industrial land use rapidly because of the great population and economic growth there.

> In Hong Kong, residential and industrial land use *is being expanded* rapidly because of the great population and economic growth there.

1. During the 1900's, the government was not requiring Hong Kong citizens to educate their children formally.
2. Now, the government is placing great emphasis on education at all levels.
3. For hundreds of years most Hong Kong farmers were growing rice, but vegetables are the primary crop today.
4. The travel industry in Hong Kong is promoting the city as a tourist attraction and an ideal location for international conferences.

PERFECT PASSIVES

The perfect passive consists of a form of *have* + *been* + the *-ed/-en* form.

> An agreement turning Hong Kong over to China in 1997 *has been signed.*

> Hong Kong *had been controlled* by the Chinese until the British took over in 1842.

> It *will have been governed* by the British for over 150 years in 1997.

Checkpoint 6

A.

Write and practice a role play to be performed by four students for the class. Write passive questions and answers that contain verbs in the present perfect tense. Each group member takes the role of one of these characters: Mrs. Lee, Mr. Lee, Henry, and Jane.

Situation: Mrs. Lee is preparing for a tea party at her house. Everyone in her family is supposed to be helping her get ready. She asks family members if they have completed their tasks. They answer either in the affirmative or the negative. Example :

floor/sweep

Mrs. Lee: Henry, *has* the floor *been swept*?

Henry: Not yet. The floor *hasn't been swept*. But I'll do it soon.

Mrs. Lee: *You are very nervous about the tea party. You want to make sure the following tasks have been done.*

guests/invite	*glasses/clean*
floor/sweep	*dishes/wash*
soup/heat	*furniture/dust*
bowls/put out	*rice/steam*
flowers/arrange	*tea/make*
cake/cut	*silver/polish*

Mr. Lee: *You are Mrs. Lee's husband. You have been given most of the cleaning jobs, and about half your work has been completed.*

Jane Lee: *You are Mrs. Lee's daughter. You have been given most of the kitchen and food preparation work to do. You have worked very hard; almost all of your tasks have been finished. You try to impress your mother with your efforts.*

Henry Lee: *You are Mrs. Lee's son. You have been assigned several tasks. You are busy and have done nothing to help.*

B.

Underline each perfect form verb in the following sentences about the history of Taiwan; then change it to passive. Pay attention to subject–verb agreement with present perfect verbs (*have* vs. *has*). Example:

Aborigines, or native people, had inhabited Taiwan before Chinese from the mainland came to live on the island.

Taiwan *had been inhabited* by aborigines, or native people, before Chinese from the mainland came to live on the island.

1. Before Dutch traders arrived and took control of a Taiwanese port in 1624, Chinese inhabitants had formed large settlements, or early cities.
2. When Koxinga, a Chinese Ming dynasty official, drove the Dutch out, Manchu soldiers had overthrown the Ming dynasty in mainland China.
3. The first Chinese-Japanese War occurred at the end of the nineteenth century, and by 1900 the Japanese had gained control of Taiwan.
4. Since the Chinese communists defeated Chiang Kai-shek's army in 1949 on the mainland, the nationalists have maintained a separate government on Taiwan.

III Focus on Stative Passives

Stative Passives

When a passive construction describes a state or situation rather than an action, it is called a *stative passive*. In the stative passive, no action is taking place; instead, the action has already occurred. Therefore, the stative passive often serves to describe a condition. The *-ed/-en* form in a stative passive acts as an adjective although it is part of a verb phrase. Compare the following sentences.

She told the story when she was *sad.*

She told the story when she was *bored.*

She told the story when she *was bored* by her work.

In the first sentence, *sad* is obviously an adjective. *Bored* in the second and third sentences is parallel to *sad* in that it describes the state or condition of the subject "she." In the third sentence, *bored* modifies "she," but a *by*-phrase follows it. In this case, "bored" acts as both an adjective and a verb. Other examples of the stative passive are given in the following sentences.

The door of the bathhouse was *locked.*

One of the cups was *broken.*

Three of their children are *married*; one *is divorced.*

Using *Get* to Form Stative Passives

The verbs *get* and, less frequently, *become* may be used to form stative passives. They replace the form of *be*. In the following sentences, the *-ed/-en* forms act as adjectives modifying the subject:

The grandparents *got married* in China. Annabelle *will get married* in the United States.

Grandma never *got tired* of writing letters to her neighbors in Japan.

Grandma's spirits *were becoming dampened* about living in San Francisco.

CHECKPOINT 7

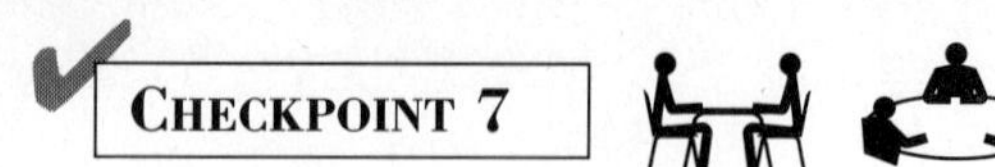

A. Complete the following paragraph with the passive form of the verbs in parentheses. Use either the present or past tense. When you finish, identify the stative passives (*-ed/-en* forms used as adjectives).

Feng shui is the ancient Chinese practice of placing and designing buildings to bring good luck. It (*invent*) ____________ about three thousand years ago. In modern Hong Kong, *feng shui* experts (*consult*) ____________ by over 80 percent of the Chinese residents. According to Prof. Tunney Lee of Hong Kong University, people in Hong Kong (*scare*) ____________ to do without *feng shui*. "It's a way of coping," he says. Apparently, the western residents of Hong Kong (*not, shock*) ____________ by it. Many of them (*attract*) ____________ to the possibility that it will bring them good fortune.

Mao Zedong tried to eliminate *feng shui*, which (*consider*) ____________ a superstition for years, but the practice (*not, yet, lose*) ____________ . It (now, *practice*) ____________ openly again in many places. Sung Siu-Kuong, a *feng shui* expert, claims it "is about direction and placement. It (*not, relate*) ____________ to the supernatural."

B. Re-read Paragraph 21 in *Yokohama, California* (page 206–207) and find the three stative passives.

ACTIVE AND PASSIVE MEANING: -ING AND -ED/-EN FORMS

Like the *-ed/-en* forms of verbs, the *-ing* forms can also be used as adjectives.

She heard that the food in San Francisco was strange and *enticing*.

She found the city *frightening* but *exciting*.

The *-ing* form suggests *cause*, while the *-ed/-en* form suggests *result* or *effect*. In the following active sentences, the adjective forms made from the verb are active in meaning when they refer to the subject (performer); they are passive in meaning when they refer to the object (receiver).

Active Sentence: The book *Yokohama, California* has fascinated many readers.

The book is *fascinating*.

Its readers are *fascinated* [by the book].

Active Sentence: The story about the Japanese acrobat's American wife didn't bore the grandchildren.

The story wasn't *boring*.

The grandchildren weren't *bored* [by the story].

In a few cases, the *-ing* form of a verb is not used as an adjective; for example, *delightful* is used instead of *delighting*, and *scary* instead of *scaring*.

The grandmother's experiences in San Francisco were *scary* at first.

Later on, she spent *delightful* afternoons drinking tea with her American friend.

Checkpoint 8 

Read the situation and then fill in the blanks with the appropriate form (*-ing* or *-ed-/en*) of the verb in parentheses.

Situation: The grandchildren never get tired of hearing the story of their grandmother's immigration to the United States.

Grandmother: Don't you ever get (*bore*) ________________ hearing the same story over and over?

Annabelle: It's the best, most (*interest*) ________________ story in the world.

Johnny: My favorite part is the boat trip. It must have been kind of (*scare*) ________________.

Annabelle: Weren't you (*frighten*) ________________ to leave home alone?

Grandmother: Yes, a little. Okay, you are such (*delight*) ________________ children that I'll tell the story one last time.

IV Focus on Special Uses of Passives

Passives with Prepositions Other Than *By*

In some common passive expressions, a preposition other than *by* is used.

Passives with Prepositions Other Than *By*

be	accustomed *to*	be	finished *with*
	ashamed *of*		interested *in*
	composed *of*		opposed *to*
	committed *to*		made (up) *of*
	covered *with* (*by*)		married *to*
	dedicated *to*		satisfied *with*
	devoted *to*		scared/frightened *of* (*by*)
	disappointed *in* (*by*)		terrified *of*
	divorced *from*		tired *of*
	dressed *in*		used *to*
	excited *about*		worried *about*

The group *was composed of* neighbors who wanted her to stay.

They *were excited about* going to the United States.

He hauled me around as if he *were ashamed of* me.

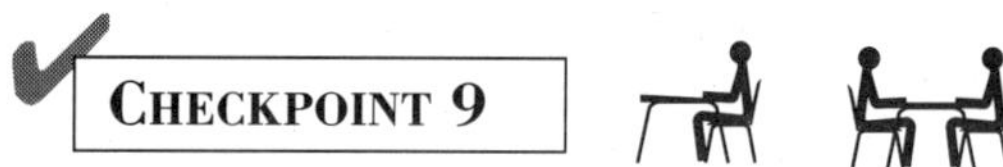

CHECKPOINT 9

A. Complete the sentences with the passive form of one of the verbs plus the appropriate preposition. Use the past tense.

accustom	satisfy
disappoint	interest
scare	tire

1. The couple moved to Oakland because they ____________________ the people who threw rocks at their house.
2. When the Japanese woman first saw San Francisco, she ____________________ the brown hills.
3. The acrobat, her neighbor, told the woman his wife ____________________ becoming her friend.
4. The neighbor ____________________ never ____________________ her tea and cakes.
5. Because of this friendship, the Japanese woman ____________________ her new country.
6. When the Japanese woman had a baby, she ____________________ her life.

B. Complete the sentences with the passive form of one of the verbs plus the appropriate preposition. Use any tense.

dedicate	marry
disappoint	cover
make	

1. The Taj Mahal in India was built by the Shah Jahan and ____________________ his wife, Mumtaz Mahal.
2. He ____________________ other women, but she was his favorite.
3. The tomb ____________________ white marble resting on a redstone platform with a prayer tower, or minaret, at each corner.
4. The center of the tomb ____________________ a dome.
5. No one who visits this magnificent structure ____________________ it.

Be Used to Versus *Used to*

The expressions *be used to* and *be accustomed to* should not be confused with *used to*, which is a way of expressing past tense. *Be used to* is followed by a gerund or *-ing* form, while *used to* is followed by a base-form verb.

> The woman *was used/accustomed to wearing* kimonos in Japan.
>
> *Did* she *use to wear* kimonos? Yes, she *used to wear* them, but now she wears dresses.

✔ Checkpoint 10

Fill in the blanks with the appropriate form (base form or *-ing* form) of the verb in parentheses.

1. Women in Vietnam used to (*wear*) ____________ the traditional costume, the *ao dai*, and many still do.
2. On festival mornings, people in Hue are used to (*see*) ____________ young women dressed in *ao dais* while riding their bicycles.
3. A guide in Vietnam said that many tourists used to (*think*) ____________ that Vietnamese clothing was just like that worn in China, but it isn't.
4. This nation of over 70 million people used to (*be*) ____________ isolated from the rest of the world; in the early 1990s it decided to open up again.
5. Journalists and filmmakers are attracted to the romance of this country where inhabitants are used to (*travel*) ____________ by rickshaw and bicycle.

Passives with Indirect Objects

Verbs that have direct and indirect objects (*tell, send, give,* etc.) can follow two patterns in the passive. The meaning is the same, but the emphasis is different, with the noun or pronoun in the subject position receiving greater emphasis.

ACTIVE:	Her husband gave her a dress.
	She *was given* a dress by her husband.
PASSIVE:	A dress *was given* to her by her husband.

Sometimes no agent or *by*-phrase accompanies the passive verb with an indirect object.

ACTIVE:	Someone *sent* her money for a ticket.
PASSIVE:	She *was sent* money for a ticket.
	Money for a ticket *was sent* to her.

Rewrite the following active sentences about the U.S. image of Vietnam. Put each in the passive in two different ways; if the *by*-phrase is not important, omit it. Example:

Thirty years ago, everyone *asked* politicians the question "Why are we in Vietnam?"

Thirty years ago, politicians *were asked*, "Why are we in Vietnam?"

Thirty years ago, the question "Why are we in Vietnam?" *was asked.*

1. Today, travelers to Vietnam give people who ask that question a very different answer from the old one.
2. Travelers send relatives enthusiastic descriptions of the beautiful, dramatic scenery.
3. Visitors tell their friends back home stories about exciting adventures in the exotic port cities of Vietnam.
4. In the early 1990s, the movie industry gave the U.S. public a romantic view of life in Indochina in the movies *The Lover* and *Indochine.*

Passive Modals

Two patterns are used with modal auxiliaries in the passive voice. Many follow this pattern: modal + *be* + *-ed/-en* form.

Passive Modals

Subject	Modal	Be	*-Ed/-En* Form	Rest of Sentence
She	*will*	*be*	*taught*	English by her friend.
She	*couldn't*	*be*	*persuaded*	to stay in Japan.
Immigrants	*can't*	*be*	*expected*	to understand the culture completely.
"Children	*should*	*be*	*seen, not heard."*	

Some past tense modals follow this pattern: modal + *have been* + *-ed/-en* form.

Visits from neighbors *would have been appreciated* by the Japanese woman.

Rocks *shouldn't have been thrown* at their windows.

Checkpoint 12

Change the following sentences to the passive voice. Delete the agent if appropriate. Example:

Children can usually learn languages more easily than adults.

Languages can usually be learned more easily by children than by adults.

1. High schools and community centers may offer adults language instruction.
2. Second language learners can pick up useful idioms from conversation.
3. Grandmother could have viewed her friendship with the American woman as an opportunity to work on her English.
4. Practicing with her friend would have helped Grandmother with pronunciation and vocabulary especially.

Causative Passives with *Have*

The verb *have* may be used to require or suggest that someone do something. This is called a *causative* expression, which can be active or passive. Usually the agent (*by*-phrase) is omitted in the passive.

ACTIVE: Grandma *had* someone *make* tea.

PASSIVE: Grandma *had* tea *made.*

ACTIVE: She *had* her daughter *do* her hair.

PASSIVE: She *had* her hair *done.*

Checkpoint 13

Change the causative expressions from active to passive. Example:

She *had* someone *make* a dress.

She *had* a dress *made.*

1. They had someone send flowers.
2. Mrs. Liao had someone prepare some egg drop soup.
3. Mari had a mechanic fix her car.
4. Takahashi had someone type his report.

PART THREE. Review and Integration

Ethnic Asians in Hawaii: When to Use Passive

Read the following sentences and discuss the appropriateness of the passive forms. Would any of them sound clearer or more natural if they were replaced by active verbs? If so, change them. If not, leave them in the passive. Be prepared to explain your decisions to the class.

1. When the 1990 U.S. census was taken, only Hawaii had a majority ethnic Asian population.
2. The largest Asian group that was counted was the Japanese (about 25%). Other large population groups there are Polynesians (the original settlers of Hawaii), Filipinos, Chinese, Koreans, and Samoans.
3. Hawaii is the only state that was once ruled by monarchs (Polynesian kings and queens).
4. Hawaii's economy is almost totally dedicated to service industries, especially tourism.
5. Pineapples (which were imported from Jamaica) and sugar cane are grown there.
6. English is spoken by almost all residents of Hawaii.
7. Many Hawaiian words are commonly used there, such as *luau* (feast) and *hula* (native dance).
8. Hawaii has been called a tropical paradise.
9. Hawaii was named the fiftieth state in 1959.

Asians in the United States: Changing Active to Passive

Rewrite the following paragraph, changing sentences to the passive where possible. Compare your version with other groups'.

Many Asians have achieved the American dream. Korean-Americans operate hundreds of small grocery stores in big U.S. cities. Indian-Americans run many of the small hotels on the West Coast and elsewhere. Indians and Pakistanis own newsstands and card shops in New York City. Cambodians control the doughnut-shop business in California. Vietnamese are a major force in the fishing industry along the Texas and Louisiana gulf coasts. People in the U.S. recognize the achievements of Asian Americans.

The "Model Minority": *-ing* vs *-ed/-en* Forms

Read the following passage. Then do the exercise that follows.

In the mid-1960's, when relaxed restrictions dramatically increased Asian immigration to the United States, the popular press, politicians, and others assigned Asian-Americans the role of "model minority." When the 1980 census

revealed that median family income for Asian-Americans actually surpassed that of whites by almost 13%, the stories surfaced with renewed intensity. . . .

The model-minority label, enviable though it might seem, has served Asian-Americans badly. It obscures real differences among Asian-Americans and exacerbates the resentment of other minority groups.

Now fill in the blanks with the *-ing* or *-ed/-en* form of the verb in parentheses based on the information in the excerpt or other information provided.

1. In the mid-1960's, U.S. restrictions on immigration were (*relax*) ____________________.
2. The stereotype that all Asians are successful in the United States is (*damage*) ____________________ to those who have problems and need help.
3. Some groups, like the Hmong tribespeople from Laos, are (*limit*) ____________________ in their ability to succeed in the United States because they are not literate.
4. Articles written after the 1980 census presented an (*exaggerate*) ____________________ view of Asian-Americans' success.
5. The figures about Asian-Americans are (*interest*) ____________________ but misleading. Asian-Americans' family incomes are higher than the average, but their individual incomes are lower.
6. Because many Asian-American families are large, there are more wage earners per family; for example, most teenagers in these families are (*earn*) ____________________ money at part-time or even full-time jobs.
7. Many Asian-Americans are well (*educate*) ____________________. The 1980 census showed that 34% of them completed at least four years of college; the U.S. national average was 16%.
8. However, three times as many Asians as whites had not finished elementary school, a (*surprise*) ____________________ number.
9. A study by the U.S. Civil Rights Commission found the (*follow*) ____________________ results.
10. Among similarly (*qualify*) ____________________ men, Chinese men earned 5% less than white men, Filipinos 7% less, and Indians 30% less.

Role Play: Using Passives

Work in groups of five. Each member of the group takes the role of one of the characters and practices using verbs in the passive voice.

Situation: The Moriyamas are a close family, but two members (Lucy and Dave) live in different cities. Therefore, the whole family rarely has a chance to get together. They have all gathered for a family dinner at Harriet and Edward Moriyama's house in San Francisco. Every member of the family wants to find out as much as possible about what's happening in the lives of the others.

Harriet Moriyama, 53, wife of Edward. *You have just been left a fortune ($2,500,000) by your uncle Takahashi in Japan. You are excited and happy.*

Edward Moriyama, 55, husband of Harriet. *You have just been promoted to president of Harriet's father's bank. You are pleased and proud.*

Lucy Moriyama, 21, daughter of Edward and Harriet. *You were voted "Most Likely to Succeed" by your class at a famous university when you were a senior. You are being considered for a fellowship to an excellent graduate school. You are delighted.*

Larry Moriyama, 18, son of Edward and Harriet. *You are in a rock band. Your grades at the high school where you are a senior are poor. You were warned last week that you may be suspended or even expelled. You are scared.*

Dave Hirasawa, 75, father of Harriet Moriyama. *You were widowed last year after 52 years of marriage. You have recently retired from the bank where you were president. You are satisfied with your life.*

Suggestions for conversation openers:

Harriet: Lucy, I'm so pleased that you were named "Most Likely to Succeed." Do you know yet if you've been granted a fellowship?

Dave: Harriet, what do you plan to do with the money you have inherited?

Role Play: Getting Acquainted

Work in groups of four. Choose one of the characters below and study the character's accomplishments. As a group, write and practice a role play to perform for the whole class.

Situation: Hedy Hoop is giving a party for some friends who have never met each other. All the guests try to get acquainted as quickly as possible by introducing themselves and asking questions to start conversations. They use a number of verbs in the passive voice in an effort to "break the ice," or get acquainted.

Hedy Hoop, 45, actress, Hollywood. Accomplishments: starring roles in 26 films, three Academy Awards, parts in eight Broadway plays, praise from theater and film critics, author of best-selling autobiography

Walter Winter, 65, journalist, New York City. Accomplishments: anchor man for a leading TV network, many awards for journalism, frequent guest on talk shows, expert on Middle Eastern affairs

Alan Abel, 34, astronaut, Florida. Accomplishments: five space missions, first man to walk on Mars, head of President's Council on Youth, popular public speaker

Betsy Fogel, 60, U.S. Senator, New Jersey. Accomplishments: first African-American woman elected to the senate, head of powerful committee on the national budget, early feminist leader, author of four best sellers on women's issues, role model to millions of young women

Example:

Betsy: You must be Alan Abel, the astronaut. I've been told that you . . .

Alan: Yes, it's true. By the way, I read that article about you that . . .

Facts About India and Taiwan: Asking Questions in the Passive

Based on the information on India and Taiwan in the table, write six questions that contain verbs in the passive voice. Exchange papers with another group and answer that group's questions. Share your answers with the whole class. Examples:

How many languages *are spoken* in India?

Is rice *grown* in Taiwan?

India and Taiwan

	India	Taiwan
Languages	English, and 14 regional dialects	Northern Chinese, or Mandarin
Agricultural products	bananas, mangoes, sugar cane, beans, potatoes, rice, wheat, tea, and cotton	bananas, pineapples, citrus fruit, vegetables, tea, sugar cane
Manufactured products	brassware, silverware, cement, chemicals, clothing, textiles, iron, steel, leather goods, machinery, paper, rugs, wool products	calculators, radios, television, clothing, iron, steel, toys, plastic goods
Money (basic unit)	rupee	yuan

Research Projects

A. Go to the library and look up information about one Asian group (Koreans, Chinese, Japanese, etc.). Write a report and share it with the class. Answer such questions as the following:

What language(s) is/are spoken by the group?

What crops are grown in this group's country?

What religions or philosophies and political system(s) are followed?

B. Research a well-known Asian-American, write a short report on him or her, and present it to the class. Possible subjects: Yoko Ono, S. I. Hayakawa, Connie Chung, Bruce Lee.

Suggestions for Writing

1. If you are keeping a journal, write an entry about one or more of the following: the behavior of U.S. women (or wives) versus that of Asian women (wives), games or sports (like karate) brought to the United States by people of other

cultures, stereotypes Americans have about Asians or about other immigrant groups.

2. Imagine that you are an immigrant who has just arrived in a new country. Write a paragraph or composition about your experiences. Use as many of the following verbs in passive constructions as possible: *fascinate*, *interest*, *bore*, *scare*, *disappoint*, *be used to*, *satisfy*.
3. Write a composition describing a journey to another country taken by you or by a relative or acquaintance. If you wish, contrast the journey with that of the couple whose story is told in *Yokohama, California*.
4. Write a composition in which you explain the concept of "the melting pot" and discuss advantages and/or disadvantages. Give several examples.
5. Write a composition agreeing or disagreeing with the concept of Asians as a "model minority." Is this phrase an accurate description or simply a stereotype? Does it help Asian residents of the United States, or does it harm them? Explain and give examples.

Unit Seven

ADVANCED SENTENCE STRUCTURE

READING: "No Longer New York Cool" by Joanne Sherman

THEME: U.S. Cities

PART ONE. The Context

The following article from the magazine *Southern Living* describes a writer's experiences in two American cities, New York and New Orleans. By deliberately exaggerating the differences between them, the author creates a humorous contrast between northern and southern attitudes in the United States.

Pre-Reading Questions

1. Of the cities in the United States that you are familiar with, which are considered the friendliest? Which are known as the least friendly?
2. What do you enjoy most about visiting a new city?
3. What was the best time you ever had visiting a new city? The worst? Explain your answers.
4. What cities are you interested in visiting in the future? Why?
5. When people think of a city, they may think of a certain landmark, a famous district, or a memorable experience. Paris, for example, is known for the Eiffel Tower, the Left Bank, and outstanding food. What comes to mind when you think of famous U.S. cities—for instance, Boston, New York, New Orleans, Chicago, Dallas, San Francisco, Los Angeles?

Preview of Key Terms and Concepts

The following idiomatic expressions appear in the reading. Guess the meaning of the expressions on the left by matching them to the definitions on the right. Put the correct letter in the blank after the expression.

1. lose one's cool ____
2. chip on one's shoulder ____
3. make eye contact ____
4. within striking distance ____
5. strike up a conversation ____
6. in retrospect ____
7. brace oneself ____
8. over the course of ____

a. during
b. at close range
c. looking back in time
d. begin speaking to someone
e. meet someone's gaze
f. resentful attitude
g. fail to maintain one's dignity or self-control
h. prepare oneself for something unpleasant or difficult

READING: "No Longer New York Cool" by Joanne Sherman

(1) I am a New Yorker. I know everything. I have cultivated* aloofness* to an art and carry a colossal* chip on my shoulder. I can walk five city blocks during lunch hour without the hint of a smile or making eye contact. I'm slick* and sophisticated, seldom impressed, able to spot a phony through a brick wall, and automatically assume that **everyone** is out to take advantage of me. If an unrelated person acts the least bit friendly I am immediately suspicious.* I'm a New Yorker and I'm darn good at it. At least I was until I spent five days in New Orleans.

(2) When the opportunity to attend the Tennessee Williams* New Orleans Literary Festival and Writers' Conference came about, I took it. Not because it was in New Orleans, but because I was desperate to get away from frigid* New York if only for a few days.

(3) The first indication that this would be an unusual trip occurred right outside the New Orleans airport. In New York, one stops a cab by stepping directly in its speeding path. It's a game we play; whoever reacts first, either by moving or stopping, loses. I had not signaled for a cab when a long Cadillac the color of a cherry popsicle* glided* to a stop and from it emerged* a smiling driver who walked toward me. I didn't panic. New Yorkers do not panic; we brace ourselves. As soon as he was within striking distance, I merely planned to hit the bridge* of his nose, a maneuver* guaranteed to stun attackers by driving their sinuses into their brains. The grinning man reached for my bags, then held open the door to the backseat. Only after assurances from the airport employees did I climb into the cherry Cadillac/cab. The driver never stopped smiling and carried on a 15-minute one-way conversation. When we arrived at my Canal Street hotel, he said "It's been a pleasure meeting you." There was no hint of sarcasm* in that man's voice or his smiling eyes, and even though I'm well trained, so very well trained, I couldn't keep from smiling back.

(4) The desk clerk was a smiler too. I bit my lips to keep from returning her smile as I waited to hear that there was no reservation for me. I had spent my entire flight rehearsing* arguments, mentally mixing the proper amounts of

---

* cultivated	carefully developed or grown
aloofness	coldness, unfriendliness
colossal	very large
slick	clever, worldly; not easily tricked
suspicious	doubting
Tennessee Williams	well-known playwright associated with the South
frigid	very cold (climate or attitude)
popsicle	sweet-flavored ice on a stick
glided	moved smoothly or slowly
emerged	came out
bridge	upper part of the bone in the nose
maneuver	movement or action
sarcasm	unkind or bitter humor
rehearsing	practicing

anger and indignation.* It was time wasted. The woman was thrilled to see me, and my name was on her list.

(5) After unpacking, I went to the fourth floor to register for the conference. Approaching the table reserved for "M thru Z" attendees, I gave my name to the woman on the other side. She, like the cabby and the desk clerk, was downright* tickled* to see me. She introduced herself, and everyone else within sight. It was a pleasant experience, though I was sure they had me confused with someone important.

(6) By the end of my first day in New Orleans, I had given up the last shreds* of aloofness. I smiled back at everyone, and a few times I found myself smiling first. Cheek cramps* kept me awake a good part of the night. During the next few days I struck up conversations with strangers everywhere.

(7) Over the course of my brief stay in New Orleans I made more new friends than I had in the previous five years. Two of the coffee-shop waitresses are now on my Christmas-card list.

(8) Although there were people attending the Writers' Conference from all over the country, the majority I met were from New Orleans and neighboring towns. I felt drawn toward* them. The word "warmth" does not adequately* convey* what radiated* from them. It was a warmth and a magnetism; it was "Southernness," and I could actually feel myself being enveloped by it. It felt real good.

(9) Several years ago, while on a three-hour bus ride to Long Island, I sat beside a man who sported* a Rolex watch, gold cuff links, and buffed fingernails. He smelled successful and rich, and, oh, so sophisticated. Of course, we never spoke. Near our destination he suddenly lunged* across me to press his face against the window.

(10) "Look!" he shouted, his voice high as he pointed to a small object by some trees. "Look! A bunny!"

(11) I looked. I had no choice, he turned my head for me. Everyone else pretended they hadn't witnessed the gentleman's temporary* lapse.* He

---

indignation	anger from losing one's dignity
downright	thoroughly
tickled	very pleased
shreds	small strips or pieces, as in torn cloth
cramps	muscle pains
drawn toward	attracted to
adequately	enough, sufficiently
convey	communicate
radiated	shone out from, like light or heat
sported	wore to appear fashionable
lunged	stretched forward suddenly
temporary	for a short time, not permanent
lapse	change from usual behavior

mumbled* an apology and buried his red face in the *Wall Street Journal*, obviously horrified* at his outburst.*

(12) In retrospect, what happened to him and what happened to me in New Orleans were the same; we lost our New York cool. He recovered his immediately, but not I. When I came back East, I was smiling. I am still smiling, still feeling their warmth and friendliness.

(13) I don't care that some of my New York acquaintances* think I should see an analyst.* I'm indebted to the people I met in New Orleans for affecting me, or perhaps infecting me, with their warmth and their friendliness.

(14) Of course I realize that New Orleans is merely a place, a geographical location. But it's not where a place happens to sit on a map that makes it unique or memorable, or even "Southern"—it's the attitude of the people who populate the place. What's really Southern about New Orleans is the people who live and work in that city, and welcome its visitors. Even without the Mississippi, or po' boys, or Bourbon Street, New Orleans would be memorable. Because the people are.

(15) Really. I know what I'm talking about. I'm a New Yorker. I might not be so cool and aloof anymore, but I still know everything.

Comprehension Questions

1. Why did the author go to New Orleans?
2. How did she get to her hotel?
3. What happened at the reception desk?
4. What does the author mean by "cheek cramps" (Paragraph 6)?
5. Why was the man from New York embarrassed by his behavior on the bus ride to Long Island?
6. In what way was the author changed by her visit to New Orleans?

Discussion Questions

1. In what region of the United States would you like to spend a vacation? Which are the most important cities in that region? What are they known for?
2. Cities such as New York, New Orleans, Chicago, and Houston were founded for various reasons. What are some of the conditions that lead to the development of cities? How do these conditions relate to geography and to the economy of the region in which they are located?

---

* **mumbled**	spoke unclearly, quietly
horrified	very shocked, upset
outburst	sudden expression of emotion
acquaintances	people one knows, but not well
analyst	psychoanalyst, psychiatrist

3. What are the most famous cities in the world? What are they known for? Why do people want to visit them?
4. How can visitors to a country find out about the culture? What are the best ways to meet natives? What kinds of places or activities do visitors to a new country/area want to learn about or experience?

PART TWO. The Target Structure: Advanced Sentence Structure

Preview of Identifying Subjects

With a partner or group, read the following sentences and draw a line separating the subject and predicate. (Return to Unit One on Basic Sentence Structure if you need to review these terms.) Underline the complete subject, and discuss the kinds of structures that subjects can include.

1. The writers' conference was held in New Orleans.
2. The majority I met were from New Orleans or neighboring towns.
3. It lasted five days.
4. Stepping directly in the path of a speeding cab must be typical behavior in New York.
5. To stop a cab is not always easy.
6. Whoever reacts first loses.

I Focus on Identifying Subjects

Subjects and How to Identify Them

Identifying a complete subject is not always an easy task. Forming a YES/NO question provides a method for doing this. In the question, the part of the sentence that the auxiliary or verb "moves before" is the subject. The complete subjects of the sample sentences above can be identified by using this technique, as in the examples below; in the sentences that require the auxiliary *do*, *does*, or *did* to form a question, the auxiliary is inserted first, then moved in front of the subject, which is underlined.

1. The writers' conference was held in New Orleans.

Was	the writer's conference	[was] held in New Orleans?
(auxiliary)	(subject)	

2. The majority I met were from New Orleans.

Were (auxiliary) the majority I met (subject) [were] from New Orleans?

3. It lasted (did last) for five days. It [did] last for five days.

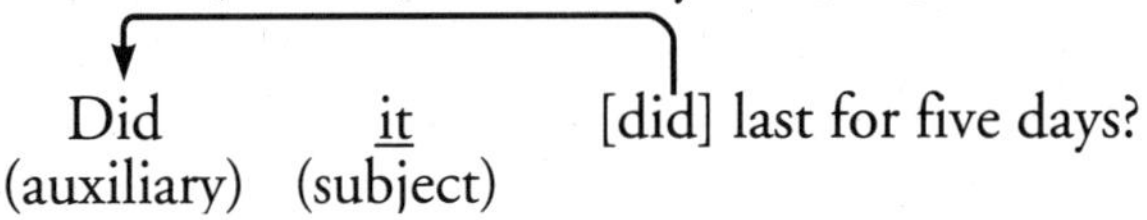

Did (auxiliary) it (subject) [did] last for five days?

4. Stepping directly in the path of a speeding cab could be typical behavior in New York City.

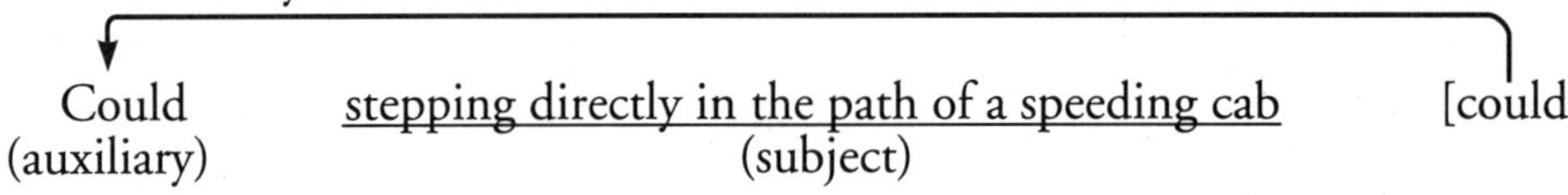

Could (auxiliary) stepping directly in the path of a speeding cab (subject) [could] be typical behavior in New York City?

5. To stop a cab is not always easy.

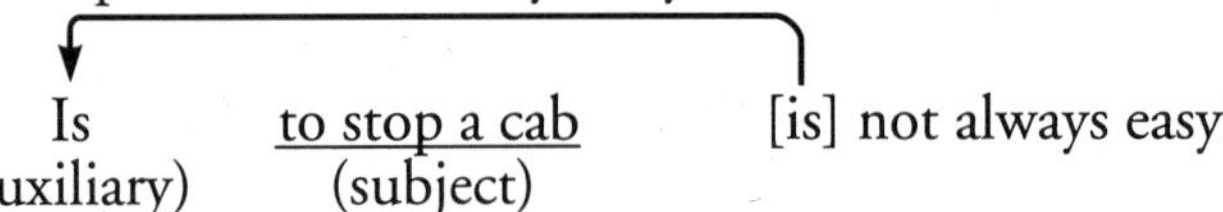

Is (auxiliary) to stop a cab (subject) [is] not always easy?

6. Whoever reacts first loses (does lose).

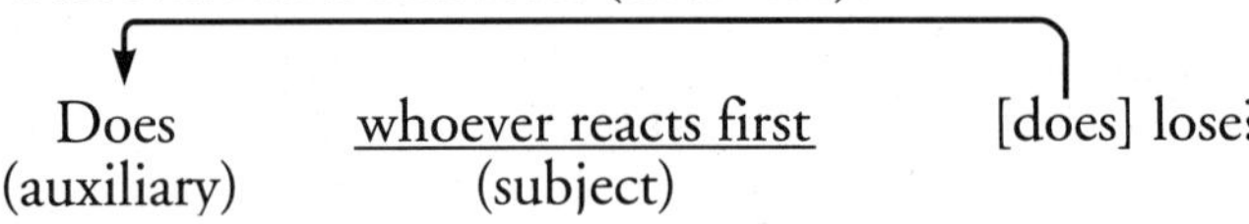

Does (auxiliary) whoever reacts first (subject) [does] lose?

CHECKPOINT 1

A.

Find the subject of each sentence by forming a YES/NO question. Underline the complete subject, and then write the question. (The number of the paragraph in which each sentence occurs is given in parentheses.) Example:

New Yorkers do not panic. (3)

Do New Yorkers not panic?

1. The grinning man reached for my bags. (3)

____

2. I had spent my entire flight rehearsing arguments. (4)

____

3. It was time wasted. (4)

____

4. The first indication that this would be an unusual trip occurred right outside the New Orleans airport. (3)

____

____

5. Two of the coffee-shop waitresses are now on my Christmas card list. (7)

____

____

6. What happened to him and what happened to me in New Orleans were the same. (12)

____

____

B.

Reread the six sentences on page 235. After each item below, insert the number of the sentence containing that structure as the subject. Example:

Noun clause (whole clause replacing noun) 6

a. Pronoun ____
b. Noun with modifiers ____
c. Gerund (*-ing* form) phrase ____
d. Infinitive (*to* + base form verb) phrase ____
e. Noun with modifying clause ____

Types of Subjects: Pronouns, Infinitives, and Gerunds

Three common noun substitutes can act as subjects: pronouns of various types and two types of "verbals"—infinitives and gerunds. The simplest substitutes are personal pronouns (*I, you, he, she, it, we*, and *they*), demonstrative pronouns (*this, that, these*, and *those*), and indefinite pronouns such as *each, everybody, everyone, anybody, anyone, somebody, someone.* (For more information about pronouns, review Unit Two, pages 56–58.)

II Focus on Infinitives and Gerunds as Subjects

Verbals Used as Subjects

Infinitives and gerunds are *verbals* that can substitute for nouns. They are called verbals because they are derived from verbs and have certain characteristics in common with verbs; for example, they can have objects or complements. When infinitives and gerunds are used as *nouns*, they can act as subjects as well as objects or complements.

Active Infinitives as Subjects

Active infinitives consist of *to* + the base form of a verb: *to stop, to go, to decide.* Negative infinitives are preceded by *not*: *not to stop, not to go, not to decide.* The sentences below include infinitives as subjects, each of which is followed by an object.

Infinitive + Object / Predicate

To visit New Orleans at Mardi Gras / is great fun.

To know New Orleans / is to love it.

To find such courteous people in New Orleans / was a surprise to the writer.

Very often in English, the infinitive subject does not appear at the beginning of the sentence; the pattern *It* + form of *be* + *adjective* or *noun* precedes the infinitive, as in the following.

It is not easy *to stop* a cab.

It was a surprise to the writer *to find* such courteous people in New Orleans.

When a sentence has an infinitive as both subject and complement (*To know* New Orleans is *to love* it), the sentence cannot be changed to begin with *It.*

Other Forms of Infinitives

Besides the active form, infinitives can have passive and progressive forms. The passive infinitive is composed of *to be* + the *-ed/-en* form of the verb: *to be stopped, to be done, to be decided.* A *by*-phrase identifying the agent or "doer" of the action expressed by the infinitive may or may not be added. Infinitives can also be progressive; they are composed of *to be* + the *-ing* form of the verb: *to be stopping, to be going, to be deciding.*

Forms of Infinitives	
Active	*To stop* a cab is not easy.
	It would be a shame *not to visit* New Orleans while you're traveling in the South.
Passive	She needs *to be driven* to her hotel.
Progressive	The tourists appear *to be enjoying* themselves.

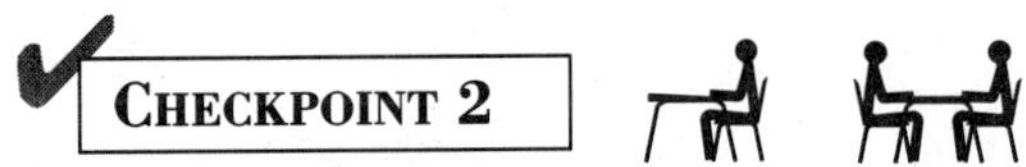

Change the following sentences that begin with infinitives to sentences with the pattern *It* + form of *be* + *adjective* or *noun.* Examples:

To visit a city as huge as New York can be an intimidating experience.

It can be an intimidating experience *to visit* a city as huge as New York.

1. To travel to a new city is an adventure.
2. To explore neighborhoods can be very pleasant.
3. To try new restaurants is usually entertaining.
4. Not to visit Greenwich Village in New York would be a mistake.
5. Not to know your way around New York could prove frustrating.
6. To be informed about U.S. cities requires some research.
7. To be traveling by train can be relaxing.
8. To experience the variety of U.S. cities takes some effort and a lot of traveling.
9. To talk with local people is always interesting.

Forms of Gerunds: Active and Passive

The gerund consists of the *-ing* form of the verb: *stopping, doing, deciding.* Gerunds are distinguished from participles, which also end in *-ing*, by their use; participles are used as adjectives, while gerunds are used as nouns.

> *Deciding* which city in Texas to visit was a difficult task for the Johnson family. (gerund)
>
> Mrs. Johnson cast the *deciding* vote in favor of San Antonio. (participle)

Negative gerunds are preceded by *not.*

> *Not knowing* the language of a country can make traveling there complicated.

Gerunds can have passive forms, composed of *being* + the *-ed/-en* form of the verb: *being stopped, being done, being decided.* Passive gerunds may or may not include a *by*-phrase identifying an agent or doer.

> *Being stopped* by the police in a strange city can be a nerve-wracking experience.
>
> No one enjoys the experience of *being stopped* because of a traffic violation.

Forms of Gerunds	
Active	*Traveling* by car in the United States is easy since most roads are good, especially the interstate highways.
	Not visiting the Lincoln Memorial while in Washington, D.C., would be unfortunate.
Passive	*Being lost* in a big city can be frightening.

GERUNDS AS SUBJECTS

The gerund, like the infinitive, can be used as a subject. The following sentences contain gerund subjects, and each gerund has an object.

Gerund + Object / Predicate

Meeting a friendly cabbie / shocked the author.

Losing his New York cool / embarrassed the man on the bus.

CHECKPOINT 3

Make up sentences with gerunds as subjects based on the cues. Use the singular form if you use a present tense verb. Example:

Visit New Orleans/change/author's opinion of the South.

Visiting New Orleans changed the author's opinion about the South.

1. Eat/coffee shop/be convenient
2. Travel/by cab from the airport to the hotel/seem to be the easiest way
3. Talk/cab driver/give author/some information
4. Attend conference/help/author's career.
5. Tell stories about New Orleans/entertain her friends

III Focus on Types of Predicates

PREDICATES: COMPLEMENTS AND OBJECTS

The *predicate* contains the verb of a clause or sentence and sometimes consists only of that verb.

The truth *hurts.*

The streets *flooded.*

An old, dilapidated building in my neighborhood *was demolished.*

In addition to the verb, a predicate may contain a subject complement construction or an object (direct or indirect) as well as other structures.

SUBJECT COMPLEMENTS

When the main verb of a sentence is a form of *be* or a linking verb, the predicate may be completed by a subject complement: an adjective, noun, or noun substitute that completes the meaning of the subject or is interchangeable with it.

I am *a New Yorker.* (noun used as a subject complement)

I'm *slick* and *sophisticated, seldom impressed.* (adjectives used as subject complements)

He smelled *successful* and *rich.* (adjectives)

It felt *real* [Standard: *really*] *good.* (adjective with modifier)

Adjectives usually follow *be* and linking verbs directly. *To be* is usually inserted before nouns or noun substitutes that follow other linking verbs.

He seemed *friendly.* (adjective as complement)

He seemed *to be* a friendly *cab driver.* (noun phrase as complement)

The waitresses appear *busy.* (adjective as complement)

The waitresses appear *to be* busy *employees.* (noun phrase)

Just as noun substitutes such as pronouns, gerunds, infinitives, or noun clauses can be used as subjects, they can also be used as subject complements.

The author's plan was *to return to New York.* (infinitive)

The most difficult part was *leaving the friendliness of New Orleans.* (gerund)

Her first thought at the airport was *when she could return to this wonderful city.* (noun clause)

CHECKPOINT 4

Return to Paragraphs 1, 5, and 9 of the reading on pages 232 and 233. Circle the predicates with *be* or linking verbs and underline all the subject complements that you find. Discuss the different types of complements used: noun, pronoun, adjective, and verbal (each of which may be accompanied by modifiers). Example:

I am <u>a New Yorker</u>. (noun as complement)

DIRECT OBJECTS

When the main verb of a sentence expresses an action, either mental or physical, it may be followed by an object. When the object receives the action of the verb directly it is called a direct object. Direct objects can be nouns or noun substitutes (pronouns, infinitives, gerunds, and noun clauses).

I know *everything.* (pronoun)

I wanted *to hear that there was a reservation for me.* (infinitive plus modifiers)

I assume *that everyone is out to take advantage of me.* (noun clause)

New Yorkers enjoy *competing for cabs.* (gerund plus modifiers)

CHECKPOINT 5

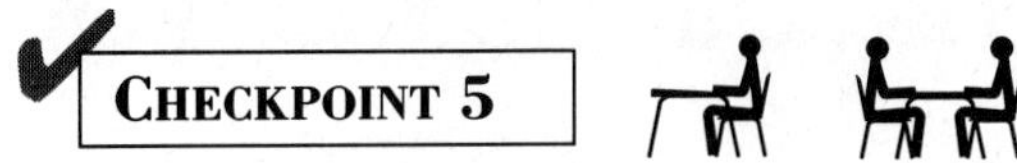

Return to Paragraphs 3, 4, and 11 of the reading on pages 232–234. Circle the action verbs and underline their direct objects, if any. Example:

In New York, one (stops) a cab by stepping directly in its path.

INDIRECT OBJECTS

When an object receives the action of the verb indirectly it is called an indirect object. Like direct objects, indirect objects can be nouns or noun substitutes (pronouns, gerunds, and noun clauses). The following sentence contains two objects, with the indirect object *before* the direct object.

	(indirect)	**(direct)**
I gave	*the desk clerk*	*my name.*
I also gave	*her*	*my credit card.*
The author gave	*what she was writing*	*a lot of thought.*

Often the indirect object, which usually refers to a person, is expressed as the object of a preposition (*to* or *for*). In these cases, the indirect object comes *after* the direct object.

	(direct)	**(indirect)**
I gave	*my name*	*to the desk clerk.*
I also gave	*my credit card*	*to her.*
They bought	*presents*	*for their children.*
She gave	*a lot of thought*	*to what she was writing.*
She devoted	*her life*	*to writing.*

CHECKPOINT 6

Rewrite the following sentences by omitting the underlined preposition and placing the indirect object between the verb and the direct object. Example:

We brought some souvenirs for our relatives.

We brought *our relatives* some souvenirs.

1. The author told interesting stories about her trip to New Orleans *to her friends in New York.*
2. When Christmas came, she remembered to send greeting cards *to the two friendly waitresses.*
3. The cab driver in New Orleans gave a positive impression of the city *to the visitor.*

4. She learned to flash a big smile *at everyone she saw.*
5. The visit to New Orleans gave a new outlook *to the woman from New York.*

(Direct and indirect objects are also discussed in Unit 1, pages 10-14.)

IV Focus on Gerunds and Infinitives as Objects

Both infinitives and gerunds can act as objects of verbs. Certain verbs are followed by gerunds, and others are followed by infinitives. A few verbs can be followed by either form.

Infinitives as Objects

Some common verbs are followed by infinitives, either immediately or after a noun or pronoun used as an indirect object.

Several writers *agreed to meet* in New Orleans again next year.

They *will encourage their friends to make* the trip also.

Verbs Followed by Infinitives

	Verb + Infinitive
agree	She *agreed to go* to New Orleans.
ask	She *asked to see* the city.
decide	She *decided not to panic.*
expect	She *expected to meet* rude people.
hope	She *hopes to return* there some day.
intend	She *intends to write* articles about her trip.
need	She *needed to attend* some meetings.
offer	She *offered to send* the waitress a card.
plan	She *planned to hit* the bridge of his nose.
promise	She *promised to keep* her cool.
refuse	She *refused to smile* at the clerk.
seem/appear	She *seemed to enjoy* herself.
want	She *wanted to stay* in New Orleans.
	Verb + Noun/Pronoun + Infinitive
ask	He *asked the woman to get* in the cab.
encourage	He *encouraged her to ask* questions.
expect	He *expected her to act* friendly.
force	He *forced her to change* her mind about cabbies.
tell	He *told her not to worry.*
need	He *needed people to like* him.
want	He *wanted the author to have* a good time.

The verbs *ask*, *expect*, *need*, and *want* can occur with both patterns. Sometimes there are significant differences in meaning between the two patterns.

He *asked to look at* the bunny.

He *asked her to look at* the bunny.

She *expected to return* to New York soon.

Her friends *expected her to return* to New York soon.

When verbs that follow the second pattern in the chart are passive, they are followed directly by the infinitive.

She *was forced to change* her mind about cabbies.

Visitors to Boston *are encouraged to walk* the Freedom Trail, which passes many important historical sites.

CHECKPOINT 7

A. Take turns asking and answering questions about cities following the pattern.

Student A: Who wants to visit New York (New Orleans/San Francisco/any U.S. city)? Why do you want to go there?

Student B: I do. I want to see the famous museums and the United Nations.

1. **Student A**: What do you (*plan/hope/expect* etc.) to do?

Student B: . . . (in New York City)
plan . . . the World Trade Center
hope . . .Broadway plays
expect . . . Central Park
intend . . . Statue of Liberty

2. (in New Orleans)
. . . jazz
. . . the French Quarter
. . . the Superdome
. . . crawfish and oysters
3. (in San Francisco)
. . . Golden Gate Bridge, Fisherman's Wharf, Chinatown, the view of the bay, the fog roll in
4. (in Washington, D.C.)
. . . Lincoln Memorial, Washington Memorial, the Capitol Building, the Senate, the White House
5. Use another city and suggest sights to see.

B. Practice writing sentences with infinitive phrases. Use the verb in parentheses to make two sentences, one active and one passive. Do not use quotation marks. Example:

The cab driver said to the author, "Have a good time in New Orleans." (*tell*)

The cab driver *told* the author *to have* a good time in New Orleans. (active)

The author *was told* by the cab driver *to have* a good time in New Orleans. (passive)

1. The hotel clerk said to her, "You should walk carefully on the wet floor." (*warn*)
2. The waitress at the coffee shop said to the woman, "You ought to try the pecan pie." (*encourage*)
3. The airline employee said to the travelers, "You must arrive at the gate thirty minutes early." (*remind*)
4. The author's editor said to her, "You may make the trip to New Orleans." (*allow*)

Infinitives with *Too* and *Enough*

Infinitives are used in idiomatic expressions with *too* and *enough*. *Too* precedes an adjective or quantity word followed by an infinitive. The "subject" of the infinitive may appear in a phrase with *for* before the infinitive.

Using *Too* with Infinitives

	Too +	**Adjective** +	**Noun** +	***for*** +	**Subject** +	**Infinitive**
We were	*too*	tired			*to go*	sightseeing.
There were	*too*	many	places	*for*	them	*to visit.*

The word *too* has a negative meaning. For example, in the first sentence above, they were *not* able to go sightseeing because they were overly tired.

Enough follows an adjective and can be followed by a noun + infinitive.

Using *Enough* with Infinitives

	(a/an)	Adjective +	***Enough*** +	Noun +	***for*** +	Subject +	Infinitive +	Rest of Sentence
She	is	sensitive	*enough*				to appreciate	New Orleans' charm.
It is	a	clear	*enough*	day	*for*	us	to fly.	

Sometimes a noun precedes *enough*.

New York has a *harbor big enough to hold* dozens of ships.

Checkpoint 8

Write a sentence that contains either *too* or *enough* for each pair of sentences. Example:

It was hot. We didn't go shopping.

It was *too* hot for us to go shopping.

1. The prices were low. We could buy souvenirs.
2. The train was crowded. They couldn't get on.
3. The sun was bright. He took some photographs.
4. The food tasted spicy. She didn't eat it.
5. The distance was short. They were able to walk.

Gerunds as Objects

Some verbs must be followed by gerunds rather than infinitives. For example, the verb *go* + gerund is used in many idioms.

go shopping	*go swimming*
go hiking	*go hunting*
go sightseeing	*go skiing*
go fishing	*go bowling*

The box shows some other common verbs followed by gerunds.

Verbs Followed by Gerunds	
appreciate	The writer *appreciated visiting* New Orleans.
avoid	New Yorkers *avoid making* eye contact with people.
consider	We *are considering traveling* to the West Coast next summer.
delay	The Johnsons *had to delay taking* a trip to Nashville when one of the children got sick.
discuss	The writers *discussed not going* to a meeting so that they could go sightseeing instead.
enjoy	New Orleanians *enjoy eating* crawfish.
keep (on)	The driver *kept smiling* all the way to the hotel.
keep from	I *couldn't keep from smiling* back.
mind	*Would* you *mind calling* me a taxi?
postpone	We *had to postpone going* to Phoenix until next fall.

CHECKPOINT 9

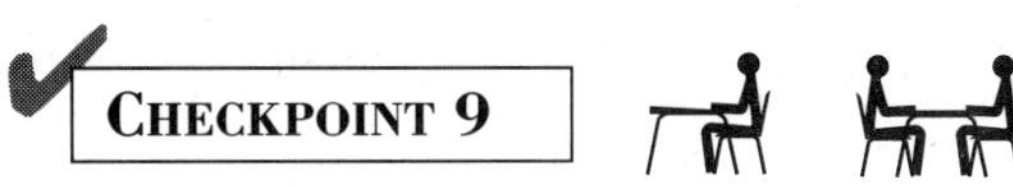

Complete the passage with either the infinitive or the gerund form of the verb in parentheses.

A group of Japanese students studying in San Francisco decided (*travel*) ____________ to the northeastern United States during semester break. They wanted (*see*)____________ the major cities in that area. They considered (*go*) ____________ to Boston, Providence, New York, Trenton, Atlantic City, and Philadelphia, but finally decided (*limit*) ____________ their travels to three cities: Boston, New York, and Philadelphia. They discussed (*leave*) ____________ right after finals, but finally agreed (*not, go*) ____________ until the following weekend.

In Boston, they especially enjoyed (*visit*) ____________ the Quincy Market and Faneuil Hall and (*sightsee*) ____________ in the North End, which is an Italian section of the city. Paul Revere's house is also located there. They expected (*people, be*) ____________ unfriendly because they had heard about "proper Bostonians," but they were forced (*change*) ____________ their minds; most people were very helpful. They encouraged the students (*ask*) ____________ questions and seemed (*enjoy*) ____________ (*answer*) ____________ them.

In New York, they had planned (*see*) ____________ the Empire State Building, the Statue of Liberty, the United Nations, Saint Patrick's Cathedral, and Rockefeller Center, as well as a few museums and universities. They went (*shop*) ____________ on Fifth Avenue, but didn't expect the prices (*be*) ____________ so high. They'll never forget (*run*) ____________ into an old friend at the United Nations. He told (*they, go*) ____________ to New York University, where he intended (*enroll*) ____________ for the spring semester. Their trip to the Statue of Liberty took so long that it kept them from (*visit*) ____________ some other sights. They had to postpone (*go*) ____________ (*skate*) ____________ at Rockefeller Center until their next trip.

They only spent a couple of days in Philadelphia; although they wanted (*stay*) ____________ longer, they needed (*get back*) ____________ to college to prepare for classes. They did manage (*see*) ____________ the Liberty Bell

and the house of Betsy Ross, who made the first U.S. flag. They plan (*return*) ____________ next year to see more of the city.

V Focus on Special Rules for Gerunds and Infinitives

Using Gerunds After Prepositions

A gerund, not an infinitive, is used after a preposition, as in the following sentences from the reading.

I can walk five city blocks during lunch hour *without making* eye contact.

I am indebted to the people I met in New Orleans *for affecting* me.

Other prepositions that often precede gerunds are *besides*, *instead of*, and *in addition to*.

Besides visiting the Statue of Liberty, we went to the South Street Seaport.

Instead of eating fish, we had hot dogs.

The preposition *by* is followed by gerunds in many expressions that explain how to do something.

One stops a cab *by stepping* directly in its path.

Whoever reacts first, either *by moving or stopping*, loses.

She learned about Southerners *by observing* their behavior.

When prepositions are used to form two- or three-word verbs, they must also be followed by gerunds.

The writers *talked about visiting* other cities.

Many *were looking forward to traveling* to Houston.

Some *were accustomed/used to attending* the conference in New Orleans.

They seldom *complain about being treated* rudely by taxi drivers in the South.

Be Used To Versus *Used To*

The expression *be used to* followed by a gerund should not be confused with *used to* followed by a base form, which is one way of expressing past time.

She *wasn't used to traveling* in the South.
(*be used to* + gerund)

She *used to think* all cab drivers were rude.
(*used to* + base form)

Checkpoint 10 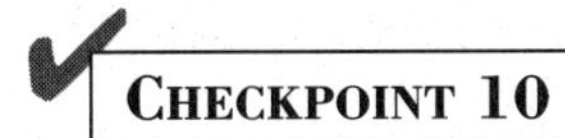 

A. Return to Paragraphs 3 and 6 of the reading (pages 232–233) and find all the gerunds. How many follow verbs? How many follow prepositions? Do any follow another part of speech?

B. Refer to the list below and write at least five sentences using two- or three-word verbs followed by gerunds. (Use a dictionary to look up any verbs you are not familiar with.) Share your sentences with a partner or group.

apologize for	*participate in*
be accustomed to	*prevent* (someone/something) *from*
be accused of	*insist on*
be excited about	*stop* (someone/something) *from*
be interested in	*talk about*
be used to	*take care of*
complain about	*take advantage of*

Examples:

We *were excited about visiting* Miami.

The snow *prevented us from leaving* on time.

Possessives with Gerunds

Like other nouns, gerunds can be preceded by possessive adjectives. Compare the following sentences.

She appreciated *his courtesy.* (possessive + noun)

She appreciated *his treating* her courteously. (possessive + gerund)

An object pronoun should not be used before a gerund in formal English.

INCORRECT: She appreciated *him* helping her.

CORRECT: She appreciated *his* helping her.

Verbs Followed by Either Infinitives or Gerunds

A few verbs can be followed by a gerund or by an infinitive with little or no change in meaning. These include *begin, start, like, hate, try, continue,* and *prefer.*

We like *traveling/to travel* to different cities on vacation.

We hate *going/to go* by bus.

Her friends have started *taking/to take* the train.

The verb *prefer* follows two different patterns depending on whether it is followed by a gerund or by an infinitive.

I prefer *visiting* cities *to visiting* rural areas.

I prefer *to visit* cities *rather than [to visit]* rural areas.

Advise also follows two patterns. An infinitive is used with an indirect object; a gerund is used when there is no indirect object.

He advised *her to visit* the Superdome.

He advised *visiting* the Superdome.

A few verbs have different meanings depending on whether they are followed by gerunds or infinitives. These include *stop*, *remember*, and *forget*. The following pairs of sentences illustrate the differences in meaning.

They stopped *to eat* lunch at a famous restaurant.

They stopped *eating* lunch there.

(In the first sentence, they stopped in order to eat. The second means they no longer go to the restaurant.)

The woman remembered *to pack* comfortable shoes.

She distinctly remembered *packing* them.

(The first sentence means that she didn't forget to pack them; the second means she recalled the activity of packing them.)

She forgot *to bring* her traveler's checks.

She'll never forget *trying* to replace them.

(The first sentence means she didn't bring her traveler's checks; the second means her experience was unforgettable).

Use the cues to make two sentences, one with a gerund and one with an infinitive. Write *S* after the second sentence if the meaning is the same or almost the same; write *D* if the meaning is different. Make sure to use appropriate verb forms. Example:

She/stop/talk to the waitress

She stopped *to talk* to the waitress.

She stopped *talking* to the waitress. *D*

1. The cab driver/remember/to buy some gas
2. The author/not forget/smile
3. New Yorkers/prefer/look serious
4. People in New Orleans/hate/be rude
5. Just about everyone in New Orleans/like/eat spicy food

Verbals After Nouns and Adjectives

The following sentences from the reading illustrate some ways that infinitives and gerunds can be used after nouns and adjectives.

I was *desperate to get way* from frigid New York.
(adjective + infinitive)

When the *opportunity to attend* the conference came about, I took it.
(noun + infinitive)

It's been a *pleasure meeting* you. (noun + gerund)

It's been a *pleasure to meet* you. (noun + infinitive)

Recognizing Types of Infinitive Phrases

A phrase that consists of an infinitive with or without modifiers can be used to express purpose. This type of phrase should not be confused with parts of the main verb or with infinitives that are objects of verbs.

The writer *has to type* her article.
(*to* as a part of main verb)

She wants *to visit* New Orleans again.
(infinitive as object of *want*)

I bit my lips *to keep from* returning her smile.
(infinitive of purpose)

Base Form versus *-ing* Form After Verbs of Perception

Verbs of perception, such as *see, watch, look at, hear, listen to,* and *feel,* can be followed by the base form or the *-ing* form of the verb.

She heard a jazz band *play/playing* at Preservation Hall in the French Quarter.

They saw the plane *take/taking* off.

The base form usually refers to the whole activity, while the *-ing* form refers to a part of it. In other words, if they saw the plane *land,* they watched the entire landing; however, if they saw the plane *landing,* they saw it during part of the time it was landing, but did not watch the entire action.

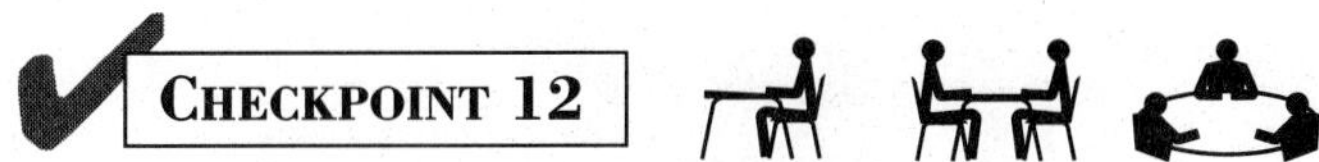

Complete each sentence with the base form or *-ing* form of the verb in parentheses. Discuss the differences in meaning.

1. She saw the sun ____________ (*rise*). She watched the sun ____________ (*shine*) in the sky.

2. We heard her plane ____________ (*leave*). We listened to the pilot ____________ (*talk*) over the loud speaker.
3. They smelled the gumbo ____________ (*cook*) on the stove. They saw the cook ____________ (*spill*) the gumbo on the floor.

Participles and Participial Phrases

Alone or as part of a phrase, - *ing* and *-ed/-en* forms (participles) can be used to modify nouns. Like infinitives and gerunds, participles are "verbals," but they act as modifiers or adjectives, not nouns. As a single-word modifier, the participle occurs *before* the noun.

There was no sarcasm in his *smiling* eyes.

The passenger had *buffed* fingernails.

A *participial phrase* occurs after the noun or noun substitute it modifies. When it provides nonessential, parenthetical information, it is set off by a comma or a pair of commas.

The cab *driven by her friend* was a Cadillac. (This phrase gives essential information about the cab.)

The cab, *gliding to a stop*, was the color of a cherry popsicle. (This phrase gives nonessential, extra information about the cab.)

It was a maneuver *guaranteed to stun attackers*. (essential)

The maneuver, *practiced in New York*, worked well for most people. (nonessential)

Participial phrases may also begin sentences; in this case they occur before the subject.

Looking out the window, the man saw a bunny.

(Information on participles is also given in Units 3 and 5.)

Checkpoint 13

A. Return to the reading on pages 232–234. Find nouns or pronouns modified by participles or participial phrases in the paragraphs and lines indicated. Write them below. Example:

Paragraph 3, lines 5 and 6 — noun *driver*
modifier *smiling*

1. Paragraph 3, line 7 — noun ____________
modifier ____________
2. Paragraph 3, line 8 — noun ____________
modifier ____________

3. Paragraph 5, line 2 noun ______________________
modifier ______________________

4. Paragraph 8, line 1 noun ______________________
modifier ______________________

5. Paragraph 8, line 5 noun ______________________
modifier ______________________

B. Find and underline other noun and participle structures in the reading.

VI Focus on Sentence Variety

Constructions can be placed in different positions in a sentence to provide extra information or to add variety and complexity.

Front (Pre-Subject) Constructions

Front constructions occur before the subject of a sentence to attract a reader's attention; placing a word, phrase, or clause in this position gives it emphasis. Most front constructions are followed by a comma.

- **Prepositional Phrase**

  In 1718, Jean Baptiste le Moyne drew plans for the city of New Orleans.

- **Participial Phrase**

  Named for the duke of Orleans, the city became the capital of the French territory in the New World.

- **Infinitive**

  To improve Spain's position in America, the Spanish crown acquired the whole territory of Louisiana in 1762.

- **Adverb of Time**

  Soon the people of New Orleans showed their displeasure with the new king.

- **Adverb of Manner**

  Furiously they fought against the Spanish governor and forced him to return to Spain.

- **Adverb of Place**

  There he remained for the rest of his life.

- **Adjective Modifying the Subject**

  Unhappy under Spanish rule, the citizens of New Orleans celebrated when France again took control of Louisiana.

- **Noun That Refers to the Subject**

  A famous document in American history, the Louisiana Purchase made Louisiana a part of the United States.

- **Adverbial Clause**

  Before Louisiana became part of the United States, the territory changed hands several times.

CHECKPOINT 14 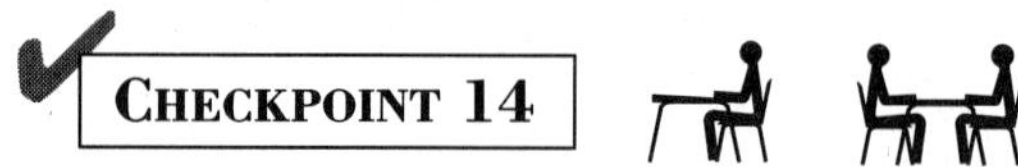

Combine the following pairs of sentences by using *part of* the information from the second sentence in the front position of the first sentence. Example:

Canal Street separates the French Quarter from the Central Business District. Canal Street is almost 200 feet wide.

Almost 200 feet wide, Canal Street separates the French Quarter from the Central Business District.

1. New Orleans lies slightly below sea level and at the level of the Mississippi River. New Orleans is protected from flooding by high banks of earth called levees.
2. The Mississippi River runs north to south. It runs through the center of the United States.
3. The port of New Orleans became one of the most important in the country. The port became important gradually.
4. The French Quarter, or Vieux Carré, contained the residences of many French and Creole families. The French Quarter is the oldest part of the city.
5. Basin Street and Bourbon Street are well known to jazz musicians. These streets are mentioned in many popular songs.

MIDDLE (POST-SUBJECT) CONSTRUCTIONS

Many constructions that occur before the subject may also be placed after the subject. Most words, phrases, or clauses in this middle position are set off by commas, which are required when the information is not essential to the meaning of the sentence.

In this position, a noun phrase that expands the subject is called an *appositive*. Adverbs of time, especially those of frequency, usually appear in this position; they are not set off by commas because they are essential.

- **Appositive**

  Mardi Gras, *an important holiday in New Orleans*, is celebrated every year.

- **Adverb of Time**

  This event *usually* occurs in February or March.

- **Participial Phrase**

  Members of the Carnival organizations, *throwing plastic beads and doubloons*, ride floats in the parades on Mardi Gras day.

- **Participial Phrase**

  The name "Mardi Gras," *taken from the French language*, means "Fat Tuesday."

- **Prepositional Phrase**

  The festive day of parades and parties, *on the Tuesday before the solemn Christian season of Lent*, gives resident and visitors a last chance to celebrate.

- **Adverbial Clause**

  Many New Orleanians, *even though they love rich food*, go on diets after Mardi Gras.

- **Adjectives That Refer to the Subject**

  Fabulous costumes, *beautiful, humorous, or exotic*, make the spectators as well as the riders fun to watch.

- **Adverb of Manner**

  Mardi Gras "Indians" *energetically* roam the streets in dazzling outfits of feathers and jewels.

- **Adjective Clause**

  Napoleon, *who ruled France in 1803*, approved the Louisiana Purchase and gave up France's claim to the New World.

CHECKPOINT 15

Combine the following pairs of sentences by putting part of the second sentence into the middle (post-subject) position. When necessary, set off the added construction with commas. Example:

> Good food seems to be an important subject in New Orleans.
>
> Good food is available in every part of the city.
>
> Good food, *available in every part of the city*, seems to be an important subject in New Orleans.

1. Cajun food has attracted national attention in recent years. Cajun food is a blend of French, African, and local cuisine.
2. Favorite Cajun dishes appear in neighborhood eateries as well as elegant restaurants. These dishes include blackened redfish, crawfish étouffé, and seafood gumbo. (Use the participle *including*.)

3. Many varieties of local fish and shellfish provide ingredients for Cajun cuisine. These are caught in the Mississippi River and the Gulf of Mexico. (Use the *-ed/en* form.)
4. The local version of the hero, hoagie, or submarine sandwich often contains fried oysters or shrimp. It is called a po' boy.
5. Paul Prudhomme deserves credit for the popularity of New Orleans food across the United States. He is a celebrated Cajun chef.

END CONSTRUCTIONS

The position at the end of the sentence may be occupied by a few of the constructions that occur in the front and middle positions. End constructions are not usually preceded by a comma. Prepositional phrases and adverbial clauses commonly occur at the end of sentences. (Adverbial clauses will be discussed in detail in Unit 9.)

- **Prepositional Phrases**

  Cajun food first became nationally known *early in the 1980s.*

- **Adverbial Clause**

  Many chefs tried to duplicate blackened redfish *when it was first introduced by Paul Prudhomme.*

Because of its distance from the subject, the end position should not be filled with modifiers that refer to the subject. These modifying words or phrases must be placed before or after the subject; otherwise, the lack of clear connection to the noun or noun substitute modified will confuse the reader.

INCORRECT: Prudhomme's restaurant has become a primary tourist attraction in the French Quarter *called K-Paul's.*

CORRECT: Prudhomme's restaurant, *called K-Paul's,* has become a primary tourist attraction in the French Quarter.

CORRECT: *Called K-Paul's,* Prudhomme's restaurant has become a primary tourist attraction in the French Quarter.

In the incorrect sentence, the participial phrase seems to refer to *the French Quarter* rather than to *Prudhomme's restaurant,* which is the subject of the sentence. In the correct versions, the modifier refers clearly to the subject.

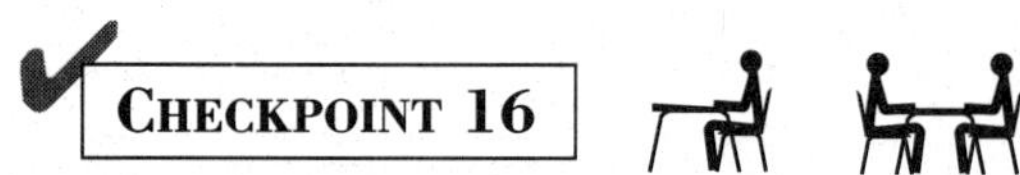

Move the italicized words to a different position in each sentence. Be sure to punctuate correctly. Example:

New Orleans has figured in the economic and cultural life of the United States *throughout the years.*

Throughout the years, New Orleans has figured in . . .

New Orleans, *throughout the years,* has figured in . . .

1. *Since the days of the early French settlers*, New Orleans' architecture has been admired.
2. The homes of early French and Creole families, *many still in good condition*, give an indication of how these settlers lived.
3. *Because of their balconies and iron filigree balustrades*, many French Quarter buildings have a European flavor.
4. Walking tours and bus trips have been organized by many different organizations and groups *to show visitors the architectural highlights*.

VII Focus on Coordination and Parallelism

Coordination of Independent Clauses

Independent clauses can be joined with one of the following coordinating conjunctions: *and, but, or, yet, for, so*, and *nor*. A comma usually precedes a coordinating conjunction that connects two independent clauses, especially long ones. The conjunctions *for* and *yet* are primarily used in formal language. *Nor* has a negative meaning and requires question word order; in other words, the auxiliary precedes the subject. (Reverse word order following negatives is discussed on page 265.)

Coordination of Independent Clauses	
and	I have a special affection for the city of Los Angeles, *and* my husband feels the same way.
but (*yet*)	We visit San Francisco often, *but* (or *yet*) we hardly ever go to Los Angeles.
or	We're thinking about spending next Christmas in Los Angeles, *or* we may go to New York City for the holidays.
or (*else*)	My friend is trying to find someone to go to L.A. with, *or* (*else*) she may have to go alone. (*Meaning*: If she doesn't find someone to go with, she may have to go alone.)
for	California welcomes millions of visitors each year, *for* tourists stimulate business.
so	California borders the Pacific Ocean, *so* it has spectacular coastal scenery and beach areas.
nor	I wouldn't want to be in California during an earthquake, *nor* would most people.
yet	The cost of living in many California coastal cities is high, *yet* their populations are continuing to grow.

The following chart summarizes the meanings of coordinating conjunctions joining independent clauses.

Meanings of Coordinating Conjunctions	
Word	**Second Clause**
and	Adds to the first and continues the same idea.
but/yet	Expresses contrast or unexpected result.
for	Gives a reason.
or	Offers a second possibility.
or (else)	Combined with the first, may have a conditional meaning.
so	Expresses result.
nor	Adds a second negative idea.

When more than two independent clauses are joined, a comma is used after each one, and the conjunction precedes the final clause.

> San Francisco is known for the fog that rolls in over the city, Los Angeles is known for the movie stars who live in surrounding areas, *and* San Diego is known for its lush, semitropical vegetation.

A. Fill in the blanks with any appropriate coordinating conjunction: *and*, *but* or *yet*, *or*, *or else*, *for*, *so*, *nor*. You may use a conjunction more than once. In some sentences, more than one conjunction can be used; discuss the differences in meaning that result when the conjunction is changed. Example:

> Los Angeles is the largest city in area in the United States, but/yet it doesn't have the largest population.

1. Most movies and television programs are produced in the Los Angeles area, ____________ many celebrated figures in the world of art, drama, and music live there.
2. Los Angeles is located in a fruit-growing region, ____________ it is in an important mining area as well.
3. Los Angeles prospered when the railway lines to the Pacific Coast were completed, ____________ it developed very rapidly after the discovery of petroleum in the 1890s.
4. Air pollution caused in part by auto exhaust has become a serious problem in Los Angeles in recent years, ____________ residents depend on cars for transportation as much as ever.
5. East of Los Angeles, the Sangre de Cristo Mountains extend north to south, ____________ the city's air pollution, called *smog*, is trapped over L.A.

6. Evidence of Hispanic culture is everywhere in Los Angeles, ____________ many residents have relocated from Mexico and various countries in Central America.
7. On any night of the week, tourists could go to a different Mexican restaurant, ____________ they could choose a place that offers the cuisine of just about any other country in the world.
8. Los Angeles now has more professional sports teams than any other city, ____________ most of them moved there from other cities.
9. Los Angeles is not usually thought of as a beautiful city, ____________ many visitors have been surprised by its charming avenues and parks.
10. Rich and famous people shop on the world-famous Rodeo Drive in Beverly Hills, ____________ the prices can be extremely high.

B. Circle the letter of the independent clause that best completes the sentence. Example:

San Francisco's peninsula lies between the Pacific Ocean and San Francisco Bay, so . . .

a. it has become a famous city in the United States
b. it has water on both sides.
c. it is located in a hilly area.

1. San Francisco was incorporated as a city in 1850, and . . .
   a. it became the western terminal of the pony express in 1860.
   b. several islands lie off the city's coast.
   c. the federal prison named Alcatraz is located there.
2. San Francisco is a great financial and commercial center, but . . .
   a. its industries include ship building, fruit canning, and printing.
   b. Don Gaspar de Portola was the first Spanish governor.
   c. it is probably best known for the Golden Gate Bridge, which links the city with counties to the north.
3. San Francisco and Los Angeles share a common cultural heritage, for . . .
   a. they have very different climates.
   b. Nob Hill and Hollywood are two famous areas.
   c. they were ruled by Spain for many years.
4. San Francisco is a modern city, yet . . .
   a. the downtown area has many skyscrapers.
   b. individual neighborhoods like Chinatown have a traditional atmosphere.
   c. a number of institutions of higher learning have been established there.
5. In San Francisco, people travel by car, or . . .
   a. they take the cable-car, an old-fashioned streetcar.
   b. there is usually a great deal of traffic.
   c. the streets of the city were very well planned.

6. San Franciscans are not like people from any other city in the United States, nor . . .
   a. they want to be.
   b. they don't want to be.
   c. do they want to be.

Parallelism

Two or more structures within any one part of a sentence (for example, two subjects or objects) must be *parallel*, or in the same form. Parallel structures are joined by coordinating conjunctions, usually *and*. Failure to make structures parallel results in an error called *faulty parallelism*. Examples:

Faulty: *Tourism and to can fruit* are important to San Francisco's economy.
Parallel: *Tourism and fruit canning* are important to San Francisco's economy.

Faulty: *The hotel where we stayed and we ate dinner at the restaurant* were both recommended in our guide book.
Parallel: *The hotel where we stayed and the restaurant where we ate dinner* were both recommended in our guide book.

Faulty: In a new city, we like *sight-seeing and to meet the local people.*
Parallel: In a new city, we like *sightseeing and meeting the local people.*

Expanding Parts of the Sentence with Coordinating Conjunctions

The conjunctions that may join parallel structures in a part of a sentence include *and, but, or, but not,* and *yet not.* No comma is used between the parallel elements unless the meaning is negative, as in the cases of *but not* and *yet not.*

San Francisco *and* Los Angeles are remarkable cities. (nouns)

Do you like to travel by bus *or* by cable car? (prepositional phrases)

Where tourists stay in San Francisco *and* what they do are subjects covered in this guide book. (noun clauses)

San Francisco was severely damaged by the earthquake of 1906, *but not* completely destroyed. (past participles)

The new stadium has been begun, *yet not* completed. (past participles)

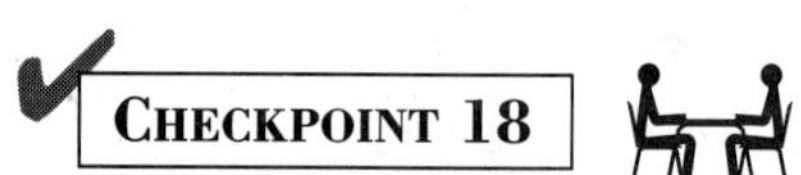

Combine each pair of sentences. Eliminate unnecessary words, and join parallel elements with *and, or, but, but not,* or *yet not.* Example:

Nell Blaine is a thin woman with gray hair. She has black horn-rimmed glasses.

Nell Blaine is a thin woman with gray hair and black horn-rimmed glasses.

1. Ms. Blaine paints floral still lifes during the winter. She paints interior scenes during the winter.
2. Ms. Blaine lives in New York City for most of the year. Ms. Blaine moves to Gloucester, Massachusetts, for the summer.
3. According to Ms. Blaine, the Massachusetts port city of Gloucester is "an authentic working-class town." According to Ms. Blaine, the Massachusetts port city of Gloucester is a fishing village.
4. Winslow Homer painted in this town. Marsden Hartley painted in this town.
5. Ms. Blaine lived in Virginia as a child. She didn't plan to stay there.
6. She spent time in New York City. She traveled to Greece.
7. In Gloucester she paints intimate landscapes. She also paints harbor views.
8. One might find lawns in these paintings. One might find gardens in these paintings.
9. She likes to paint distant boats in her harbor pictures. She likes to paint islands in her harbor paintings.
10. Polio, which she contracted in 1959, has confined her to a wheelchair. Polio has not prevented her from painting.

VIII Focus on Paired Conjunctions

A pair of conjunctions can coordinate elements in a sentence; they may occur with nouns, verbs, phrases, and clauses. Common pairs of conjunctions are *both . . . and, not only . . . but also, either . . .or*, and *neither . . . nor.*

Both . . . and

Both . . . and refers to two nouns or noun substitutes and emphasizes the similarity or relatedness of the elements. When *both . . . and* occurs in the subject, the subject is always plural. Examples:

Both Houston *and* Dallas are important cotton cities. (subject)

Houston and Dallas *both* produce *and* market crops such as cotton and fruit. (verb)

Houston is known for *both* rice *and* sugar. (object of preposition)

Not only . . . but Also

Not only . . . but also means "both" but emphasizes the second element. When it occurs in the subject, the verb agrees with the *nearest* subject.

Not only movies *but also* a famous television program has been written about the famous Texas lifestyle. (subject)

Dallas was *not only* a popular show *but also* one of the longest-running series in television history. (subject complement)

Not only can be paired with *but* (without *also*) and with *but . . . as well.*

The weather in Houston is *not only* hot *but* humid.

Houston is *not only* hot *but* humid *as well.*

CHECKPOINT 19  

Rewrite each sentence using *both . . . and* or *not only . . . but also.* It may be necessary to make other changes in agreement and number. Example:

Cowboy boots have become a symbol of Texas, and oil wells have become a symbol of Texas too.

Both cowboy boots *and* oil wells have become symbols of Texas.

Not only cowboy boots *but also* oil wells have become symbols of Texas.

1. The railroads have made Dallas an important location in the transportation industry, and the airlines have done this too.
2. Oil companies have made important strikes, or discoveries, in the Dallas area, and they have made important strikes, or discoveries, in the Houston area.
3. Legends have grown about Dallas and legends have grown about Houston as a result of their suddenly acquired wealth.
4. The millionaire cowboy has become a Texas stereotype, and the woman in blue jeans and diamonds has become a Texas stereotype.
5. Many ranchers in the Texas countryside raise cattle. Many ranchers in the Texas countryside grow fruit in the orchards.

EITHER . . . OR

In negative sentences, *either* means the opposite of *both.* In other words, it means neither of the two possibilities. The following pairs of sentences show the difference between *both . . . and* and *either . . . or.**

He has been to *both* Houston *and* Dallas.

I haven't been to *either* Houston *or* Dallas.

(I haven't been to Houston, and I haven't been to Dallas.)

---

* *Either* can be followed by *one* or *of the* plus a noun or noun substitute, or by *of them*:

I haven't been to either one.

I haven't been to either city.

I haven't been to either of them.

Houston is *both* an oil town *and* an agricultural center.

El Paso isn't *either* an oil town *or* an agricultural center.

(El Paso isn't an oil town, and it isn't an agricultural center.)

Either . . . or in affirmative sentences means that one of two choices is possible.

The oil industry will *either* recover from the recession *or* continue to be less profitable than it was in past decades.

Either Dallas *or* Houston is home to the largest number of self-made millionaires.

It is possible to reach Dallas quickly *either* by train *or* by airplane.

Neither . . . nor

Neither . . . nor is used in the same way as *either . . . or*; it has the same meaning that *either . . . or* has in negative sentences. The meaning of *neither . . . nor* is always negative, but the verb is affirmative.

Neither Houston *nor* Dallas existed in the eighteenth century.

The territory of Texas was *neither* claimed *nor* explored by the Puritans who settled colonial America.

Subject-Verb Agreement with Paired Conjunctions

Both . . . and is the only pair that requires a plural main verb when used in the subject. When *not only . . . but also, either . . . or,* or *neither . . . nor* coordinate elements in the subject, the verb agrees with the element closest to it.

Both my aunt and my uncle *enjoy* living in Houston.

Either my sister or my brothers *have* taken the car to Dallas.

Either my brother or my sister *has* taken the car to Dallas.

Neither her friends nor her mother *has* talked with her since she moved to Texas.

Neither her mother nor her friends *have* talked with her since she moved to Texas.

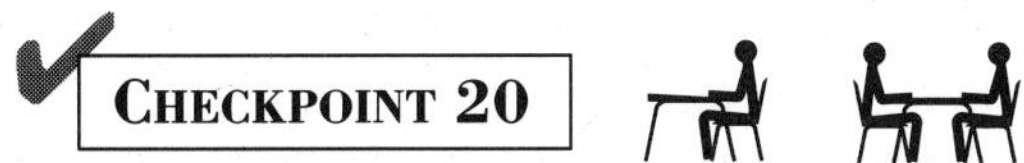

A. Fill in the blanks with *is* or *are*. Example:

Either Dallas or Houston __is__ the largest city in Texas.

1. Neither their parents nor their cousin __________ in Texas now.
2. Both Susan and Fred __________ fond of Texas country music.

3. Either Sam or you ____________ going to dance the "Texas Two-Step" with me.
4. Not only the "Two-Step" but also the "Cotton-Eyed Joe" ____________ easy to learn.
5. Either July or August ____________ the hottest month in Houston.

B. Working with a partner, rephrase each sentence using *either . . . or* or *neither . . . nor*. Example:

> We aren't going to Astroworld this year, and we're not going to Six Flags over Texas.
>
> We aren't going to *either* Astroworld *or* Six Flags over Texas this year.
>
> We're going to *neither* Astroworld *nor* Six Flags over Texas this year.

1. That restaurant doesn't serve a Texas barbecue, and it doesn't serve a fish fry.
2. Who can find rodeos outside of Texas? Who can find big working ranches outside of Texas?
3. My uncle didn't want to stop in Houston, and he didn't want to stop in Dallas.
4. You couldn't find your guide book, and you couldn't find your map of Houston.
5. The Johnson Space Center isn't open today, and the skating rink at the Houston Galleria isn't open today.

CHECKPOINT 21

Answer your classmates' questions about U.S. cities they have visited, using *either*, *neither*, *both*, or *but not*. You may want to look at a map of the United States as you do this exercise. Example:

> Los Angeles/San Francisco?

Student A: Have you ever been to Los Angeles or San Francisco?

Student B: I've been to both San Francisco and Los Angeles.

> I've been to neither San Francisco nor Los Angeles.
>
> I've been to San /Francisco, but not to Los Angeles.

1. Houston/Dallas?
2. Miami/Tampa?
3. Tucson/Phoenix?
4. Santa Fe/Las Vegas?
5. Boston/Providence?
6. Chicago/Minneapolis?
7. City of your choice/City of your choice?

IX Focus on Special Sentence Structure Rules

Negative

Some unusual English sentences begin with a negative adverbial word or expression, such as *no, nowhere, at no time, never, seldom, rarely,* and *hardly (ever).* These sentences, like those beginning with *not only,* use question word order for emphasis. The first word in the verb precedes the subject.

> *Never had she met* friendlier people.
>
> *At no time was she* nervous about being an unescorted woman.
>
> *Rarely does a New Yorker feel* so comfortable with strangers. *Seldom had the man seen* a real rabbit.

Checkpoint 22

At the beginning of each of the following sentences, use the negative word or phrase in parentheses. Change the word order and remove any other negative in each sentence. Example:

> We haven't visited a hotter city than Phoenix, Arizona. (*Never*)
>
> Never have we visited a hotter city than Phoenix, Arizona.

1. We haven't seen sunsets more beautiful than those in the Arizona desert. (*Seldom*)
2. We hadn't experienced such a change in climate as that between northern and southern Arizona. (*In no other state*)
3. We visited Phoenix, but we also visited Flagstaff in northern Arizona and Tucson, which is near the Mexican border in southern Arizona. (*Not only*)
4. It doesn't snow in Phoenix or Tucson. (*Hardly ever*)
5. We haven't seen such spectacular scenery as that of the Grand Canyon. (*Rarely*)

Connecting Adverbs

Connecting adverbs are used to provide logical transitions between sentences; they are especially common in writing. These connecting, or conjunctive, adverbs can be grouped according to meaning, although subtle differences do exist among the members of each group.

Meanings of Connecting Adverbs	
Continuing the same idea	*also*
	in addition
	besides
	moreover
	likewise
Emphasis	*in fact*
	indeed
	as a matter of fact
Contrast	*however*
	still
	nevertheless
	in contrast
Direct opposition	*on the other hand*
	on the contrary
Result	*therefore*
	thus
	consequently
	as a result
Summary	*in conclusion*
	in short
	in summary or in sum

A connecting adverb may occur in various positions in the sentence.

> Before leaving for Texas, you should buy several books. *Also* you must obtain traveler's checks. (front position)
>
> You must *also* get traveler's checks. (middle position)
>
> You must obtain traveler's checks *also*. (end position)

Often the linking word begins a sentence and is followed by a comma. If the sentence is closely related to the one before it, a semicolon may be used instead of a period and the second sentence does not begin with a capital letter.

> Robert was interested in applying to Rice University; *therefore,* he planned a visit to the campus in Houston.
>
> Rice has an excellent Engineering department; *in addition,* its science facilities are outstanding.
>
> Robert had good grades and wonderful recommendations; *nevertheless,* he was not admitted to Rice.

CHECKPOINT 23

Use the linking adverbs from the chart on page 266 to join independent clauses; in most cases, the adverbs replace coordinating conjunctions such as *and* and *but*. Add conjunctions of emphasis where indicated. Be sure to punctuate correctly. Example:

> Harvard is the most famous university in the Boston area, *and* it is the oldest one. (emphasis) It is the oldest in the United States.
>
> Harvard is the most famous school in the Boston area; *moreover*, it is the oldest. *Indeed*, it is the oldest in the United States.

1. Harvard is the oldest and most prestigious university in the area, *but* MIT (the Massachusetts Institute of Technology) is almost as famous.
2. *And* MIT is known as one of the very finest technical schools in the world. (emphasis) It has produced a number of famous graduates.
3. Students from many countries go to MIT to study science and engineering, *but* not all of them stay in the United States after graduation.
4. The cost of education at the two universities is high, *yet* most graduates agree that it is worth the price.
5. The campus of Harvard is known for its architectural beauty. (emphasis) Many buildings date back to the seventeenth century.

SUBORDINATING CLAUSES

In addition to joining clauses with coordinating conjunctions like *and*, *but*, and *so*, speakers and writers of English can join clauses by subordinating them. Subordinate clauses are explained in detail in the next three units.

PART THREE. Review and Integration

There's No Place Like Home: Types of Subjects

A. Write a description of your hometown (location, climate, interesting features, and so on) using sentences that contain different types of subjects: nouns, pronouns, gerunds, infinitives. Refer to pages 237–241 if necessary. Examples:

> *Getting* around is easy in ____________________ (your hometown), which is very small. (gerund as subject)

To grow up in a city like my home town, ______________________, is a unique experience. (infinitive as subject)

B. With a group, draw a map of your ideal town. Each town must contain the following: business district, shopping center, residential areas (houses and apartments), streets, parks, hospitals/clinics, fire and police departments. Take turns presenting your town plans to the other groups, and discuss your reasons for placing the elements where you did.

Life in U.S. Cities: Gerunds and Infinitives

Complete the following sentences with gerund or infinitive forms of any appropriate verb. Choose from the list below or use your imagination.

visit (museums, etc.)	*take* (pictures, cabs, etc.)	*play*
meet (Chicagoans, etc.)	*go* (sightseeing, etc.)	*eat*
travel	*return*	*see*

1. Once I decided ______________________ by train to Chicago.
2. ______________________ was something I had always wanted to do.
3. It was fun ______________________, but I hated ______________________.
4. Also, it was difficult for me ______________________.
5. In Chicago, I especially enjoyed ______________________.
6. Besides ______________________, I tried ______________________.
7. Around Lake Michigan, it was great ______________________.
8. I'm not used to ______________________.
9. Now that I'm back home, I look forward to ______________________.

Lost in the Desert: Gerunds and Infinitives

Read the following situation and do the exercise.

While driving alone from Houston to Los Angeles, you fell asleep and drove off the road. Your car was completely destroyed. You are in a desert, far from any city or town. You haven't seen another car for hours. Listed below are items you have in your car. You also have a small canvas bag that will hold ten small or five large items. Choose the items you will take with you on your search for help.

When you have finished, write complete sentences using verbs like *need*, *prefer*, *consider*, *plan*, *want*, *hope*, *expect*, and *keep*. Use the correct forms (gerunds or infinitives) following the verbs. Examples:

I would plan *to take* the flashlight with me.

I'd consider *carrying* the soda, but not the potato chips.

Compare your answers with other groups' and discuss your reasons for making your choices.

1. snakebite kit
2. hammer
3. pocket knife
4. map of the U.S.
5. compass
6. sunscreen
7. mystery novel
8. flashlight
9. pack of batteries
10. box of 1,000 matches
11. towel
12. raincoat
13. blanket
14. small transistor radio
15. deck of playing cards
16. shaving mirror
17. shampoo
18. baseball cap
19. deodorant
20. mouthwash
21. bar of soap
22. insect repellent
23. six-pack of soda
24. pack of candy bars
25. gallon of water
26. thermos of hot coffee
27. jar of peanut butter
28. bag of potato chips

Famous Women in U.S. Cities: Sentence Combining

Write two or three sentences in which you combine all the sentences in each group. Try using different sentence patterns, including appositives, paired conjunctions (*not only . . . but also*, *both . . . and*, *either . . . or*, *neither . . . nor*), and connecting adverbs like *however*, *in addition*, and *therefore*. Then decide which version you like best. Hints about which structures to use are given for the first group of sentences about Marie Laveau. Example:

Marie Laveau came from Haiti, an island in the Caribbean Sea.

A. *New Orleans and Marie Laveau*

Marie Laveau came from Haiti.

Haiti is an island in the Caribbean Ocean. [appositive]

Marie was the slave of a Louisiana man.

Marie was called a witch. [*both . . . and*]

Marie was called a priestess of voodoo.

Voodoo is sometimes called black magic. [appositive]

Marie Laveau used herbs to make her magic potions.

Marie Laveau used bones to make her magic potions.

She sold her potions to the people.

The people came to her for help.

The people were of many kinds.

Marie Laveau is buried in St. Louis Cemetery Number One.

Thousands of tourists visit Marie's tomb every year.

Her legend remains.

But that is not all.

Her house can still be seen.

The house is in the French Quarter.

Her wax form can still be seen.

The form is in the New Orleans Wax Museum.

B. *Chicago and Jane Addams*

Jane Addams caught a fever.

She was two years old then.

The fever was terrible.

Jane Addams became crippled.

Her back was crooked.

Jane was different from everyone else.

She didn't become sad.

She didn't become angry.

She liked people.

She kept busy.

She enjoyed her life.

Jane grew up.

Jane was upset about children.

The children were poor.

The children had to work long hours.

They worked at factories.

The children didn't have food.

The children didn't have clothing.

They played in the streets.

They didn't have a place to go.

Jane spent a lot of money.

She established Hull House.

Hull House was comfortable.

It was a place for children.

It was a place for the children's families.

It was free.

Restaurant Role Play: Paired Conjunctions

In groups of three, decide which character below each student will play. Then write a dialogue in which each character uses paired conjunctions several times while in a New Orleans restaurant. Refer to the list of menu items given below. Practice the dialogues and then take turns performing them in front of the whole class.

1. You are a waiter or waitress in an elegant restaurant. You want the customers to order as much food as possible because you want a large tip. Make suggestions using these structures: *both . . . and* and *not only . . . but (also)*.
2. You are an indecisive customer. You want to have a fabulous dinner, but you can't decide what to order. You change your mind several times and use the structure *either . . . or.*
3. You are a picky customer. You have come to this restaurant with #2 even though you didn't want to. You had a terrible dinner here last month, and nothing the waiter suggests sounds good to you. You reject his/her suggestions with the structure *neither . . . nor.*

Appetizers	*Main Course*	*Desserts*
Shrimp Cocktail	*Crawfish Etouffé [ay-too-fay]*	*Bananas Foster*
Crabmeat Imperial	*Prime Rib*	*Cherries Jubilee*
Chicken Liver Paté	*Trout Amandine*	*Ice Cream with Praline Sauce*
Garden Salad	*Grilled Soft Shell Crabs*	*Bread Pudding with Rum Sauce*

Scrambled Sentences: Linking Adverbs

Unscramble each sentence and add correct punctuation. Example:

carefully he know New York well he study map does have very will therefore not to a

He does not know New York well; therefore, he will have to study a map very carefully.

1. capital map we the nobody find Texas not state capital furthermore that knew could of on the
2. rather car travel bus Carlos however would I to prefers by take my
3. are my like to November going either cold friends in Houston not consequently or they weather do Miami
4. located been she without nevertheless had her before hotel problem to never Chicago see any

Suggestions for Writing

1. If you are keeping a journal, write an entry about one or more of the following: your favorite city, your least favorite city, a city that you would like to visit, how you would change the city/town you live in if you could.
2. Write a letter to a friend advising him/her about how to prepare for a visit to a specific U.S. city. Do some research if necessary.
3. Write a composition comparing two American cities, or write about two comparable cities, one in the United States and one in another country (perhaps two capitals). Some possible topics to include are language, population, architecture, history, and recreational activities.
4. Imagine that you are visiting a major U.S. city (for example, New York, Los Angeles, Miami, Dallas) in the year 2050. Describe what the city will be like in the future. Include discussions of some or all of the following: the population, methods of transportation, pollution (or the lack of it), types of jobs, recreation, families.

Unit Eight

ADJECTIVE CLAUSES

READING. "From Song to Sound: Bing and Elvis" by Russell Baker

THEME. Popular Music in the United States

PART ONE. The Context

Russell Baker (1925–) wrote the following article on the occasion of Bing Crosby's death, which occurred shortly after the death of Elvis Presley. Both Crosby (1901–1977) and Presley (1935–1977) gained wide popularity and admiration as singers; their singing styles still influence popular music. Crosby was best known for his soothing versions of ballads and love songs, while Presley was known as the "king of rock 'n' roll."

Pre-Reading Questions

1. What type of music do you enjoy? Do you prefer classical or popular music? Why?
2. Why do people listen to music? What types of music do you play while relaxing, dancing, driving, studying?
3. Who are the most popular singers in the world? What characteristics make them so popular?

Preview of Key Terms and Concepts

The following terms and concepts are referred to in the reading. Try to guess their meanings by filling in the blanks in the sentences that follow.

generational puzzle

mass culture

rags-to-triumph pattern

Depression America

rock 'n' roll

climb the wall

1. People who are annoyed and extremely irritated by something are said to ______________________________.
2. ______________________________ is lively, often loud music that appeared early in the 1950s.
3. The story of Horatio Alger, a poor boy who became a successful businessman, illustrates a ______________________________.
4. The inability of many parents and their children to understand each other is a ______________________________.
5. Symphonic music is part of high culture, whereas folk songs and rock 'n' roll belong to ______________________________.
6. For many families, neither essential goods nor luxury items were affordable in ______________________________.

READING. "From Song to Sound: Bing and Elvis" by Russell Baker

(1) The grieving* for Elvis Presley and the commercial exploitation* of his death were still not ended when we heard of Bing Crosby's death the other day. Here is a generational* puzzle. Those of an age to mourn* Elvis must marvel* that their elders could really have cared about Bing, just as the Crosby generation a few weeks ago wondered what all the to-do* was about when Elvis died.

(2) Each man was a mass* culture hero to his generation, but it tells us something of the difference between generations that each man's admirers would be hard-pressed* to understand why the other could mean very much to his devotees.*

(3) There were similarities that ought to tell us something. Both came from obscurity* to national recognition while quite young and became very rich. Both lacked formal music education and went on to movie careers despite a lack of acting skills. Both developed distinctive* musical styles which were originally scorned* by critics and subsequently* studied as pioneer developments in the art of popular song.

(4) In short, each man's career followed the mythic rags-to-triumph pattern in which adversity* is conquered, detractors* are given their comeuppance* and estates,* fancy cars and world tours become the reward of perseverance.* Traditionally, this was supposed to be the history of the American business striver,* but in our era of committee capitalism it occurs most often in the mass entertainment field, and so we look less and less to the board room for our heroes and more and more to the microphone.

---

* **grieving**	expressing sorrow for a loss, usually a death
exploitation	the use of something or someone to make a profit
generational	concerning the generations, i.e. parents and children
mourn	grieve
marvel	show wonder or surprise
to-do	fuss, excitement
mass	common, appealing to large groups of the population
be hard-pressed	have a difficult time
devotees	followers, fans
obscurity	being unknown, not conspicuous
distinctive	individual, unique
scorned	showed contempt or hatred for
subsequently	later, afterward
adversity	trouble, hard times
detractors	critics, people who make negative statements
comeuppance	deserved punishment or criticism
estates	large, expensive homes with land
perseverance	persistence, staying with something
striver	one who tries or competes

(5) Both Crosby and Presley were creations of the microphone. It made it possible for people with frail* voices not only to be heard beyond the third row but also to caress* millions. Crosby was among the first to understand that the microphone made it possible to sing to multitudes* by singing to a single person in a small room.

(6) Presley cuddled* his microphone like a lover. With Crosby the microphone was usually concealed,* but Presley brought it out on the stage, detached* it from its fitting,* stroked it, pressed it to his mouth. It was a surrogate* for his listener and he made love to it unashamedly.

(7) The difference between Presley and Crosby, however, reflected generational differences which spoke of changing values in American life. Crosby's music was soothing;* Presley's was disturbing.* It is too easy to be glib* about this, to say that Crosby was singing to, first, Depression America, and, then, to wartime America, and that his audiences had all the disturbance they could handle in their daily lives without buying more at the record shop and movie theater.

(8) Crosby's fans talk about how "relaxed" he was, how "natural," how "casual and easygoing." By the time Presley began causing sensations, the entire country had become relaxed, casual and easygoing, and its younger people seemed to be tired of it, for Elvis's act was anything but soothing and scarcely* what a parent of that placid* age would have called "natural" for a young man.

(9) Elvis was unseemly,* loud, gaudy,* sexual—that gyrating* pelvis*!—in short, disturbing. He not only disturbed parents who thought music by Crosby was soothing but also reminded their young that they were full of the turmoil* of youth and an appetite for excitement. At a time when the country had a population coming of age with no memory of troubled times, Presley spoke to a yearning* for disturbance.

---

* **frail**	weak, delicate
caress	touch lovingly
multitudes	large crowds
cuddled	held affectionately
concealed	hidden
detached	separated
fitting	connection to a base
surrogate	replacement
soothing	relaxing, calming
disturbing	troubling, causing discomfort
glib	overly simple, easy
scarcely	hardly
placid	calm, not easily excited
unseemly	inappropriate, not proper
gaudy	showy, tasteless
gyrating	twisting, turning
pelvis	hip bone
turmoil	confusion
yearning	strong desire

(10) It probably helped that Elvis's music made Mom and Dad climb the wall. In any case, people who admired Elvis never talk about how relaxed and easygoing he made them feel. They are more likely to tell you he introduced them to something new and exciting.

(11) To explain each man in terms of changes in economic and political life probably oversimplifies the matter. Something in the culture was changing. Crosby's music, for example, paid great attention to the importance of lyrics. The "message" of the song was as essential to the audience as the tune. The words were usually inane* and witless,* but Crosby—like Sinatra a little later—made them vital.* People remembered them, sang them. Words still had meaning.

(12) Although many of Presley's songs were highly lyrical, in most it wasn't the words that moved audiences; it was the "sound." Rock 'n' roll, of which he was the great popularizer, was a "sound" event. Song stopped being song and turned into "sound," at least until the Beatles came along and solved the problem of making words sing to the new beat.

(13) Thus a group like the Rolling Stones, whose lyrics are often elaborate*, seems often to the Crosby-tuned ear to be shouting only gibberish,* a sort of accompanying background noise in a "sound" experience. The Crosby generation has trouble hearing rock because it makes the mistake of trying to understand the words. The mutual* deafness may be a measure of how far we have come from really troubled times and of how deeply we have come to distrust the value of words.

Comprehension Questions

1. How are the backgrounds of Crosby and Presley similar?
2. How did the invention of the microphone change popular music? What was significant about the way each singer used the microphone?
3. What did the older generation like about Crosby's music? What did this group dislike about Presley and his music?
4. What role do the lyrics (words) play in Crosby's music? In Presley's music?
5. Do you think the author prefers one singer to the other? If so, how does he show his preference?

Discussion Questions

1. Music plays an important role in U.S. culture. It is included in religious and political ceremonies, and it provides people with entertainment—for example, concerts and symphonies. People in the United States also use music to relax and

---

*	
inane	empty
witless	unintelligent
vital	important, crucial
elaborate	complicated
gibberish	nonsense words
mutual	shared, in common

to enliven social occasions. What are some of the ways that music is used in another culture that you know of? How are those uses similar to the uses of music in the United States? How are they different?

2. Bing Crosby and Elvis Presley both became celebrities of great importance. What qualities, if any, do they have in common with today's musical celebrities? To what group(s) in the population do these celebrities appeal?
3. What musical themes, such as love, are universal—that is, the subject of songs in all cultures? What subjects do song writers especially like to write about? Why? Give examples. What are some of the most unusual subjects of songs you have heard? What makes them unusual?

PART TWO. The Target Structure: Adjective Clauses

I Focus on Identifying and Analyzing Adjective Clauses

Preview of Adjective Clauses

Fill in the blanks in the following sentences with any words or structures you wish:

_______________ was a singer who _______________

_______________.

_______________ is a style of music that/which _______________

_______________.

Because you have just read Russell Baker's article about Bing Crosby and Elvis Presley, you might have filled in the blanks this way:

Bing Crosby was a singer who *had a long career.*

Elvis Presley was a singer who *shocked many people with his style of singing.*

Rock 'n' roll is a style of music that *is very lively and loud.*

Rock 'n' roll is a style of music which *became popular in the United States in the 1950s.*

The clauses that begin with *who, that,* and *which* are adjective clauses. Each one modifies (describes or identifies) a noun: *singer* or *style.*

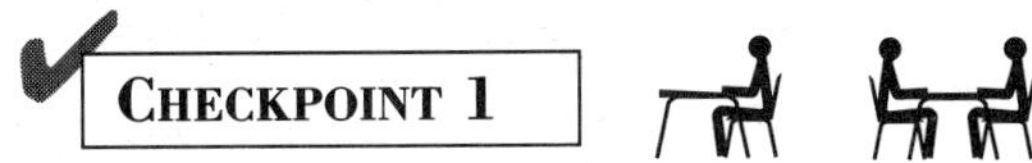

Go back to the reading on page 277 and find clauses beginning with *that* and *which* in paragraph 3, and one beginning with *who* in paragraph 9. These are adjective clauses. Draw a circle around the noun that is modified, or described, by the clause and underline the adjective clause.

Try to form some conclusions about the words used to introduce adjective clauses. Which are used with people? Which are used with places or things?

INTRODUCTION TO ADJECTIVE CLAUSES

An adjective clause is one type of dependent (subordinate) clause. It cannot stand alone as a sentence; it must be connected to an independent (main) clause. In addition, an adjective clause follows the noun or pronoun it modifies.

Examples of Sentences with Adjective Clauses

Main Clause	Adjective Clause
Bing Crosby was a **singer**	*who had a soothing voice.*
Rock 'n' roll is **music**	*that has a rapid rhythm.*
The microphone is a **device**	*which allowed Bing and Elvis to entertain large audiences.*

USING RELATIVE PRONOUNS

Adjective clauses usually begin with the relative pronouns *that*, *which*, or *who* (*whom*, *whose*). These pronouns substitute for the nouns they modify.

> The singer *who/that made rock (rock 'n' roll) popular* was Elvis Presley. (*who/that* = the singer)
>
> The song *that/which is playing* is "Hound Dog." (*that/which* = the song)

Who can only refer to a person, *which* can only refer to a thing, and *that* can refer to a person or a thing. Relative pronouns can refer to both singular and plural nouns.

> One rock *song that* Elvis often sang began, "You ain't nothin' but a hound dog."
>
> Other rock *songs that* he made popular were "Blue Suede Shoes" and "Jailhouse Rock."

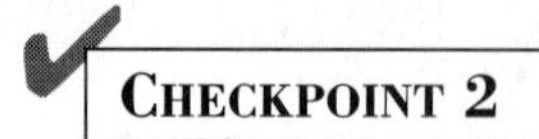

A. Each of the following sentences contains a noun modified by an adjective clause. Circle the noun and underline the adjective clause that modifies it. Example:

The (instrument) that Elvis first learned to play was the guitar.

1. In the 1970s, disco was popular music that made people want to dance.
2. "Rap" is talking music written for the most part by young men who live in big cities.
3. "Salsa" is an example of Latin American music that has become well known in the United States.
4. Many radio stations that are popular in the United States specialize in "classic" rock, or tunes from the fifties and sixties.
5. In the year 2000, will we be listening to songs that were written by computers?

B. Complete the following sentences with adjective clauses

1. The Beatles were musicians who . . .
2. Bing Crosby was a singer who . . .
3. Elvis was a performer who . . .
4. Barbra Streisand is . . .
5. [Your own choice] is . . .

ADJECTIVE CLAUSES WITH INDEFINITE PRONOUNS

Adjective clauses are often used with indefinite pronouns.

Indefinite Pronouns		
anyone	someone	any
anybody	somebody	much
anything	something	many
everyone	some	most
everybody	no one	other
everything	nobody	one
all	nothing	that
none	those	

When adjective clauses accompany these pronouns, the meaning of the sentence can change significantly.

Anyone can be a star. (indefinite pronoun alone)

Anyone who has talent and luck can be a star.

Everyone has heard of the Beatles.

Everyone who enjoys popular music has heard of the Beatles. (indefinite pronoun with adjective clause)

The adjective clause in the second sentence above limits *anyone* to any person in a specific group, those who have talent and luck. The adjective clause in the fourth sentence limits *everyone* to those who enjoy popular music.

CHECKPOINT 3 

Take turns doing A and B. (A) Give clues that include adjective clauses to refer to a person or thing in your classroom. (B) Guess their identities. Follow these sample patterns and the examples below.

Pattern 1 (Person): I'm thinking of *someone who/that . . .*
somebody who/that . . .

Pattern 2 (Thing): I'm thinking of *something that . . .*
something which . . .

Example:

Student A: I'm thinking of someone who is sitting in the front row.

Student B: You're thinking of Maria.

Student A: No, I'm not. I'm thinking of somebody who wears glasses.

Student B: You're thinking of Luan.

Student A: That's right!

COMBINING SHORT SENTENCES WITH ADJECTIVE CLAUSES

By using adjective clauses, writers can add variety and interest to their style; they can also avoid repetition and "pack" their sentences with more information. For example, the following sentence with two adjective clauses combines three short sentences.

The song *that Maria is playing* was a hit *that Elvis Presley recorded in 1970.* (The song was a hit. Maria is playing it. Elvis Presley recorded it in 1970.)

CHECKPOINT 4 

Combine each pair of sentences to make *one* sentence with an adjective clause. Example:

Bing Crosby sang Christmas songs. The Christmas songs became American classics.

Bing Crosby sang Christmas songs *that became American classics.*

1. Bing got his start with a band. The band consisted of a small group of friends.
2. Some of Bing's movies were set on islands. The islands had tropical climates and beautiful scenery.
3. Bing's many movies added to his popularity. The popularity brought him fortune.
4. Bing's sons gave him some professional support. The support helped his career.
5. Bing became involved in many forms of entertainment. The forms of entertainment allowed people to forget their problems for a while.

II Focus on the Relative Pronoun as Subject

When the relative pronoun is the subject of the adjective clause in which it occurs, the clause is called "subject-type." This name refers to the grammar of the adjective clause, not to the role of the noun or pronoun modified by the clause.

Relative Pronoun as Subject

Persons

The singer *who/that* made rock 'n' roll famous was Elvis.
(relative pronoun *who/that* = *subject of adjective clause)*

Things

The guitar is the instrument *that/which* was his favorite.
(relative pronoun *that/which* = ***subject of adjective clause)***

Checkpoint 5

Circle the appropriate relative pronouns; in some sentences, there is more than one correct answer. All the relative pronouns are used as *subjects* of the adjective clauses. Example:

> Many people (*who,*) *which,* (*that*) love popular music still listen to Bing Crosby's music.

1. Bing Crosby's mother, Kate, was a strong woman (*who, which, that*) greatly influenced her four sons.
2. In Spokane, Washington, high school instructors (*who, which, that*) used to teach Bing remembered him as a lazy student.
3. Bing's father played the mandolin and four-string guitar, instruments (*who, which, that*) introduced music into the Crosby household.
4. A Pacific Coast tour (*who, which, that*) lasted from 1925 to 1926 began Crosby's career.

5. Audiences (*who, which, that*) were accustomed to the traditions of the musical comedy and vaudeville* often didn't appreciate Bing's singing style.

III Focus on the Relative Pronoun as Object

Contrasting Subject- and Object-Type Adjective Clauses

A relative pronoun can also serve as the object of the verb in an adjective clause. "Decombining" a sentence that contains an adjective clause makes it easy to determine how the relative pronoun is used.

Combined sentence:

Paul McCartney is a Beatle *who continues to make albums.*

"Decombined" sentence:

Paul McCartney is a Beatle. He continues to make albums.

This decombined sentence shows that the relative pronoun *who* is a subject in the adjective clause because it substitutes for *he*. Therefore the clause is subject-type.

Combined sentence:

Paul McCartney is a Beatle *who(m) I first saw in 1967.*

"Decombined" sentence:

Paul McCartney is a Beatle. I first saw him in 1967.

The decombined sentence shows that the relative pronoun is the object of the verb in the adjective clause because it substitutes for *him*. Therefore the clause is object-type.

Object-Type Clauses

As in subject-type clauses, different relative pronouns may introduce object-type clauses: *who*, *whom*, *that*, and *which*. The major difference between subject-type and object-type clauses is that the relative pronoun may be omitted in object-type clauses, but *not* in subject-types:

***Subject-type*:**

INCORRECT: John Lennon is the Beatle married Yoko Ono.

CORRECT: John Lennon is the Beatle *who/that* married Yoko Ono.

Object-Type

CORRECT: The Beatles sang tunes people all over the world enjoyed. (relative pronoun omitted)

---

* **vaudeville** a form of popular theater consisting of a variety of comedy and musical acts

CORRECT: The Beatles sang tunes *that* people all over the world enjoyed.

In formal writing, the relative pronoun *whom* is used to refer to a person or persons in object-type clauses. *That* may also be used, or the relative pronoun may be deleted. In informal speech, *who* is sometimes used in object-type clauses, but this usage is not technically correct. To refer to things, *that*, *which*, or no pronoun may be used to introduce an object-type adjective clause.

Relative Pronoun as Object

Persons

Most musicians *whom* we see on television also give live concerts.

Most musicians *that* we see on television also give live concerts.

Most musicians we see on television also give live concerts.

(relative pronoun = object of verb *see*)

Things

The concert *that* I wanted to see was sold out.

The concert *which* I wanted to see was sold out.

The concert I wanted to see was sold out.

(relative pronoun = object of infinitive *see*)

CHECKPOINT 6

A. 

Read the following situation and take turns making up sentences that contain object-type clauses. Use different relative pronouns. Begin the sentences "They enjoyed/liked/appreciated . . . "

Situation: Talented musicians in high schools all over the United States were invited to New York City to compete in a contest at Carnegie Hall. All of them had a wonderful time. Example:

They received attention in their hometown newspapers.

They enjoyed the attention *(that)* they received in their hometown newspapers.

1. They visited famous museums.
2. They saw several Broadway plays.
3. They tried new restaurants.
4. They met professional musicians.
5. They made new friends.

B.

Circle any appropriate relative pronoun (X means *no* relative pronoun). In some cases more than one answer may be correct. Remember that you must use a relative pronoun in a subject-type clause. Example:

The music (*whom*, (*that*,) (*X*)) Elvis enjoyed as a child was gospel singing.

1. Elvis's relatives were mostly poor Mississippi farming people (*whom, that, X*) he loved deeply.
2. In 1943 when Elvis was eight, his father bought him a guitar (*whom, that, X*) he enjoyed and soon learned to play.
3. "Old Shep" was a song (*whom, that, X*) Elvis sang at the Mississippi-Alabama Agricultural Fair.
4. At a movie theater in Memphis, Tennessee, Elvis got a job (*whom, that, X*) he soon lost because he watched all the movies.
5. Sun Recording Studio was the organization (*whom, that, X*) gave Elvis his first break.
6. "That's All Right" was the first song (*whom, that, X*) Elvis recorded at Sun Recording Studio.
7. Elvis copied some movements (*whom, that, X*) he had first seen in gospel performers.
8. These unusual twisting motions caused the teenaged girls (*whom, that, X*) came to see Elvis perform to scream and faint.
9. Elvis's hairstyle was another feature (*whom, that, X*) was controversial.
10. In the fifties, Memphis and New Orleans were cities (*whom, that, X*) people visited when they wanted to hear good music.

IV Focus on the Relative Pronoun as Object of a Preposition

Relative pronouns that introduce adjective clauses can also be objects of prepositions. In formal writing or speech the preposition precedes the relative pronouns *which* or *whom*.

The concert *at which* I saw Elvis was great.

The musicians *with whom* Elvis performed were talented.

In informal writing or speech, the preposition can appear at the end of the clause. In this case, the relative pronouns *that* or *whom* or the omitted relative pronoun pattern may be used.

The concert *that* I saw him *at* was great.

The concert (X) I saw him *at* was great.

The musicians *whom* Elvis performed *with* were talented.

The musicians (X) Elvis performed *with* were talented.

It is important to remember to include the preposition in the sentence. The meaning is not clear if it is omitted:

INCORRECT: The group whom Eric Clapton appeared was the Beatles.

CORRECT: The group whom Eric Clapton appeared *with* was the Beatles.

CORRECT: The group Eric Clapton appeared *with* was the Beatles.

Relative Pronoun as Object of Preposition

Persons

The girl ***with whom** Elvis fell in love* while serving in the army later became his wife. (formal)

The girl ***whom** Elvis fell in love **with*** . . . (less formal)

The girl *(X) Elvis fell in love **with*** . . . (informal)

The girl ***who/that** Elvis fell in love **with*** . . . (informal)

Things

The country ***to which** Elvis went* as a soldier was Germany. (formal)

The country ***that/which** Elvis went **to*** . . . (less formal)

The country *(X) Elvis went **to*** . . . (informal)

CHECKPOINT 7

A.  

Write as many sentences as possible that contain adjective clauses with relative pronouns as objects of prepositions. Each sentence will provide information about a musical instrument from the list below. Look in a dictionary or other reference book if you need information about the various instruments. Try to use several different prepositions. Follow the pattern given. When you have finished, exchange papers with another group and check each other's answers.

Instruments	Prepositions
harmonica	with
violin	on
drum	or
trumpet	to
etc.	etc.

A/an ____________ is an instrument ____________ (preposition/relative pronoun) ________________________________ (adjective clause).

A *piano* is an instrument *on which* there are 88 keys.

A *piano* is an instrument (*that*/*X*) there are 88 keys *on*.

A guitar is an instrument *with which* many singers accompany themselves.

A guitar is an instrument (*that*/*X*) many singers accompany themselves *with*.

B.

Complete the following sentences any way you wish. Examples:

I know a teenager *to whom* Harry Connick Jr. gave his autograph.

There's a fabulous restaurant in this neighborhood *at which* many celebrities have eaten.

A. I know a	teenager	with whom . . .
	movie star	to whom . . .
	teacher	for whom . . .
B. There's a	tropical island	on which . . .
	fabulous restaurant	at which . . .
	test tomorrow	after which . . .
	great TV program	on/before which . . .

V Focus on the Relative Pronoun as a Possessive

The relative pronoun *whose* is used to show possession. It may refer to both people and things. When the relative pronoun is used as a possessive, the noun it modifies must follow the pronoun immediately.

Relative Pronoun as a Possessive

Persons

The singer *whose music* Jane enjoys the most is Julio Iglesias.

(The singer is Julio Iglesias. Jane enjoys *his music* the most.)

Things

This is the guitar *whose strings* are broken.

(This is the guitar. *Its strings* are broken.)

An adjective clause beginning with *whose* can also act as the object of a preposition, as in the following sentence:

Some entertainers *on whose television programs* Elvis appeared became great Presley fans.

(Some entertainers became great Presley fans. Elvis appeared *on their television programs.*)

CHECKPOINT 8

A.

Use the cues to write a definition sentence for each of the following. Every sentence must contain an adjective clause with *whose*. When you have finished, exchange papers with another group and check each other's answers. Example:

> convertible/car/top/down
>
> A convertible is a car *whose top can be put down.*

1. piano/instrument/keys/ivory
2. blues/music/roots/ African American
3. reversible raincoat/coat/inside/outside
4. flag/piece of cloth/design/meaning
5. hybrid/plant/parents/different species
6. mobile home/vehicle/inside space/home

B. 

Rewrite each pair of sentences as one sentence that contains an adjective clause of possession. Form the adjective clause from the second sentence. Example:

> A man is playing the banjo. His guitar is broken.
>
> A man *whose guitar is broken* is playing the banjo.

1. He took his guitar to a shop. He called the shop's owner yesterday.
2. A friend went with him. He heard the friend's band in California.
3. A singer plans to join the band. His recording contract was just canceled.
4. The singer has been practicing with a female vocalist. Her father is a famous opera singer.

VI Focus on the Punctuation of Adjective Clauses

PUNCTUATION OF ADJECTIVE CLAUSES: RESTRICTIVE VERSUS NONRESTRICTIVE

Adjective clauses can be classified as restrictive or nonrestrictive according to their use in a sentence.

Restrictive clauses are essential to a sentence; they cannot be removed from a sentence without changing its meaning. They are needed to distinguish nouns from others of the same group, or to identify or limit the noun that is described. These clauses are *not* set off by commas.

> People *who admired Elvis* never talk about how relaxed and easygoing he made them feel.

The musician *who sang "Hound Dog"* was Elvis Presley.

Music *that relaxes people* is usually slow.

Adjective clauses that are *not* essential to the meaning of the sentences in which they are used are called *nonrestrictive*. They are not used to identify or limit a noun; rather, they provide extra, parenthetical information about it. They are preceded and followed by a comma.

Elvis Presley, *whom many rock singers imitated and admired*, died in 1977.

"White Christmas," *which is one of the world's favorite holiday songs*, made Bing Crosby famous in many countries.

Both Bing and Elvis used the microphone, *which allowed them to project their voices to large numbers of people.*

The first two examples show that adjective clauses that modify proper nouns are always nonrestrictive because proper nouns are one-of-a-kind and cannot be restricted. Note that the relative pronoun *that* is never used to begin non-restrictive clauses.

Checkpoint 9

A.

Complete the sentences with restrictive and nonrestrictive clauses. Examples:

A singer who has been popular for many years is Ray Charles.

My favorite instrument, which is the piano, is easy to play.

Restrictive	Nonrestrictive
1. A singer who. . .	My favorite singer, who . . .
2. An instrument that . . .	My favorite instrument, which . . .
3. Music that . . .	Music, which . . .
4. The song that . . .	That song, which . . .
5. Rock 'n' roll that. . .	Rock 'n' roll, which . . .

B.

Use a pair of commas to set off nonrestrictive clauses (those giving extra information about a noun). Add no punctuation to sentences with restrictive clauses. Example:

The high school officials who were responsible for Elvis's education did not approve of his style. (no commas)

Beale Street, which is in Memphis, had lots of clubs that featured blues music.

1. Adolescents who listened to Elvis's music were often scolded by their parents.
2. Elvis's pelvis which wiggled and twisted during his performances shocked older audiences.
3. "Heartbreak Hotel" which was Elvis's first RCA release has a special "echo" effect.
4. In 1956 Elvis recorded a song that had been sung by Carl Perkins; it was called "Blue Suede Shoes."
5. Elvis's fans who often tore the shirt off his back forced their hero to stay in his hotel rooms on tour.

Expressions of Quantity with Adjective Clauses

Adjective clauses often occur after pronouns of quantity (*one, both, many, much, some,* etc.) or superlatives used as nouns followed by the preposition *of.* These clauses are always nonrestrictive.

> Bing Crosby's wives, *both of whom* were beautiful women, stopped working when they married him.
>
> Bing Crosby had many children, *one of whom* played a character on the TV series "Dallas."
>
> Bing Crosby made many movies, *the most famous of which* were the "Road" movies.

This pattern may also be used with other nouns, not just expressions of quantity and superlatives.

> I have read several books, *the titles of which* I have forgotten, about Elvis Presley's life.

Checkpoint 10

Complete sentences A and B with adjective clauses that contain expressions of quantity or superlatives; make the clauses from the numbered sentences given. When you finish, compare your answers to those of other pairs or groups. The first one has been done for you.

A. Mary has twelve instruments, . . .

1. She bought all of them herself.
   . . . all of which she bought herself.
2. Two are trumpets.
3. The most expensive is a piano.
4. She plays one at a nightclub.

B. That rock 'n' roll band has five members.

5. Two are guitar players.

6. The youngest is a Native American.
7. I have met one of them.
8. Each member has a great voice.

VII Focus on Positions of Adjective Clauses

Adjective Clauses with Prepositional Phrases

Adjective clauses are sometimes preceded by prepositional phrases.

> Two singers *of the twentieth century* who have profoundly influenced American popular music are Bing Crosby and Elvis Presley.

If a noun is modified by both a prepositional phrase and an adjective clause, the prepositional phrase always comes first.

Other Positions

Adjective clauses may follow a noun or a noun phrase in one of several different positions in a sentence. The following base sentence has three different positions where adjective clauses might appear.

> Base sentence: Bob Hope made films with Bing.

Since there are three nouns in the sentence (*Bob Hope*, *films*, and *Bing*), three adjective clauses could be added to it, one for each noun.

> Bob Hope, *who later became a famous comedian*, made films *that were called the "Road" movies* with Bing, *whose reputation was at its peak.*

In this example, the first and third adjective clauses are nonrestrictive because they modify proper nouns; the other clause is restrictive because it limits or restricts the noun (*films*) it modifies.

Complete the sentences with adjective clauses. Before filling in the blanks, discuss the clauses to determine which fits each blank best. The first clause has been filled in for you.

1. Recording artists <u>whose songs have become popular in the previous year</u> are nominated for music industry awards ______________________________ in January of the following year, a time ______________________________.
    - that are called the Grammies
    - when the year's statistics are known
    - whose songs have become popular in the previous year

2. Top categories ______________________________ include "Song of the Year," ______________________________, and "Album of the Year," ______________________________.

which includes more songs than the "Single" category
that Grammy awards are given for
for which five artists were nominated in 1993

3. Singers ______________________________ hope the judges ______________________________ will choose their songs, ______________________________.

that are nominated
which will become even more popular if they win
who vote

4. Two categories ______________________________ are Reggae, ______________________________, and Instrumental, ______________________________.

which is music not accompanied by lyrics
which is a style of singing from Jamaica
that are less well known

VIII Focus on Clauses of Time and Place

Some adjective clauses begin with *when* and *where*, sometimes called "relative adverbs"; these words substitute for the adverbs *then* and *there*. The following is an example from the reading.

> At a time *when* the country had a population coming of age with no memory of troubled times, Presley spoke to a yearning for disturbance.
>
> (At a time . . . , Presley spoke to a yearning for disturbance. *Then* the country had a population coming of age with no memory of troubled times.)

In very formal writing, time and place clauses are often expressed as the objects of prepositions. For example, the relative clause in the preceding sentence could be written:

> At a time *during which* the country had a population . . .

In the following sentence, the adjective clause gives information about a place.

> Graceland is the house *where Elvis Presley lived with his family for several years.*
>
> (Graceland is the house . . . . Elvis Presley lived *there* with his family for several years.)

Again, in more formal style, the sentence could be written with a prepositional phrase instead of *where.*

Graceland is the house *in which* Elvis Presley lived . . .

CHECKPOINT 12

A. Complete each sentence by adding a predicate and an adjective clause of time or place. You may want to refer to the reading at the beginning of the chapter. When you have finished, exchange papers with another group, and check each other's answers. Example:

An Elvis Presley concert ...

An Elvis Presley concert was a place where teenaged girls screamed and fainted.

1. An estate . . .
2. A boardroom . . .
3. The depression in America (the 1930s) . . .
4. Wartime in America (1941-1945) . . .
5. The death of Elvis . . . occasion . . .

B. Each of the following sentences with adjective clauses contains an error. Make the corrections and compare your group's answers with those of another group. Example:

A guitar player which my father knows studied with the Beatles' friend.

A guitar player whom my father knows studied with the Beatles' friend.

1. Someone has musical talent still needs to practice.
2. The song that the Beatles first recorded it is still played on the radio.
3. Ringo Starr who has made several solo albums was the drummer.
4. The television program whose the Beatles first appeared on was the Ed Sullivan program.
5. Beatle George Harrison, who he became interested in Eastern religions, spent some time in India.

PART THREE. Review and Integration

Facts About Bing and Elvis: Sentence Combining

A. Form an adjective clause beginning with *preposition + relative pronoun* from the second sentence in each pair. In the first sentence, put the adjective clause after the noun the clause modifies. The preposition that should be used to begin the adjective clause is italicized, along with the noun or pronoun to be replaced. Example:

> Early in his career, Bing Crosby had a partner.
>
> He got his start *with the partner.*
>
> Early in his career, Bing Crosby had a partner *with whom* he got his start.

1. During fifty-one years Bing recorded more than 1600 songs. He made 100 films *in fifty-one years.*
2. Bing's band, "The Rhythm Boys," played to enthusiastic audiences in Los Angeles night clubs. The Whitman orchestra played "back-up" music *for "The Rhythm Boys."*
3. Bing's four oldest sons followed their famous father into the entertainment field. Bing recorded the album "A Crosby Christmas" *with his sons* in 1950.
4. Bing Crosby had two wives. *One of them* was Dixie Carrol.
5. Kathryn Grant wrote a book. She described her life with Bing *in this book.*

B. Combine the following pairs of sentences with adjective clauses that begin with *whose.* The words to be replaced are in bold print. Example:

> Elvis Presley starred in several movies. **Their popularity** was due to his singing.
>
> Elvis Presley starred in several movies *whose popularity* was due to his singing.

1. Elvis was popular with Hollywood filmmakers because of his politeness and professionalism. **His film career** began in 1956.
2. His first movie was very successful. **Its story** was set at the end of the American Civil War.
3. Elvis's movie *King Creole* was set in New Orleans. **Its officials** declared a holiday, "Elvis Presley Day," for the city's school children.
4. *G.I. Blues* followed Elvis's release from the U.S. army. **The army's most famous soldier of 1958** had served his tour of duty in Germany.
5. A Hollywood "prison" was the scene of *Jailhouse Rock.* **The prison's inmates, or "jailbirds,"** danced around with Elvis.

C. Combine the following pairs of sentences about a piano competition by using adjective clauses of any type.

1. Kristen played a piece. It was a lively sonata.
2. The next piece was by Beethoven. Her friend played the piece.

3. Jane looked very serious. Her piece came from an Italian opera.
4. The composer's mother loved the next piece. He had written it for her.
5. The winning contestant smiled happily. She had played her piece perfectly.

Information About Jazz: Varying the Relative Pronoun

Improve the passage about the origins of jazz by rewriting it using a variety of relative pronouns. Underline *that* wherever it occurs as a relative pronoun and substitute *who, whom*, or *which* (accompanied by prepositions, if appropriate) or use the pattern with deleted *that*. Rewrite the passage; then exchange your group's work with another group and check it. Possible changes for the first two adjective clauses are given below.

Jazz is music that listeners say brings joy. The way that jazz came about and the reason that it came into being are unknown. But there is one thing that everyone knows: New Orleans is the city that gave birth to jazz. Musical sources in New Orleans that musicians drew on were the brass bands that played military music in the streets, street musicians that entertained residents and tourists, operas that people attended at the French Opera House, and musical church services that African Americans participated in.

Buddy Bolden is the man that is usually recognized as the first musician that played jazz. Bolden's introduction to music occurred during the Mardi Gras parades that passed near his home in uptown New Orleans.

The band that Bolden put together in New Orleans had most of the elements that experts consider essential to this type of music. The band that he played with improvised, or made up, the music as they went along. Their music had a quality that was called "hot."

Bolden's instrument, the cornet, was the horn that the great Louis Armstrong later played. The name that Bolden was given was "The King." This is a tradition that was carried into the Elvis Presley era. Elvis, after all, was the musician that was called "The King" in the 1950s.

Possible changes:

Jazz is music <u>which</u> listeners say brings joy. The way <u>in which</u> . . .

Improving Style with Adjective Clauses

Improve the style of the following paragraph by changing the underlined sentences into adjective clauses and joining them to the independent clauses that precede them.

Three limited edition dolls were created by the Hasbro Toy company in late 1993. <u>The dolls look just like Elvis Presley</u>. Elvis's fifty-ninth birthday was celebrated on January 8. <u>The birthday dolls were made for Elvis's fifty-ninth birthday.</u> They went on sale for $50. <u>The $50 includes a certificate and a signature.</u> Elvis is represented by three 12-inch figures. <u>Two of the figures are "Elvis Teen Idol" and "Jailhouse Rock."</u> Other dolls were planned for an introduction on August 16. <u>Other dolls include "The Gold Suit" and "Military" models.</u> <u>August 16 marks the anniversary of Elvis's death.</u>

Identifying Types of Adjective Clauses

Return to the reading on pages 277–279. Find adjective clauses of each type listed below, and write the number of the paragraph in which the clause occurs. Then copy each clause with the noun it modifies. Example:

Subject-type with *that*

paragraph __*3*__ <u>similarities that ought to tell us something</u>

Subject-type with *which* (2)

paragraph ______ ________________________________

paragraph ______ ________________________________

Object of preposition (2)

paragraph ______ ________________________________

paragraph ______ ________________________________

Subject type with *who* (2)

paragraph ______ ________________________________

paragraph ______ ________________________________

Time with no relative pronoun

paragraph ______ ________________________________

Time with *when*

paragraph ______ ________________________________

Possessive

paragraph ______ ______________________________

Object-type with no relative pronoun

paragraph ______ ______________________________

An Imaginary Dialogue Between Bing and Elvis: Forming Adjective Clauses

Look over the chart summarizing Bing's and Elvis's careers and then do the exercise that follows.

	BING	ELVIS
Personal lives	1930: married Dixie Carrol; who died in 1952. 1933: Gary born; Dixie and Bing had three more sons later. 1955: married Kathryn Grant; she gave birth to Bing's only daughter.	1955: signed RCA contract 1956: had four #1 records 1968: daughter, Lisa Marie, born to Elvis and Priscilla Presley 1977: last live concert in the city of Indianapolis, Ind.
Homes	1901: born, Tacoma, Wash. grew up in Spokane, Wash. 1943: Toluca Lake mansion burned down. later life: Hillsborough estate on San Francisco peninsula	1935: born in Tupelo, Miss. 1948: moved to Memphis 1957: moved to Graceland with parents (later, wife Priscilla) 1960s: "Circle G" ranch horse farm
Movies/TV shows	*King of Jazz,* first film *High Society,* sang "True Love" to Grace Kelly Christmas special with sons	*Flaming Star,* Elvis played a "half-breed" Native American. *G.I. Blues* film made after discharge from army "Aloha from Hawaii" on TV

The following imaginary dialogue between Bing Crosby and Elvis Presley is missing all adjective clauses. Fill in the missing clauses, if necessary using the summary chart about the two men's lives and careers. Form the clauses from the sentences in parentheses. Example:

Elvis: I read several books about you ______________________________ (I will never forget them).

Elvis: I read several books about you *that I will never forget.*

Bing: I've heard a lot about you, Elvis. You have a tremendous number of fans ______________________________ (they still play your music).

Elvis: You're pretty famous yourself, Bing. I was told you had a career ______________________________ (you made more than 100 films during this career).

Bing: It's hard to believe, but it's true. But the one ______________________________ (I remember it the best) is the first film ______________________________ (I made it).

Elvis: Is that the one ______________________________ (you sang "True Love" to Grace Kelly in it)? I loved that one.

Bing: Thanks. But the movie ______________________________ (Grace Kelly and I starred in it) was *High Society,* not *King of Jazz,* my first film. You made a lot of films, too, Elvis. Tell me about your favorite role.

Elvis: Well, *G.I. Blues* was the film ______________________________ (it was the most fun to make), but the one ______________________________ (the critics liked it the most) was *Flaming Star.* Did you happen to see that one?

Bing: Was it filmed the year ______________________________ (I married my second wife then), 1955?

Elvis: It was actually later than that. Nineteen fifty-five was the time ______________________________ (I had just signed a contract with RCA then).

Bing: I remember reading about some year ______________________________ (you had four number one hit singles then). I couldn't believe it.

Elvis: That was 1956. I was pretty amazed myself. That was the greatest year of my life, except 1968, ______________________________ (our daughter was born then). She was a beautiful baby ______________________________ (we named her Lisa Marie).

Bing: You had only one child, didn't you? I had a few more. And two wives, ______________________________ (both of them were actresses). Dixie was the wife ______________________________ (she had my first four sons). These were the boys ______________________________ (they appeared on my Christmas special). Kathryn, ______________________________ (I had my only daughter with her) was the woman ______________________________ (I was married to her longer).

Elvis: Hmm. I was married only once, but we did have two houses. Graceland, ______________________________, (I lived there with Priscilla, Lisa Marie, and my parents) was in Tennessee. But the ranch in Mississippi, the

"Circle G," was the place ______________________________ (we went there to relax).

Bing: One of our houses, ______________________________ (Dixie and I lived there at Toluca Lake), burned down in 1943.

Elvis: That's too bad. Did you rebuild?

Bing: No. The next place ______________________________ (I lived for a length of time there) was an estate in Hillsborough, ______________________________ (it is on the San Francisco peninsula).

Elvis: Sure is nice to meet you after all this time. You were one of the best singers ______________________________ (they came before me).

Bing: You and I both did a number of things as singers ______________________________ (they had never been done before). Hope to see you again soon.

Categories Game: Packing Sentences with Meaning

Divide into teams of three or four students. Your teacher will select a category or let you choose one of your own. Write a definition sentence for all the nouns that belong to the category that you can think of in five minutes. You *must* use an adjective clause in each definition. Your teacher will give you 0-3 points for each sentence depending on how complicated its structure is and how "packed" with information it is. For example, sentence 1 might be worth only one point, and sentence 2 might be worth two, and sentence 3, worth three points.

1. The piano is a musical instrument that has a keyboard.
2. The piano is a musical instrument whose strings sound when the keys are struck.
3. The piano, which is played expertly by Ray Charles, is a musical instrument that has a keyboard.

Suggested categories: musical instruments, types of music, places to listen to music, machines that play music, move stars, movies

Debate: Bing Versus Elvis

In small groups, discuss arguments for the superiority of either Bing or Elvis as a singer and entertainer. Refer to the reading selection (and the grammar exercises) for vocabulary and content. Prepare arguments that contain a number of adjective clauses of all types: subject, object, object of preposition, possessive; include restrictive and nonrestrictive clauses. Then choose a speaker from your group to debate a speaker from another group.

Role Play: Using Adjective Clauses

Situation: Your favorite musical performer is appearing live in concert in your hometown in a few days. This is a once-in-a-lifetime event. Form groups of four people and in each group decide who will take each of the following roles. Write a short skit, practice your parts, and perform the skit in front of the class. Use adjective clauses. (Choose names for the characters.)

Character #1: *You are one of this performer's greatest fans. You want to attend his concert very much. You are failing chemistry and have a big chemistry test the day after the concert. You try to persuade your parents to let you go.* (Sample sentence: "This is an event *that I can't miss.*")

Character #2: *Your parents have allowed you to buy a ticket to the concert. You want your friend to come with you. You are an excellent student and offer to tutor your friend in chemistry.* (Sample sentence: "I can help ______________________________ (name) with the material *he needs to know for the test.*")

Mother: *You think this performer is vulgar, crude, and a bad influence on your child. You are determined to keep your teenager away from the concert.* (Sample sentence: "______________________________ is the most disgusting performer *that I have ever seen.*)

Father: *Although you are not offended by this performer, you are concerned about your child's academic record. You think your teenager should stay home the night of the concert to study for his/her test the next day.* (Sample sentence: "Can't you see him some other time *when you don't have to study for a test?*")

Suggestions for Writing

1. If you are keeping a journal, write an entry on your fantasies about fame. Would you like to be rich and famous like Bing Crosby or Elvis Presley? Do money and fame necessarily bring happiness? How would you feel about revealing your private life to the public?
2. Do you and your parents (or children) differ in your attitudes toward music, dress, dating, or some other kind of behavior? Write a composition about the generation gap in regard to one or more of the above issues.
3. Write a composition in which you compare a contemporary singer with either Bing Crosby or Elvis Presley. Consider their singing styles, audience appeal, lyrics, and any other points you think are significant.
4. Write a composition in which you compare and contrast two musicians or types of music in the United States (or in another country).
5. Write a composition in which you discuss different types of music from another culture that you know about.

Unit Nine

Adverb Clauses

READING. From *Black Elk Speaks* by John G. Neihardt

THEME. Native Americans

PART ONE. The Context

In *Black Elk Speaks* by John G. Neihardt, Black Elk, a leader of the Sioux people from the upper midwestern part of the United States, tells his life story. The Sioux tribe is one of several hundred that had been living in the Americas for over ten thousand years before the first European explorers arrived. The passage that follows is from chapter one; it explains the origin of the pipe that many tribes of Native Americans ("Indians") smoked on ceremonial occasions. It also reveals the reverence for the land and all living creatures that characterizes Native-American religions.

Pre-Reading Questions

1. Do you know the early history of your country or your parents' country? Was there a group of original inhabitants? Did the population of the country change over time? If so, what significant events contributed to that change?
2. Unlike Native Americans, most people in North America today view the land as property, either public or private. Landowners may, within limits, do what they please with their land. Has this attitude affected the environment? If so, how?
3. A characteristic of Native-American culture is respect for old people and the wise stories they can tell. How does your culture view older people? Are they encouraged to tell stories to the young? If so, what kind? Do the stories teach lessons?

Preview of Key Terms and Concepts

To help familiarize yourself with important words and ideas in the chapter, determine the meaning of the terms on the left by matching them to the definitions on the right. Put the correct letter after each term. Discuss your answers with a partner or group, and ask your teacher about any terms you're not sure of.

1. warrior ____
2. vision ____
3. bison ____
4. scout ____
5. buckskin ____
6. tepee ____

a. cone-shaped tent used by some Native-American tribes
b. large, shaggy oxlike animal with a rounded back; a buffalo
c. soft leather made from the skins of animals
d. courageous fighter or person with experience in war
e. something seen by a person in a dream or dreamlike state
f. person sent out ahead of an army or other group to gather information

READING: From *Black Elk Speaks* by John G. Neihardt

(1) My friend, I am going to tell you the story of my life, as you wish; and if it were only the story of my life I think I would not tell it; for what is one man that he should make much of his winters, even when they bend him like a heavy snow? So many other men have lived and shall live that story, to be grass upon the hills.

(2) It is the story of all life that is holy and is good to tell, and of us two-leggeds sharing in it with the four-leggeds and the wings of the air and all green things; for these are children of one mother and their father is one spirit.

(3) This, then, is not the tale of a great hunter or of a great warrior, or of a great traveler, although I have made much meat* in my time and fought for my people both as boy and man, and have gone far and seen strange lands and men. So also have many others done, and better than I. These things I shall remember by the way, and often they may seem to be the very tale itself, as when I was living them in happiness and sorrow. But now that I can see it all from a lonely hilltop, I know it was the story of a mighty vision given to a man too weak to use it; of a holy tree that should have flourished* in a people's heart with flowers and singing birds, and now is withered;* and of a people's dream that died in a bloody snow.

(4) But if the vision was true and mighty, as I know, it is true and mighty yet; for such things are of the spirit, and it is in the darkness of their eyes that men get lost.

(5) So I know that it is a good thing I am going to do; and because no good thing can be done by any man alone, I will first make an offering and send a voice to the Spirit of the World, that it may help me to be true. See, I fill this sacred* pipe with the bark* of a red willow;* but before we smoke it, you must see how it is made and what it means. These four ribbons hanging here on the stem are the four quarters of the universe. The black one is for the west where the thunder beings live to send us rain; the white one is for the north, whence* comes the great white cleansing wind; the red one for the east, whence springs the light and where the morning star lives to give men wisdom; the yellow for the south, whence come the summer and the power to grow.

(6) But these four spirits are only one Spirit after all, and this eagle* feather here is for that One, which is like a father, and also it is for the thoughts of men that should rise high as eagles do. Is not the sky a father and the earth a mother, and are not all living things with feet or wings or roots their children? And

---

* made meat	hunted
flourished	grew stronger, prospered
withered	dried up, died
sacred	holy
bark	covering of a tree
willow	tree that has long, thin leaves and bends easily
whence	from which, from where (formal or archaic)
eagle	large bird of prey whose feathers are sacred to Native Americans

this hide* upon the mouthpiece* here, which should be bison hide, is for the earth, from whence we came and at whose breast we suck as babies all our lives, along with all the animals and birds and trees and grasses. And because it means all this, and more than any man can understand, the pipe is holy.

(7) There is a story about the way the pipe first came to us. A very long time ago, they say, two scouts were out looking for bison; and when they came to the top of a hill and looked north, they saw something coming a way off, and when it came closer, they cried out, "It is a woman!," and it was. Then one of the scouts, being foolish, had bad thoughts and spoke them; but the other said: "That is a sacred woman; throw all bad thoughts away." When she came still closer, they saw that she wore a fine buckskin dress, that her hair was very long and that she was young and very beautiful. And she knew their thoughts and said in a voice that was like singing: "You do not know me, but if you want to do as you think, you may come." And the foolish one went; but just as he stood before her, there was a white cloud that came and covered them. And the beautiful woman came out of the cloud, and when it blew away the foolish man was a skeleton* covered with worms.

(8) Then the woman spoke to the one who was not foolish: "You shall go home and tell your people that I am coming and a big tepee shall be built for me in the center of the nation." And the man, who was very much afraid, went quickly and told the people, who did at once as they were told; and there around the big tepee they waited for the sacred woman. And after a while she came, very beautiful and singing, and as she went into the tepee this is what she sang:

With visible breath I am walking.
A voice I am sending as I walk.
In a sacred manner I am walking.
With visible tracks I am walking.
In a sacred manner I walk.

---

* **hide**	animal skin
mouthpiece	the part of a pipe or musical instrument held in the mouth
skeleton	the supporting framework of bones in a body

And as she sang, there came from her mouth a white cloud that was good to smell. Then she gave something to the chief, and it was a pipe with a bison calf* carved* on one side to mean the earth that bears and feeds us, and with twelve eagle feathers hanging from the stem to mean the sky and the twelve moons, and these were tied with a grass that never breaks. "Behold!"* she said. "With this you shall multiply and be a good nation. Nothing but good shall come from it. Only the hands of the good shall take care of it and the bad shall not even see it." Then she sang again and went out of the tepee; and as the people watched her going, suddenly it was a white bison galloping* and snorting,* and soon it was gone.

(9) This they tell, and whether it happened so or not I do not know; but if you think about it you can see that it is true.

(10) Now I light the pipe, and after I have offered it to the powers that are one Power, and sent forth a voice to them, we shall smoke together. Offering the mouthpiece first of all to the One above—so—I send a voice:

(11) Hey hey! hey hey! hey hey! hey hey!

(12) Grandfather, Great Spirit, you have been always and before you no one has been. There is no other one to pray to but you. You yourself, everything you see, everything has been made by you. The star nations all over the universe you have finished. The four quarters of the earth you have finished. The day, and in that day, everything you have finished. Grandfather, Great Spirit, lean close to the earth, that you may hear the voice I send. You towards where the sun goes down, behold me; Thunder Beings, behold me! You where the White Giant lives, behold me! You where the sun shines continually, whence come the day-break star and the day, behold me! You where the summer lives, behold me! You in the depths of the heavens, an eagle of power, behold! And you, Mother Earth, the only Mother, you who have shown mercy to your children!

(13) Hear me, four quarters of the world—a relative I am! Give me the strength to walk the soft earth, a relative to all that is! Give me the eyes to see and the strength to understand, that I may be like you. With your power only can I face the winds.

(14) Great Spirit, Great Spirit, my Grandfather, all over the earth the faces of living things are all alike. With tenderness have these come up out of the ground. Look upon the faces of children without number and with children in their arms, that they may face the winds and walk the good road to the day of quiet.

(15) This is my prayer; hear me! The voice I have sent is weak, yet with earnestness* I have sent it. Hear me!

---

* calf	young buffalo, cow, or other large animal
carved	formed from wood or other material with a sharp instrument such as a knife
behold	look (formal or archaic)
galloping	running
snorting	breathing loudly through the nose
earnestness	seriousness

(16) It is finished. Hetchetu aloh!

(17) Now, my friend, let us smoke together so that there may be only good between us.

Comprehension Questions

1. How old do you think Black Elk was when he told this story? How do you know?
2. Based on the reading, what conclusions can you draw about the Native-American view of animals and birds? Is this view unusual?
3. What kind of life has Black Elk lived?
4. What does Black Elk say about the "mighty vision"? Why hasn't it died along with the people's dream?
5. What is the legend of the pipe? How did the Sioux people receive it?

Discussion Questions

1. Many scientists and historians believe that the first Americans came to Alaska by walking over the Bering land bridge. Later it was covered by water and became the Bering Strait. After crossing the land bridge, the first Americans migrated south throughout the Americas. What does this suggest about the connection between Native Americans and Asian groups?
2. Black Elk uses a decorated pipe in his ceremony. The Native-American tribes are famous for various crafts in which they are very skilled. What kinds of crafts made by Native Americans are you familiar with?
3. The Native-American tribes adopted different lifestyles depending on the region in which they lived and what resources were available in that region. The Sioux, for example, had a nomadic lifestyle; they lived in portable homes and followed the buffalo. What are some other nomadic peoples in the world? What are their reasons for moving around?
4. Another group of Native Americans, the Pueblos, lived close together in villages that contained dwellings resembling apartment houses. Other tribes lived in longhouses that provided shelter for extended families. Which of the Native-American lifestyles would you prefer? Why?

PART TWO. The Target Structure: Adverb Clauses

I Focus on Subordinators and Punctuation of Adverb Clauses

Preview of Adverb Clauses

With a partner, read the following sentences and draw a line separating the two clauses in each one. The first one has been done for you. Then answer the questions after the sentences.

> This is not the tale of a great hunter, / although I have made much meat in my time.
>
> Because it means all this, the pipe is holy.
>
> If the vision was true and mighty, it is true and mighty yet.

1. Which of the clauses in each sentence is *dependent* (not a complete sentence)? Find it and underline.
2. Circle the word that introduces each dependent clause. Which clause expresses a reason? a contrast? a condition?

Overview of Adverb Clauses

Like adjective clauses, adverb clauses are called "dependent" because they must be connected to independent clauses. Although they contain a subject and predicate, adverb clauses are incomplete thoughts. Like adverbs, they modify either the verb in the main (independent) clause or the whole clause, and many answer the questions *When?*, *Where?*, *How?*, *Why?*, and *For what purpose?* The sentences above illustrate three types of adverb clauses: (A) contrast, (B) cause or reason, and (C) condition. Other types include time, place, manner, opposition, result, and purpose.

Subordinators

The words that introduce adverb clauses indicate their type. Examples of these connecting words, called subordinators or subordinating conjunctions, include *when*, *after*, *as soon as*, *although*, *as*, *because*, and *if*. These conjunctions have special meanings that express a relationship between the dependent or *subordinate* clause and the main, or independent, clause.

Subordinating Conjunctions That Introduce Clauses

Time	Reason	Contrast	Condition
after	because	although	if
before	since	even though	unless
when	as	though	in case (that)
whenever	now that		provided (that)
while/as	as long as	**Opposition**	whether or not
since		while	whether . . . or
until/till	**Result/Purpose**	whereas	
as soon as	in order that		**Manner**
once	so that	**Place**	as
as long as	such that	wherever	the way
by the time (that)		where	as if/as though

CHECKPOINT 1

A. Find the two sentences that contain adverb clauses in the paragraph in the "Overview of Adverb Clauses" on page 311. Underline the clause and circle the subordinating conjunction that introduces it. Put *S* over the subject of the adverb clause and *V* over the verb.

B. Return to the first paragraph of the reading (page 307) and find the adverb clauses beginning with *as*, *if*, and *(even) when*. Write *S* over the subject and *V* over the verb in each adverb clause.

Punctuation of Adverb Clauses

An adverb clause usually appears at the beginning or end of a sentence. If it precedes the main clause, a comma follows it; if the adverb clause ends a sentence, no comma is necessary.

> *Because it means all this*, the pipe is holy.
>
> The pipe is holy *because it means all this*.

An exception occurs with clauses of contrast or opposition, which are often preceded by commas when they end the sentence.

> The buffalo is thriving in the United States today, *although it was nearly extinct just a few decades ago*.

Checkpoint 2

A. 

Return to the two paragraphs you worked on in Checkpoint 1. Which adverb clauses that you underlined precede the independent clause? Which ones follow the independent clause? Discuss the differences in punctuation with your partner or group.

B. 

Insert commas in the following paragraph where necessary.

Whenever Black Elk spoke everyone listened. He was a highly respected leader even though he was old. Because Black Elk remembered the history of his people he knew a great deal about all the families. Whereas his family had many members other Sioux families were very small.

II Focus on Adverb Clauses of Time and Place

Time Clauses

Adverb clauses that express a time relationship generally begin with one of these subordinators: *when, as soon as, whenever, while, after, before, since, once, until,* and *by the time that.* Some of them, such as *when, once,* and *as soon as,* are very similar in meaning, as the examples in the box show.

Adverb Clauses of Time	
Conjunctions	**Time Clauses**
when (at that time)	*When* they finished the pipe, they spoke about Black Elk's life.
whenever (each time)	*Whenever* he welcomed a guest, the chief offered the pipe to show hospitality.
until/till (up to a time)	Indian tribes were the only inhabitants of North America *until* the Europeans came.
before	They came from Asia over land *before* North America and Asia were separated by the Bering Sea.
once, as soon as (immediately after)	The lives of Native Americans began to change *once* white settlers arrived.
while, as (during a time)	*As* the number of settlers increased, the number of Indians decreased.
by the time (that) (before/up to a time)	*By the time* Congress passed the Indian Removal Act (1830), their population had been reduced by almost two-thirds.
since (from a time up to now)	They have regained some rights in state and federal courts *since* they began to protest their treatment in the 1960s.
as long as (for all that time)	*As long as* their cultures are remembered, they will serve as examples of people who tried to live in harmony with nature.

CHECKPOINT 3

A. 

Fill in the letter of the subordinating conjunction that best completes each sentence. Return to the reading if you are unsure of an answer. Example:

__a__ Black Elk told the story of his life, he decided to share a pipe of willow bark with his visitors.

a. Before
b. While
c. Since

1. He began the story _____ they had smoked.
   a. before
   b. while
   c. once

2. The visitors listened ____ he finished his story.
   a. when
   b. until
   c. after
3. ____ he was speaking, they were sitting on the ground.
   a. While
   b. After
   c. Before
4. The Sioux have known about the pipe ____ a beautiful woman appeared to them in a vision.
   a. after
   b. since
   c. when
5. A good-smelling cloud came out of her mouth ____ she spoke.
   a. after
   b. until
   c. as

B.

Combine each pair of sentences using the subordinating conjunction in parentheses. Make sure to punctuate correctly.

1. Native Americans inhabited the continent.
   European settlers arrived in North America. (*before*)
2. The European newcomers began taking over territories.
   They forced Native Americans to move off their lands. (*once*)
3. The Sioux under Crazy Horse won a great victory at little Big Horn in Dakota Territory.
   George Armstrong Custer and his U.S. soldiers were defeated. (*when*)
4. Many Native-American tribes fought the incoming settlers.
   Chief Geronimo was defeated in 1886 at Wounded Knee, the last battle between Indians and the army. (*until*)
5. The Sioux couldn't hunt bison any longer.
   Their old way of life disappeared. (*as soon as*)

Special Tense Rules with Time Clauses

Sentences that contain time clauses sometimes require the use of certain verb tenses.

- The present tense, not the future, is used to express future time in a time clause. The future tense is used only in the main clause.

  When the tepee *is* ready, the Sioux people *will leave* to hunt the buffalo.

- Progressive forms are often used in clauses that begin with *as* or *while*.

  While the warriors *were performing* a ceremonial dance, the chief prepared the pipe.

- A perfect tense verb must be used in an independent clause joined to a *since*-clause that refers to a past action or situation.

  Native Americans *have inhabited* this continent since they *arrived* here thousands of years ago.

✔ Checkpoint 4

A.

Use the cues and the time words in parentheses to make sentences with *future* time clauses about the situation given below. Use *we* as the subject if no subject is supplied.

Situation: Imagine that it is late spring, 1868. Red Cloud and Sitting Bull, two great Sioux chiefs, are making plans for their people. Example:

winter come/move tepees (*as soon as*)

As soon as winter comes, we will move the tepees.

OR We will move the tepees as soon as winter comes.

1. rain stop/not move (*until*)
2. make clothes/buffalo hides dry (*after*)
3. warriors gather/smoke pipe (*as soon as*)
4. scouts leave/they/prepare horses (*before*)
5. spring arrive/return here (*when*)

B.

Read the following passage from *Black Elk Speaks* and find all the clauses that begin with *when*. Try using a different conjunction (*after*, *as soon as*, *once*, etc.) Does the meaning change? If so, is the change slight or significant? Discuss your conclusions with your partner.

There is a story about the way the pipe first came to us. A very long time ago, they say, two scouts were out looking for bison; and when they came to the top of a high hill and looked north, they saw something coming a way off, and when it came closer, they cried out, "It is a woman!," and it was. Then one of the scouts, being foolish, had bad thoughts and spoke them; but the other said: "That is a sacred woman; throw all bad thoughts away." When she came still

closer, they saw that she wore a fine white buckskin dress, that her hair was very long and that she was young and very beautiful. And she knew their thoughts and said in a voice that was like singing: "You do not know me, but if you want to do as you think, you may come." And the foolish one went; but just as he stood before her, there was a white cloud that came and covered them. And the beautiful young woman came out of the cloud, and when it blew away the foolish man was a skeleton covered with worms.

Adverb Clauses of Place

Most clauses that begin with *where* are adjective clauses; in those clauses *where* can be replaced by *in which*, *on which*, or *at which*. Some *where*-clauses are adverbial, however. In the following sentences, the adjective clause modifies a noun (*places*), but the adverb clause modifies a verb (*had lived*).

> Native Americans were forced to leave the places *where they had lived for centuries.* (adjective clause)
>
> They had lived *where they could follow their traditional lifestyles.* (adverb clause)

In the adjective clause, *where* can be replaced by *in which*, but *where* in the adverb clause cannot.

Wherever and adverbs ending in *-place* or *-where*, such as *anywhere*, *somewhere*, *everywhere*, *anyplace*, and *no place*, can also introduce adverb clauses of place.

Adverb Clauses of Place	
Conjunctions	**Clauses of Place**
where	At first they hunted *where they wanted to.*
wherever	They could follow the bison *wherever they went.*
anyplace, etc.	They could live *anyplace* they wanted.

Read the following sentences and underline the clauses that begin with *where* or any other words that refer to place in each pair. Determine which is an adjective clause and which is an adverb clause, and write *adjective* or *adverb* after each sentence. Examples:

> They met where the rivers crossed. ___adverb___
>
> They met at a place where the rivers crossed. ___adjective___

1. In the film *Little Big Man*, Dustin Hoffman played a scout who witnessed the battle at little Big Horn, where Custer was defeated by Crazy Horse.

   ____

2. As a scout for the Sioux, the character played by Hoffman rode wherever Crazy horse sent him. ______________
3. In the film *Dances with Wolves*, Kevin Costner's character traveled where no other white people were living. ______________
4. The motion picture *The Last of the Mohicans* was set in the seventeenth-century northeastern United States, where the French and Indian War was in progress. ______________
5. The most exciting scene involved a fight between Native-American warriors on a mountain where one fell to his death. ______________

III Focus on Adverb Clauses of Manner and Reason

Adverb Clauses of Manner

Adverb clauses of manner answer the questions *How?* or *In what way/manner?* Many begin with *as* or *(in) the way.*

Navajo blankets are still made *as they were made centuries ago.*

In recent decades, people in the United States have changed *in the way they view Native Americans and their cultures.*

Clauses of manner can also begin with *as if* or *as though*; they usually follow the verbs *act, look, appear, feel,* or *seem.*

Black Elk looks *as if/as though* he is tired.

Native Americans did not act *as if / as though* they owned the land.

In spoken English, *like* is often used instead of *as if* or *as though*, but *like* is not a conjunction. Using *like* to join clauses should be avoided in formal speech and writing.

FORMAL: The child acted *as if* she wanted to ride the horse.

INFORMAL: The child acted *like* she wanted to ride the horse.

Adverb Clauses of Manner

Conjunctions	Clauses of Manner
as (in) the way	Native Americans are no longer viewed *as/the way* they were in colonial times.
as if as though	People now feel *as if/as though* Native Americans have been treated unjustly.

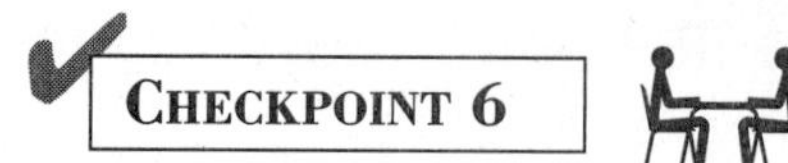

Combine the following pairs of sentences, using the conjunction in parentheses. Example:

> The Plains tribes constructed tepees. Their ancestors had taught them. (*the way*)
>
> The Plains tribes constructed tepees the way their ancestors had taught them.

1. The braves told stories. Their adventures had just happened. (*as if*)
2. The warriors led the boys in battle. Their fathers had showed them how to fight. (*as*)
3. The paintings on the tepee looked old. They had been drawn a hundred years before. (Delete "old"; *as though*)
4. Eagle feathers were hung from the peace pipe. They always had been. (*the way*)

Adverb Clauses of Reason

Adverb clauses of reason answer the question *Why?* and typically begin with the following conjunctions: *because, since, now that,* or *as long as.** For example, the *because*-clause below answers the question "Why will I first make an offering and send a voice to the spirit of the world?"

> *Because no good thing can be done by any man alone,* I will first make an offering and send a voice to the spirit of the world.

Adverb Clauses of Reason

Conjunctions	Clauses of Reason
because	The forced removal of eastern Native Americans to land west of the Mississippi is called the Trail of Tears *because* many people died on the journey.
since	Thousands of Cherokees had to live on reservations in Oklahoma *since* settlers forced them to move from their native lands in the mountains of western Tennessee and North Carolina.
as long as	"*As long as* you are here, let us have a special celebration," said Black Elk to the visiting chiefs.
now that	*Now that* the mistreatment of Native Americans is being recognized, their ways are more respected and studied.

* In informal English, *as* can begin adverb clauses of reason: *As* Black Elk was the tribe's leader, he explained the peace pipe.

Since and *as long as* are also used in time clauses, but in reason clauses their meanings are different; the context generally makes clear which meaning of these conjunctions is intended. *Now that* is used only in reason clauses that refer to the present time.

Using *Because* to Join Clauses

If *because* is used incorrectly, the relationship between clauses is not logical, as in the following examples.

ILLOGICAL: Native Americans loved nature *because they didn't pollute the land and water.*

LOGICAL: *Because Native Americans loved nature,* they didn't pollute the land and water.

OR Native Americans didn't pollute the land and water *because they loved nature.*

ILLOGICAL: Black Elk was very old *because his back was bent.*

LOGICAL: *Because Black Elk was very old,* his back was bent. OR Black Elk's back was bent *because he was very old.*

Using *(in Order) to*

The expression *(in order) to* is not a conjunction, but it is similar in meaning to *because* and *since.* The following sentences illustrate different ways of expressing the same meaning.

The chiefs gathered *because* they wanted to discuss strategy.

The chiefs gathered *in order to* discuss strategy.

The chiefs gathered *to* discuss strategy.

✔ Checkpoint 7

A. 

Ask questions beginning with *Why?* and answer them in any way that is logical, using the cues. The answers should be complete sentences that contain the conjunctions in parentheses. Give more than one answer if possible. Example:

Black Elk/be/happy to speak to the author? (*since*)

Q: *Why was* Black Elk happy to speak to the author?
A: He was happy to speak to the author *since* he was eager to pass on the history of his people.

OR *Since* the author was his friend, he was happy to speak to him about his life.

1. The history of Native-American tribes/be/interesting? (*because*)
2. There/be/much to learn from Native Americans? (*since*)
3. We/want/hear story/Black Elk? (*now that*)
4. Black Elk/talk/for hours? (*because*)
5. Black Elk/offer/pipe? (*since*)

B.

Combine the following pairs of sentences, using subordinating conjunctions that show reason. Give multiple answers for each pair of sentences.

1. Native Americans of the Plains between the Mississippi River and the Rocky Mountains fought wars against the settlers who were coming west. The newcomers were taking their lands and killing off the buffalo.
2. William Cody was given the name "Buffalo Bill." People said he killed 400 buffalo in one day.
3. The buffalo was the basis of the Plains peoples' culture. Food, clothing, houses, tools, and weapons were made from different parts of this animal.
4. The tepee was made of many buffalo skins sewn together. It was lightweight and easily folded for traveling.
5. The Plains peoples used a complicated system of smoke signals. Messages could be transmitted a great distance.

IV Focus on Adverb Clauses of Purpose and Result

Adverb Clauses of Purpose and Result

Adverb clauses of purpose and result are like reason clauses in that they express cause and effect. Purpose clauses answer the questions *For what purpose?* or *Why?* and most commonly begin with *in order that* or *so that.*

Now, my friend, let us smoke together *so that* there may be only good between us.

The Sioux learned to ride horses *in order that* they could be better hunters and warriors.

Result clauses follow special patterns with *so . . . that* and *such . . . that.*

so + adjective or adverb + *that*

In the book, Black Elk is *so old that* he can remember several generations of his people.

Black Elk speaks *so clearly that* all members of the council can hear him.

such + *a/an* + (adjective) + noun + *that*

Lame Deer was *such a wise medicine man that* he became famous among the Rosebud Sioux.

So . . . that is often used with quantity words like *many, much, few,* and *little* + a noun. *Such . . . that* is often used with expressions like *a lot of* or *a number/wealth/ quantity of.*

There were *so many* tribes in North America at one time *that* no one could have listed them all.

There were *such a lot* of buffalo at one time *that* no one believed they could disappear.

Adverb Clauses of Purpose and Result

Conjunctions	Clauses of Purpose and Result
PURPOSE	
so that	Black Elk told stories *so that* the lessons he had learned would not be forgotten.
in order that	The author wrote the stories down *in order that* they could be read and studied by others.
RESULT	
so . . . that	Black Elk was *so* wise *that* other chiefs looked up to him. He spoke *so* wisely *that* they respected him. He told *so many* stories *that* his listeners could hardly remember them all.
such . . . that	He had learned *such* a large number of stories *that* he could tell them for days.

CHECKPOINT 8

A. Fill in the blanks with *so that, so . . . that,* or *such . . . that.*

In the frozen land of the Northwest territories, it is ______ cold ____________ very few species of plants and animals can survive. The clothes made by women of the Inuit and Aleut tribes who live there are ______ well made ____________ their jackets and boots keep the hunters and voyagers comfortably warm. The clothing is not only warm but also lined with duck feathers to absorb perspiration ____________ it does not freeze on the wearer's skin. These women are ______ skillful workers ____________ they also make "kayaks," or one-person boats. A kayak must be waterproof and also very lightweight ____________ it can be carried great distances over land. This boat

is ______ much like clothing ____________ the Inuit say they "wear" a kayak, like a jacket.

B. Combine the following pairs of sentences by using *so . . . that* or *such . . . that.* Example:

There were great leaders among the forest tribes. We still recognize many of their names today: Hiawatha, King Philip, Black Hawk, Red Jacket, Sequoyah, and Osceola.

There were *such* great leaders among the forest tribes *that* we still recognize many of their names today: Hiawatha, King Philip, Black Hawk, Red Jacket, Sequoyah, and Osceola.

1. Chief Hiawatha of the Onondagas in the North was an effective politician. He persuaded six tribes to join one great nation called the Iroquois.
2. In the southern mountains, the Cherokee Sequoyah was creative. He invented an alphabet his people could read.
3. When Osceola led the Seminoles in the swamps of Florida, these Native Americans were brave. They fought U.S. soldiers rather than be forced to move to Oklahoma.
4. The Seminoles were skillful warriors. They were never defeated by the U.S. military and still inhabit the southern swamplands today.

PHRASES OF PURPOSE

Clauses of purpose that begin with *so that* and *in order that* may be reduced to phrases with *in order to* + the base form of the verb or *to* + the base form.

Native Americans built structures *in order that* they could take advantage of the behavior patterns of specific fish. Native Americans built structures (*in order*) *to* take advantage of the behavior patterns of specific fish.

They built underwater fences *so that* they could guide and trap fish.

The built underwater fences *to* guide and trap fish.

PHRASES OF RESULT

Clauses of result that contain the pattern *so . . . that* may sometimes be reduced to a phrase that consists of *too . . .* + the infinitive. This may be done when the verb in the subordinate clause is negative. A change in the subject can be expressed in a prepositional phrase with *for.*

The history of Native Americans is *so important that* we must never forget it.

The history of Native Americans is *too important* for us *to* forget.

There were *so many* tribes *that* people don't know all of them.

There were *too many* tribes *(for people) to* know.

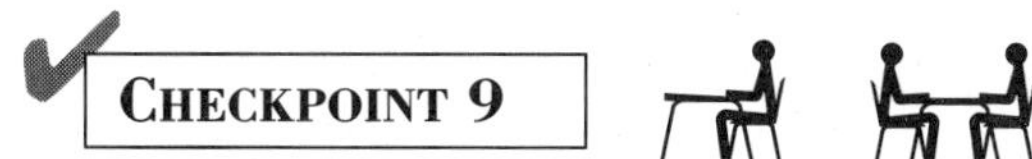

Reduce the clauses of result or purpose to phrases. Example:

> The women cleaned and dried vast quantities of fish so that they could store the food for winter months.
>
> The women cleaned and dried vast quantities of fish *in order to* store the fish for winter months.

1. All parts of the fish were so useful that the Native-American women didn't waste any of it.
2. Oil was extracted so that the women could use it in cooking.
3. Killer whales are so dangerous that most fisherman don't try to catch them.
4. Fisherman must be careful in order that they can avoid the many logs in the water that come from the timber industry.

V Focus on Adverb Clauses of Contrast and Opposition

Adverb Clauses of Contrast

An adverb clause of contrast changes the idea of the independent clauses by adding an unexpected or surprising element. The conjunctions that introduce these clauses are similar in meaning to the words *but* and *however.* They include *although* (informally, *though*) and *even though.*

Because it expresses a shift in the direction of thought, a contrast clause is usually set off by a comma even when it follows the independent clause.

> This, then, is not the tale of a great hunter or of a great warrior, or of a great traveler, *although I have made much meat in my time and fought for my people both as boy and man, and have gone far and seen strange lands and men.*

Adverb Clauses of Contrast	
Conjunctions	
although/though	*Although* the copper of North American tribes is beautiful, it is not as valuable as the gold used by South American tribes.
even though	The European settlers weren't interested in copper, *even though* it was beautiful.

Combine the following pairs of sentences by using contrast clauses. Use different subordinating conjunctions. Example:

> Cahokia, in southern Illinois, is the site of the greatest pyramid constructions north of Mexico City. Very few people in North America know of its existence.
>
> *Although very few people in North America know of its existence*, Cahokia, in southern Illinois, is the site of the greatest pyramid constructions north of Mexico City.

1. Until the eighteenth century, Cahokia's population was greater than that of any colonial city in North America. Not a single person lives there today.
2. Approximately 50 of the original 120 pyramids can still be seen today. Farmers and settlers dug into the site without any thought of preserving the buildings.
3. Little is known about the people who built Cahokia. Archaeological investigations show that construction started as early as A.D. 600.
4. We do not know much about the people of Cahokia. Their reasons for choosing a location on the Mississippi River to be a communication, transportation, and trade center are obvious.
5. The total drainage area of the Mississippi–Missouri rivers system is larger than that of any rivers in the world except the Amazon and the Congo. The Mississippi is only the fourth-longest river in the world.
6. Archaeologists haven't found any evidence of a political empire at Cahokia. As a trade empire, its river routes were longer than the distances from Moscow to Madrid or from London to Istanbul.
7. The site is thousands of miles from the Gulf Coast or from Wyoming. Shell objects from the Gulf and carved stones from the Yellowstone Park area have been found at Cahokia.

ADVERB CLAUSES OF OPPOSITION

Like clauses of contrast, adverb clauses of opposition add a different idea to that of the independent clause. But opposition clauses add information completely *opposite* that in the independent clause. Clauses of opposition are usually introduced by *while* or *whereas*. *While* can introduce time clauses as well as clauses of opposition; the context shows which meaning is intended.

Clauses of Opposition	
Conjunctions	
while	Black Elk was Oglala Sioux, *while* Lame Deer was Rosebud Sioux.
whereas	*Whereas* Lame Deer was young in the 1930s, Black Elk was old.

Like clauses of contrast, clauses of opposition are usually preceded by a comma when they follow the independent clause. Either idea may be introduced by the subordinating conjunction without any real difference in meaning other than greater emphasis on the independent clause.

> *While* the Navajos were nomadic, the Pueblos inhabited permanent homes. (emphasis on the Pueblos)
>
> The Navajos were nomadic, *while* the Pueblos inhabited permanent homes. (emphasis on the Navajos)

A. Use the cues to make sentences that contain clauses of opposition with *while* or *whereas*. Example:

> Plains people / . . . hunters/Pueblos . . . farmers
>
> *Whereas* the Plains people were hunters, the Pueblos were farmers.

1. Inuits' climate . . . cold/Seminoles' climate . . . hot
2. Inuit . . . Alaska/Seminole . . . Florida
3. The boats used by the forest tribes of the Northeast . . . "canoes"/those used by the Inuit of the Northwest . . . "kayaks"
4. The forest tribe Ottawa . . . deer and birds/Sioux . . . buffalo
5. Pontiac . . . Ottawa chief/Red Jacket . . . Shawnee

B. Compose sentences that contain *contrast* or *opposition* clauses. Combine the pairs of sentences using *although*, *even though*, *while*, or *whereas*. Example:

> Television shows have created a stereotypical picture of the Native-American warrior who hunts buffalo. Actually many different Native-American cultures exist.
>
> *Although* television shows have created a stereotypical picture of the Native American warrior who hunts buffalo, actually many different Native-American cultures exist.

1. The Apaches of Arizona and New Mexico were a great fighting tribe. The Hopis, Pueblos, and Zunis lived peacefully in the same area of the Southwest.

2. The Pueblos lived in cities. The Navajos were sheep farmers who moved from place to place in the desert.
3. Many tribes have a tradition of weaving objects from wool. No weaving is more beautiful or unusual than the rugs and blankets of the Navajo.
4. The Pueblos built houses on cliffs, or steep hills, many centuries ago. A number of these buildings are in good condition today.

VI Focus on Conditional Clauses: Real Conditions

Preview of Conditional Clauses

Return to Paragraphs 1, 7, and 9 (pages 307–309) of the reading and find the clauses that begin with *if.* Circle the word *if* and underline the clause it introduces. What time does each clause refer to: the present, the future, or the past? Find the verb in each *if*-clause. Does it match the time of the condition in each sentence? If not, in which one(s) is it different? What conclusions can you draw about verb tense in conditional sentences?

Real and Unreal Conditional Clauses

Conditional clauses are dependent clauses that usually begin with *if*; the accompanying independent or main clause expresses the <u>result</u> of the condition. Conditional clauses can express two kinds of conditions: real (possible) or unreal (hypothetical or impossible). The differences in meaning between these two types are indicated by the verb forms they call for; unreal conditionals require the use of special forms in both the dependent and independent clause.

The conditions in paragraphs 7 and 9 of the reading are real, or possible. The first one refers to present time, and the second one refers to future time.

> If you *want* to do as you think, you *may come.*
> (The condition is possible; in fact, the scout does approach the woman.)
>
> If you *think* about it, you *can see* that it is true.
> (The condition is possible. The result clause could also be expressed "You *will* see that it is true.")

The condition in Paragraph 1 may seem to refer to past time, but it actually does not. The past form (*were*) expresses hypothetical or unreal meaning, not past time.

> If it *were* only the story of my life, I think I *would not tell* it.
> (The condition is *unreal* since it is *not* only the story of his life; more than his life is involved.)

The following sentences illustrate some differences in verb forms between real and unreal conditions in the present or future.

> REAL (present): If Black Elk *has* visitors, he usually *offers* them a pipe.

REAL (future):	If Black Elk *has* visitors tomorrow, he *will offer* them a pipe.
UNREAL (present):	If Black Elk *had* visitors, he *would offer* them a pipe. (He has no visitors right now.)

Read the following paragraph from *Black Elk Speaks*. Then underline the conditional clause in the sentences that follow the paragraph. Which express real conditions? Which express unreal conditions? Discuss your answers with your partner.

It is the story of all life that is holy and good to tell, and of us two-leggeds sharing in it with the four-leggeds and the wings of the air and all green things; for these are children of one mother and their father is the spirit. Examples:

> <u>If it is true that we have the same mother and father as animals and birds</u>, then all creatures are brothers and sisters. <u>real</u>
>
> <u>If animals and plants were treated as human beings</u>, fewer species would become extinct. <u>unreal</u>

1. People will preserve their environment if they consider all life holy. ________
2. If people are sharing the planet equally with all other creatures, they must respect the rights of animals and birds. ________
3. North America might not have such serious problems with industrial pollution if people saw the world as Black Elk did. ________
4. Many North Americans would have behaved in a more environmentally responsible way if Europeans had followed the example of Native Americans. ________

Real Conditions: Present or Future

When the *if*-clause refers to a real present or future event, the tense of the verb in the clause is present. (The auxiliaries *will* and *be going to* are not used in an *if*-clause, even when the verb has future meaning.) The verb in the independent (result) clause may be present or future, depending on the meaning intended. The following chart illustrates the correct use of verbs in real present or future conditions.

Present/Future Real Conditions

	Condition	Result
PRESENT	If corn *receives* proper care,	it *grows* well.
FUTURE	If the cornfields *look* dry,	we *will water* them.
	Result	**Condition**
PRESENT	We *make* cornbread and grits	if our crop *is* big enough.
FUTURE	The corn plants *won't grow*	if there *is* a drought (dry period).

The conjunctions *when* or *whenever* can usually substitute for *if* in real conditions expressing generalizations.

If/ *When*/ *Whenever* there is a drought, the corn crop fails.

To refer to a situation that is only remotely likely to occur in the present or future, the auxiliary *should* + base form is sometimes used in the *if*-clause. As in all present or future real conditions, the verb in the independent clause is either present or future.

If you *should go* to Mesa Verde, you *will see* some beautiful ruins. (possible but unlikely)

If you *go* to Mesa Verde, you *will see* some beautiful ruins. (possible)

CHECKPOINT 13

A. 

Take turns asking and answering the question "What will you do if . . .?" based on the cues. Give any answer that is logical and true (real). Remember not to use *will* or *be going to* in the *if*-clause. Example:

lose/wallet

Student A: What *will* you *do* if you *lose* your wallet?

Student B: If I *lose* my wallet at work, I'*ll check* with the Lost and Found department.

1. lose/car keys
   checkbook
2. tomorrow/be/hot
   cold
   rainy

3. there/be/flood
   hurricane
   earthquake
   fire

B.

Using *if*-clauses, combine the following sentences about the Pima tribe in the southwestern United States. Example:

> The corn may be ripe tomorrow. Then the Pima tribe will harvest it.
>
> If the corn *is ripe* tomorrow, the Pima tribe *will harvest* it.

1. There may be enough only for the Pima. Then they won't sell it to other tribes.
2. The corn may be especially good this year. Then the Pima can make a large profit.
3. The Pima may be very successful. Then they will offer thanks to the Spirit of the World.
4. The land may not be rich enough for next year's corn. Then the Pima will plant new fields.
5. At times, the Pima become wealthy. In that case, they share their good fortune with their friends.

Using *Unless* to Introduce Conditions

The conjunction *unless* sometimes introduces a condition. Because *unless* means *if . . . not,* the verb in the *unless*-clause is usually affirmative.

> *If* corn plants *aren't watered,* they wither and die.
> (negative verb in *if*-clause)
>
> *Unless* corn plants *are watered,* they wither and die.
> (affirmative verb in *unless*-clause)
>
> Irrigation wouldn't be possible *if* canals *didn't exist.*
> (negative in *if*-clause)
>
> Irrigation wouldn't be possible *unless* canals *existed.*
> (affirmative in *unless*-clause)

If the verb in the conditional clause is affirmative, the verb in the main clause is changed to negative when *unless* is substituted for *if.*

> *If* people work together, they *can save* the environment.
> (affirmative verb in *if*-clause)
>
> *Unless* people work together, they *cannot save* the environment.
> (negative verb in main clause)

✔ CHECKPOINT 14

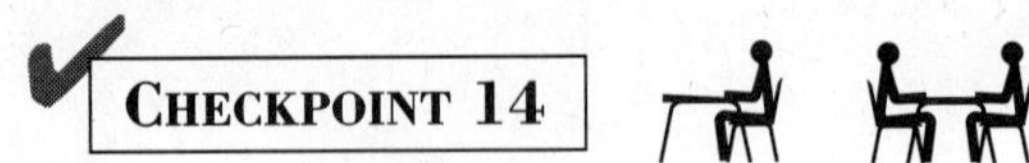

Change the conjunction in each sentence from *if* to *unless* or vice versa. Make any changes to the verbs that are necessary. Example:

> *If* everyone becomes concerned about the environment, the world *will* probably *be saved* for future generations.
>
> *Unless* everyone becomes concerned about the environment, the world *will* probably *not be saved* for future generations.

1. Plant and animal species will survive if we think of all the living things as relatives.
2. The forests may disappear if industries continue to use great numbers of trees.
3. Unless we control the chemical dumping in our rivers, pollution will enter our water supply.
4. There will be too much garbage in the world unless we recycle.
5. If we live responsibly, we will improve our environment.

WHETHER OR NOT, IN CASE, PROVIDED (THAT), ONLY IF

The subordinators *whether or not, in case,* and *provided that* have special meanings when they are used instead of *if* to introduce conditional clauses. *Whether or not* usually emphasizes that the action in the main clause will happen *regardless of the action in the conditional clause.*

> We will visit the pyramids at Cahokia *whether or not* you come with us to Illinois.
>
> OR
>
> We will visit the pyramids at Cahokia *whether* you come with us to Illinois *or not.*

Sometimes *whether or not* simply expresses a choice or alternative, as in this sentence from the reading.

> This they tell, and *whether* it happened so *or not* I do not know.

In case usually emphasizes being prepared for the action in the conditional clause, which may or may not happen.

> Let's put up the tepee *in case* it rains today.

Provided (that) and *only if* (*only . . . if*) have about the same meaning: that the action in the condition is *mandatory* or *required.*

> Tepees can be quickly and easily built *provided that/only if* the proper materials are available.

(They can be built quickly and easily *only if* the proper materials are available.)

CHECKPOINT 15

Combine the pairs of sentences, using the subordinators *whether or not, in case, provided (that),* or *only if.* Try combining them in more than one way and note any changes in meaning. Discuss your choices with your partner or group. Example:

We will visit the reservation. It rains.

We will visit the reservation *whether* it rains *or not.*
OR

We will visit the reservation *only if* it rains.

1. She will look for gifts to take home. She has room for them in her suitcase.
2. There will be a tour bus. You want to ride.
3. Native-American crafts will be available. Tourists want to buy them.
4. You can get beautiful baskets and pottery. You bring cash, travelers checks, or credit cards.

PAST REAL CONDITIONS

Sentences with past real conditions are less common than present and future ones. They explain that if one action or event occurred (or didn't occur) in the past, another one occurred (or didn't occur) as well.

If Native Americans *killed* buffalo, they *used* them for practical purposes, such as food and clothing.

If they *didn't shoot* the buffalo, they sometimes *drove* them over cliffs.

VII Focus on Present Unreal Conditions

PRESENT UNREAL CONDITIONS: HYPOTHETICAL VERSUS CONTRARY TO FACT

Conditional sentences can also express an *unreal* or hypothetical condition. Although present unreal conditions refer to present time, the verb in the conditional clause occurs in the past tense form. Only one form of the verb *be, were,* is used for all persons; if the verb is progressive, *were* is followed by the *-ing* form of the main verb.* The verb in the independent clause consists of *would* + base form. To express possibility or ability, *could* replaces *would. Might* is also used instead of *would* to express possibility.

---

* Like present unreal conditions, wishes about the present use past forms:
I wish you *were* here.
He wishes he *lived* among the Navajo.

If Black Elk *were* alive/*were living* today, he *might/would feel* better about the way people are treating the environment.

- **Hypothetical Conditions**. A present unreal clause can refer to a *hypothetical* condition, that is, a situation in which an event or action is *extremely unlikely* to occur.

Present Hypothetical Conditions
If the Pima corn *grew* as tall as trees, it *would provide* food for many tribes. **(But corn rarely grows this tall.)**
Many food products *wouldn't exist* if farmers *didn't plant* corn. **(But corn is an important crop.)**
We *might get* tired of cornbread if we *ate* it every day. **(We don't eat it every day, so we're not sure.)**
If they *were able* to travel anywhere, they *might go* to Pueblo Grande. **(But it is unlikely.)**

The auxiliary verb *would* is *not* used in the *if*-clause unless it expresses the meaning "willing to." In this case, *would* is the past form of *will* and is used to express a hypothetical condition.

If you *would feed* the horses, I *would appreciate* it.

(If you *were willing to feed* the horses, I *would appreciate* it.)

- **Contrary-to-Fact**. In a contrary-to-fact situation, there is *no possibility at all* that an event or action will occur. The same verb forms are used in present contrary-to-fact conditionals as in hypothetical conditionals.

Present Contrary-to-Fact Conditions
If I *were* a Pima, I *would have* many special agricultural skills. **(I am not a Pima.)**
If she *lived* among the Navajo, she *could make* beautiful weavings. **(She doesn't live among them.)**
If they *didn't water* the corn plant, it *would die*. **(They do water the corn plant.)**
If she *were living* in Phoenix, she *would need* a car. **(She isn't living in Phoenix.)**

CHECKPOINT 16 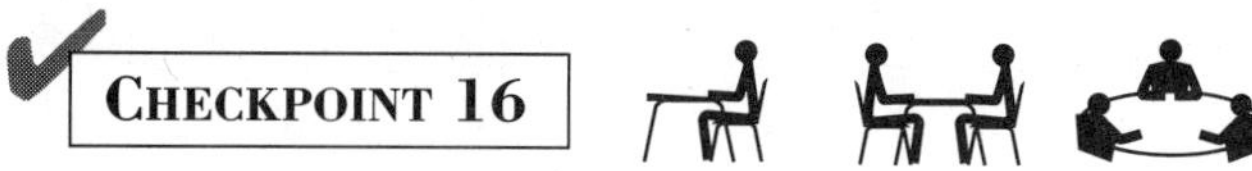

A. Black Elk said all living things were brothers and sisters sharing the world. Imagine being one of the animals, birds, or plants listed below. Make up sentences based on the following patterns. Take turns saying your sentences.

If I *were* a(n) ____________, I *would/could/might* + base form . . .

If I ____________ (past tense form) . . ., I *would/could/might* + base form . . .

Examples:

If I *were* an eagle, I *could fly.*

If I became an eagle, I *would fly* over a mountain.

deer	salmon	whale	snake	rabbit	turkey
buffalo	alligator	corn plant	oak tree	horse	bear
owl	flower	mushroom	banana	cactus	wolf

B. Imagine that it is the year 1630 and you are a European settler in North America. You are given a chance to join a Native-American tribe. Read the descriptions of three tribes' lifestyles and decide which tribe you would join. Write a paragraph containing present unreal conditional sentences to describe your life in the tribe. For example, how *would* you *live* if you *were* a ____________? What *would be* important to you if you *joined* the ____________ tribe?

1. The *Iroquois* are forest people of the Northeast. They live in wigwams or oval homes of tree bark over pole frames with only one door and a hole in the top for smoke from fires to escape. Iroquois villages are situated on river banks to allow easy travel by canoes, lightweight boats made from branches of trees, leather, and tree bark. Iroquois men hunt and track animals and birds with long bows and arrows. They are good fighters and often wage war against their enemies. Women grind corn into meal for bread; they also make clay pots and prepare meat for the winter.

2. The *Sioux* are people of the Midwest and western plains whose way of life is based on the buffalo. They used to hunt on foot, but since 1600 they have ridden horses to hunt the buffalo with short bows and arrows. The tribe holds great celebrations after successful hunts to thank the Great Spirit. Warriors tell stories about the hunt. Boys are considered men when they kill their first buffalo. The people use every part of the animal: for food, clothing, tools, weapons, and their homes (tepees). Made from buffalo skins placed over poles, tepees are triangular in shape and very lightweight. They must be easy to move because the Sioux move from place to place following the buffalo. The Sioux communication system consists of smoke signals, combinations of fast and slow puffs of smoke controlled by passing a blanket over a fire.

3. The *Tlingit* live along the Pacific Coast from Oregon to Alaska. They eat mostly salmon, fish which come up the northwestern rivers to lay their eggs. The Tlingit fish with spears and nets; they catch enough salmon in a few days to last many months. They live in permanent wooden homes called long houses, which are sometimes fifty feet long and large enough for several families. These people

are known for beautifully carved and painted totem poles that tell the history of a family; each person in the family has the name of an animal, which is his/her symbol or totem. The Tlingit have different canoes for different waters: small canoes for rivers and lakes and canoes big enough to hold fifty people for ocean travel.

VIII Focus on Past Unreal Conditions

Past Unreal Conditions: Expressing Hindsight and Regret

In unreal conditional sentences that refer to the past, the main verb consists of *would have* + the *-ed/-en* form. The verb in the *if*-clause consists of *had* + the *-ed/-en* form.* As they do in other conditions, *could* and *might* replace *would* with the meanings of ability or possibility.

Past Unreal Conditions

If Black Elk *had been* president, he *would have protected* the environment.

Industry *wouldn't have polluted* the rivers and oceans if Black Elk *had made* the laws.

What *would have happened* if the settlers *had not taken* the Native Americans' land?

If they *hadn't taken* the Native Americans' land,

. . . they *could have learned* a great deal from the Native-American culture. (ability)

. . . all the people *might have lived* together in peace. (possibility)

Would is used in the main or result clause but is *not* used in the *if*-clause of a past unreal condition.

INCORRECT: If the European settlers *would have known* how damaging their attitudes were, they *might have treated* Native Americans more respectfully.

CORRECT: If the European settlers *had known* . . .

Meaning in Past Unreal Conditions

Whereas present or future sentences that contain unreal conditions often express *imaginary* situations or conjecture, past unreal conditions often express *regret* or *hindsight*. Compare the meanings in the following pairs of sentences. The first in each pair is present unreal; the second, past unreal.

---

* Wishes about the past also use *had* + *ed/en:*

They wish/wished they *had built* their tepee before the snow started.

North Americans today *wouldn't hunt* animals and birds for sport if they *thought* of those creatures as brothers and sisters.

North Americans *wouldn't have hunted* animals and birds for sport if they *had thought* of those creatures as brothers and sisters.

Lame Deer *would be* a candidate for president in 1998 if he *decided* to run.

Would Black Elk *have run* for president if the Sioux *had encouraged* him?

CHECKPOINT 17

A. Return to the description of Native-American lifestyles on page 334. Imagine what your life *would have been* like if you had been a member of one of these tribes. Write a paragraph that begins, "If I *had been* a ____________, I would have ____________ . . ." When you have finished, exchange papers with a partner and check the verbs. Example:

> If I *had been* an Iroquois, I *would have lived* in the forest.

B. Read the following passage and do the exercise that follows it.

Pueblo Grande, an old Hohokam settlement, became the site of the modern city of Phoenix. Here the Hohokam built the most complex system of canals in North America and turned this extremely hot and dry desert area into a thriving city. The canals were lined with clay, so they were watertight. With them, the Hohokam transported water to irrigate their crops of maize, squash, cotton, and chilis. Because the U.S. settlers wanted to use the system of canals, they established a new city on the ruins of Pueblo Grande.

Maize, or Indian corn, was probably grown in North America as early as 3500 B.C. By 300 B.C. the important plant was the basis for an entirely new technology. Corn was the staple food of the entire continent before the arrival of the Europeans. Even today it is the staple food of the southwest United States.

Before Columbus introduced it to Europe, corn was unknown in the "Old World." Early settlers in North America ate corn chowder, cornbread, corn tortillas, hominy, grits, and popped corn. They fed corn to their pigs, turkeys, and chicken. Also they learned to manufacture whisky, alcohol, starch, fuel, and tobacco pipes from corn.

Complete the following sentences to make past unreal conditions based on the information from the reading. Example:

> If the Hohokam hadn't built canals at Pueblo Grande, . . .
>
> If the Hohokam hadn't built the canals at Pueblo Grande, *they wouldn't have been able to fertilize their crops.*

1. The canals wouldn't have been airtight if . . .
2. The settlers wouldn't have established a new city at Pueblo Grande if . . .
3. . . . if Columbus hadn't brought it to Europe.
4. Early settlers . . . chowder, tortillas, and hominy if . . .

5. What would domestic animals . . . if (or unless . . .)
6. If maize . . . North America, . . .
7. If . . . , . . .
8. . . . if . . .

IX Focus on Special Rules for Conditional Sentences

Past Conditions with Present Results

It is possible to mix time in both real and unreal conditional sentences when a past event or action has a present result. (The opposite would of course be logically impossible.) The following sentence from the reading contains a past condition and present result that are both possible.

If the vision *was* true and mighty, it *is* true and mighty yet.

In unreal conditional sentences in which time references are mixed, the *if*-clause follows the rules for forming past unreal conditions, and the main clause follows the rules for forming present unreal results; that is, the *if*-clause refers to past time, and the main clause refers to present time.

Mixed Time in Unreal Conditions

If Black Elk *had become* president, the United States *would be* a different country today. **(But he didn't become president.)**

If people *had begun* protecting the environment sooner, the water supply *might be* cleaner and safer now. **(But they didn't begin soon enough.)**

Would the world *be* different if Native-American cultures *had been* fully *preserved*? **(But they weren't fully preserved.)**

Checkpoint 18

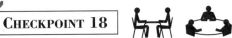

By asking and answering questions based on the cues, speculate about what North America and South America would be like today if they had never been colonized. Make up as many answers as you can think of.

If the Americas *had never been colonized*, . . .

Example:

Population/be (like)?

Q: If the Americas *had never been colonized*, what *would* the population *be* like now?

A. The population *would* probably *be* smaller.

1. How big/cities?
2. How many species/animals?
3. Family life/be like?
4. Politics/be like?

Conditional Clauses Without *If*

In formal or literary English, *if* is sometimes omitted from conditional sentences, and the subject and auxiliary verb are inverted. The word order in the main clause is not affected by the omission of *if* in the conditional clause. In real conditions, the auxiliary *should* introduces the conditional clause when *if* is omitted.

> *If we travel* to Arizona, we *will visit* several Native-American ruins.
>
> *If we (should) travel* to Arizona, we *will visit* several Native-American ruins.
>
> *Should we travel to* Arizona, we *will visit* several Native-American ruins.

In unreal conditions, *were* or *had* introduce conditional clauses without *if.*

Present unreal:

> If Black Elk *were* alive today, he *would applaud* the efforts of environmentalists.
>
> *Were* Black Elk alive today, he *would applaud* the efforts of environmentalists.

Past unreal:

> If Custer *had been* a better general, he *might not have fought* a battle at Little Big Horn.
>
> *Had* Custer *been* a better general, he *might not have fought* a battle at Little Big Horn.

Rewrite the conditional clause in each sentence without *if*; the main clause does not require any changes. For negative conditions put *not* after the subject. Exchange your sentences with a partner and check each other's work. Example:

> If beaver hats *had not become* popular in the seventeenth century, the fur trade in North America *would not have grown* into such a big industry.
>
> *Had* beaver hats *not become* popular in the seventeenth century, the fur trade . . .

1. If you should travel to the Hudson Bay area, you will probably hear about the famous trading company of that name.
2. If the climate in northeastern North America were milder, bears and other fur-bearing animals would not be so numerous.

3. Finding the skins of the beavers would have been much more difficult for the Europeans if the Native Americans in that area had not traded with them.
4. If the Native Americans hadn't known how to trap the animals and process them into marketable skins, the Europeans would have had to develop these skills themselves.
5. If fashions had not changed in the nineteenth century, beaver hats for men might still be popular.

What if . . . ?

The expression *what if* has the same meaning as a conditional clause, but in a reduced form. It can be used to express real or unreal conditions and has the meaning *What will/would happen if . . . ?* or *What would have happened if . . . ?* Compare the following pairs:

We're planning a picnic tomorrow. *What will we do if* it rains?

We're planning a picnic tomorrow. *What if* it rains?

What would have happened if the buffalo had become extinct?

What if the buffalo had become extinct?

It's amazing to think that the people of Cahokia might still live in pyramids.

What if the people of Cahokia still lived in pyramids?

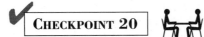

Change each sentence to a shortened version with *what if.*

1. I wonder what would have happened if Christopher Columbus had never come to the Americas.
2. It is amazing to think about the possibility that North America could still be unknown in Europe.
3. What would have happened if Squanto's tribe had never been exposed to European diseases?
4. Imagine that the Plains Indians still hunted buffalo throughout the western United States.

X Focus on Reduction

Reduction of Time Clauses

To improve the style of sentences, clauses are often reduced. Adverb clauses that begin with *after, before, when, while,* and *since* can be reduced to phrases.

To reduce an adverb clause, the subject is omitted, and the verb is changed to an *-ing* form.

When the Hohokam built their irrigation canals, they used clay to make them watertight.

When building their irrigation canals, the Hohokam used clay to make them watertight.

Note that adverb clauses can be reduced only *when the subjects of the dependent and independent clauses refer to the same person(s) or thing(s).* In the following sentences, only the first adverb clause can be reduced.

When *the Hohokam* built their irrigation canals, *they* used clay to make them watertight. (same subject)

After *the Hohokam* built their irrigation canals, *their crops* could be watered. (different subjects)

When the verb phrase of the subordinate clause contains a form of *be* the clause can be reduced by deleting that form and its subject.

When you are in Arizona, you could visit the ruins at Pueblo Grande.

When in Arizona, you could visit the ruins at Pueblo Grande.

I plan to go there *while I am visiting my sister.*

I plan to go there *while visiting my sister.*

A. Read the following sentences and write *S* after a sentence if the subjects of the independent clause and the subordinate clause are the same. Write *D* if they are different. If you wrote *S*, change the subordinate clause to a phrase, and rewrite the sentence. If a pronoun is used in the main clause, you may have to replace it with the noun from the reduced clause. Example:

When people drive along the Pacific Coast of Washington, Canada, and Alaska, they can see an amazing variety of birds and animals. *S*

When driving along the Pacific Coast of Washington, Canada, and Alaska, people can see an amazing variety of birds and animals.

1. Whales migrate through the waters, while other mammals such as otters, sea lions, and seals are catching fish for food.
2. Herds of migrating whales gather around the rocks of Vancouver Island while they are singing their beautiful deep songs.
3. Here visitors will see the largest totem pole in the world while they are sailing into the Aleut Bay.
4. After the Kwakiutl tribe made the 173-foot pole, they carved twenty-two figures in the red cedar wood.

B. Using the conjunctions in parentheses, expand the cues to make sentences with time clauses, and then reduce the clauses. Example:

Native Americans hunted buffalo/learn to ride horses. (before)

Native Americans hunted buffalo *before they learned to ride horses.*

Native Americans hunted buffalo *before learning to ride horses.*

1. They became even better hunters/master horseback riding. (*soon after*)
2. The Sioux ride horses/they could also hunt and fight. (*while*)
3. The braves returned to the camp/skin the animals. (*before*)
4. All the members of the tribe celebrated/cook the buffalo meat. (*while*)

More Reduction: Conjunctions Versus Prepositions

Problems in the formation of sentences may arise when prepositions are confused with conjunctions. Of course, a few words, such as *before* and *after*, can act as either prepositions or conjunctions in different contexts.

Before winter arrived, the Sioux moved their camp. (conjunction)

The Sioux moved their camp *before winter*. (preposition)

Before and *after* are exceptions: usually prepositions and conjunctions have different forms. In general, prepositions must be followed by nouns or noun phrases, and conjunctions must be followed by clauses that include a subject and verb.

- *While* Versus *During*. *While* is a conjunction that can introduce a time clause. *During* is a preposition followed by a noun or noun phrase.

  INCORRECT: They talked *during* they smoked.

  CORRECT: They talked *while* they smoked.

  CORRECT: They smoked *during* their conversation.

- *Because* Versus *Because of*. The conjunction *because* introduces a clause, but the expression *because of* is a two-word preposition followed by a noun or noun phrase. *Due to* is another preposition that has the same meaning. When *due to* introduces a clause, it is followed by *the fact that*.

  Because water was scarce, the Hohokam conserved it.

  Due to the fact that water was scarce, . . .

  Because of the scarcity of water, the Hohokam conserved it.

  Due to the scarcity of water, . . .

- *Despite* and *In spite of*. The expressions *despite* and *in spite of* are prepositions. But when followed by *the fact that* these expressions are used as conjunctions and can introduce clauses.

Prepositions:

Despite the intense heat, the Pima flourished in the desert.

The Pima flourished in the desert *in spite of* the intense heat.

Conjunctions:

In spite of the fact that the winters were long and cold, the Iroquois flourished in the northern forests.

The Iroquois flourished in the northern forests *despite the fact that* the winters were long and cold.

Checkpoint 22 

Read the Native-American creation myth and replace the underlined clauses with prepositional phrases that have the same meaning. The first one has been done for you.

At the beginning of time, because everything was dark [*because of the darkness*], people couldn't see each other on one side of the world. But people on the other side had a great deal of light. They didn't want to share it due to the fact that they were greedy. Fox went to the other side to steal the sun but failed because the sun was hot. His tail was burned and to this day is hairless. Then Buzzard tried and, because his claws were sharp, he grabbed the sun and put it on his head. In spite of the fact that Buzzard had had a good idea, he too failed. His head was burned and to this day is bald. Then Grandmother Spider tried. Despite the fact that she was extremely small, the spider was very clever. She made a clay pot and huge web. She used these to catch the sun and bring it to the other side of the world. So, because she was so brave and intelligent, the Cherokee people received not only light but also fire and pottery.

Using *Even* with Conjunctions

The word *even* is often used to emphasize or intensify the meaning of conjunctions, such as *when*, *before*, *after*, *if*, and *though*. *Even* is not a conjunction, however, and it can *never* introduce a clause by itself.

INCORRECT: We know a great deal about Native-American cultures *even* many tribes have disappeared.

CORRECT: We know a great deal about Native-American cultures *even though* many tribes have disappeared.

CORRECT: Many people began to recognize the beauty of Native-American art *even before* it became popular.

When *even* is used before *if* it means that the action in the main clause will occur regardless of the action in the *if*-clause.

Some species of plants and animals would become extinct naturally *even if* people tried to preserve them.

CHECKPOINT 23

Read each sentence and fill in the missing conjunction: *when*, *before*, *after*, *if*, or *though*.

1. Even ___________ most people have heard of Sitting Bull and Geronimo, few modern history books mention Chief Joseph.
2. Many Native Americans continued to fight with bow and arrow even ___________ the Europeans introduced guns.
3. We can learn about Native-American culture even ___________ we never travel to a reservation.
4. There had been wars among tribes in North America even ___________ the European settlers arrived.
5. Custer's men stayed and fought at Little Big Horn even ___________ they learned that they were outnumbered.

PART THREE. Review and Integration

Who Did It? Tenses in Time Clauses

Read each group of sentences and answer the question that follows. More than one correct answer may be possible. Discuss your answers in groups.

1. Black Elk was telling the story when Red Cloud arrived.
2. Black Elk had told the story when Chief Joseph arrived.
3. Black Elk told the story when Sitting Bull arrived.

Q: Who heard the whole story?

4. The Blackfeet make clothes when they have hides.

5. The Crows will make clothes if they have hides.
6. The Sioux will make clothes when they have hides.

Q: Who may *not* have a chance to make clothes?

7. Once Red Cloud arrived at Black Elk's tepee, he smoked the pipe.
8. Before Chief Joseph arrived at Black Elk's tepee, he smoked the pipe.
9. When Sitting Bull arrived at Black Elk's tepee, he smoked the pipe.

Q: Who didn't share his pipe with Black Elk?

Oral Practice: General Time Clauses

Using the cues, make up sentences that contain general time clauses. Example:

People/nervous/when . . .

People get nervous when they speak in public.

1. People/nervous/when . . .
   upset/when . . .
   confused/when . . .
   tired
   bored
2. A person/dial 911/as soon as . . .
   drive/gas station/as soon as . . .
3. I . . . /whenever/toothache
   headache
   stomach ache
   homesick
   hungry

Native-American Legends: Reason or Cause

Combine the following sentences, using a coordinating conjunction that expresses reason or cause (*because, since, now that,* etc.). Give multiple answers for each pair of sentences and then determine which sentence your partner or group prefers.

1. Native Americans lived close to nature. Their stories show a belief in the mysterious powers of mountains, rivers, and rocks.
2. Holy men of the Pueblo tribes often go to four sacred mountains. The Pueblos believe the mountains have the power to give rain and to make medicine.
3. Among the Native-American tribes of the Northwest, the sun, moon, and stars were thought to travel freely around the sky. They were considered human.
4. The Sioux and Cheyenne believe in the magical powers of sacred objects. Members of these tribes say they feel life flowing through the holy pipe.

5. Conventional logic cannot be used to analyze Native-American legends. Stories reflect different tribal traditions rather than factual or scientific information.
6. The legends are often beautiful and amusing but always much more than simply entertaining. They are believed.

Let Me Suggest . . .

Complete the sentences in any way that is logical. Example:

As long as you have the time, . . .

As long as you have the time, you can help us build a tepee.

Now that it's morning, . . .

Now that it's morning, we can go fishing.

1. As long as you have the time, . . .
the money, . . .
the energy, . . .
the interest, . . .
2. Now that it's morning, . . .
noon, . . .
evening, . . .
midnight, . . .

Expressing Mixed Feelings: Contrast

Take turns completing these patterns. Give multiple answers for each one. Use the cues in parentheses in #1 if you wish.

1. Although I enjoy summer, . . . (hot)
restaurants, . . . (expensive)
movies, . . . (scary)
vacation, . . . (boring)
2. ____________ is a wonderful (city) despite the fact that . . .
school
country
neighborhood
3. Even though . . ., it is (they are) exciting
interesting
educational
delicious

Expressing Opposition

Write a paragraph in which you contrast two members of your class who seem to be completely opposite. Use *while* and *whereas* in sentences that contain clauses of opposition. Share your paragraphs with other students and check the clause structure and punctuation.

Write another paragraph about two different cities, countries, or tribes of Native Americans. Check each other's papers.

Father and Son: Present Unreal Conditions

Read the situation and then use the cues to make sentences that contain present hypothetical or contrary-to-fact conditions. Pay careful attention to the forms of the verbs you use.

> Situation: Lame Deer is talking to his young son Black Eagle. He is using hypothetical conditions to tell Black Eagle what the boy would do/be doing if he were older. He also talks about what would happen if he didn't do certain things. Example:
>
> be/older
> have/more responsibility
>
> If you *were* older, you *would have* more responsibility.

1. be following/buffalo
   have to carry/tepee
2. be riding/horse
   care for it/by yourself
3. not/feed horse
   it/get sick
4. lose/bow and arrows
   not/be prepared for hunt
5. take/buffalo meat
   have food/several days
6. ride horse/too hard
   it/collapse

Rewriting History: Past Unreal Conditions

Read the following paragraphs. Then write a paragraph using past hypothetical conditions. Examples:

> The Pilgrims *wouldn't have survived* the winter if the Native Americans *hadn't helped* them.
>
> Squanto *wouldn't have learned* English if he *hadn't been* a slave.

1. The early settlers at Plymouth, called Pilgrims, succeeded in establishing an agricultural community with the help of two Native-American tribes in the area: the Wampanoag and the Massachusetts. The English newcomers survived the winter of 1620–21 because of the Native Americans' assistance; with their

help, the English learned to plant corn, pumpkins, beans, and squash. Because the Pilgrims had emigrated from cities and towns in Europe, they didn't know about farming. They learned about agriculture from the friendly and generous native people. Eventually, the American colonial economy was based on the cultivation of Native-American crops: corn, tobacco, and cotton.

2. A famous member of the Wampanoag tribe named Squanto provided food for the Pilgrims' first Thanksgiving feast. Squanto had learned English as a slave in Europe and had traveled to several European countries. (He had been captured by Europeans who came to New England before the Pilgrims arrived.) Since he spoke English, he was particularly effective in teaching the Pilgrims. Squanto died in 1622 from one of the many diseases brought to North America by the Europeans. Thousands of Squanto's fellow Native Americans died from these previously unknown diseases to which they had no resistance. As they died, the Pilgrims took over their land and possessions.

Custer's Last Regret: Past Unreal Conditions

Situation: George Armstrong Custer is thinking about the terrible defeat of his army by the Sioux Chief Sitting Bull at Little Big Horn in 1876. Of course, he wishes the outcome of the battle had been different; he expresses regret, or hindsight, about a number of things that happened there.

Combine each pair of sentences into one sentence that contains a past unreal condition; make whatever changes are necessary in phrasing and verb forms. Example:

Sitting Bull was a great leader. He inspired his warriors to fight bravely.

If Sitting Bull *hadn't been* a great leader, he *wouldn't have inspired* his warriors to fight bravely.

1. I took my troops to the Dakota Territory. We encountered the enemy at Little Big Horn.
2. Crow warriors joined the Sioux at Little Big Horn. The Native-American army was enormous.
3. My soldiers felt too confident. The Sioux Chief Red Cloud had lost a war with U.S. troops in Wyoming.
4. Sitting Bull was angry. The U.S. army had come into the Sioux sacred lands.
5. The Crow and Sioux forces destroyed my army. Native Americans gained new hope for freedom and independence.

The Biggest Fish: Conjunctions Versus Prepositions

Situation: You and the members of your group are Tlingits from the Northwest fishing for salmon. The salmon are traveling upstream to lay their eggs. You are talking as you try to catch as many of them as possible. Complete the sentences in any way that is logical.

1. The salmon came upriver because of . . .
2. We must trap and spear many fish because . . .
3. The fish come here every year despite the fact that . . .
4. Many of them die on their journey despite their . . .
5. We can't go home now in spite of the fact that . . .
6. Our nets are at the bottom of the river because . . .
7. My son is getting very cold in spite of . . .
8. We will stay here for three days because of . . .

Suggestions for Writing

1. If you are keeping a journal, write an entry on one or more of the following: stereotypes about Native Americans, native people in a country other than the United States, Native Americans' attitudes toward nature or the environment, Native-American religion, arts and crafts, or reservation life.
2. Write a description of a ritual as you have seen it: a wedding, a funeral, a christening, etc. Use as many time clauses beginning with *when*, *before*, *after*, *as soon as*, etc. as possible. Example:

   As soon as the music starts, the bride comes down the aisle.

3. Write a composition about differences between Native Americans and settlers/immigrants to the United States, or compare two Native-American tribes you have read or heard about.
4. Write a letter to someone in another country describing some characteristics of Native Americans or outlining their history. Use information from the unit.
5. Imagine that Black Elk has come back to life. Write him a letter about some of the changes that have occurred since his death in people's attitudes toward Native Americans and the environment. Express your feelings about the customs and beliefs of Native Americans and their treatment by European settlers.

Unit Ten

NOUN CLAUSES

READING. "Sticker Shock at the Ivory Tower" by Susan Tifft

THEME. Higher Education in the United States

PART ONE. The Context

The following article from *Time* Magazine, "Sticker Shock at the Ivory Tower," describes the rising costs of higher education in the United States, especially at famous private universities like Harvard, Yale, and Stanford.

Pre-Reading Questions

1. "Sticker shock" means surprise at the price tag (sticker) of an item or service; it usually refers to the prices of new cars, but it may also refer to other things. Have you ever experienced sticker shock? What products or services made you feel this way?
2. The article that follows mentions "Chivas Regal pricing" at American private universities. Chivas Regal is an expensive brand of Scotch whisky that is sometimes considered a symbol of high social status. Can you think of brand names of other status symbols, such as cars, clothing, or footwear? What are they? What North American universities do you think of as status symbols?
3. In your opinion, how valuable is a university education? Should families go into debt and make great sacrifices to send their children to famous schools? Why or why not?
4. Why do you think the academic world is sometimes called the "ivory tower," a place without any connection to the real world?

Preview of Key Terms and Concepts

The following terms and concepts are referred to in the reading. Read the definitions and then complete the sentences that follow with a partner.

patchwork quilt — bed cover sewn from small pieces of different kinds of cloth; figuratively, anything made from a number of different parts

hardware — equipment, often the parts of a computer; can also include any facilities, such as buildings

take a toll — have a negative effect. Comes from money (toll) taken from travelers on certain roads; often refers to loss of property or human lives

fringe benefits — extra costs paid for by employers in addition to salaries, such as health insurance and retirement plans

let-them-eat-cake attitude — unsympathetic attitude toward the poor (from a remark attributed to French Queen Marie Antoinette about the poor who had no bread in France before the French Revolution)

bottom-line	as an adjective, an economic term referring to concern about profits (from the last line in a financial statement, which shows profit or loss). Also used as a noun phrase without a hyphen: the bottom line

1. Sending their children to good schools can ______________________ on parents, both emotionally and financially.
2. Maria took an entry-level position with an accounting firm when she graduated; the starting salary wasn't very high, but the ______________________ were excellent.
3. Members of a privileged class who send their children to expensive private schools are sometimes accused of having a ______________________ toward those whose children must attend public schools.
4. Some observers believe universities would be more successfully managed if administrators paid more attention to ______________________ matters, but others feel that too much attention to profits is inappropriate at educational institutions.
5. A school board is often made up of people of different races, backgrounds, philosophies, and interests. Because of these differences, it has been called a ______________________.
6. Many businesses have found that the initial expense for computerization is high, but the investment in computer ______________________ and software pays off over a period of time.

READING: "Sticker Shock at the Ivory Tower" by Susan Tifft

(1) When the College Board released its annual cost survey showing that private school tuitions would rise an average of 9% this fall, Kellie Kenner raced for her calculator. Since the 20-year-old junior entered Emory University two years ago, her total bill, including tuition, has jumped from $13,900 to $16,100, an increase of almost 16%. Despite a patchwork quilt of aid that includes scholarships, loans and an on-campus job, Kenner's father, a train conductor, must now pay $6,000 out of pocket to send his daughter to school this year . . . To help make ends meet, her mother recently took a job as a data processor. "I told my parents I'd go somewhere else," Kenner says, "but they wanted me to stay."

(2) As their children register for the new school year, most parents, like Kenner's, are willing to scrimp* and sacrifice. But they are increasingly outraged at the platinum* price tags. For nine years, hikes in tuition and other fees have averaged roughly twice the rate of inflation,* boosting* bills at elite* private schools like Sarah Lawrence and Princeton to the edge of the $20,000-a-year

---

* scrimp	spend as little money as possible
platinum	like a precious metal; very expensive
inflation	tendency of costs to increase over time
boosting	raising, increasing
elite	the best or highest in a group

mark. And the spiral* shows no sign of stopping. By 2005, according to the investment firm Paine Webber, the price of a college education is likely to climb to $62,894 annually.

(3) As the bills mount,* many parents suspect that institutions are kicking up their fees at will, knowing that families will pay almost anything to give their child the cachet* of a Harvard or Yale degree. "It's Chivas Regal pricing," says Kalman Chany, president of Campus Consultants Inc., a Manhattan-based financial-aid consulting firm. "The most selective schools can afford to charge what they want because they've got lines out the door of people who want to go there."

(4) College administrators vehemently* reject that accusation. Increasing tuition charges, they say, merely reflect their own increasing expenses. In particular, they cite soaring* costs for building construction and maintenance; salary-inflating battles to woo* and keep top-flight* faculty members, especially in science and business; and the dizzying price of keeping up with technology, ranging from computerized card catalogs to the latest in lab paraphernalia.* Hardware and faculty often go hand in hand:* when Duke lured physicist John Madey away from Stanford, it promised to build a lab for his free-electron laser research. Cost: $5 million.

(5) Cuts in federal student aid during the Reagan years have also taken a toll, forcing schools to contribute more from their own coffers.* Like other labor-intensive* businesses, colleges feel the bite of rising fringe benefits. At Brown, for instance, outlays* for employee health-care premiums have quintupled* since 1986. Then there is the need, fostered* by feverish* admissions competition, to provide more and better student services—such as tennis courts and state-of-the-art* gyms.

(6) Aggressive fund raising has eased the crunch* to some extent. As many as 60 schools are now conducting drives with goals of more that $100 million;

---

* spiral	gradual rise, usually circular
mount	increase
cachet	special mark of approval or high standing
vehemently	with great energy or anger
soaring	rising quickly; flying like a bird or airplane
woo	try to attract a person (usually in a romantic sense)
top-flight	excellent, first-class
paraphernalia	equipment
hand in hand	together
coffers	cash boxes
labor-intensive	requiring many workers
outlays	expenses
quintupled	multiplied by five
fostered	encouraged
feverish	intense, excited
state-of-the-art	very modern, up-to-date
crunch	high-pressure situation

three are seeking to break the $1 billion mark. But changes in the tax code have made giving less attractive, and many endowments* are still feeling the aftershocks* of the 1987 market crash. "How can we look so rich, yet feel so poor?" asks Donald Kennedy, president of Stanford, which faces a projected* $11 million shortfall* this year.

(7) One reason for public skepticism* is that some elites convey a let-them-eat-cake attitude—a result, no doubt, of their enormous wealth and the knowledge that they are the purveyors* of one-of-a-kind* diplomas. Harvard, for example, cautiously spends only 4% to 5% of the annual income it earns from its $4.1 billion endowment, the largest in the country. . . . The rest is reinvested. Despite its secure position, Harvard felt the need to jack up* this year's tuition and other fees 6.5%, to $19,395. "What we distribute from endowment may sound low today, but it did not in 1979," explains Harvard president Derek Bok, alluding* to a period when stock returns* were disappointing.

(8) But even a Harvard cannot afford whatever it wishes. Nearly 60% of major research universities report that they are cutting back as they re-examine the long-held* and costly* belief that they must offer a full range of disciplines.* In April, Washington University announced plans to shut down its sociology department. Columbia University is phasing out* linguistics.* "There has got to be more focused investment," says Robert Zemsky, director of the higher education research program at the University of Pennsylvania, which urged in a report last week that schools close marginal* campuses and adopt* more businesslike budgeting practices.

---

* **endowments**	gifts (usually large sums of money) donated to universities and other institutions
aftershocks	smaller earthquakes that follow large ones; negative effects that are felt some time after an event
projected	expected in the future
shortfall	difference between the planned or needed amount and the smaller actual amount
skepticism	doubtfulness
purveyors	providers, suppliers
one-of-a-kind	unique
jack up	raise, increase
alluding	referring
returns	benefits resulting from an investment of time or money
long-held	believed or observed for a long time
costly	expensive
disciplines	fields of study, majors
phasing out	gradually eliminating
linguistics	study of the nature and structure of languages
marginal	barely acceptable
adopt	put into practice

(9) Calls for fundamental change and bottom-line thinking are sure to upset some in the education establishment. But the consequences* of not changing are already apparent. Tired of sticker shock at the pricey* privates, more and more families are turning to state-supported schools, where the total bill this year averages $6,671 for an in-state resident.

(10) When the Justice Department announced in August that it was investigating some 20 private colleges for price fixing* in the areas of tuition and financial aid, the news elicited* shocked gasps* from the ivory tower. Last week the Government added six more schools to the list, including Bryn Mawr and Wellesley. Many administrators fear that if Washington concludes that students should be like baseball players—free agents able to dicker* for the most attractive aid packages—the ensuing* bidding* wars could boost* charges for less sought-after* candidates. "Do we really want to turn colleges into bazaars* where students say, Cornell offered me so much, now what can you do to top that?'" asks one college president. In fact, such free-market* decision making is already common, despite the decades-old practice among many top schools of meeting annually to discuss the aid packages being offered to their applicants.

(11) Whatever comes of the Justice Department inquiry, there is little relief in sight for most students and their over-extended* parents. The causes that drive up tuition bills today are likely to worsen in the years to come. One key factor is an imminent* faculty shortage. A study released by the Andrew W. Mellon Foundation last week predicts that there will be only eight candidates for every ten teaching positions in the arts and sciences during the decade beginning in 1997, a development that is sure to inflate professorial salaries. In a time-honored* bit of corner cutting,* some schools are already increasing their student-faculty ratios. Others are thinking about involving undergraduates in teaching and putting their best professors on video.

---

* **consequences**	results
pricey	expensive, high-priced
price fixing	setting prices illegally, not allowing free competition
elicited	brought or drew out
gasps	sudden intakes of breath
dicker	reach an agreement about price or salary
ensuing	following
bidding	from bid (v): to offer more than one's competition
boost	raise, increase
sought-after	desirable
bazaars	outdoor markets without fixed prices
free market	competitive; based on a capitalistic economic system
over-extended	already in debt, suffering financially
imminent	approaching quickly
time-honored	traditional; accepted because of a long existence
corner cutting	way to save money

(12) None of these expedients* is desirable. Yet higher education, like the health-care industry, must either contain costs now or risk becoming the monopoly* of the wealthy, a condition that would be socially undesirable. The alternative is ever increasing prices, with the costs spread among parents, students, federal and state government, and private donors. Quality, as educators never tire of saying, costs money—and there is no easy solution. Laments* Frederick Bohen, senior vice president at Brown University: "We're talking about a bunch of lousy choices."

Comprehension Questions

1. Why are parents of college students angry about school fees? .
2. How do college administrators defend their decisions to increase tuition?
3. What steps are universities taking to raise money and reduce expenses?
4. Why is the Justice Department investigating a number of private colleges?
5. What future difficulties are predicted for North American universities?

Discussion Questions

1. Is a college education essential in all professions/careers? Which fields do not require advanced study? Do too many people go to college instead of finding jobs or attending a trade school or community college after high school?
2. Education is one factor in achieving success, but does not guarantee it. What qualities are necessary for success? What is your personal definition of success?
3. Institutions of higher learning are structured in different ways. Some have an extensive "core" curriculum which requires all students to take a broad program of courses in various fields. What are the advantages and disadvantages of this structure? What courses would you require all students to take if you were a college administrator? Which ones, if any, would you consider eliminating from the "core" curriculum? Why?

---

* **expedients**	quick solutions, not necessarily the best ones
monopoly	control by one group
lament	grieve, complain, regret

PART TWO: The Target Structure: Noun Clauses

I Focus on General Rules for Noun Clauses: Introductory Words and Word Order

Preview of Noun Clauses

The following pairs of sentences have approximately the same meaning. Read each pair and answer the questions that follow. Discuss your answers with a partner or group.

1. A. You get what you pay for.
   B. The quality of something that you buy depends on the amount of money you're willing to pay for it; if you buy something cheap, you shouldn't expect good quality.
2. A. He's got what it takes.
   B. He has the necessary qualities for the task that needs to be done.
3. A. It's who you know, not just what you know, that counts.
   B. Often your knowledge and talent will not bring you as much success as the influential people that you know.

1. Which sentence of each pair, A or B, communicates more directly and efficiently? Why?
2. Analyze sentence A in the first pair. Draw a line between the subject and predicate and another line between the verb and its object. Is the object a single noun or a noun clause?
3. The structure *what you pay for* is a noun clause. Circle the introductory word in this clause and in the noun clauses in 2A and 3A. Underline the whole clause in each of these sentences. (There are two in 3A.) Can you draw any conclusions about the types of words that can introduce noun clauses?
4. The noun clause in 1A is the object of the verb *get*. How are the noun clauses in 2A and 3A used?
5. The noun clauses you have analyzed are similar to questions in the way they begin. How are these clauses *different* from questions?

Introduction to Noun Clauses

If you preferred sentence A in each pair of sentences above, you recognized that using noun clauses often helps writers to be more direct and expressive than they could be if they used other structures. Like adjective and adverb clauses, noun clauses are called *dependent* because they must be connected to independent clauses in sentences. They can appear in any position in a sentence where nouns or noun substitutes could be used—for example, as subjects, objects of various kinds, or subject complements.

Many noun clauses begin with question words, such as *who* and *what*; others begin with *if, whether, that*, and *-ever* words like *whoever* and *whatever*.

Words That Introduce Noun Clauses				
what	how	when	if	whatever
who	how much	where	whether (or not)	whoever
whom	how many	why	that	whomever
whose	how often			whichever

The following sentences illustrate some uses of noun clauses. The first example shows that a noun clause subject is singular; therefore, a present tense verb ending in *-s* is used.

> *Where their children go to college* concerns parents.
> (subject of sentence)
>
> Many students are discovering *that they can get a good education at community colleges and state universities.*
> (object of verb)
>
> Their concern is *whether they can get the kind of education they want and need.*
> (subject complement)
>
> Parents are angry about *how high tuitions have risen, especially at private colleges and universities.*
> (object of preposition)
>
> They cannot afford to pay *what these schools cost.*
> (object of a verbal: infinitive)

✔ CHECKPOINT 1

Return to the reading on pages 353–357. Find the noun clause used as the object of an infinitive in paragraph 3, the noun clause used as a subject in paragraph 7, and the noun clause used as an object in paragraph 8. Analyze the noun clauses with your partner or group. What words introduce them? What are the subject and predicate in each?

WORD ORDER IN NOUN CLAUSES

In noun clauses, question word order is not used, although many noun clauses begin with question words. This is true even when the sentence containing the noun clause is a question. Compare the following sentences.

> INCORRECT: We don't know *how* **will we** pay for college.

CORRECT: We don't know *how* **we will** pay for college.

INCORRECT: When is Maria going to decide *which college* **will she** attend?

CORRECT: When is Maria going to decide *which college* **she will** attend?

CHECKPOINT 2 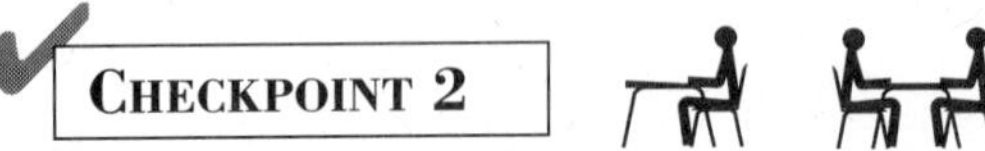

Substitute the noun clause in parentheses for the underlined noun phrase. Then determine whether the clause is used as a subject, object of a verb, object of a verbal, object of a preposition, or subject complement. Write your answer after each rewritten sentence. Example:

> A problem for parents is extremely high fees at universities.(what parents must face)
>
> What parents must face is extremely high prices. Subject

1. Administrators can't always predict increases in tuition. (when tuition will increase)
2. The media have been concentrating on administrators' thoughts about this subject. (what administrators think)
3. Their concern is fund-raising. (how much money the school can raise)
4. Why do administrators want to increase their endowments? (what they receive from endowments)

II Focus on Noun Clauses Derived from Questions

Noun Clauses from Information Questions

Noun clauses derived from information questions begin with the question words *who, whom, whose, what, which, why, when, where,* and *how.* Notice that in the second sentence, the word *does* is not used in the noun clause, and that question word order does not occur in any of the noun clauses.

Noun Clauses from Information Questions

Question	Sentence with Noun Clause
What college are you going to?	I haven't decided *what college I am going to.*
How much does tuition cost?	*How much tuition costs* depends on the college you choose.
Where is Harvard?	He doesn't know *where Harvard is.*
Why is college so expensive?	We want to know *why college is so expensive.*
Who is your advisor?	She doesn't know *who my advisor is.*

CHECKPOINT 3

A.

Combine the following questions and statements to form sentences with noun clauses. In the second sentence replace the word *this* with a noun clause made from the question. The clauses may be used as subjects, objects of verbs, verbals, or prepositions, or as subject complements. Example:

> Why is tuition rising so fast? We wonder about this.
>
> We wonder (about) *why tuition is rising so fast.*

1. How will her parents save enough money to send her to college? John has asked me this.
2. When is my application due? I am concerned about this.
3. How long does the semester last? Another question is this.
4. Where will my family get the money for school fees? This is a cause for worry.
5. What kinds of financial aid do colleges offer? He wants to know this.

B.

Take turns asking and answering information (*wh-*) questions about each other. If you know the answer to a question, answer it. If you don't know the answer, respond with a sentence containing a noun clause. Use as many different question words and phrases as you can, such as *how, how long, how often, why, where, who, whom, whose.* Follow this pattern:

Student A: What is (Student C)'s major?

Student B: His/her major is Engineering. OR

I don't know *what his/her major is.*

Student B: Where does (Student A) live?

Student C: He/she lives in the dorm. OR I'm not sure where he/she lives.

NOUN CLAUSES FROM YES/NO QUESTIONS

Another type of noun clause is based on questions that have the answer "Yes" or "No," such as the following:

> Does your brother intend to go to college? Yes/No.

When a noun clause is based on a YES/NO question, it begins with *if* or *whether,* which have almost the same meaning. The words *or not* often follow *whether,* either immediately or at the end of the noun clause, but they are not needed.

> YES/NO question: Do all children in the United States have to go to kindergarten?

Sentences with noun clauses:

They are wondering ***if/whether*** **all children in the United States have to go to kindergarten.**

They are wondering ***whether (or not)*** **all children in the United States have to go to kindergarten.**

YES/NO Question: Are there six grades in elementary school?

Sentences with noun clauses:

He is asking ***if/whether*** **there are six grades in elementary school.**

He is wondering ***whether*** **there are six grades in elementary school** (***or not***).

CHECKPOINT 4 

Take turns responding to the questions. Make up sentences that begin with such expressions as *She asked, I wonder, They don't know,* or *She has no idea,* followed by a noun clause. Give additional information if you can. Example:

Is Anna going to go to Harvard?

I have no idea *whether she is going to go to Harvard.* She didn't tell me she had applied there.

1. Was Harvard the first college founded in the United States?
2. Was Oberlin College the first co-educational college in the United States?
3. Did President Lincoln sign the Land-Grant College Act into law?
4. Is Michigan State University a land-grant college?
5. Did the states receive money for colleges from the sale of federal land?
6. Is Princeton University located in Connecticut?
7. Are Yale's school colors red and white?
8. Is Berkeley a state university in Texas?
9. Did George Washington attend college?

(The answers to these questions are given on page 381.)

III Focus on Noun Clauses Beginning with THAT and -EVER Words

NOUN CLAUSES BEGINNING WITH *THAT*

Many noun clauses begin with the connecting word *that.* Like other types of noun clauses, this type can also appear as a subject; as an object of a verb, verbal, or preposition; or as a subject complement.

Many parents suspect *that institutions are kicking up their fees at will.* (object of verb)

The College Board released its annual survey showing *that private school tuitions would rise an average of 9 percent this fall.* (object of present participle *showing*)

One reason for public skepticism is *that some elites convey a let-them-eat-cake attitude.* (subject complement)

Although noun clauses beginning with *that* may be used as subjects, such clauses are not commonly used, especially in speech. Instead *it* is used as a subject and the noun clause is delayed. In the following pairs of sentences, both versions are correct, but the second is much more common.

That tuitions are rising rapidly is clear.

It is clear *that tuitions are rising rapidly.*

That Harvard is an excellent university is well known.

It is well known *that Harvard is an excellent university.*

Adjective Versus Noun Clauses Beginning with *That*

Adjective clauses can also begin with *that*, but adjective and noun clauses serve very different purposes in a sentence. Compare the following sentences.

The college *that I would like to attend* is in Ohio. (adjective clause modifying the noun *college*)

I told my friend *that I would like to attend a college in Ohio.* (noun clause object of the verb *told*)

A. Return to Paragraphs 1 and 3 on pages 353 and 354. Find three noun clauses beginning with *that*. Identify which are used as objects of verbals and which is used as the object of a verb.

B. Return to Paragraphs 7 and 8 on page 355. Underline the clauses that begin with *that*. With your partner or group, decide which are adjective clauses and which are noun clauses by asking these questions: Does the clause modify a noun? Does the clause replace a noun—as a subject, object, or complement?

C. Read the following passage about land-grant colleges in the United States and do the exercise.

The Land-Grant College Act of 1862, also called the Morrill Act, encouraged the states to establish colleges that would provide affordable education for middle-class citizens, not just the wealthy. Sponsored by Representative Justin Smith

Morrill of Vermont, the bill was signed by President Abraham Lincoln; his predecessor, James Buchanan, had vetoed a similar bill proposed by Morrill.

The law gave each state 30,000 acres of federal land for each of its representatives in Congress. The land was to be sold to raise funds to endow one or more colleges in each state. The law required these colleges to provide instruction in agriculture and mechanical arts, such as engineering and mining, as well as the liberal arts, and sciences, and military tactics. Among the earliest land-grant colleges were Michigan State, Rutgers (New Jersey), and the Universities of Vermont and Wisconsin. Many land-grant colleges are now among the finest universities in the United States. Their success greatly influenced the development of education in the U.S.; they made the study of "practical" subjects respectable and proved that higher education could be provided at a very reasonable cost.

Based on information about land-grant colleges, make up sentences with noun clauses beginning with *that* used as subjects, objects, or complements. In the main clause of your sentences, use expressions such as these.

> *It is known/a fact that* . . . OR . . . *is known/a fact.*
>
> *History shows that* . . .
>
> *The law required that* . . . OR *was required by the law.*
>
> *These colleges showed/proved that* . . .

Examples:

> It is a fact *that the Land-Grant Act of 1862 led to the establishment of colleges in many states.*
>
> *That the Land-Grant Act of 1862 led to the establishment of colleges in many states* is a fact.
>
> History shows that *Rep. Justin Smith Morrill sponsored the bill.*

USING *THE FACT THAT*

Often the connector *that* is preceded by *the fact.* For example, the noun clauses in the following sentences could begin with either *that* or *the fact that.*

> *(The fact) that tuitions are rising rapidly* is clear.
>
> *(The fact) that Harvard is an excellent university* is well known.

The fact that can also introduce noun clauses that act as objects and complements.

> One reason for the increase in tuitions is *the fact that universities spend a great deal on labs and hardware to recruit top-flight faculty.* (subject complement)
>
> Students and parents resent *the fact that schools seem insensitive to applicants' financial difficulties.* (object of verb)

CHECKPOINT 6

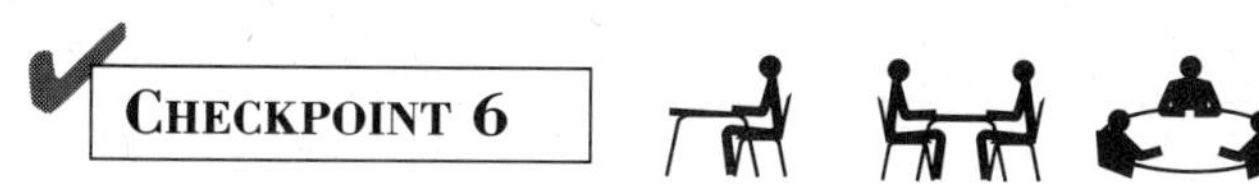

A. Read about the three Ivy League colleges described below. Then use the information to complete the sentences that follow with noun clauses beginning with *The fact that.* (The term "Ivy League" refers to the ivy that grew on the buildings of the earliest U.S. colleges, which were modeled on those in England.)

HARVARD UNIVERSITY, the oldest college in the United States, is located in Cambridge, Massachusetts, on several hundred acres on the banks of the Charles River, across from Boston. It was founded in 1636. Approximately 20,000 students attend Harvard, which has seventeen academic departments, or disciplines. There are fifty libraries at Harvard that contain about eight million books. Harvard's colors are red and white; its athletic teams are called the "Crimson." Among the many famous graduates of Harvard are Presidents Franklin D. Roosevelt and John F. Kennedy.

PRINCETON UNIVERSITY is located in Princeton, New Jersey, south of New York City. It was founded in 1746 as a school for Protestant ministers. Approximately 5,000 students attend Princeton, which has twenty departments and lies on 2200 acres. Princeton's colors are orange and black; its mascot is the tiger. The physicist Albert Einstein and the philosopher Bertrand Russell were faculty members at Princeton. President Woodrow Wilson was a Princeton alumnus.

YALE UNIVERSITY, founded in 1701, is in New Haven, Connecticut, northeast of New York City. Approximately 9,000 students attend Yale, which has 5.7 million volumes in its libraries. There are 720 acres for athletics at Yale. Yale's colors are blue and white, and its teams' mascot is the bulldog. President George Bush went to Yale; President Bill Clinton and Hillary Rodham Clinton graduated from Yale Law School.

Example:

The fact that Harvard was founded in 1636 makes it the oldest of the three schools.

1. ______________________________
makes it the youngest of the three schools.
2. ______________________________
means that it is the school located the farthest to the north.
3. ______________________________
means that it is the school located the farthest to the south.
4. ______________________________
makes it the school with the largest student population.
5. ______________________________
makes it the school with the smallest student population.
6. ______________________________
means that many students probably wear those colors to the school's football games.

7. ____
makes it a university with a good research facility.

8. ____
means that it used to have a connection to the church.

9. ____
suggests that boating may be popular there.

10. ____
shows that sports are extremely important there.

B. Use the information about the three Ivy League schools to complete the following sentences. Give your opinions and reactions to the information. Use both *that* and *the fact that* noun clauses. In some sentences you can use *it* and a noun clause after the verb. Examples:

The fact that Harvard has fifty libraries amazes me.

That Harvard has fifty libraries amazes me.

It amazes me *that Harvard has fifty libraries.*

1. ____
surprises me.
____
surprises me.
It surprises me ____.

2. I hadn't realized ____.
I hadn't realized ____.

3. ____
makes it a ______________ school.
____
makes it a ______________ school.

4. ____
was news to me.
____
was news to me.

5. ____
____.

Expressions Used with *That*-Clauses

Noun clauses beginning with *that* are often used with certain common expressions beginning with *it is* plus an adjective, a noun, or a participle.

It is *clear that parents will have trouble paying the bills.*

It is *a fact that Oberlin College was the first co-educational college in the United States.*

It is *surprising that some famous universities cannot meet their budgets through endowments.*

Here are some other expressions that are commonly followed by noun clauses with *that.*

It's apparent	a shame	shocking
obvious	a pity	disturbing
strange		known
(un)fortunate		
(un)lucky		

CHECKPOINT 7

Read the following passage. Then use *it is* expressions with noun clauses to comment on the information. Use as many expressions as possible to begin sentences of your own.

The population of the United States consists almost entirely of immigrants, or descendents of immigrants, yet English as a Second Language is not offered in many communities' schools. Although many institutions do offer ESL courses, other school systems have not made ESL part of their curriculum and place non-English speaking students in classes with native speakers of English. Many of these ESL students learn English well from their school environment. Others do not have sufficient opportunities to develop the ability to communicate well in English. These students usually have problems in school.

The best level at which to begin second language training is pre-school or kindergarten. Early programs give all non-native speakers a chance to achieve proficiency in the English language relatively quickly and easily.

Many universities offer some kind of ESL training. Some university ESL programs are part of academic programs designed for students who are pursuing a degree. Many international students, as well as residents, immigrants, and refugees, enroll in these ESL programs as part of their course work; unfortunately, they usually do not receive credit from ESL courses toward their degree. Other ESL programs are in language institutes that require students to complete English training before matriculating at a university.

Follow the pattern of these sentences to respond to the ideas in the passage.

> *It is a fact that* the population of the United States consists almost entirely of immigrants.
>
> *It is surprising that* ESL is not offered in many communities.

NOUN CLAUSES THAT BEGIN WITH *-EVER* WORDS

In noun clauses that begin with the *-ever* words *whoever, whomever, whatever,* and *whichever, -ever* refers to any person or thing.

> Even Harvard cannot afford *whatever it wishes.* (*whatever* = anything)
>
> My friends and I have an agreement. *Whoever graduates from college first* must give a party for the others. (*whoever* = anyone who)
>
> Janet's parents will send her to *whichever college she chooses.* (*whichever* = any)

Words that end in *-ever* do not always introduce noun clauses. For example, in the following sentence from the reading, the structure that begins with *whatever* is called an "absolute construction".

> Whatever comes of the Justice Department inquiry, there is little relief in sight for most students . . .

The absolute construction beginning with "Whatever" modifies the whole sentence that follows it; since it does not substitute for a noun, this structure is *not* a noun clause.

Read the situation and then complete the sentences with the best *-ever* word (*whoever, whomever, whichever, whatever*).

Situation: Jack wants to be admitted to Wheat University, a famous North American school. He would enter as a freshman next fall.

1. Jack is trying to do ______________________ is required by the Admissions Office at Wheat.
2. He has telephoned ______________________ he could to get information.
3. A university employee told Jack that ______________________ applies to Wheat has to take the American College Test (ACT).
4. He is willing to live in ______________________ is assigned to him for housing.
5. When Jack went for an interview, he was prepared to speak with ______________________ he met in the office.

6. And he was ready to discuss _______________________ the interviewer asked about.

IV Focus on Direct and Indirect Speech

Noun Clauses in Indirect Speech

Direct (quoted) speech uses the *exact words* of the speaker, but indirect (reported) speech does not. There are other differences as well: in punctuation, verb tense, word order, and pronoun use.

Punctuating Direct Speech

The following chart illustrates the rules for punctuating direct or quoted speech. The identification of the speaker (*she said*, *added*, *asked*) can come before or after the quoted speech, or it may interrupt the speech.

Punctuating Direct Speech	
"I'm going to college now," she said.	The first letter of a quoted sentence is always capitalized. A comma separates the speaker's *exact words* from the identification of the speaker. Quotation marks surround the exact words. The comma at the end of the exact words goes *inside* the quotation marks. A period ends the whole sentence.
"I'll graduate," she added, "in four years."	If the exact words of the speaker are interrupted by the identification of the speaker, two sets of quotation marks are used. The comma after the first part of the quoted speech goes *inside* the first set of quotation marks; the period goes inside the second set. A comma after the identification of the speaker sets it off from the exact words.
"My university is excellent. Have you heard of it?" she asked.	If more than one sentence is quoted, both go inside one set of quotes. Because the second sentence here is a question, a question mark is used inside the quotes, and no comma is needed before the identification of the speaker.

Add the necessary punctuation and capitalization to the sentences. Example:

My counselor is advising us about colleges Sara said.

"My counselor is advising us about colleges," Sara said.

1. I need to talk to him I have to apply soon her friend said.
2. You should come Sara said to the meeting today.
3. Her friend answered I have an exam.
4. Where is your exam Sara asked.
5. It's either in the library she answered or the math building.
6. Here comes the counselor now do you think we should talk to him wondered Sara's friend.
7. Hi, Mr. Slade Sara shouted my friend and I need to speak with you.
8. Can't you be more dignified her friend complained you're embarrassing me.
9. Mr. Slade won't bite you Susan I know because he's my uncle said Sara smiling broadly.

Noun Clause Objects in Indirect Speech

Direct quotations can be changed to indirect or reported speech containing noun clauses used as objects. The first of the following sentences illustrates direct speech. In the second, the speaker's words are reported in a noun clause object of the verb (*is saying*), which may be followed by *that*, although *that* is not necessary. Quotation marks are not used in reported speech.

QUOTED: My friend Jack is saying, "I want to go to college."

REPORTED: My friend Jack is saying (that) he wants to go to college.

Tense Changes in Indirect Speech: Present to Past

Another important difference between quoted and reported speech involves the use of verb tenses. In reported speech, if the main verb of the sentence is in the past tense, the verb in the noun clause usually changes to the past as well. The past tense is appropriate because the idea is reported *after* it was first spoken. As in all cases of reported speech, if the noun clause comes from a question, the word order changes.

Changing Present to Past in Indirect Speech	
Direct (Quoted)	**Indirect (Reported)**
"Our community college ***has*** a two-year degree program," the teacher *said*.	The teacher *said* that their community college ***had*** a two-year degree program.
(The main verb, *said*, is past, so the verb in the noun clause changes to the past when the statement is reported.)*	
"***Are*** there going to be more students at the community college next year?" *asked* the parent.	The parent *asked* if there ***were*** going to be more students at the community college next year.
(The word order changes from question order in the direct quote to statement order in the noun clause. In addition, the past form *were* is used instead of *are*.)	
"Who ***teaches*** physics at the school?" asked the student.	The student *asked* who ***taught*** physics at the school.
(The word order stays the same in the indirect question because the question in the quoted speech is subject-type—see page 31.)	

The following chart gives the non-past and past forms of auxiliary verbs, including modals; this information is useful in changing direct speech to indirect speech.

Forms of Auxiliary Verbs in Indirect Speech

Non-past	Past
do, does	did
have, has	had
will	would
may	might
can	could
must	had to
am, is, are	was, were

* In informal speech, the present tense verb, *has*, might be retained because it expresses a generalization that remains true in the present.

CHECKPOINT 10 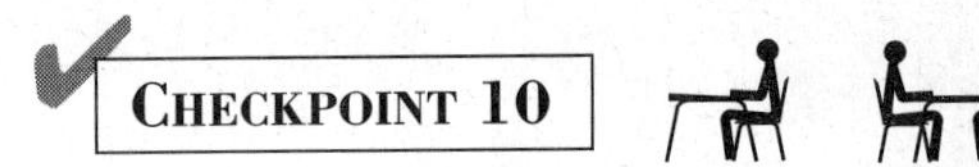

Change the main verb to the past tense and make any changes necessary in the main clause. Underline the changes. Examples:

> Ann says she is going to speak to her advisor about colleges.
>
> Ann said she was going to speak to her advisor about colleges.
>
> Her friend asks if Ann will apply to college soon.
>
> Her friend asked if Ann would apply to college soon.

1. My advisor says that the two-year college is going to offer more programs next year.
2. He adds that the government may give more money to this type of school.
3. The newspaper reports that many students can't afford the higher tuition of a university.
4. Jane's guidance counselor tells her that she must apply to the community college because it may be the best kind of school for her.
5. She says that some of the non-academic skills programs don't have strict requirements and that many different types of people can benefit from them.

MORE TENSE CHANGES IN INDIRECT SPEECH: PAST TO PAST PERFECT

If the main verb of the sentence is in the past, a past tense verb in quoted or direct speech usually becomes *past perfect* in reported speech.

QUOTED:	"***Did*** many foreign students ***apply*** to the university this fall?" the teacher *asked.*
REPORTED:	The teacher *asked* if many foreign students ***had applied*** to the university this fall.
QUOTED:	"Who ***was*** in charge of registration last year?" the new student *wanted to know.*
REPORTED:	The new student *wanted to know* who ***had been*** in charge of registration last year.

Because the main verb in the reported sentence is past, the verb in the noun clause becomes past perfect. Notice that question word order is changed to statement order in the first example; no change in word order is necessary in the second example because the question is subject-type.

PRONOUN CHANGES IN INDIRECT SPEECH

Another difference between quoted and reported speech involves changes in the use of pronouns. These changes reflect differences in point of view between speaker and reporter. In the following example the point of view changes from the first person plural (*we*) to the third person plural (*they*).

QUOTED: "How can *we* look so rich, yet feel so poor?" asks Donald Kennedy, president of Stanford.

REPORTED: Donald Kennedy asks how *they* can look so rich, yet feel so poor.

In the following example, both the possessive pronoun (*my*) and the subject pronoun (*I*) have to be changed.

QUOTED: "*I* told *my* parents *I'd* go somewhere else," Kenner says.

REPORTED: Kenner says that *she* told *her* parents *she'd* go somewhere else.

CHECKPOINT 11

Change the following examples of quoted speech to reported speech. Remember to change the verbs in the noun clauses when necessary and to pay attention to pronoun changes. Example:

My advisor said, "You must take mathematics next semester."

My advisor said that I had to take mathematics next semester.

1. "I really don't want to take it," I replied.
2. "After all," I added, "I failed last semester."
3. He answered, "Then you should take it as soon as possible."
4. "It's like climbing back on a horse," he added, "after you've fallen off."
5. I smiled weakly and said, "I was never much of a rider."

MODALS IN INDIRECT SPEECH

Modal auxiliaries do not change from past to past perfect; they change onlyfrompresent/future to past. Even when *could*, *should*, and *would* refer to present or future time, they do not change forms in indirect statements. In the following example, the modal does not change.

QUOTED: "*Could* your friend have helped the new students during registration?"the teacher asked.

REPORTED: The teacher asked if my friend *could* have helped the new students during registration.

CHECKPOINT 12

A. 

Complete the sentences by changing the questions to reported speech. Use the past perfect where necessary. In some cases, no change is possible.

1. "Where should we pick up our registration cards?"
   I asked ______________________________

2. "How many students came here from China?"
   My friend wondered ______________________________
3. "Where were the ESL teachers trained?"
   Mrs. Lee wanted to know ______________________________
4. "Do we have to have our books on the first day of class?"
   I wasn't sure ______________________________
5. "How many students would pass this test?"
   She asked ______________________________

B.

Return to the reading on pages 353–357. Underline all quoted speech. With your partner or group, rewrite at least two of these passages using indirect speech. Example:

> "I told my parents I'd go somewhere else," Kenner said, "but they wanted me to stay."
>
> Kenner said (that) she had told her parents she would (she'd) go somewhere else, but they wanted to stay.

V Focus on Special Rules for Noun Clauses

Base Form Verbs in Noun Clauses

Some noun clauses beginning with *that* are used as objects after certain verbs and adjectives that stress necessity or importance. These expressions require that the verb in the noun clause be in the base form (the infinitive of the verb without *to*), as in this sentence. For example:

> the base form of *to be* = *be*
>
> the base form of *to have* = *have*

Some of the verbs that are followed by this type of noun clause are *ask*, *demand*, *insist*, *require*, *suggest*, and *recommend*; some adjectives are *important*, *necessary*, and *essential.*

> He *asked* that we *get* to class early for the exam.
>
> Ann's advisor *recommended* that she *study* a foreign language.
>
> It is *important* that you *be* prepared for the test.
>
> It is *essential* that private universities *have* large endowments in order to meet their expenses.

In some cases, an infinitive phrase can replace a noun clause to express necessity and importance.

He asked us *to get* to class early for the exam.

It is important for you *to be prepared* for the test.

It is essential for private universities *to have* large endowments in order to meet their expenses.

✔ CHECKPOINT 13 

Play the roles of a school counselor and a student being advised. Brainstorm statements they might make and prepare a short skit.

Situation: The *student* is talking about his/her problems in academic, social, and family life. The *counselor* gives advice and guidance using the verbs and adjectives listed below.

Verbs	**Adjectives**
suggest	*essential*
recommend	*important*
advise	*necessary*

Example:

Student: My father is upset about my grades.

Counselor: I suggest that you tell your father that you are working hard.

NOUN CLAUSES MODIFYING NOUNS

Occasionally a noun clause explains the meaning of a noun; in this case the clause acts as an appositive rather than as a modifier.

John just heard the news *that he had been accepted for study at Berkeley.*

The idea *that knowledge is power* is widely held.

CLAUSES WITHIN CLAUSES

Both dependent and independent clauses can include other clauses. The following example contains three clauses: the independent clause includes a noun clause as an object, and the noun clause includes an adjective clause modifying the noun *colleges.*

Jane told us **that she had applied to three colleges** *that have programs in Naval Architecture and Marine Engineering.*

In the following sentence, there are four clauses (one independent and three dependent: adverb, adjective, and noun). Try to identify them.

Because she knows how important good training in engineering is, Jane wants to attend the university that has the best reputation in that field.

PART THREE: Review and Integration

Identifying Noun Clauses

Read the passage and underline all the noun clauses.

That some of the very finest universities in the country had humble beginnings as land-grant colleges or other government-funded state universities testifies to the success of public higher education in the United States. For example, the University of California at Berkeley, usually referred to simply as Berkeley, is one of the great learning centers in the United States. Perhaps what it is most famous for is the political and social activism of the students and others who live nearby. UCLA (University of California at Los Angeles) and other California state schools also demonstrate that public institutions of higher learning can become prominent research centers.

The state colleges in Texas, like those in California, are noted for their academic excellence. What makes the Texas system unique is how the state schools are funded. The fact that money comes directly to the schools from drilling on state-owned oil fields makes it unusual among public university systems. The result of this arrangement is that the Texas legislature does not set the schools' budgets. What the schools receive cannot be controlled by elected politicians to the degree that budgets at other state university systems are. The flagship school, the University of Texas, has a library that is considered one of the best in the country.

"Ten Questions" Game: Noun Clauses from YES/NO Questions

Take turns standing in front of the class and being "it." The person who is "it" thinks of another student in the class, a teacher in the ESL program, or a textbook the class is using. Classmates try to identify the person or book by using sentences with noun clauses to get information; the noun clauses must begin with *if* or *whether*, as in the following.

I'd like to know if you're thinking of a (book, person, man, woman, etc.).

Please tell me *if/whether* . . .

I'd like to know *if/whether* . . .

My question is *if/whether* . . .

The person who is "it" answers "yes" or "no." If no classmate has guessed the name of the person or book after ten questions have been asked, the person who is "it" wins the game.

Group Research Report

Divide into groups. Go to the library or consult an encyclopedia to research one of the suggested topics or a topic of your choice related to the subject of education. Compare your research with that of other members of the group. In class, take turns presenting your data in groups, acting as "experts" on your topic. Give information to the rest of the class when a classmate asks an indirect question about the topic using indirect speech with noun clauses. You may begin a question in one of these ways.

I'd like to know why (or if) . . .

Please tell us when (whether, if, how) . . .

Would you please speak about how (whether or not) . . .

My question is why (how, if, when, where) . . .

Suggested research topics:

1. Gallaudet College for the Deaf
2. Land-grant colleges
3. TOEFL
4. Educational Testing Services (ACT, SAT, GRE)
5. Types of scholarships offered at ______
6. Sources of funding at local institutions of higher education

Recognizing Clause Types

Read the *Time* Magazine article "Is an Ivy Degree Worth Remortgaging the Farm?" and do the exercise that follows.

(1) In his autobiography, *The Education of Henry Adams*, the author somewhat sourly recalls teaching at Harvard in the 1870's. What seemed to perplex* Adams was the naive* faith of his students that their education somehow had a purpose and a utility. When he finally asked an undergraduate student what he intended to get out of his studies, Adams was startled by the answer: "The degree of Harvard College is worth money to me in Chicago."

(2) The only aspect of this century-old anecdote* that might be dated is Adam's surprise. This year, when Harvard sifted through 12,843 applications to fill 1,605 places . . . , undoubtedly many of these would-be students (and their parents) were motivated by equally crass* considerations. Popular wisdom

*	
perplex	puzzle
naive	simple, unsophisticated
anecdote	story
crass	materialistic, undignified

asserts that getting a pedigree* from an Ivy League school is worth more in terms of future income and social standing than attending any of several dozen other academically rigorous colleges and universities.

(3) With a Yale man in the White House and two others in key Cabinet posts, it is easy to assume that sociological evidence buttresses* this collegiate pecking order. But, in truth, it is nearly impossible to calculate the value of, say, a Princeton degree compared with one from a selective but less prestigious* school. Totting* up the comparative educational backgrounds of honorees listed in *Who's Who* may reveal something about those admitted to Princeton, but little about the quality of the experience there. For how do you separate out the effects of an elite university from such life-shaping factors as family background and IQ? And when do you measure alumni success—at age 25, when young men and women may still be temporarily riding on the reputation of their colleges, or at 70, when such credentials belong to the distant past?

(4) This is not to feign* ignorance of how the world really works. An Ivy education does carry with it useful social networks, external prestige and the self-esteem that comes with winning the college-admissions version of the Publishers' Clearing House Sweepstakes.* But these advantages tend to be small and transitory,* especially when compared with the weight that anxious parents attribute to them. "For certain kinds of jobs, a Harvard degree might help you get a foot in the door," says economist Robert Klitgaard, the author of *Choosing Elites*. "But if you look at outcomes—earnings and social status—it is very hard to make the case that going to Harvard is worth eight times going to UCLA, which is roughly the difference in their tuitions."

(5) If there is a message in all this for high school seniors and their parents nervously prepping* for the college gauntlet,* it is simply "Relax." To its credit, American higher education remains infinitely less hierarchical than that of Japan or France. In a nation of second chances, no college admissions office—not even Harvard's—has the power to either guarantee success or withhold it.

• pedigree	proof of superiority
buttresses	supports
prestigious	honored
totting	adding
feign	pretend
Publisher's Clearing House Sweepstakes	contest sponsored by magazine publishers
transitory	short-lived
prepping	preparing
gauntlet	ordeal, test

Now find the noun, adverb, and adjective clauses in the passage. Put a rectangle around the first word in a noun clause and underline the rest. Circle the first word in an adverb clause and underline the rest. Put a triangle around the first word in an adjective clause and underline the rest.

Discuss the characteristics of the three types of clauses and the differences among them. Answer such questions as the following:

Adjective clauses

1. What noun or pronoun does the clause modify?
2. How is the relative pronoun used? (As subject, object, possessive?)

Adverb clauses

1. What type of adverb clause is it (time, manner, cause, condition, etc.)?
2. Does the clause modify the verb or the independent clause as a whole?

Noun clauses

1. How is the clause used? (as subject, object, complement?)
2. Does the clause come from a question? If so, is it a YES/NO or an information Question?
3. Is the clause used in direct or indirect speech?

Role Playing: University Meeting

Read the following situation and then divide into three groups (students, administrators, and reporters) to prepare and act out the role play.

> Situation: There have been many changes in your university in areas such as the school calendar, curriculum, tuition, athletic programs, the grading policy, and policies concerning faculty. The student news station is broadcasting a live meeting between concerned students and university administrators. The student newspaper has sent reporters to cover the event.
>
> Students: You have come to ask the administrators about the changes in your school, both those taking place at the present and those planned for the future. You like the school and are worried about the changes you have heard about. You are respectful but insistent and want truthful answers to your questions. Take turns asking questions of any type (YES/NO, information, "Or").
>
> Administrators: You are responsible for changing many of the school's policies. You are under pressure from your supervisors in the state capital, the Board of Trustees, and angry faculty members. You want to reassure the students without giving them much information. Answer the questions as diplomatically as possible.
>
> Reporters: You take notes on the questions asked by the students and the answers given by the administrators. Use quoted or reported speech to make sentences that you can use in your article. Take turns reading your reports to the rest of the class. Examples:

Student X asked why the tuition was going up 25 percent next semester. President Jones said that the university could not pay its bills without the increase in tuition.

Student Y asked when the new library would be completed. Dean Garcia said that he didn't know the exact date.

Reading a College Catalogue: Base Form Verbs in Noun Clauses

This entry from Rocky End University's catalogue lists required courses and electives as well as suggestions for students who want to complete a Baccalaureate (B.A.) degree. Read the information and then do the exercise.

REQUIREMENTS FOR THE BACCALAUREATE DEGREE (B.A.)

Freshman Composition	3 hours
Literature	6 hours
Mathematics	6 hours above the 1000 level or a passing grade on a competency test
Science	11 hours, including 2 hours of laboratory and Biology. Electives include Chemistry, Geology, and Physics.
Art	3 hours. Electives include Fine Arts, Communications, Music, and Drama.
Social Sciences	6 hours. Electives include Economics, Sociology, Political Science, Geography, Anthropology, and History.

In addition, computer literacy and research proficiency are recommended. Students should try to declare a major concentration and complete basic requirements before junior year. Attendance at classes and graduation is requested.

Restate the university's guidelines by using these patterns.

It is **essential** that a student *take* freshman composition.

The university **requires** that students *take* math.

It is **not essential** that every undergraduate *study* history.

Rocky End **suggests** that each sophomore *complete* basic requirements before the end of the year.

Write sentences on these or other ideas. In your sentences, practice using the verbs and adjectives on the left.

ask	Economics
demand	Geology
insist	History
(not) require	Literature
recommend	Computer literacy
suggest	Sociology
	Drama
important	Science
(not) necessary	Music
(not) essential	Graduation

Suggestions for Writing

1. If you are keeping a journal, write an entry in which you give your opinions on one of the following: the cost of a college education, the advantages and/or disadvantages of working while going to school, what a college education means to you and/or to your family.
2. Write a letter to a friend in another country describing what he or she should expect to spend if s/he goes to college in your country. Explain the costs (tuition, fees, living expenses) and the sources of financial aid, such as grants, scholarships, loans, and on-campus employment. Add any other information you consider important.
3. Pretend that you are a reporter for a college newspaper. Write a short article in which you begin with a narrative to attract the readers' attention, like the brief story about Kellie Kenner in the *Time* article at the beginning of the chapter. Use direct and indirect speech if possible. Suggested topics: parking problems on campus, dormitory conditions, the quality of food in the cafeteria(s), credit for ESL courses.
4. Write a composition arguing for or against one of the following:
   College Is Not for Everyone
   Universities Should Prepare Students for Jobs
   Ivy League Education Is Overrated

Answers to questions on page 362.

1. Yes	6. No
2. Yes	7. No
3. Yes	8. No
4. Yes	9. No
5. Yes	

APPENDIX I

Irregular Noun Plurals

Some nouns require spelling changes to form their plurals.

The -y *Rule*

When a noun ends in a *y* that is preceded by a *consonant,* in the plural the *y* changes to *i* followed by *es*. Examples:

Singular	**Plural**
lily	lilies
family	families
baby	babies
lady	ladies
country	countries

When the final *y* is preceded by a vowel, no spelling change is necessary: *keys, trays, toys, monkeys, bays.*

More Irregular Plurals

Some nouns have an irregular plural form that requires an internal spelling change or an *en* ending.

Singular	**Plural**
a clever *man*	clever *men*
a crazy *woman*	crazy *women*
a funny *child*	funny *children*
an *ox*	some *oxen*
a *foot*	both *feet*
a false *tooth*	false *teeth*
a blind *mouse*	three blind *mice*
a *person*	*people* or *persons*

Singular nouns that end in *f* or *fe* often have a *v* in the plural.

Singular	Plural
a sad *wife*	sad *wives*
the *knife*	the *knives*
a *life*	*lives*
a *half*	both *halves*
one *leaf*	some *leaves*
a *loaf*	two *loaves*

Exceptions:

belief/beliefs *chief/chiefs,*
roof/roofs *cliff/cliffs*

Some nouns, including the names of several animals, have the same form in the singular and the plural.

Singular	Plural
a *deer*	*deer*
a *fish*	six *fish*
a *sheep*	*sheep*
a *series*	three *series*
one *means*	several *means*
a *species*	five *species* of animals

A few nouns are always used in the plural. Some common ones are *clothes, police, groceries, measles,* and *mumps.** These nouns have no singular form; however, *policeman* and *policewoman* have both singular and plural forms.

The wife's *clothes are* very stylish.

The *police were* already on their way when the wife called the psychiatrist.

Many of the *groceries* we bought *were* on sale.

Some other nouns that come in pairs are always plural: *scissors, glasses, pants, trousers, pajamas, jeans, slacks, shorts.* The only way to count them is to use the word *pair,* as in these examples.

The husband bought two *pairs* of glasses.

The woman bought three *pairs* of slacks, a *pair* of shorts, and two *pairs* of jeans.

A few nouns that end in *s* are *never* plural—for example, *news, mathematics, physics.*

The *news* of the woman's adventures *is* exciting.

Mathematics is my favorite subject, and *physics is* my second favorite.

---

* Although the nouns *measles* and *mumps* end in *-s,* they can be used with either a singular or plural verb:

Measles is a common childhood disease.

Mumps are contagious.

A small group of English words that were borrowed from Greek and Latin continue to use their Greek and Latin plural forms. Some common ones are given in the chart.

Greek/Latin Plurals

Singular	**Plural**
an *alumna*	*alumnae* (feminine)
an *alumnus*	*alumni* (masculine)
the *antenna*	the *antennae*
a *formula*	*formulae*
the *appendix*	the *appendices* (or *appendixes)**
a *bacterium*	*bacteria*
a *medium*	*media*
a *memorandum*	*memoranda*
an *analysis*	*analyses*
the *basis*	the *bases*
a *hypothesis*	*hypotheses*
a *cactus*	*cacti* (or *cactuses*)
one *criterion*	several *criteria*
a *phenomenon*	*phenomena*

CHECKPOINT A

A. 

In the following memo from Mrs. Johnson to Dr. Watson, fill in the correct plural forms from the list before each paragraph.

TO: Dr. Fred Watson

FROM: Mrs. Mary Johnson

man	creature	person
memorandum	fish	ox
species		

I've written several ____________ to you already. You ____________ are among the strangest ____________ on earth. Even ____________ in the sea or dumb animals like ____________ would never treat their fellow ____________ with such cruelty! You and my husband are two of the most horrible ____________ I know.

* The plural *appendices* correctly refers to added sections of books, while *appendixes* refers to the plural of a human internal organ. *Appendixes*, however, is becoming common in both senses.

patient appendix child
criterion woman

What ______________ have you used to decide that I should be one of your psychiatric ______________? I shudder to think of your being responsible for other ______________ and even little ______________. I thought your specialty was ______________ (appendix), anyway.

charge bacterium cliff means

I will use whatever ______________ I can to escape from here and press ______________ against you. I know the hospital is surrounded by high ______________, and the lake across which I must swim is full of dangerous ______________. What do I care?

leaf tree glass
meal tooth

In our next session, I plan to make my move! I can make weapons from the ______________ that come with my ______________. Even the ______________ in my mouth can be dangerous weapons!! Beware, doctor. Before the ______________ fall from the ______________ I swear I will be a free woman.

B. Give the plural forms of the following nouns. You may use a dictionary to check your answers. When you finish, put the nouns in four groups according to the way their plurals are formed.

1. wife ______________
2. person ______________
3. tooth ______________
4. glass ______________
5. hero ______________
6. fish ______________
7. deer ______________
8. knife ______________
9. child ______________
10. series ______________
11. leaf ______________

12. watch ____________
13. loaf ____________
14. sheep ____________
15. tomato ____________
16. man ____________

GROUPS

____________	____________	____________	____________
____________	____________	____________	____________
____________	____________	____________	____________
____________	____________	____________	____________

Collective Nouns

Collective nouns are words like *family* or *team* that refer to groups; they are usually considered singular in American usage, although the British often use them as plurals.

> *American usage:* The public *is* concerned about crime. *British usage:* The public *are* concerned about crime.

Some common collective nouns are *audience, clergy, committee, crowd, faculty, majority, minority, public, senate, staff,* and *team.*

> The *committee meets* every Wednesday.
>
> The *crowd cheers* wildly every time the team scores.
>
> The House will consider the law after the *Senate votes.*

Sometimes a problem arises with choosing a pronoun to refer to a collective noun. In the following sentences, common sense requires using a plural pronoun to refer to a collective noun.

When the *audience* left the theater, they went *their* separate ways.

The *team* will go to the game in *their* cars.

APPENDIX II

Uncountable Nouns

Abstractions
anger
beauty
communication
courage
darkness
danger
democracy
fatigue
honesty
hunger
intelligence
love
patience
racism
sadness
time, etc.

Fields of Study
Biology
Chemistry
Engineering
History
Mathematics
Physics
Psychology
Statistics, etc.

Foods
beef
bread
broccoli
butter
celery
cheese
corn
fish
meat
pasta
pepper
pizza
pork
rice
salt
sugar, etc

Gases
air
carbon dioxide
helium
hydrogen
oxygen
smog, etc.

General
art
baggage
clothing
equipment
furniture
hardware
homework
housework
information
jewelry
luggage
money
music
postage
scenery
slang
traffic
transportation
vocabulary
work

Gerunds
eating
fishing
manufacturing
reading
swimming, etc.

Languages
English
French
German
Spanish
Swedish
Vietnamese, etc.

Liquids
beer
coffee
gasoline
glue
honey
milk
tea
water
wine, etc.

Solids
aluminum
cement
chalk
copper
cotton
gold
glass
grass
hair
iron
paper
plastic
sand
soap
wood
wool, etc.

Weather
fog
hail
heat
humidity
mist
lightning
rain
sleet
snow
wind

APPENDIX III

Articles with Place Names

I. *The* is used with

A. Countries that have collective names

Examples: *The* Netherlands
The Philippines
The United Arab Emirates
The United States of America

B. Oceans, seas, deserts, mountains, and rivers

Examples: *The* Amazon River
The Atlantic Ocean
The Red Sea
The Rocky Mountains
The Sahara Desert

C. The names of universities when *University* is first

Examples: *The* University of Nebraska
The University of Texas

II. *The* is *not* used with

A. Large geographical areas:

Cities. Examples: London, Tokyo, Chicago (exception: the Hague)
States, Provinces. Examples: Louisiana, Massachusetts, Saskatchewan
Countries. Examples: Cambodia, France, Mexico
Continents. Examples: North America, Europe, Asia

B. Lakes, streets (avenues, roads, boulevards) and parks

Lake Michigan, Lake Ontario (but *The* Great Lakes, *The* Great Salt Lake)
Main Street, Fifth Avenue, River Road, Sunset Boulevard
Glacier National Park, Central Park

C. Universities or colleges when the primary name precedes *College* or *University*

Examples: Harvard University
Georgetown University
Smith College

APPENDIX IV

Verb Forms

Base Form	Simple Past	*-ed/-en* Form
arise	arose	arisen
awake	awoke	awoken
be	was/were	been
beat	beat	beaten
become	became	become
begin	began	begun
bend	bent	bent
bet	bet	bet
bind	bound	bound
bite	bit	bit
bleed	bled	bled
blow	blew	blown
break	broke	broken
breed	bred	bred
bring	brought	brought
broadcast	broadcast(ed)	broadcast(ed)
build	built	built
burst	burst	burst
buy	bought	bought
catch	caught	caught
choose	chose	chosen
cling	clung	clung
come	came	come
cost	cost	cost
creep	crept	crept
cut	cut	cut
deal	dealt	dealt
dig	dug	dug
do	did	done
dive	dove/dived	dived
draw	drew	drawn
drink	drank	drunk
drive	drove	driven
eat	ate	eaten
fall	fell	fallen
feed	fed	fed
feel	felt	felt
fight	fought	fought
find	found	found
fit	fit	fit
flee	fled	fled

fly	flew	flown
forbid	forbade	forbidden
forget	forgot	forgotten
forgive	forgave	forgiven
freeze	froze	frozen
get	got	gotten
give	gave	given
go	went	gone
grind	ground	ground
grow	grew	grown
hang	hung	hung
have	had	had
hear	heard	heard
hid	hid	hidden
hit	hit	hit
held	held	held
hurt	hurt	hurt
keep	kept	kept
kneel	knelt	knelt
know	knew	known
lay	laid	laid
lead	led	led
leave	left	left
lend	lent	lent
let	let	let
lie	lay	lain
light	lit/lighted	lit/lighted
lose	lost	lost
make	made	made
mean	meant	meant
meet	met	met
pay	paid	paid
put	put	put
quit	quit	quit
read	read	read
ride	rode	ridden
ring	rang	rung
rise	rose	risen
run	ran	run
say	said	said
see	saw	seen
seek	sought	sought
sell	sold	sold
set	set	set
shake	shook	shaken
shine	shone/shined	shone/shined
shoot	shot	shot

show	showed	shown
shrink	shrank	shrunk
shut	shut	shut
sing	sang	sung
sink	sank	sunk
sit	sat	sat
sleep	slept	slept
slide	slid	slid
slit	slit	slit
speak	spoke	spoken
speed	sped	sped
spend	spent	spent
spin	spun	spun
split	split	split
spread	spread	spread
spring	sprang	sprung
stand	stood	stood
steal	stole	stolen
stick	stuck	stuck
sting	stung	stung
stink	stank	stunk
strike	struck	struck
swear	swore	sworn
sweep	swept	swept
swim	swam	swum
swing	swung	swung
take	took	taken
teach	taught	taught
tear	tore	torn
tell	told	told
think	thought	thought
throw	threw	thrown
understand	understood	understood
upset	upset	upset
wake	woke/waked	woken
wear	wore	worn
weave	wove	woven
weep	wept	wept
win	won	won
wind	wound	wound
withdraw	withdrew	withdrawn
write	wrote	written

SOURCES

Material quoted verbatim is cited on the Acknowledgments page. The following material provided the background information on which readings and exercises are based.

Page

36 *Yankee* Magazine, March 1991, p. 70

48 "The Dogs and the Fox" and other fables by Aesop in this unit are adapted from *Aesop for Children* (Chicago: Rand McNally, 1947).

59 All stories about James Thurber are adapted from *The Little, Brown Book of Anecdotes* (Boston: Little, Brown, 1985).

86 Information on national holidays in this and succeeding checkpoints is from *The New World Family Encyclopedia* (New York: Standard International Library, 1955).

102–3 "My Own Ten Rules for a Happy Marriage" is adapted from James Thurber, *Thurber Country* (New York: Simon & Schuster, 1981), pp. 41–51.

110 Checkpoint 1: Andres Viglucci and Leslie Casimir, "New Immigrants' Children Pick English in Survey," (New Orleans) *Times-Picayune,* July 7, 1993, A-4.

116 Checkpoint 5: Margaret L. Usdansky, "No Correct Space for Filling in Race, Ethnic Groups Say," *USA Today,* July 7, 1993.

131 This reading and part A of Checkpoint 15: Leopoldo Castedo, *A History of Latin American Art and Architecture from Pre-Colombian Times to the Present,* trans. Phyllis Freeman (New York and Washington: Praeger, 1969).

133 Checkpoint 15, part B: Betty Leddy, "La Llorona in Southern Arizona," *Perspectives in Mexican American Studies 1* (1988): 9–16.

137 Checkpoint 19: Tony Hillerman, *New Mexico, Rio Grande, and Other Essays* (Portland, Oregon: Graphic Arts Publishing Co., 1974), pp. 63-91.

154–55 Part B: Marguerita B. Melville, "Hispanics: Race, Class, or Ethnicity?" *Journal of Ethnic Studies* 16, no. 1: 67–82.

155–56 Reading 2: Arthur L. Campa, "Spanish Traditional Tales in the Southwest," *Perspectives in Mexican-American Studies* 1 (1980): 2–7.

156–57 Reading 3: Larry Rohter, *New York Times,* June 20, 1993, pp. 1, 11.

180 Checkpoint 12, Part B: *American Writers,* Supplement III, Pt 2 (New York: Charles Scribners' Sons, 1991).

181 Checkpoint 13, Part B: *Historical Times Illustrated Encyclopedia of the Civil War,* ed. Patricia L. Faust (New York: Harper & Row, 1986).

182 Checkpoint 13, Part C: *Current Biographies* (New York: H.W. Wilson, 1957–1986).

184–87 Checkpoints 14, Part C, and 15, Part C: *American Writers.*

190–91 Checkpoint 17, Part B: Chris Waddington, "Portraits of a People," (New Orleans) *Times-Picayune,* December 18, 1993, E1 and E3.

197 The exercise on Henry Ossawa Tanner is adapted from Romare Bearden and Harry Henderson, *Six Black Masters of American Art* (New York: Doubleday, 1972), pp. 41–59.

213–15 Checkpoints 5, Part B, and 6, Part B: *The World Book Encyclopedia* (World Book, Inc., 1990).

216 Checkpoint 7: Susan Hornick, "How to Get That Extra Edge on Health and Wealth," *Smithsonian* (August 1993): 70–75.

219 Checkpoint 10: Polly Hamilton, "The Mist Off Perfume River," *New York Times Magazine*, November 23, 1993, pp. 72–77.

220 Checkpoint 11: Molly O'Neill, "Why Are We in Vietnam?" *New York Times Magazine*, November 23, 1993, p. 71.

222 First reading: Richard L. Worsnop, "Asian Americans: The Issues," *CO Researcher* (December 13, 1991): 947–54.

222–23 "Trapped on a Pedestal: Ethnic Asians in the United States," *Dollars & Sense* (March 1990): 12–15.

261 Checkpoint 18 exercise: Edgar Allen Beem, "Drawn to Gloucester," *Yankee* Magazine (June 1991): 74-79.

283–96 Exercises on Bing Crosby are adapted from Ken Barnes, *The Crosby Years* (New York: St. Martin's Press, 1980) and Bob Thomas, *The One and Only Bing* (New York: Grosset & Dunlap, 1977). Exercises on Elvis Presley are adapted from Larry Geller, *If I Can Dream: Elvis' Own Story* (New York: Simon & Schuster, 1989) and Earl Greenwood, *The Boy Who Would Be King* (New York: Dutton, 1990).

297 Scott Aiges and John McCusker, "Jazz Men: The End of the Beginning," (New Orleans) *Times-Picayune,* October 11, 1993, A1 and A10.

298 "The King in Brief," (New Orleans) *Times-Picayune*, January 8, 1994, E1.

323–39 Exercises on Native Americans are adapted from Jack Weatherford, *Native Roots* (New York: Crown Publishers, 1991).

343–45 Exercises on Native-American legends are adapted from Richard Erdoes and Alfonzo Ortiz, *American Myths and Legends* (New York: Pantheon Books, 1984).

347–49 Exercises on Native Americans are adapted from Weatherford, *Native Roots.*

363–65 Exercises on Asia are adapted from *Encyclopedia Brittanica*, 1993; s.v. "Colleges, Land Grant" and "Colleges, Ivy League."

INDEX

PHOTO CREDITS

Page

37 Marlborough St.
Bela Kalman
Stock, Boston

40 Arthur B. Davies
detail: Unicorns (Legend–Sea Calm)
The Metropolitan Museum of Art, Bequest of Lizzie P. Bliss, 1931. (31.67.12)

104 Diego Rivera
detail of mural: Corridor of the National Palace
Schalkwijk/Art Resource, NY

158 Jacob Lawrence
The Great Migration: "In the North, the Negro had better educational facilities." (1940–1941). Tempera on gesso on composition board, 12 x 18".
The Museum of Modern Art, New York.
Gift of Mrs. David M. Levy.
Photograph © 1995 The Museum of Modern Art, New York

227 NYC/5th Ave.
Patrick Donehue,
Photo Researchers, Inc.

227 Louisiana New Orleans, French Quarter
Dennis J. Cipnic
Photo Researchers, Inc.

274 Bing Crosby
UPI/Bettman

274 Elvis Presley
UPI/Bettman